The Historical Archaeology of Shadow and Intimate Economies

UNIVERSITY PRESS OF FLORIDA

Florida A&M University, Tallahassee
Florida Atlantic University, Boca Raton
Florida Gulf Coast University, Ft. Myers
Florida International University, Miami
Florida State University, Tallahassee
New College of Florida, Sarasota
University of Central Florida, Orlando
University of Florida, Gainesville
University of North Florida, Jacksonville
University of South Florida, Tampa
University of West Florida, Pensacola

The Historical Archaeology of Shadow and Intimate Economies

EDITED BY
JAMES A. NYMAN, KEVIN R. FOGLE,
AND MARY C. BEAUDRY

University Press of Florida
Gainesville · Tallahassee · Tampa · Boca Raton
Pensacola · Orlando · Miami · Jacksonville · Ft. Myers · Sarasota

Published in the United States of America.

This book may be available in an electronic edition.

24 23 22 21 20 19 6 5 4 3 2 1

Library of Congress Cataloging-in-Publication Data
Names: Nyman, James A., editor. | Fogle, Kevin R., editor. | Beaudry, Mary Carolyn, 1950– editor.
Title: The historical archaeology of shadow and intimate economies / edited by James A. Nyman, Kevin R. Fogle, and Mary C. Beaudry.
Description: Gainesville : University Press of Florida, 2019. | Includes bibliographical references and index.
Identifiers: LCCN 2018046978 | ISBN 9780813056326 (cloth : alk. paper)
Subjects: LCSH: Informal sector (Economics)—History. | Capitalism—Social aspects—History. | Organized crime—History. | Business enterprises—Corrupt practices—History.
Classification: LCC HD2341 .H57 2019 | DDC 330—dc23
LC record available at https://lccn.loc.gov/2018046978

The University Press of Florida is the scholarly publishing agency for the State University System of Florida, comprising Florida A&M University, Florida Atlantic University, Florida Gulf Coast University, Florida International University, Florida State University, New College of Florida, University of Central Florida, University of Florida, University of North Florida, University of South Florida, and University of West Florida.

University Press of Florida
2046 NE Waldo Road
Suite 2100
Gainesville, FL 32609
http://upress.ufl.edu

Contents

Figures

Tables

Preface

What became the intimate economic perspective, the concept developed and explored among the chapters in this volume, primarily began while James Nyman was conducting research on the historical interactions between American Indians and European settlers in the late seventeenth and early eighteenth centuries in North America. While he was studying a collection of colonoware vessels produced by Native American potters in unique, hybridized forms that suited the needs of the European settlers along the Gulf Coast region and the associated food rituals the settlers adopted in the New World, a historical phenomenon revealed itself. Daily encounters between Europeans and Native Americans resulted in creative negotiations of culture and identity as both groups began to confront the unfamiliar and incorporated it in their lives. Often undersupplied, European colonists along the Gulf Coast, as elsewhere in the New World, relied heavily on their indigenous neighbors for supplies such as food and utilitarian vessels to offset their meager rations and supplies or to help them focus on cash crops other than those needed for subsistence. On plantations and farmsteads and in garrisons, familiar cultural practices intersected with foreign foods and materials, resulting in cuisines and accoutrements for food rituals that had the qualities of hybrids—they simultaneously exhibited tradition and accommodation.

The idea Nyman kept returning to during this research was intimacy, in that in the early years of European colonization it was common for Native American producers and European consumers to interact consistently in intimate contexts. Native American peoples were still a visible part of the cultural landscape. Europeans hired them as help both inside and outside their homes and pursued intermarriage with them. These close, intimate interactions provided additional opportunities for deeply meaningful exchanges to occur among neighbors and partners. This historical pattern inspired a greater discussion about exchange in intimate contexts, for goods and services that developed in the context of larger trades for furs and slaves that drove the expansion of markets in the New World and beyond. As a concept however, social scientists associate the term intimacy with sexuality and physical intimacy, in essence overlooking the larger world of transactions that occur among social actors in intimate contexts through time. Because of this, Nyman and Fogle sought to further explore and expand the concept of intimate economies by inviting a diverse group of scholars to participate in a thematic session at the 2015 Society for Historical Archaeology conference in Seattle, Washington.

That session, titled "Intimate Economies: Independent Production in the Past," sought to explore how small-scale independent production at the level of individuals, households, or communities existing outside but alongside larger economic systems played a role in shaping and reinforcing the boundaries of social bonds and identities. The idea that would become the intimate economic perspective emerged from the work done during this session. While the focus then was centered on small-scale production in intimate contexts, the concept we explore in the present volume grew to involve discussions of how important relationships develop, are maintained, and/or become redefined between social actors when they participate in intimate economic transactions outside major political or governmental structures. The approach, in essence, evolved to provide a way to describe and analyze important exchange systems that have powerful impacts on those who participate in them, even if they may or may not interpenetrate larger global capitalist economic structures and may in fact be virtually invisible when the focus is on the macroeconomic scale. What emerged from the 2015 SHA session was an enlarged concept that had room for important explorations of meaning, cultural identity and its rearticulation, power, and emotion. The contributors to this volume continued the work of expanding the concept as it was initially framed in 2015 and the results are expertly illustrated in this volume.

We are grateful to the original participants in the 2015 SHA session, especially Ryan J. Bradley, Dwayne Scheid, Matthew M. Palus, and Flora Vilches (whose conference papers do not appear here) and Charles Cobb, who served as a valuable discussant for this session. We also acknowledge and thank enormously our contributors to the volume for their hard work, dedication, and patience. We also thank everyone who supported us and assisted us in completing the volume, particularly Director Meredith Babb at the University Press of Florida. James would like to dedicate this volume to his parents, Allan and Maryann, for inspiring him to explore, and his wife Brooke for her unwavering support and patience. Kevin dedicates this volume to Abigail, Grant, and Blair, who make everything possible. Kevin and James would also like to thank Mary Beaudry, who served as a discussant for the 2015 session and now serves as a co-editor and contributor. Mary's willingness to provide carefully considered comments no matter where she is in the world, her insightful contributions to this volume, and her unwavering mentorship have improved this work exponentially. We are grateful to our friend and colleague.

James A. Nyman, Concord, New Hampshire
Kevin R. Fogle, Gordonsville, Virginia
Mary C. Beaudry, Boston, Massachusetts

1

The Intimate Economies Perspective

JAMES A. NYMAN AND KEVIN R. FOGLE

Social scientists often link the term intimate economies to sex work, particularly to prostitution (see Lyttleton 2014; Wilson 2004). While the phrase certainly includes this form of intimate transaction, the reality is that it encompasses many forms of intimate exchange. This reality is what we hope to illuminate in part through this volume. We also wish to begin a conversation about the deeply meaningful connections that are created when things are exchanged. The *Oxford English Dictionary* defines intimacy, a value-laden term that carries multiple meanings (Zelizer 2005), as "1. (a) the state of being personally intimate; intimate friendship or acquaintance; familiar intercourse; close familiarity; (b) euphemism for sexual intercourse; (c) closeness of observation, knowledge, or the like. 2. Intimate or close connection or union. 3. Inner or inmost nature; an inward quality or feature." The polysemy of the term means that conceptualizations of "intimate economies" can transcend the realm of exchange involving sexual encounters.

How can archaeologists see intimate economic transactions and their effects in the past? Where do these situations arise and how do they relate to market exchanges in the larger sense? In the most basic form, we see intimate economies flourishing on the edges, outside of formal organized markets. Intimate economic transactions happen at different, sometimes smaller scales. They can be clandestine but typically exist free of major restrictive oversight. Indeed, people are constantly blending their economic activities with their intimate relations in a variety of situations (Zelizer 2005). Human beings engage in countless exchanges of ideas, goods, and/or services with intimate partners or incorporate objects exchanged in such settings into intimate contexts such as homes or other personal spaces.

Intimate economies are about the deeply meaningful relationships that form between people when goods or ideas are exchanged. Essays in this volume explore the meaning and consequences of intimate economies and the intimate exchanges and the long-term repercussions that may result. The intimate economic perspective we describe here and our colleagues articulate in this book is meant as a framework through which archaeologists can examine small-scale exchange and its social ramifications.

Transactions are at the heart of intimate economies—exchanges of materials, services, and/or information that create or reinforce relationships, connections, or bonds and that have meaningful consequences. Such transactions may be based on an exchange of equivalencies or, more commonly, of inequivalencies. Inequivalent exchange creates a state of indebtedness between two or more parties and sustains a complex connection between them well beyond the moment of transaction (see Graeber 2011). An intimate economy is one in which social actors in close connection intersect with the exchange of money or other tangible/intangible commodities with the result that the individuals involved define social roles, obligations, and/or rights (*sensu* Zelizer 2005).

Our approach to the study of intimate economies provides a way to describe and analyze important exchange systems that have powerful impacts on those who participate in them, even if they may or may not interpenetrate larger, global, capitalist economic structures and may in fact be virtually invisible when the interpretive focus leans to the broad scale. In a sense, an intimate economies perspective allows for discussions of how subcultures emerge and how social solidarity within a subculture may evolve.

In developing this volume, we wished to present the intimate economic perspective to a broad audience of historical archaeologists in the hope that others might explore patterns of localized exchange and intimate relations through this novel approach. Our goal is to provide an evocative lens through which archaeologists and other scholars can examine how people develop and maintain or redefine relationships when they participate in small-scale intimate economic transactions.

Intimate economic exchanges are often made between parties based on real, perceived, or misplaced trust—for example, between friends, family, neighbors, partners—for goods, services, and/or information (Zelizer 2005). During intimate exchanges, social boundaries and identities are negotiated, close connections are created, and relationships are reinforced. Materials (tangible or intangible, alienable or inalienable) come to embody an emotional value in these transactions: both the producer and the consumer attach meaning to them (*sensu* Bridge and Smith 2003). While prostitution is certainly a form of such exchange, it is but one example of intimate economic relations.

Intimate economies, as we see them, are closely associated with embodiment theory because the things that are being exchanged in these transactions include ideas and not just goods. The nature and closeness of the relationships that form informs not only what people exchange but also how they use them to express their sense of identity, which is shaped by the transaction and the emerging relationship. What we are describing is firmly rooted in perspectives traditionally associated with postprocessual thought. While we accept this, we also acknowledge the importance of a more integrated approach to intimate economies that embraces the possibilities that positivist approaches offer.

The contributors in this volume develop ways of detecting and analyzing exchange systems for which traditional (usually Marxist or "post-Marxist" modern world theory) analysis is ill-suited or fails to recognize. The volume also serves to outline a typology of what this kind of approach looks like for other scholars of history and historical archaeology while rejecting the notion that overarching structures of capitalism render small-scale, intimate economies irrelevant or as merely futile and ineffective forms of resistance.

Traditional economic analyses tend to conjure mental images of dusty account books and long lists of goods produced or sold. One unique and defining aspect of this volume is that we contextualize the economic framework at a very personal and relatable scale. By exploring the everyday relationships that are at the core of every transaction, monetary or otherwise, we can help elucidate the underlying motivations, intentions, and emotions that drive localized economies. It helps, however, to situate the reader within the genealogy of the intimate economic perspective through a brief survey of how previous scholars have conceptualized the intersection of intimacy and social exchange.

Current Approaches to Intimate Economic Activity

The concept of intimate economies is a relatively new idea among archaeologists and is better known among cultural anthropologists. The few archaeologists who have applied the term intimate economies use it to specifically address the economies of sexuality and sensuality. A good example is the edited volume *The Archaeology of Colonialism: Intimate Encounters and Sexual Effects* (Voss and Casella 2011). The authors in this volume seek to answer questions about the sexual and sensual dynamics of colonial encounters to reveal how archaeology can elucidate the aspects of these kinds of relationships forged through colonial interactions. As Voss and Casella state, such encounters are multifaceted and generate types of sexual relationships from the exotic to the coerced and abusive. They argue that in studies of colonial, colonized, and postcolonial societies, archaeologists have tended to minimize conversations about sexuality. Their volume gives contemporary scholars the opportunity to reexamine and reimagine how their research on place, material culture, and representation in archaeology could speak to issues of sexuality and colonialism.

Sexuality and colonialism are areas of interaction that are affected by and inform intimate economies. The contributors of our volume show how intimacy and economics can overlap in multiple and diverse contexts including Native American whaling sites on Long Island, Caribbean plantations, colonial Jamestown, pilgrimage sites in Ireland, Appalachian moonshiner sites, and the pitch tar industry in Oulu, Finland.

Perhaps the most well-known application of intimate economies as a theoretical lens is Ara Wilson's *The Intimate Economies of Bangkok* (2004). The heart of Wilson's volume is globalization in the modern age, the intersection between the global market economy and "intimate economies." Wilson uses the term to encapsulate how everyday practices and beliefs, particularly those associated with the intimate realities related to gender roles and sexuality, become closely entwined with the logics of global capitalist practices. In her carefully analyzed case studies, Wilson reveals how objects, ideologies, and practices associated with intimate aspects of social lives such as sex, kinship, gender roles and other social identities become inextricably linked with global capitalist culture. While Wilson's study emphasizes sexuality and the personal expression of gender roles, it centers on a contemporary example from a specific geographic area

(Thailand) that focuses on the intersection of globalization, the practices of daily routines, and personal senses of identity. As Wilson writes, her aim is to "capture the deeply felt orientations and entrenched practices that make up what people consider to be their personal or private lives and their individual selves" (Wilson 2004, 11). While we agree that these are important aspects of human life that are affected by intimate economies, we assert that this is a limited perspective on both what intimacy means and on what an intimate economy entails.

The roots of our conceptualization of intimate economies can be traced to White and Dillian's examination of exchange at multiple scales in the past. In *Trade and Exchange: Archaeological Studies from Prehistory and History* (2010), White and Dillian acknowledge that the social dynamics of exchange in the past were just as meaningful as the objects that were exchanged. They therefore align themselves with the substantivist approach to exchange. We recognize that the intimate economy perspective thus shares a genealogical link to substantivist thought, particularly in terms of its association with the social contexts of economic behavior, the symbolic and ideological dimensions of exchange, and the relationships between people and objects. However, we do not wish to limit ourselves by allying solely with substantivist thought and entering the debate between formalist and substantivist approaches (see Cook 1973; Gudeman 1986; Polanyi 1968; Prattis 1982). We believe it is important for scholars to examine the relationships that emerge between social actors during intimate systems of exchange using epistemological lenses that incorporate the best of both processual and postprocessual theory.

While White and Dillian's fascinating volume focuses on materiality as a way to understand the connection between people and objects, particularly objects that are foreign or exotic, we argue that it is equally important to examine the relationships between people involved in intimate exchange. We see this perspective as a complementary approach to White and Dillian's approach to understanding exchange in the past, just at a different scale and with a different scope. White and Dillan's book advanced the discussion of economics in archaeology by addressing broader anthropological issues such as power, identity, and meaning. In this book we attempt to step beyond White and Dillian's focus on materiality to examine the complex interpersonal relationships that underpin systems of exchange.

One recent volume that comes the closest in scope to how we perceive intimate economies operating in the past is *The Social Archaeologies of Trade and Exchange: Exploring Relationships among People, Places, and Things* (2010). In this volume, the essays Bauer and Agbe-Davies have selected address the social context and consequences of exchange and how transactions have the ability to create, alter, or reinforce relationships between people and things. This volume presents one of the most innovative perspectives on trade since the 1970s and their progressive approach is one we strive to build on. As Agbe-Davies and Bauer suggest, a revitalization of archaeological studies of trade in archaeology could develop if postprocessual themes such as agency and materiality are integrated with more traditional positivist approaches (Agbe-Davies and Bauer 2010, 13–15). As the editors state, the study of trade and its influence on social lives is not and should not be the exclusive domain of processual studies (Agbe-Davies and Bauer 2010, 14–15). Instead, there is ample room for scholars to explore the concept of exchange through a processual-plus lens. We share Bauer and Agbe-Davies's view that exchange is fundamentally a social process between people. The goal of our book, however, is to elucidate how intimacy and emotion are fundamental aspects of exchange in subaltern or independent economies that are integral to establishing, maintaining, or redefining relationships.

We see the work outlined in this volume as a natural progression in thought. The authors integrate postprocessual themes of interpretation, materiality, meaning, social identities, and the everyday experiences of individuals engaged in exchange with traditional approaches couched in pattern recognition or modeling. Although we share similarities in tone and, in part, theme with the Bauer and Agbe-Davies collection, we emphasize the emotional, intimate connections that develop when people exchange objects, ideas, or obligations and how those connections influence relationships and senses of identity. These moments are deeply meaningful, even if they are fleeting, because complex negotiations of power, social roles, and identity that have ramifications for human social actors at multiple scales are embedded in them. Agbe-Davies and Bauer (2010, 16) acknowledge by way of citing the work of John Edward Terrell (2001, 69) that there are often overlapping emotional, social, and sometimes sexual dimensions to economic exchange that create connections that can go beyond cultural or even geographic boundaries, and the chapters in their volume provide a tantalizing glimpse of how this operated in historical contexts.

This book expands the definition of intimate economies so that scholars, historians, and people grappling with issues of subcultures and/or social exchange at multiple scales can consider intimacy as multivarious. Intimacy is central to various types of relationships between individuals as embodied selves and participation in relational, versus simply economic transactions affects how people come to see themselves on an intimate level and how they see themselves in the world, as individuals and as members of groups. This approach may offer valuable new insights to archaeologists.

While this volume complements other studies of exchange, its distinguishing feature is the authors' desire to get at the complex, sometimes dark and dirty, and deeply meaningful relationships that form between actors in situations of intimate exchange. Each chapter offers fresh insights into the mechanisms and outcomes of intimate exchange. The essays highlight the reality that economic activity and intimate relations took place in the past in a host of contexts, including slave quarters, farming hamlets, and household craft workshops. James A. Nyman examines how people and places can be bound together through a diverse network of informal intimate exchanges. He considers the survivance of Native American groups in nineteenth- and twentieth-century Maine. From an intimate economies framework, Nyman examines how a thriving peripheral trade with local Euroamerican communities created avenues for the cultural resilience of Native populations but also built enduring bonds between Native Americans and those who consumed the goods they produced.

Sami Lakomäki, Timo Ylimaunu, and Ritva Kylli examine the introduction of alcohol into seventeenth-century Sápmi, the country of the Sámi people in northern Fennoscandia. Here, as elsewhere, liquor helped entangle the indigenous Sámis into the emerging global, Eurocentric networks of production, commerce, and consumption. Yet seeing alcohol only as a colonizing substance distorts the complexity of the social relationships liquor created in early modern Sápmi where highly ritualized exchanges of alcohol developed in Sámi culture. Crucially, in many cases the Sámis used alcohol to redefine their relations with outsiders on their terms and to expand social networks that contested those constructed by the colonial states. Liquor became a central force in creating and extending indigenous social webs and spaces.

Kirk French examines the social and economic impact of moonshining in western North Carolina within tight-knit local communities. He uses archaeological surveys, historic documents, and oral histories to illustrate the complex relationships surrounding the manufacture and sale of illicit whiskey and the memorialization of the moonshine trade that developed in parts of Appalachia.

Marika Hyttinen, Timo Ylimaunu, Titta Kallio-Seppä, Markku Kuorilehto, and Paul R. Mullins look at the site of a pitch-tar mill on Pikisaari Island near Oulu, Finland, an island where thousands of barrels of tar were cooked into pitch tar every year during the eighteenth and nineteenth centuries. Archaeological excavations by the authors, however, have revealed an unexpected metalworking trade on the island that produced buttons, brooches, and other metal artifacts. These objects may have been imbued with magical properties because of the liminal nature of the island landscape. The fact that these objects were created and traded offers a perspective on everyday life and the conceptions of the world in the isolated island of Pikisaari.

In their archaeological research on French sugar plantations in Martinique and Guadeloupe, Heather Gibson and Kenneth G. Kelly examine the strategies enslaved communities developed to survive difficult circumstances, provide for their material needs, and develop social and economic networks that extended far beyond the boundaries of their individual plantations. These strategies were based on small-scale, intimate economies that cut across slave villages, plantation communities, and importantly, "master-slave" relations. Using the creole concept of *se débrouiller*, or "getting by," Gibson and Kelly examine the material assemblages of enslaved laborers, considering evidence of consumption and own-account production that reshaped the economic and social landscape of these two islands.

Kevin R. Fogle considers the intimate economies the enslaved community built and maintained on Witherspoon Island, a nineteenth-century cotton plantation in South Carolina. Fogle explores the impact of household and community involvement in intimate economic practices that the plantation management at times sanctioned, expressly forbade, or tacitly accepted. When the archaeological evidence is examined in conjunction with documentary records for Witherspoon Island, a fragmentary glimpse emerges of production, consumption, and exchange within this large enslaved community on an absentee plantation. The economic engagement of these resourceful families reveals a web of budding relationships among slaves, merchants, and poor whites that slaveholders feared could jeopardize planter hegemony across the antebellum South.

Matthew Reilly employs an approach to microhistory inspired by feminist scholarship that replaces the local or micro scale with the intimate scale to address the attachments among people, places, and things that are crucial for understanding life on the plantation landscape. Using historical and archaeological data from a poor white tenantry on the margins of a Barbadian sugar plantation during and after the period of slavery, Reilly explores the nature of interaction, exchange, and attachment among poor whites and enslaved and free Afro-Barbadians. Reilly suggests that while local focuses on labor and alienation can help us understand the inner workings of global capitalism at the macro and micro levels, privileging the intimacies of everyday life can highlight the most vulnerable aspects of the functioning of plantation economies.

Melisa Salerno, Jimena Cruz, and Andrés Zarankin examine the global reach of the nineteenth-century sealing industry in the South Shetland Islands of Antarctica that were the home of thousands of sealing workers. Employers provided some money in advance so sealers could purchase gear and agreed to provide food for the long voyages. Historical documents and archaeological evidence recovered at the sealing camps on the South Shetland Islands suggest regular constraints on supplies and reveal the efforts workers made to build their own shelters, obtain their own food, and mend and produce their own clothes. Beyond the guiding principles of capitalism, sealers had to create an innovative and collaborative economy in order to survive in a remote and harsh environment.

Allison Manfra McGovern's study examines the social and economic interconnectedness of two nineteenth-century Algonquian households during the whaling era. Though they were geographically distant from the white settlements nearby, the Montaukett residents of Indian Fields, an Algonquian village in eastern Long Island, New York, were intimately entangled in local and global economic activities and social networks. Archaeological and documentary data demonstrate that Montaukett people were part of a complex web of activities that transcended local geographical boundaries, as their participation in whaling, seafaring, and agriculture often led to absences from home. Residents who stayed home sustained their households through hunting, fishing, service work, and small-scale craft production. Their labor and their consumption were integral to the successes of capitalism. But mapping Montaukett labor patterns and movement demonstrates that social and kin networks were more prominent than relations established through work. Such networks did not result simply from whites forcing Montauketts into a conscripted labor class; they were networks of survival that helped minimize risk while men and women sought work outside their homes and villages. McGovern argues that Montaukett survival was maintained through these social and kin-based relationships.

In her study of beads in eighteenth-century Louisiana, Diana DiPaolo Loren focuses on the animation of glass in the lives and on the bodies of Native Americans. Pierre LeMoyne d'Iberville's journal of his travels along the Mississippi River from 1699 to 1702 is punctuated with notations of the presents he gave to Native Americans to facilitate alliances. Other early colonial accounts of French and Native American interactions in the Lower Mississippi Valley often included discussions of the items Europeans needed for trade with Native Americans. French travelers always included glass beads in such gifts, which they described as "trinkets." Loren finds that such offhand descriptions of the beads belie how Native Americans embodied this new material in presentations and performances of self on the colonial landscape.

Jade Luiz examines the thriving prostitution marketplace in nineteenth-century Boston, Massachusetts. Her study of a brothel in Boston's North End reveals not only that the establishment was advertised and rated but also that the residents of the brothel developed strategies for coping with the reality of being purchased for ostensibly intimate acts that were in fact commercial transactions. This included using aliases to mask true identities and providing a wide array of ancillary services to brothel clients such as special meals and drinks that were consumed in an ersatz middle-class setting. These supplementary offerings suggest that the visiting clients purchased a particular style of fantasy experience alongside intimate sexual acts, fulfilling fantasies related to distorted middle-class domesticity, homosocial male camaraderie, and erotic performance. Luiz examines the archaeological evidence of embodiment, artifacts related to dress, personal adornment and presentation of self, personal hygiene, and self-medication that help reveal the range of intimate transactions that took place in the brothel.

In her study of the initial English settlement at Jamestown, Beverly A. Straube examines over 200 obsolete coins and exonumia that are unusual for the American context. Straube considers these numismatic objects as evidence of an undocumented scheme of token currency that the joint-stock Virginia Company planned in 1609 to incentivize disaffected members of its colony. These individuals, who constituted the labor force, were integral to the company's success even though they were not shareholders and did not stand to profit from Virginia's resources. Straube finds that the Virginia Company attempted to initiate a practice of paying workers in scrip, a move intended to address the turbulent emotional atmosphere of its colonial community by offering immediate monetary rewards to its workers. The act of using obsolete coins as an internal currency offers a unique perspective on the deceptive intimate economy the Virginia Company planned for James Fort.

Eleanor C. Casella's survey of holy wells in County Roscommon, Ireland, takes a spiritual approach to intimate economies by analyzing folklore, oral history, and material remains. Casella examines the nature of votive offerings and sacrifices the supplicants who visited the wells left in the hope of securing a cure for bodily ailments and imperfections. She argues that through such offerings the "givers" established intimate relationships with the spirit of the patron saint linked to the well and that these transactions at holy wells helped reinforce and recreate traditional religious beliefs and shape individual and community identities.

This volume goes beyond broad-view, top-down political economic perspectives on production and social hierarchy. The intimate economic perspective it presents acknowledges complex historical relations of class and power while evaluating the emotional and intimate factors inherent in economic transactions. These emotional aspects are equally as important (or sometimes more important) than the things exchanged and are integral to the creation and maintenance of important connections between actors.

References Cited

Agbe-Davies, Anna S., and Alexander A. Bauer. 2010. Rethinking Trade as a Social Activity: An Introduction. In *The Social Archaeologies of Trade and Exchange: Exploring Relationships among People, Places, and Things*, edited by Alexander A. Bauer and Anna S. Agbe-Davies, 13–28. New York: Routledge.

Bauer, Alexander A., and Anna S. Agbe-Davies, eds. 2010. *The Social Archaeologies of Trade and Exchange: Exploring Relationships among People, Places, and Things*. New York: Routledge.

Bridge, Gavin, and Adrian Smith. 2003. Intimate Encounters: Culture-Economy-Commodity. *Environment and Planning D: Society and Space* 21:257–268.

Cook, Scott. 1973. Economic Anthropology: Problems in Theory, Method, and Analysis. In *Handbook of Social and Cultural Anthropology*, edited by John Honigmann, 795–860. Chicago: Rand McNally.

Graeber, David. 2011. *Debt: The First 5,000 Years*. New York: Melville House.

Gudeman, Stephen. 1986. *Economics as Culture: Models and Metaphors of Livelihood*. London: Routledge.

Lyttleton, Chris. 2014. *Intimate Economies of Development: Mobility, Sexuality and Health in Asia*. New York: Routledge.

Polanyi, Karl. 1968. The Economy as Instituted Process. In *Economic Anthropology: Readings in Theory and Analysis*, edited by Edward E. LeClair Jr. and Harold K. Schneider, 122–143. New York: Holt, Rinehart and Winston.

Prattis, J. I. 1982. Synthesis, or a New Problematic in Economic Anthropology. *Theory and Society* 11:205–228.

Terrell, John Edward. 2001. Archaeology, Material Culture, and the Complementary Forms of Social Life. In *Fleeting Identities: Perishable Material Culture in Archaeological Research*, edited by P. B. Drooker, 58–75. Carbondale: Southern Illinois University Press.

Voss, Barbara L., and Eleanor Conlin Casella, eds. 2011. *The Archaeology of Colonialism: Intimate Encounters and Sexual Effects*. Cambridge: Cambridge University Press.

White, Carolyn L., and Carolyn D. Dillian, eds. 2010. *Trade and Exchange: Archaeological Studies from Prehistory and History*. New York: Springer.

Wilson, Ara. 2004. *The Intimate Economies of Bangkok: Tomboys, Tycoons, and Avon Ladies in the Global City*. Berkeley: University of California Press.

Zelizer, Viviana A. 2005. *The Purchase of Intimacy*. Princeton, NJ: Princeton University Press.

2

Potatoes, Baskets, and Power

Indigenous Persistence in Maine

JAMES A. NYMAN

Anecdotes on Exchange and Intimacy in a Rural New England Town

A few years ago, my wife and I left the hectic world of graduate school and moved to New Hampshire. Having grown up in New England, it was important for us to live in a place that captured what we love most about the region. This meant a rural, quiet place away from Boston or Portsmouth with room to stretch but steeped in history. We are fortunate that New England is rich with towns like these, big and small. Our home was built in the 1850s on a hill above the Piscataquog River. It is quiet and shady, and in the fall it is ablaze with color and the smells from wood stoves. The subsection of the larger town we live in is a neighborhood called Chase Village. It is a nucleated mix of historic and more modern houses situated on the hill and along the river below. Where we chose to settle fit an idealized sense of what we were searching for to satisfy our personal tastes. What we discovered over time, however, is a connection much deeper and more meaningful than we had anticipated. This connection stems directly from the intersection between place and the relationships we have developed with our fellow residents of Chase Village through the exchanges among us. It has come to redefine our own identities in part and has heightened our emotional attachment to the community we are a part of.

There are few fences in Chase Village. Boundaries between properties are respected, but they are also fluid according to a set of pre-approved, unspoken conditions established among family and close neighbors.

Extended family and neighbors are often invited and encouraged to hike through or hunt in the forested lands behind people's homes, for example. This setting provides a sense of closeness and interconnectedness between families that dwell in the neighborhood. While fluidity between boundaries exists, invitations are also reciprocal, or in a sense invitations are typically returned through similar or often larger exchanges. For example, our neighbor Mr. Harris (names changed to protect privacy) sometimes plows snow from our driveway. This service is never requested in advance but is performed out of a sense of being neighborly. We return this favor by allowing Mr. Harris to cut and collect logs from downed trees on our property. He burns them in the winter in his wood stove to heat his home. There is an exchange here between close neighbors of relative equivalencies in this example—a service for a commodity. It is practical, but it also serves to reinforce the bonds between our neighbor and ourselves, laying the foundation for the opportunity of continued similar exchanges in the future. This relationship also reinforces a highly local shared identity in Chase Village that centers on the sense (real or imagined) that neighbors in this place look out for each other.

In another example, Adam, a neighbor with whom we share a property line to our east, raises chickens. In the summertime his chickens roam between our backyards as there is no physical barrier to prevent them. The chickens eat ticks and other garden pests in our yard and we leave them be so they can fatten on insects and produce eggs in their coop. In return, Adam provides us eggs by the dozen through the summer as part of an unspoken bargain between neighbors. He sells the rest of the eggs from a cooler by the roadside to the tourists passing through Chase Village. The eggs are various sizes and are shades of blue or tan with dark freckles. They are far from the kind of eggs we are familiar with from the grocery store, but they are delicious, and we have delighted in incorporating them into our meals all summer long. Similarly, we trade tomatoes from our garden for the Turks turban and blue Hubbard squash Adam grows. These varieties have deep historic roots in New England, but before we moved to Chase Village we had never heard of them. They have become staples in our home; we incorporate them along with the eggs Adam's chickens produce in new and hybrid dishes we enjoy. In a sense my wife and I have developed a personal cuisine that is heavily influenced by the things we have procured through intimate exchanges among our neighbors.

These exchanges could be understood as forms of gift exchanges, but they also have elements of a kind of barter economy (see Humphrey and Hugh-Jones 1992), as a service (plowing snow, giving animals access to land for forage) is being exchanged for goods (firewood, unlimited eggs) without money and the reciprocal bilateral exchange is nearly immediate, although some delay in time occurs. As Humphrey and Hugh-Jones point out (1992, 2), there is not always a clear boundary between barter and gift economies, and the two can coexist and share characteristics. The transaction where Adam gives us eggs has the outward appearance of being a gift, but it is really barter in disguise. This highlights the complexity of such transactions here, even at such a small scale, but also illustrates elements of tactic and self-interest present in gift exchanges that anthropologists such as Bourdieu (1977) emphasize.

Other exchanges occur in Chase Village outside gift/barter systems that involve the exchange of money for goods and services but are equally pertinent. For example, our house is our first, and as new homeowners we needed all the equipment one needs to manage and maintain a dwelling and its surrounding property. In short, we needed a lawn mower. Rather than purchasing a new one from a big-box retailer, and there are many in southern New Hampshire, our neighbors advised us to "just go see Charles." Charles, a resident of Chase Village, lives on the fringes between the nucleated neighborhoods in town and is employed as a contractor on navy projects. On the side he refurbishes and sells used lawn mowers to the locals as a part-time business and hobby. He is known around town for this side business, which relies on the commodities others obtained in larger markets to wear out, break down, and get discarded in order to be refurbished and redistributed to an intimate network of consumers in the village. To purchase one of his mowers, a person travels to his home and wades through a sea of rebuilt examples of all makes and models, each lovingly rehabilitated by Charles. The lawn mowers are purchased with cash, and each is priced according to its age and degree of wear. Each purchase also comes with the guarantee that if it ever needs service or breaks down, Charles would repair it at no cost. Charles is not an official retailer, and one does not inquire how he reports the money he makes from his side business during tax season. In essence, Charles operates his business parallel to larger markets but also, somewhat, in the shadows.

Purchasing the mower from Charles accomplished something less tangible, because beyond the transaction itself a friendship developed between us that is deeply meaningful. And that friendship is reinforced and incrementally strengthened through subsequent exchanges. The social relationship forged in this exchange is incidental to the initial market exchange, but it exists in the larger framework of how Chase Village forms social bonds and expresses a common identity rooted in Yankee thrift and self-reliance. Everybody gets their mower from Charles here instead of going to the larger, faceless stores in Concord. It is another part of the shared culture of Chase Village.

The exchanges described above reinforce bonds but also ensure that self-interests are preserved within the neighborhood. This is particularly important in a region that can experience extreme winters or summers of drought and poorly producing gardens. The farther away we travel from the core of Chase Village and the deeper we go into other sections of the main town, the less we feel an intimate connection to the other residents, the less commonality we sense beyond a shared pride in the history of the larger community. As a result, we are less likely to enter into similar exchanges with residents outside the boundaries of the neighborhood we inhabit and the relationships we have already formed. We are newcomers though, and over time we may develop other relationships through social exchange that could cut across neighborhoods or even other nearby towns.

One might define a neighborhood as a tightly delineated subset or nucleus of close social interaction within a larger town. The glue that holds these spatially defined areas together is the social networks that develop typically through face-to-face socialization. Intimate, close social interactions create living social neighborhoods. While archaeologists may preoccupy themselves with the social patterns of commonality or bond exhibited in archaeological contexts in tightly defined subsets of towns to identify the presence of neighborhoods, I argue that the residents of the Chase Village neighborhood in rural New Hampshire are organized in a social network with bonds between actors that are defined through participation in intimate economic transactions. These transactions, exchanges of goods that are loaned temporarily, bartered, or gifted, and the ideas that are exchanged with them, exist outside of, but often parallel to larger markets. The exchanges and the relationships that form because of them are deeply meaningful because they both create and reinforce a sense of place and belonging, based on a shared understanding of unspoken "rules" and social norms common within the tightly defined social network of the neighborhood and an identity shaped by the sense of historical connection to place and belonging.

These exchanges occur every day in neighborhoods across the country. None of us rely in total on gift or barter economies, however. The residents of Chase Village are also residents of the larger town and of the modern world of market exchange conducted in physical retail stores and through the online marketplace. The exchanges in such settings are fleeting and do not necessarily provide the framework through which deep social bonds are formed. There are costs and benefits inherent in every social exchange (*sensu* Blau 1964; see also Cook and Rice 2006; Emerson 1976; Firth 1967; Sahlins 1965). That said, beyond reducing exchange to just evaluations of costs and benefits, the intimate economic exchanges highlighted in the examples above are meant to underline the need to evaluate both the forces of power and social structures and the influences of emotions to get at the deeper meanings underlying these forms of exchange.

Revealing these highly personal anecdotes highlights the personal, small scale at which these transactions occur and illustrates the deeply meaningful results of these exchanges that go well beyond the simple reinforcement of social bonds. Of importance are the deep connections to place we have developed and the way we have rearticulated our identities in this setting, based on our participation in transactions on an intimate scale. We bring objects procured through small-scale personal transactions into the intimate spaces of our homes, we rely on labor provided by close neighbors to help us literally shape our personal landscape, we have developed close relationships with people with whom we deal, and through the intersection of participating in these transactional relationships and dwelling in this place we have come to embrace a rearticulation of our identities as New Englanders and as people who belong to Chase Village. This identity is expressed through the objects we use in and around our home, the relationships we foster and maintain in our neighborhood, and the food we prepare for our meals.

How we participate in the intimate economy of Chase Village has come to shape how we perceive ourselves as residents of the community and of New England and has heightened our emotional attachment to place. We have experienced lasting effects beyond brief moments of exchange—the forming of relationships, an emotional attachment to place, and a rearticulation of our identities as residents who participate in the local economies, as adults, as homeowners, as New Englanders. We find ourselves at the intersection of place, small-scale economic transaction, the forming of bonds and connections, and the rearticulation and/or reinforcement of identity. This intersection is where intimate economies operate.

For an archaeologist, the question becomes how might similar intimate economic transactions have operated in the past and how can archaeologists address them? The ethnohistoric case study that follows is presented as a way to illustrate how the intimate economic perspective intersects with contemporary research on historical interactions between indigenous peoples and Euroamericans in New England. The scale, of course, is different from the scale of my interactions in Chase Village, which in no way should be considered as a way to compare cultural equivalencies. Instead, the purpose is to illustrate how exchange among Native American producers and Euroamerican consumers in intimate contexts, who were "neighbors" by force of conquest and attempted subjugation, fostered cross-cultural connections with deeply meaningful consequences.

The Persistence of Indigenous Populations in Maine: Labor, Production, and Intimate Exchange

When Europeans arrived in New England, the cultural pattern that emerged was similar to others across North America. In the early years of settlement, European colonizers relied on Native American populations to offset the difficulties of navigating life on a new continent. To assure their survival, settlers depended on provisions, guidance, and labor from indigenous people. Despite the widespread disruptions engendered by the expansion of European colonizers into their territory, the diseases and new material culture Europeans introduced into their worlds, and the inherent violence associated with the spread of colonialism, Native American people found creative ways to respond to the pressures of the period in order to survive (see McGovern, this volume). They did so in a way that accommodated change and at the same time ensured a kind of cultural continuity with the past (see Silliman 2009). I argue that participation in intimate economic transactions provided and continues to provide such opportunities for Native American communities.

Archaeologists pay much attention to how indigenous peoples incorporated European goods into their lives (e.g., Loren 2010; Matthews 2010; Nassaney 2004; Rubertone 2001; Silliman 2009). Of equal interest should be how Europeans and Euroamericans incorporated the crafts and foods American Indians produced into their own daily lives. Illustrations of this phenomenon include how Native American peoples in Maine and Canada participated in intimate economic transactions with Euroamericans to obtain the crafts Native Americans produced. Throughout the Northeast, Euroamerican consumers developed relationships with objects they had procured from small-scale indigenous producers on the fringes of Euroamerican towns and settlements. The relationship forged between producers of Native American crafts and consumers of these goods contributed and continues to contribute to indigenous survivance strategies. These strategies helped mitigate the consequences of colonialism and the settler colonial legacy (see Wolfe 2006).

By the mid-nineteenth century, after over a century of European expansion into Maine, most Native American peoples of the state were forced to live in greatly reduced territories, usually on portions of their land that were remote and out of the way (Scully 1995). Treaties signed in the late eighteenth century preserved some Native American sovereignty over this remaining territory, at the expense of ceding most other Indian lands in the region. Over the course of the late eighteenth and nineteenth centuries, the Abenaki, Maliseet, Micmac, Passamaquoddy, and Penobscot—the Maine Indian nations that constitute the Wabanaki Confederacy—gradually saw their sovereignty eroded as Euroamericans continued to trespass into their territory in violation of established treaties. In an 1831 Supreme Court decision, Chief Justice John Marshall categorized Native American tribes as "domestic dependent Nations" (Brimley 2004, 13). The relationship between Indian nations and the United States became paternalistic in that the decision implied Indian nations were sovereign but were thought to be incapable of exerting that sovereignty (Brimley 2004, 13). The decision determined that Native American tribes were dependents of the federal government and established a trust relationship whereby the U.S. government would protect Indian nations. A year later, another Supreme Court decision established that states could not encroach on the sovereignty of Native American groups: state laws would not apply on tribal lands unless Congress granted that power to states. Tribes thus became nations within states (Brimley 2004). The state of Maine, however, largely ignored this ruling and limited the rights of Native American people, compelling them to fight for survival (Scully 1995).

From the time of initial European expansion into their territory, the indigenous peoples of Maine engaged in close interactions with traders and settlers, providing them with the services and goods they needed to survive and produce other commodities (see Bourque 2004). As their territory dwindled along with their ability to procure traditional subsistence resources, Wabanaki peoples found themselves on the fringes of Euroamerican farmsteads and settlements (see McBride and Prins 2009). Euroamerican settlers relied on their Native American neighbors to act as hunting guides and as providers of foodstuffs to supplement those they produced and sold themselves (McBride 1990). During the nineteenth century, although they were legally confined to their reservations, the Wabanaki maintained a mobile lifestyle across the interior of Maine. They returned to camp on their ceded traditional lands so they could hunt and fish, even though they were trespassing in the eyes of the state (Pawling 2016). While some Euroamericans complained, others disregarded the trespassers, either accepting them as harmless or accommodating them through agreements forged through personal relationships (Pawling 2016, 625).

In the late eighteenth century, Wabanaki craftsmen adapted their woodcraft traditions to weave maple, cedar, spruce, and ash splint baskets in forms Euroamerican settlers needed for domestic or utilitarian purposes (McBride 1990). McBride argues that Wabanaki craftsmen tailored their traditional skills of crafting birch bark canoes and bark boxes to create products European and Euroamerican consumers needed (McBride 1990, 11). In addition to splint baskets, Wabanaki craftsmen produced wooden spoons and troughs, poles for beans, buckets, churns, and the casks Euroamerican settlers used around their farms and dwellings (McBride 1990). Native American artisans tailored their designs to their customers' tastes, particularly in terms of decoration and form. Euroamerican consumers needed splint baskets for storing clothing and hats and for other forms of storage such as containers for knitting materials (Bourque and Labar 2009). The Wabanaki artisans sold their wares door to door, often camping on the edges of Euroamerican settlements in the nineteenth

Figure 2.1. Potato pickers, circa 1950. Photo by George French. Courtesy of the Maine State Archives, George French Collection.

century. Some enterprising Micmac artisans even traveled as far as Boston and New York City to sell their wares door to door (McBride 1990).

By the late nineteenth century the potato industry had begun to flourish in northern Maine. Lacking mechanical harvesters, potato farmers relied on large labor forces, including mixed groups of Euroamericans and indigenous laborers. The ideal tool on all farms in northern Maine during harvest time were Indian-made potato baskets (Figure 2.1). As McBride (1990, 20) writes, "Wabanaki Indians who 'hunted ash' and made baskets in the Aroostook area usually participated in the annual potato harvest. Between 1920 and 1965, potato picking and basket weaving were integral factors in the migrational seasonal working patterns of thousands of Wabanaki Indians."

While the Wabanaki were being increasingly marginalized in Maine during this period, tourists began to flock to the state to take advantage of the scenic beauty and to hunt and fish. Traditional Wabanaki baskets and snowshoes became tourist collectables (Bourque and Labar 2009). Maine Native Americans sold their wares from roadsides and from tents in empty lots. As they had done for years, they would travel to the coast and camp on the fringes of the wealthy tourists' resorts. From these

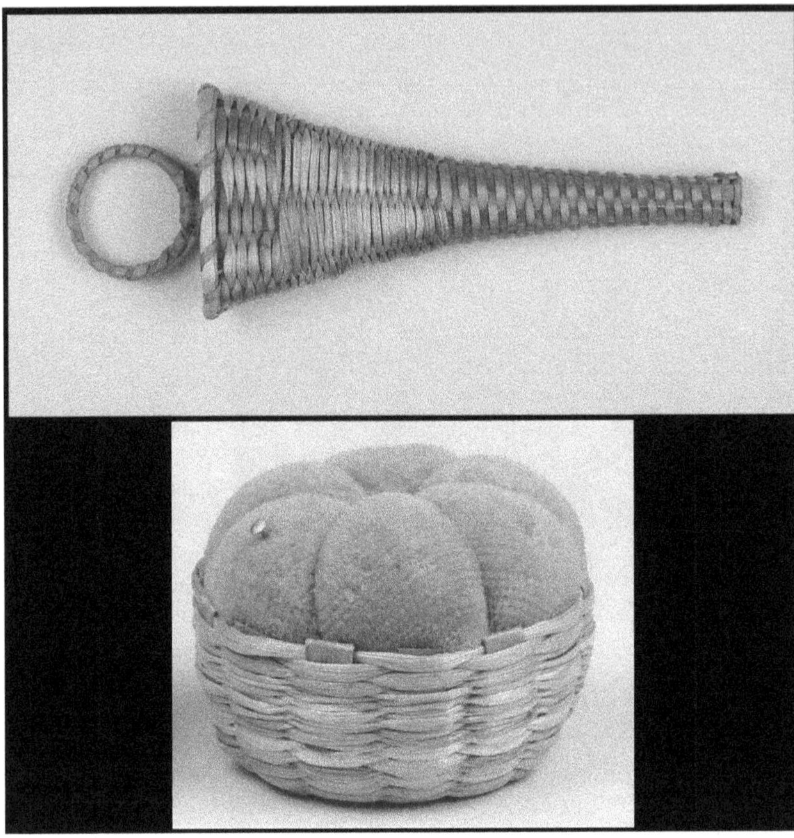

Figure 2.2. Penobscot Indian scissor case (*above*) and pin cushion (*below*), produced circa 1934 by Native American artisan Theresa Camilla Lyon. HM3035 and HM3036; Hudson Museum, University of Maine.

camps, Native American artisans would weave baskets and collect nearby resources of ash and spruce to produce their crafts. Baskets were particularly popular; sportsmen used them as packs and as sturdy luggage containers. Wabanaki artisans also responded to the desires of their consumers by creating new "fancy baskets." They adjusted their traditional crafts to accommodate European tastes with creative weaving techniques and colored, patterned designs. Many "rusticator" tourists sought these fancy baskets as collectibles (McBride 1990). Wabanaki basket makers produced both traditional storage boxes in highly decorative and highly specialized forms, including objects such as scissor cases and bases for pin cushions (Figure 2.2). Such objects returned with their Euroamerican consumers to major cities in the northeast to be used in their homes.

Emerging from these interactions with tourists were materially embodied examples of the paradox of globalization—what Cobb and DePratter (2012, 452) describe as the simultaneous unfolding of homogeneity and heterogeneity: "at the same time that Western technologies, styles, and tastes seem to be rapidly circulating and pervasive, local traditions are continuously reworking them into idiosyncratic variants on a theme." For Maine Native American craftspeople, interactions with Euroamericans on the fringes of their farms, cities, and resorts produced opportunities for their deeply ingrained traditions and practices to meet within a space of negotiation and creativity, resulting in the emergence of new examples of Wabanaki-made baskets to appeal to Euroamerican needs and tastes.

Unlike other parts of the East, in Maine, the Native Americans were never removed. They still live in the region. As Pawling (2016) notes, while they were meant to stay on reservations, Wabanaki peoples were mobile throughout the nineteenth century, returning to the lands they had lost to Euroamerican settlers to hunt and fish. They also moved seasonally to provide labor in the coastal fisheries and inland orchards. Although relegated to the fringes of settlements, Native Americans in Maine remained a visible part of the landscape and were, for the most part, consistent neighbors near white settlements in certain regions of the state. Pawling contends that this mobility was a "key expression of their collective identity and their sense of homeland" (Pawling 2016, 636). In retaining their mobility and pursuing subsistence strategies on their traditional lands while also acting as guides and producers for Euroamericans, Native Americans in Maine maintained an intimate connection to their homeland despite the federal government's attempts to confine them to reservations. They remained visible parts of the landscape even though they lived on the peripheries of Euroamerican settlements.

The historic relationship between Native Americans in Maine and Euroamericans is not a harmonious one. Maine Indians faced patterns of systemic racism throughout the nineteenth century, as they still do today. Their transactions with Euroamericans however fostered cross-cultural connections with deeply meaningful consequences that served the self-interests of all parties. The lasting effects of these transactions are deeply meaningful at various scales. As consumers, Euroamericans became comfortable bringing Native American–made objects into their homes and using them in their daily lives. The familiar and the foreign suddenly intersected within Euroamerican homes and in the fields of Northern

Maine. In Aroostook County, both Euroamerican and Native American laborers in potato fields relied on splint baskets Native Americans had made into the twentieth century. These laborers, who were paid to pick fresh potatoes by the barrel, filled those barrels using Native American–made baskets. Thus, the Wabanaki-made basket was not merely a utilitarian tool; it was also an object that was intimately connected to the livelihood of the workers. Negotiations in which deeply ingrained traditions and practices met in a space of cultural negotiation emerged out of the relationship between Native producers and Euroamerican consumers.

Discussion: An Intimate Economy Perspective of the Persistence of Indigenous People in Maine

As archaeologists, we are concerned with change through time at many scales. We use material culture, including the boxes, baskets, and associated tools Maine indigenous artisans produced and their associated basket-making traditions that date to the time before European contact and continue today to examine change. In what terms, however, do we describe or explain these transformations?

Johnathan Freidman (1994, 118) writes that "making history is a way of producing identity, insofar as it produces a relation between that which supposedly occurred in the past and the present state of affairs." I caution that we must be careful about contributing directly or indirectly to the disarticulation of contemporary Native Americans from their past and legitimating the settler colonial agenda of erasing Native Americans (see Wolfe 2006). When we rely too heavily on narratives that privilege "decline" as the dominant force behind changes in Native society following the expansion of Europeans into North America, that is exactly what we are doing. This narrative is most often invoked when discussing the effects diseases had on Native American groups, but it has also been used to discuss changes in cultural expressions (e.g., Axtell 1997; Cook 1998; Crosby 1976; Quimby 1966; Reff 1991; South 2002; Spicer 1961). For example, Rice (1987, 457) suggests that in situations where there are differences in values between a "traditional" society and one that is more dominant (as in situations of colonialism), acculturation is the major force behind changes in the production of crafts.

While most archaeologists have discarded acculturation theory as a legitimate way to understand changes in American Indian societies and cultural expressions, we must be careful of its legacy. Silliman (2009) indicates that a more constructive way of understanding the complex processes occurring in situations of colonial entanglement is through the lens of cultural accommodation, persistence, and the intersection between change and continuity. Still, we must acknowledge what is at stake if we do not address the creative ways Native American people worked to mitigate the deeply disruptive consequences of European expansion into their territory and the continued presence of Euroamericans today.

Echoing Liebmann's (2012, 32) sentiments, it is not my intention to "deny the magnitude and consequences of post-1492 colonialism for Native Americans—as this risks trivializing the brutality of European imperialism for Indigenous populations." Indeed, the consequences of colonial expansion, including the introduction of foreign diseases, clearly contributed to changes in Native American society across North America. My point is if we do not also acknowledge the creative ways Native American people responded to the consequences of European expansion, we risk the danger of ignoring Native Americans' resilience in the face of adversity and potentially obscuring Native American peoples in the present.

As scholars continue to examine the period of European expansion into North America and the relationships that formed between Europeans and Native American populations, the challenge is finding ways of addressing the complex interactions and strategies indigenous persons followed as they navigated colonial institutions and entered into intimate economic relationships with Euroamericans through the production and exchange of crafts that do not presuppose "cultural decline." I argue that an appropriate, nuanced, and ultimately more interesting way to think about objects such as the hybrid forms of baskets Native Americans produced in Maine in the late nineteenth century is as expressions of both continuity with indigenous traditions and history and the accommodations Native American artisans made to appeal to newly introduced ideas and tastes of Euroamerican consumers (*sensu* Morgan and MacDonald 2012). Hybridization theory provides space for Native American agency and the choices and strategies they used to mitigate the consequences of European expansion. Similar to Cobb and DePratter's thoughts on colonowares, hybrid ceramic vessels that incorporate European, African, and Native American elements and hybrid products such as fancy baskets are "a profound testament to the creative agency of peoples striving to maintain a sense of self and community" (Cobb and DePratter 2012, 455).

Native American baskets produced by skilled Maine Indian artisans are the material evidence of negotiations Native Americans and Euroamericans made as they dealt with the forces of colonialism at multiple scales.

Among Wabanaki artisans, basketmaking continues to be an important tool through which cultural continuity is practiced. As Jennifer Neptune, a Penobscot Indian and a staff member at the Maine Indian Basket Makers Alliance, related in 2007, "Baskets are everything in our culture. . . . Baskets really saved our people when settlement and logging wiped out fishery" (Alvarez 2007). Today, Wabanaki Indian baskets are considered art pieces. Many are exhibited in museums across the country, including the Abbe Museum in Maine near Acadia National Park. The lasting legacy of Native American participation in the intimate economic production of utilitarian and fancy baskets on the fringes of Euroamerican settlements, I argue, is directly associated with larger Native American strategies for cultural survivance in the face of incredible adversity. Maine Indians remain a part of the Maine landscape, as they have since time immemorial. For example, in the 1930s, Penobscot Indians Leo and Florence Shay set up a stand in a vacant lot in Lincolnville, which is located along the coast (Figure 2.3). From this roadside stand the Shays wove baskets for sale to summer tourists. Their stand was a part of the Lincolnville landscape for sixty years. I remember seeing this stand as a boy and the sweet smell of the baskets. That was my first interaction with American Indians. Generations of my family members traveled through Lincolnville and purchased baskets from the Shays, some for use, and some as decoration or collectibles. In ways similar to this, New England families such as my own interacted with Native American artisans in Maine and brought Native American crafts into their Euroamerican homes and applied them to the practices of their daily lives. Meanwhile, Maine indigenous people remained and continue to remain a visible part of the landscape.

The example of intimate exchanges between indigenous Maine Indians and Euroamerican settlers presented in this chapter underscores how exchanges conducted outside formal, large market systems between producers and consumers who share intimate connections and relationships associated with the transactions have lasting, meaningful repercussions in terms of how meaning became ascribed to objects, to relationships, and expressions of identity.

Euroamerican consumers brought Indian objects as they applied Indian-made objects to the reproduction of their household practice and

Figure 2.3. Indian basket makers at a Penobscot Indian Camp, Lincolnville, Maine. Courtesy of the Penobscot Marine Museum.

relied, in part, on Native American wage labor on farms, cutting timber, and in coastal fisheries (McBride and Prins 2009, 16). Likewise, Indian producers remained highly mobile and a part of the Maine landscape despite the nearly overwhelming forces of settler colonialism that would undermine their sovereignty and relegate them to the past. Instead, Native American laborers and artisans responded to Euroamerican expansion through creative accommodations that simultaneously contributed to the survivance of many cultural traditions. With this final point, I suggest that inherent within the intimate economic transactions between Maine Indians and Euroamerican settlers are issues of power closely associated with Native American cultural survivance strategies and agency.

This example from Maine is not unique. In the early eighteenth century, small Native American tribes living on the coast of South Carolina responded similarly to European expansion. They did so by serving as producers for Lowcountry plantations, providing foodstuffs cooked or delivered in Native American–made vessels produced in strikingly traditional European forms (Nyman 2011). Similarly, along the Gulf Coast there is evidence that Native American potters made European-style vessels for colonial plantations using traditional materials and methods (see Cordell 2001; Waselkov and Gums 2000), creating hybrid vessels that materially represented cross-cultural negotiations between producers and consumers with intimate connections. Shannon Dawdy points out that in eighteenth-century New Orleans, colonial French settlers understood the importance of food rituals as a part of diplomacy among Native Americans in the Gulf region (Dawdy 2010, 394). The policy of reciprocal hospitality between the two cultures required the French to consume the things they were offered, which sometimes included dog meat (Dawdy 2010, 394–395). In these instances, both food and ideas about eating were being exchanged and adopted, so that the French became increasingly comfortable incorporating the strange and the exotic into their ideas of what constituted a proper French meal. They also became comfortable with transforming these strange new foods in ways that were familiar but had a distinctly local flavor (Dawdy 2010, 402). Dawdy (2010, 409) remarks that the French seemed eager to eat Native American foods and took pleasure in the "wild" tastes of the frontier. The result was a cuisine with the quality of a hybrid—one that emerged out of the paradox of globalization as a unique variation of French cooking greatly influenced by local flavors.

The point of presenting these examples is to remind scholars to confront older narratives centered on cultural decline and reframe them to acknowledge Native American creativity and agency despite the violence inherent in colonial expansion. Archaeologists have the opportunity to explore how intimate intercultural contact and exchanges resulted in Europeans and Euroamericans expressing and/or rearticulating their identities through incorporating Native American goods into their daily practices. Cultural exchanges were never unilateral, and the goods Native Americans produced to meet the needs of consumers they were in close, intimate contact with are often expressions of the relationships themselves. The hybrid basket forms Native Americans produced were, in a sense, an embodiment of the intercultural negotiations partners made as a result of confronting Euroamerican expansion into their world.

References Cited

Alvarez, Maribel. 2007. Weaving Survival and Art: Maine Indian Basketmakers Alliance. Arts in a Changing America. Accessed October 2017. https://artsinachangingamerica.org/weaving-survival-memory-and-art-maine-indian-basketmakers-alliance-from-the-archives-of-artography/.

Axtell, James. 1997. *The Indians' New South: Cultural Change in the Colonial Southeast.* Baton Rouge: Louisiana State University Press.

Blau, Peter M. 1964. *Exchange & Power in Social Life.* New Brunswick, NJ: Transaction Publishers.

Bourdieu, Pierre. 1977. *Outline of a Theory of Practice.* Cambridge: Cambridge University Press.

Bourque, Bruce J. 2004. *Twelve Thousand Years: American Indians in Maine.* Lincoln, NB: Bison Books.

Bourque, Bruce J., and Laureen A. Labar. 2009. *Uncommon Threads: Wabanaki Textiles, Clothing, and Costume.* Seattle: University of Washington Press.

Brimley, Stephen. 2004. Native American Sovereignty in Maine. *Maine Policy Review* 13(2):12–26.

Cobb, Charles R., and Chester B. DePratter. 2012. Multisited Research on Colonowares and the Paradox of Globalization. *American Anthropologist* 114(3):446–461.

Cook, Karen S., and Eric Rice. 2006. Social Exchange Theory. In *Handbook of Social Psychology,* edited by John Delamater, 53–80. New York: Springer.

Cook, Noble David. 1998. *Born to Die: Disease and New World Conquest, 1492–1650.* Cambridge: Cambridge University Press.

Cordell, Ann S. 2001. *Continuity and Change in Apalachee Pottery Manufacture: A Technological Comparison of Apalachee-Style and Colono Ware Pottery from French Colonial Old Mobile and Mission San Luis de Talimali.* Archaeological Monograph, Center for Archaeological Studies. Mobile: University of South Alabama.

Crosby, Alfred. 1976. Virgin Soil Epidemics as a Factor in the Aboriginal Depopulation in America. *William and Mary Quarterly* 33:289–299.

Dawdy, Shannon Lee. 2010. "A Wild Taste": Food and Colonialism in Eighteenth-Century Louisiana. *Ethnohistory* 57(3):389–414.

Emerson, Richard M. 1976. Social Exchange Theory. *Annual Review of Sociology* 2:335–362.

Firth, Raymond. 1967. *Themes in Economic Anthropology.* London: Tavistock.

Freidman, Jonathan. 1994. *Cultural Identity & Global Process.* London: SAGE Publications.

Humphrey, Caroline, and Stephen Hugh-Jones, eds. 1992. Introduction: Barter, Exchange and Value. In *Barter Exchange and Value: An Anthropological Approach,* edited by Caroline Humphrey and Stephen Hugh-Jones, 1–20. New York: Cambridge University Press.

Leibmann, Matthew. 2012. The Rest Is History: Devaluing the Recent Past in the Archaeology of the Pueblo Southwest. In *Decolonizing Indigenous Histories; Exploring Prehistoric/Colonial Transitions in Archaeology,* edited by Maxine Oland, Siobhan M. Hart, and Liam Frink, 19–44. Tucson: University of Arizona Press.

Loren, Diana DiPaolo. 2001. Social Skins: Orthodoxies and Practices of Dressing the Early Colonial Lower Mississippi Valley. *Journal of Social Archaeology* 1:172–189.

———. 2010. *The Archaeology of Clothing and Bodily Adornment in Colonial America.* Gainesville: University Press of Florida.

Matthews, Christopher N. 2010. *The Archaeology of American Capitalism*. Gainesville: University Press of Florida.

McBride, Bunny. 1990. *Our Lives in Our Hands: Micmac Indian Basketmakers*. Gardiner, ME: Tilbury House Publishers.

McBride, Bunny and Harald E. L. Prins. 2009. *Indians in Eden: Wabanaki and Rusticators on Maine's Mount Desert Island, 1840s–1920s*. Camden, ME: Down East Books.

Morgan, David W., and Kevin C. MacDonald. 2012. Colonoware in Western Colonial Louisiana: Makers and Meaning. In *French Colonial Archaeology in the Southeast and Caribbean*, 117–151, edited by Kenneth G. Kelly and Meredith D. Hardy. Gainesville: University of Florida Press.

Nassaney, Michael S. 2004. Native American Gender Politics and Material Culture in Seventeenth-Century Southeastern New England. *Journal of Social Archaeology* 4(3):334–367.

Nyman, James A. 2011. The Ashley Series as Native American Persistence: Lowcountry Indians in the Period of European Expansion. MA thesis, University of South Carolina.

Pawling, Micah. 2016. Wabanaki Homeland and Mobility: Concepts of Home in Nineteenth-Century Maine. *Ethnohistory* 63(4):621–643.

Quimby, George Irving. 1966. *Indian Culture and European Trade Goods: The Archaeology of the Historic Period in the Western Great Lakes Region*. Madison: University of Wisconsin Press, Madison.

Reff, Daniel. 1991. *Disease, Depopulation, and Culture Change*. Salt Lake City: University of Utah Press.

Rice, Prudence M. 1987. *Pottery Analysis: A Sourcebook*. Chicago: University of Chicago Press.

Rubertone, Patricia. 2001. *Grave Undertakings: An Archaeology of Roger Williams and the Narragansett*. Washington, D.C.: Smithsonian Institution Press.

Sahlins, Marshall. 1965. Exchange Value and Diplomacy of Primitive Trade. In *Essays in Economic Anthropology*, edited by June Helm, 95–129. Seattle: American Ethnological Society.

Scully, Diana. 1995. Maine Indian Claims Settlement: Concepts, Context, and Perspective. Accessed October 2017. http://www.mitsc.org/documents/21_Body.doc.pdf.

Silliman, Stephen. 2009. Change and Continuity, Practice and Memory: Native American Persistence in Colonial New England. *American Antiquity* 74(2):211–230.

South, Stanley. 2002. *Archaeological Pathways to Historic Site Development*. New York: Kluwer Academic/Plenum Publishing.

Spicer, Edward H. 1961. *Perspectives in American Indian Culture Change*. Chicago: University of Chicago Press.

Waselkov, Gregory A., and Bonnie L. Gums. 2000. *Plantation Archaeology at Rivière aux Chiens, ca. 1725–1848*. Prepared for the Alabama Department of Transportation. Mobile: University of South Alabama, Center for Archaeological Studies.

Wolfe, Patrick. 2006. Settler Colonialism and the Elimination of the Native. *Journal of Genocide Research* 8(4):387–409.

3

Webs of Drinking

Alcohol, Colonialism, and Social Relations in Early Modern Sápmi

SAMI LAKOMÄKI, TIMO YLIMAUNU, AND RITVA KYLLI

In Sápmi, the homeland of the indigenous Sámi people that stretches from today's central Norway through northern Sweden and Finland to northwestern Russia, excavations at early modern settlement and trading sites often yield fragments of bottle glass (Harlin 2007, 157–161; Harlin 2009, 123). Usually interpreted as the remains of liquor bottles that Scandinavian, Finnish, and Russian traders carried to the Sámi country, these tiny finds raise large questions about the economic and political networks that ordered northernmost Europe during the seventeenth and eighteenth centuries, when emerging states and globalizing commerce expanded to the area from the south. The spread of such capitalist and colonial networks from western Europe across the globe has long been the stuff of historical archaeology (Orser 1996), and alcohol trade has often been seen as a central component of this process. Distilling liquor on an industrial scale began in Europe in the sixteenth and seventeenth centuries, and European alcohol soon spread globally through the widening commercial and political webs explorers, invaders, merchants, and missionaries built. From the North American fur trade to the African slave trade, alcohol became a key commodity in the growing exchange between indigenous peoples and newcomers. In other contexts, colonial elites used it to mobilize local labor for colonial plantations, mines, and other enterprises. Alcohol helped incorporate indigenous peoples into the emerging Eurocentric world-system as producers of raw materials, workers, and consumers of colonial goods (Akyeampong 1996; Diduk 1993;

Figure 3.1. This silver drinking vessel with partial gilding was made for the Sámi trade in Tornio, one of the main centers of the Swedish *boalvars*, in 1793. In 1902, museum collectors acquired it from the Sámi community in Aanaar (Inari), northern Finland. Like similar elaborately crafted artifacts, it probably played a central role in social and spiritual rituals involving alcohol among the Sámis. Courtesy of the National Board of Antiquities, Finland.

Dietler 2006, 234, 239–241; Scaramelli and de Scaramelli 2005, 143–150; Smith 2008; Willis 2002).

Yet the history of alcohol exchange in early modern Sápmi complicates the familiar narrative of liquor as a harbinger of capitalism and colonialism. To be sure, alcohol linked Sámi men and women to distant producers, consumers, and financiers across Europe in novel ways. Distilled in Scandinavian and Russian towns or even farther afield, transported to the Sámi country in glass bottles manufactured in southern factories, and often drunk from silver vessels urban artisans crafted, liquor epitomized the new economic and social relations and materialities early modern colonialism and commerce created. Nevertheless, historical archaeologists should not assume that Europeans or their cultural understandings of economy and exchange dominated the emerging networks that connected indigenous peoples to European manufacturers, merchants, and capitalists. In fact, in the seventeenth and eighteenth centuries, much of the liquor circulating in the Sámi homelands did not change hands in transactions that we would today easily identify as capitalistic trade—or indeed as "trade" of any kind. While Swedish, Finnish, Norwegian, and Russian merchants certainly carried large quantities of inebriants to

Sápmi, they sold only part of their stock and gave the rest to Sámis as gifts in elaborate rituals that accompanied trade. Crown officials and priests, too, shared liquor with Sámis in reciprocal gift exchanges. Finally, Sámis circulated large amounts of alcohol among themselves in marriage ceremonies, feasts, and rituals of hospitality and offered it to spiritually powerful beings.

These diverse exchanges invite scholars to rethink the role of alcohol in the expansion of colonialism and capitalism in early modern northern Europe. Instead of transforming the Sámi country into a colonized market that operated according to the logic of capitalism, the complex ways liquor circulated among people and between humans and nonhumans created a multilayered landscape of personal, often intimate, relations that were not only economic but also social, familial, political, spiritual, emotional, and sexual. Colonists did not wield unilateral control over these webs. Alcohol undoubtedly helped colonial traders, officials, and priests forge economic and political contacts with Sámis, but it also helped Sámis mold these relationships after indigenous cultural models. Even more important, Sámis used colonial inebriants to weave social, economic, and spiritual networks that were not colonial at all. Sámis exchanged and shared liquor among themselves to expand their own connections and relationships, contesting the networks built by colonists. Although alcohol entangled Sámis in far-reaching commercial markets and webs of emerging state power, it also maintained, even extended, indigenous networks and spaces.

This chapter explores the intimate economies of alcohol exchange in seventeenth- and eighteenth-century Sápmi in order to reenvision the social and economic landscape of northernmost Europe during the early modern expansion of colonialism and capitalism. Concentrating on the Sámi communities in what is today Sweden and Finland and on their encounters with Swedish merchants, officials, and missionaries, we argue for a fine-grained and multifaceted understanding of this landscape.[1] Instead of discovering a European "center" from which webs of economic and political connections spread across a northern "periphery," our analysis uncovers a far more complex world of multiple overlapping, interlocking, and frequently competing indigenous, colonial, and hybrid networks in which the meanings of intercommunity trade, relations between indigenous people and colonial newcomers, and identities were constantly negotiated through exchange and consumption.

Toasting with the *Boalvars*: Negotiating the Rules of Intercultural Exchange

Sámi communities have long participated in multiple exchange networks that extend from the Arctic Ocean to continental Europe and Britain. By the Middle Ages, they had forged complex economic relations with the neighboring Scandinavian, Finno-Ugric, and Slavic peoples who funneled the furs and fish Sámis harvested to southern commercial hubs such as Novgorod, Hanseatic cities, and English ports (Fjellström 1985, 63–67; Hansen and Olsen 2004, 136–139; Mulk 1996, 47–50). The structures of this exchange transformed dramatically in the sixteenth and seventeenth centuries, as medieval kingdoms in southern Scandinavia and Russia began consolidating into centralized states and sought to expand their power north to Sápmi. Swedish kings were particularly eager to assert control over the lucrative economic networks in the north. In 1602, the Crown ordered that special trading sites, known as marketplaces, be established across the Sámi country and decreed that all commerce with Sámis had to take place at these locations at prescribed times under the supervision of royal officials (Hansen 1990, 69–70; Hansen and Olsen 2004, 243–246). Swedish merchants, known among Sámis as *boalvars* (Itkonen 1948, 223), toured the marketplaces every winter, offering Sámis industrial and agricultural products such as cloth, metal tools, and flour in exchange for reindeer, beaver, marten, fox, and bear furs; clothing made from skins; fish; and dairy products from reindeer (Hansen 1990, 63–64; Högström 1747, 245–246; Rheen 1983, 58; Tornæi 1983, 63–64). During this period, Sámis also continued to look for other opportunities for long-distance exchange, frequenting Norwegian and Russian trading sites on the Atlantic and Arctic coasts (Hansen 1990).

Intoxicating beverages have a long history in the exchange between Sámis and their neighbors. Beer and mead are ancient Scandinavian products (Sköld 1999, 63) and may have been offered to Sámis for centuries before the early modern expansion of the trade between Sámis and Scandinavians (Kvist 1992a, 197). By the 1590s, Swedish merchants had added a more recent innovation, distilled liquor, to the supplies they carried to Sámi country for exchange (Fellman 1915, 50, 54, 56). It was an immediate success. Sámis soon learned to value the strong sensory effects of alcohol: it came to be used as a medicine, as a medium for attaining spiritual states in shamanistic ritual, and as a social and ceremonial drink consumed communally at weddings, funerals, and feasts (Sköld 1999). After the mid-seventeenth century, Swedish officials and priests routinely listed distilled liquor as one of the main items the *boalvars* carried to the annual trade fairs at the marketplaces in Sápmi (Fellman 1910, 179, 268; Rheen 1983, 58; Tornæi 1983, 63). In Swedish towns specializing in the Sámi trade, alcohol production became a major industry (Mäntylä 1971, 204–205, 512). Alcohol was also carried to Sápmi from much farther away: some Norwegian and Swedish merchants even imported French wines to the marketplaces and coastal trading sites (Högström 1747, 127; Rheen 1983, 59).

Clearly, alcohol was ubiquitous in the flourishing long-distance exchange in Sápmi. Yet exactly how it changed hands between the foreign merchants and Sámis was far more complex than simple descriptions of volume imply. Exploring the diverse cultural forms this exchange took greatly complicates our understanding of colonial commerce in early modern northern Europe. It is evident that *boalvars* sold large amounts of liquor to Sámis during the annual trade fairs, for this is how Swedish officials, priests, and other observers usually described the exchange. According to them, alcohol was an expensive commodity. In the 1670s, at the Jáhkámáhkke (Jokkmokk) marketplace, a jug (2.6 liters) of distilled spirits cost one weight of silver. This was half of the price of a reindeer skin and a quarter of the price of a live reindeer (Rheen 1983, 58; Sköld 1999, 66). Almost a century later, the *boalvars* of Tornio, one of the main Swedish towns on the southern borderlands of Sápmi, estimated that a jug of liquor was worth the entire skin of a female reindeer (Tamelander 1941, 53, 59).

Such clearly commercial transactions were only one way that liquor passed from the traders to Sámis, however. Often, the exchange of alcohol was far more deeply embedded in webs of mutual services and socializing that bound Sámis and the merchants together in intimate ways. Many *boalvars* traveling through Sápmi needed Sámis to haul their goods and paid for transportation with alcohol (Fellman 1910, 369). Others offered alcohol to indigenous shamans in exchange for their services, for example putting spells on their rivals or performing other magical tasks (Ervast 1956, 32; Lundii Lappi 1983, 39). Still others passed idle moments during the trade fairs by drinking with their Sámi friends and acquaintances, sometimes just to socialize, sometimes possibly to attract or hire sexual partners among indigenous women (Fellman 1910, 466; Tornæi 1983, 40). Liquor, then, lubricated quotidian and intimate cross-cultural encounters between Sámis and merchants.

Most important, much of the alcohol carried to Sápmi was exchanged in elaborate gift-giving rituals that accompanied the encounters between Sámis and *boalvars*. Swedish officials and priests who frequented the marketplaces during the trade fairs often described how generously the merchants shared their liquor with potential indigenous trading partners. Sometimes the *boalvars* spent entire nights visiting Sámis' lodges and offering them liquor (Fellman 1910, 461, 467). Sámis expected, even demanded, such generosity. When they visited the merchants' huts to negotiate about trade goods and prices, they would not conclude a deal before receiving a drink. Sometimes the *boalvars* had to offer liquor to Sámis before any commercial negotiations could even begin (Mäntylä 1971, 111; Tornæi 1983, 62–63). Often alcohol constituted only a part of a complex flow of reciprocal gifts. In 1831, a Swedish priest explained that trading would typically begin with the *boalvar* giving his Sámi partner a dram of liquor to welcome him together with other small gifts. The Sámi would then respond by offering cooked meat to the merchant, who, in turn, distributed more alcohol to the Sámi and his relatives and friends (Laestadius 1831, 82–83).

The materiality of the drinking rituals Sámis and merchant engaged in constructed the identities and relationships of the participants. When Henrik Lyttraeus, a wealthy merchant based in Tornio, died in 1773, his estate included one "Lapp goblet" and eleven "Lapp spoons," all made of silver, probably by Swedish artisans for the Sámi trade. Although Lyttraeus may have intended to sell some of these items to Sámis, at least one of them was described as "old," suggesting that Lyttraeus had used it himself when transacting business with Sámis (Tamelander 1941, 83). Similar artifacts occur in the probate inventories of other Tornio merchants (Tamelander 1941, 39, 68–69, 120). This implies that *boalvars* distributed their gifts of liquor to Sámis in elaborate silver vessels designed to display the wealth and power of their owner. Drinking together from such conspicuous vessels was meant to create strong personal ties of trust and partnership between merchants and Sámis.

These commensal rituals of trust emerged in a context of deepening interethnic distrust. Throughout the seventeenth and eighteenth centuries, expanding Swedish settlements, mining activities, and aggressive missionizing in Sápmi worried many Sámis, who complained that "their forefathers were in ancient days the owners of all of Sweden" but the Swedes had "driven them away" (Högström 1747, 39). Swedes, in turn, considered Sámis to be uncivilized, potentially dangerous pagans and were particularly afraid of indigenous witchcraft (Lundii Lappi 1983, 33, 38; Fur 2006, 85). More than anything else, they claimed that Sámis were entirely untrustworthy. In Swedish writings of the era, Sámis were routinely portrayed as "insidious" (Tudero 1983, 22) and "full of deceit and treachery" (Tornæi 1983, 63). In particular, they were believed to be "most perfidious and unscrupulous in trade" (Graan 1983, 15) and ready to cheat any Swede who entered into business with them (Fellman 1910, 247–248, 281).

In the middle of such suspicions, rituals of gift giving and collective drinking constituted one way of building personal relations and trust across the troubled ethnic boundary. Such relations were crucial for both sides. For Sámis, a merchant's willingness to share liquor, an expensive exotic substance, transformed him from a stranger to a partner and created a basis for lasting collaboration. Personal trust and long-term relationships were also important to the *boalvars*, for they typically sold their goods to Sámis on credit and had little choice but to rely on Sámis to show up at the next year's fair to pay their debts (Fellman 1910, 281; Tornæi 1983, 63).

Ironically, however, gifts of liquor also corroded relations of trust between Sámis and *boalvars*. Almost from the start, each group accused the other of abusing the practice of gift giving. In 1674, for example, peddlers from Tornio reportedly swindled fishing sites from the Suonttavaara villagers after first making them drunk with generous gifts of liquor (Hiltunen 2006, 65). Other Tornio merchants were accused of "filling [Sámis] with spirits" to lure them into less-than-profitable deals (Mäntylä 1971, 111). But the *boalvars* had their share of complaints, too. A priest who knew the Tornio merchants well and probably reported their opinions claimed in 1672 that many times a Sámi might promise to enter into a trade relationship with a merchant just to receive gifts of alcohol; after drinking the free liquor, the Sámi would fail to deliver the goods he had promised to sell to the Swede (Tornæi 1983, 63).

To some extent these accusations may have reflected tensions between two contrasting cultural understandings of exchange. Reciprocal exchange had long characterized most social relationships in Sámi communities (Mulk 1996, 47, 63–66), while capitalist enterprise, often funded by foreign businessmen, increasingly shaped the economy of early modern Sweden (Söderberg 2006, 53–57). Yet it is easy to exaggerate this difference. The Sámis, too, used money when transacting business with outsiders, keenly compared prices of Swedish goods, and haggled with merchants (Fellman 1910, 280–281; Högström 1747, 244–245; Lundii Lappi 1983, 40; Tornæi 1983, 62–63). On the other hand, social responsibilities created by kinship, marital ties, and community membership continued to shape the economic strategies and decisions of most Swedes (Hemminki 2014, 15, 20).

Instead of reinforcing fundamental cultural differences between Sámis and newcomers, the debates surrounding gifts of alcohol crystallized the deep ambiguity of all Sámi-Swedish exchange and relations. Just as the act of sharing liquor could represent either a sincere effort to create a mutually beneficial partnership or an attempt to cheat, every transaction between Sámis and the *boalvars* contained these two possibilities. The constant barrage of reciprocal accusations demonstrates that both groups distrusted the other and wondered whether there was any moral obligation to treat the ethnic other honestly. Alcohol, then, galvanized Sámi and Swedish identities and the very idea that a deep ethnic and cultural boundary separated the two peoples. Moreover, it forced Sámis and colonists alike to ask what kinds of moral and social rules applied to exchanges with those considered social outsiders at a time when the number of such exchanges was rapidly increasing. Instead of being simply a signal of the expansion of capitalism to Sápmi, the liquor trade constituted a dynamic field of meaningful practices and discourses that participated in crafting the cultural framework of the market economy in northernmost Europe.

Drinking with the Crown's Men and Priests: Kingdom and Subjects in Sápmi

In addition to the *boalvars*, officials of the Swedish Crown and priests carried considerable amounts of alcohol to the Sámi communities. Indeed, during the seventeenth century, sharing and consuming liquor assumed an important part in ritualized encounters in which Sámis and the king's men negotiated the relationship between Sámis and the expanding state. Alcohol also lubricated everyday contact between Sámis and Swedish officials, often in ways that obscured the culturally constructed ethnic, social, and political boundaries between the two groups.

In Sweden, the early modern period was an era of consolidation and expansion of political power. In the sixteenth century, the loosely organized kingdom began transforming into a centralized, bureaucratic state. At the same time, its rulers initiated a campaign to extend their power from the old heartlands of the kingdom in what is now southern and central Sweden north to the Sámi country, drawn by the lucrative maritime trade of the Arctic Ocean (Hansen and Olsen 2004, 261–262). The expansion meant asserting control over the Sámi people. By the mid-1500s, kings were sending their bailiffs to Sámi communities annually to collect tribute and administer justice according to Swedish law (Kvist 1992b, 64–65). During the next century, the Lutheran Church, which the monarch headed, launched an aggressive missionary offensive in Sápmi in an effort to convert Sámis and integrate them spiritually to the kingdom (Kylli 2012, 34–94). Early modern European political elites interpreted these actions as transforming the Swedish king into a sovereign over Sámi subjects.

Despite these efforts, Sámis continued to pose a problem to Swedish state making. During the seventeenth and eighteenth centuries, the presence of representatives of the state and the Church on Sámi homelands, far from the major centers of Swedish power and population, remained thin. Bailiffs and priests typically toured Sámi communities only once a year, and even after permanent vicarages were built across Sápmi, most priests merely visited them for some weeks or months. Sámi mobility, too, complicated state building in the north. As Sámi families traveled widely to exploit diverse natural resources across vast areas, the king's men often had trouble collecting taxes and priests could not always even find their parishioners (Fur 2006, 63; Hiltunen 2006, 83–84; Högström 1747, 100). In addition, Sámis were constantly crossing the state borders that Sweden and its rival kingdoms were drawing to divide Sámi homelands among themselves. Many Sámis, who were now allegedly Swedish subjects, spent long periods in nominally Dano-Norwegian or Russian territory, paid taxes to the king of Denmark-Norway or the emperor of Russia, and participated in Dano-Norwegian or Russian court sessions and church rituals (Fellman 1912, 74–76; Hansen and Olsen 2004, 269; Tornæi 1983, 24–25; Tudero 1983, 10). In the eyes of Swedes, such behavior eroded Sámis' ties to the kingdom and raised questions about their loyalty.

These ambiguities meant that the relationship between Sámis and the kingdom of Sweden was constantly defined and debated in local encounters among Sámis, crown officials, and priests, often in contexts in which Sámis possessed considerable power. When we focus on these negotiations, early modern Sweden appears less like a conquering colonial state and more like an emergent, unstable network of deeply personal relationships based on reciprocal rights and obligations. These relationships certainly bound Sámis to the expanding kingdom, but they also entangled the king's men and priests in Sámi communities in complex ways.

Alcohol was a key medium in the negotiations between Sámis and the Swedish officials and priests. When a Swedish bailiff or priest left his home for the annual winter tour in Sámi country, he needed reindeer to haul his supplies, men to drive the animals, and guides to lead him through the unfamiliar territory. Only Sámis could provide all three. In the seventeenth century, the Crown began demanding that Sámis provide transportation for state and church officials visiting Sápmi. Even though this was a legal obligation, government officials and priests commonly paid Sámis for their services, and liquor soon became one typical form of payment (Tornæi 1983, 55). Besides transportation, officials and clergymen in Sámi homelands frequently had to procure food from the locals. Again, many purchased provisions with alcohol. Not surprisingly, priests traveled in Sápmi with considerable stores of liquor (Lakomäki et al. 2017). These exchanges of alcohol highlight the complexities of power on the Sámi homelands. On the one hand, liquor enabled Swedish officials and priests to enter Sápmi; on the other, the Swedes' generous gifts of alcohol to the locals demonstrate how much their presence in the north depended on Sámis and was shaped by Sámi customs.

Negotiations between Sámis and crown officials and priests took on a more ceremonial form when the Swedes would arrive at an indigenous village. Gabriel Tuderus, a priest in eastern Sápmi in the 1660s and 1670s, told how Sámis would assemble outside their village to welcome a visiting bailiff or priest and escort him to the settlement in a festive procession. Once in the village, the Sámis would offer the visitor a rich meal and give him warm skin boots and gloves. The visitor would reciprocate by distributing liquor and bread (Tudero 1983, 55). Tuderus's contemporary in the Ume River region witnessed similar practices among western Sámis. According to him, when a Swedish bailiff arrived at a Sámi village, the locals would greet him with cheese and meat. The bailiff would then offer three spoonfuls of liquor as a "gift of greeting" to the Sámis, who would bow and thank God for allowing them to meet in health (Lundii Lappi 1983, 31). In 1738, another clergyman in eastern Sápmi wrote that Sámi village elders presented Swedish priests and judges with pelts of beaver, bear, reindeer, and wolf. In exchange, they received alcohol and other gifts (Ervast 1956, 28).

These rituals defined the relationship between Sámi communities and the Swedish kingdom as a reciprocal alliance kept alive by a continuous flow of gifts. Although this was not an alliance between equals, the alcohol royal officials and priests distributed symbolically demonstrated that the king recognized the right of Sámis to receive gifts and protection in return for their taxes, gifts, and collaboration. Moreover, in the context of Swedish claims of sovereignty over Sápmi, the gifts of liquor constructed Sámi villages as Sámi spaces that crown officials could enter only on Sámi terms by participating in the networks of gift giving that had long shaped political, social, and economic relations throughout Sápmi.

The establishment of the crown-sanctioned marketplaces across Sápmi was a more forceful effort to assert Swedish power and presence on Sámi homelands. In addition to sites of commerce, the marketplaces were designed as centers of crown law and church ritual that would tie Sámis to the kingdom as subjects. When large numbers of Sámis assembled at these places during the annual trade fairs, they met not only Swedish merchants but also bailiffs, judges, and priests who had come to collect tribute, organize court sessions, and teach Christianity. According to Swedish law, any Sámi who failed to appear at the marketplaces during the trade fairs would be punished by a fine (Fur 2006, 62–63, 68–69). As early as the 1680s, policymakers in Stockholm discussed the possibility of stationing crown officials permanently in the marketplaces to enforce the king's rule more effectively in Sápmi (Fellman 1910, 382). While these plans did not materialize until much later, during the late seventeenth and eighteenth centuries the Crown built churches, and in some cases also vicarages, in the marketplaces in an attempt to transform these sites into more formidable embodiments of Swedish authority on the indigenous landscape (Kylli 2012, 37–56).

But even in the marketplaces, the relations between Sámis and Swedish officials continued to be expressed and negotiated through rituals of reciprocal gift giving in which alcohol played a major role. When Sámis arrived at a marketplace for an annual gathering, they were often greeted by the visiting crown bailiff, who welcomed them with a generous distribution of exotic beverages and agricultural produce. In 1607, for example, the king's men feasted Sámis of the Ume district with sixteen liters of liquor, 1,400 liters of beer, butter, bread, and meat. As Swedish historian Roger Kvist notes, Sámis may have understood the taxes they paid at the marketplaces as return gifts for such displays of generosity from the Crown (Kvist 2004, 2).

When Swedish priests began living more permanently at the vicarages in the marketplaces, alcohol exchange continued to shape their economic and social relations with Sámis. Clergymen stationed in Sápmi were poorly paid and lacked many of the benefits their colleagues in the southern parishes enjoyed (Kylli 2005, 46–49). To supplement their livelihoods, many priests engaged in farming and refined part of their crops into liquor, which they used to pay Sámis for extra provisions and various kinds of services (Kylli 2012, 67–68; Lassinantti 1969, iv). But the importance of alcohol extended beyond economic exchanges. Some priests and their family members socialized with their Sámi neighbors over a cup of liquor. Around 1700, for instance, Aili Jönsdotter, the wife of the Guovdageaidnu (Kautokeino) vicar, often served visiting Sámis spirits and drank with them (Riksarkivet 1695, 1713). Such sharing of alcohol helped weave priestly families intimately into indigenous social webs. For example, Aili Jönsdotter and her children gradually assimilated in the Guovdageaidnu Sámi community after her husband's death (Rasmussen 2011, 65). The circulation and consumption of alcohol created intimacy that eroded the imagined cultural, social, and ethnic boundaries many Swedes drew between "civilized" Swedish priests and "savage" Sámis.

Ironically, as alcohol increasingly linked the lives of Sámis and newcomers in Sápmi, Swedish policymakers in Stockholm were growing concerned about the effects of drinking on Sámis. Although many priests produced and drank liquor themselves, others argued that alcohol promoted sinful practices among Sámis and was an obstacle to their conversion (Fellman 1910, 209; Lundii Lappi 1983, 11, 15, 31, 33). State and ecclesial officials discussed the possibility of banning liquor in Sámi homelands as early as the 1680s (Fellman 1910, 382). In 1723, the Crown finally prohibited the sale of alcohol in marketplaces across Sápmi until the official part of the annual trade fairs had been finished. Later in the eighteenth century, the Crown periodically forbade the production and consumption of liquor throughout the kingdom (Kvist 2004, 3–4). In the

Sámi homelands, these prohibitions meant a unilateral attempt on the part of the Crown to redefine the relationship between indigenous communities and Sweden. While the gifts of liquor bailiffs and priests distributed to Sámis had signaled at least a symbolic Swedish recognition that Sámis were active partners in an alliance based on cooperation, the bans on alcohol consumption construed a far more hierarchical and one-sided relationship between the Crown and its indigenous subjects.

Swedish officials lacked the power to enforce the prohibitions in Sápmi, however. Throughout the mid- and late eighteenth centuries, Sámis routinely bought alcohol illegally from Swedish *boalvars* or carried it home from Norwegian trading sites on the Atlantic and Arctic coasts (Fellman 1910, 213–214, 266–268, 277; Lakomäki et al. 2017). This commerce contested Swedish sovereignty and borders in the north and maintained Sápmi as an indigenous space defined by indigenous webs of mobility and exchange. Just as the liquor bans represented the Crown's effort to turn the Sámi homelands into Swedish territory, the continuing alcohol trade fostered Sámi networks that cut through state borders and undermined state control.

Liquor, Kinspeople, and Spirits: Alcohol Exchange in the Sámi World

While scholars who explore the intersections of alcohol and colonialism are often primarily interested in how liquor flowed in emerging capitalist and imperial networks, in Sápmi, colonial intoxicants also circulated in exclusively indigenous social webs. Built on kinship, reciprocity, and ritual, these overlapping and interlocking webs bound Sámi families to one another, to their ancestors, and to the other-than-human beings who control the cosmos. Focusing on how alcohol moved within this Sámi world demonstrates how Sámis indigenized colonial liquor and employed it to create, even expand, indigenous social, economic, and spiritual networks during an era of intense colonization. Rather than simply a colonial commodity that chained Sámis to the invaders' projects of trade and state building, liquor became an important material element of a vibrant indigenous landscape.

Sámis integrated alcohol in their social and ritual lives during the seventeenth century. Since liquor was an expensive exotic substance with powerful spiritual and medicinal effects, they used it as a valued gift that they gave to particularly honored persons. Gifts of alcohol also became crucial for initiating and maintaining social relationships, especially with people and beings with high status and strong power.

Gifts of alcohol were especially important in courtship and marriage rituals that united families and created new alliances among them. In the seventeenth and eighteenth centuries, Sámi courtship was a long process of negotiation that sometimes stretched over several years, during which time the families involved regularly exchanged gifts (Rheen 1983, 10–11; Tudero 1983, 18). Although practices varied across the wide Sámi homelands, alcohol played a key symbolic role in this gift giving everywhere. In the region of the Pite and Lule Rivers, a man visiting the parents of the woman he wanted to marry for the first time brought one to three jugs of liquor as a gift. If the woman's father accepted the gift, the families began negotiating the terms of the marriage seriously. Over the following years, the suitor would continue to visit the woman's family, each time sharing more liquor with his future in-laws, as the families discussed the details of the gifts they would exchange (Graan 1983, 27). Ritualized distribution and consumption of alcohol gave rhythm to these meetings. In the Tornio River drainage area, for example, the suitor's spokesman would first offer a round of drinks to the woman's family. Then, kneeling down, he would perform a long speech honoring the woman's father and praising the suitor while a goblet circulated among the woman's kinspeople (Tornæi 1983, 42–43). At the wedding, the direction of the gifts, including alcohol, was often reversed. In many eastern Sámi communities, for instance, it was the bride's family who served the relatives of the groom and other guests food and liquor (Tudero 1983, 19).

Elaborate material culture was an essential element of these rituals of drinking. According to one seventeenth-century Swedish priest, during the marriage negotiations, wealthy Sámis offered liquor to their prospective in-laws from a goblet with a spoon (Tornæi 1983, 43). Although he does not mention it, these items were probably made of silver in Stockholm, Bergen, or other Scandinavian cities. Such artifacts were popular trade goods among Sámis, and in the late 1700s the probate inventories of prosperous Sámis often listed silver goblets, tankards, and spoons (Fjellström 1962, 146–194; Kansallisarkisto 1796–1806). Silver drinking vessels were also valued gifts during courtship. For example, in the Lule River region, the first gift a man made to his future father-in-law was customarily a goblet of silver (Rheen 1983, 11). Silver vessels and spoons were expensive items. The Sámis regarded them highly because silver was a permanent form of wealth that never lost its value (Fjellström 1985, 481, 501). Silver also carried a host of spiritual meanings. Sámis believed that silver had sacred power that could be mobilized for a wide variety of ritual, magical, and healing purposes (Fjellström 1962, 205–206). In more than one way, then, drinking rituals associated with courtship and weddings gave the families of the groom and the bride an opportunity to perform their wealth, power, and generosity.

For a family, such performances were crucial for attracting allies and establishing intimate connections with other families near and far. Extensive supralocal marriage networks that linked families across hundreds of kilometers were crucial for survival among Sámis (Aikio 1998). They provided families with broad social safety nets and access to multiple alternative resources, both of which were vital in the harsh northern environment. When facing hard times at home, many people migrated to their in-laws or returned to their natal communities in search of better economic opportunities (Fellman 1912, 74–75; Hansen 2005, 177). Other families dispersed periodically even during normal years. In the river valleys of what is now northern Sweden, men spent summers fishing in the forested lowlands, while women and children joined reindeer-herding villages in the Scandinavian Mountains (Graan 1983, 35), probably making use of marital and other kinship connections to these communities. Extensive webs of in-laws and other relatives were especially important for nomadic reindeer herding, an emerging subsistence strategy that expanded rapidly through Sápmi during the seventeenth and eighteenth centuries. Families who owned large herds of reindeer needed grazing lands at environmentally diverse locations and typically gained access to pastures through webs of kinship (Brännlund 2015, 22).

Gifts of alcohol helped Sámis both construct and reproduce such extensive networks of kin. In 1672, one Swedish priest described how Sámis liked to "travel around and visit" one another (Graan 1983, 50). Nicolaus Lundius, another clergyman with a Sámi background, told how parents enjoyed visiting their children who had married elsewhere (Lundii Lappi 1983, 35). According to Lundius (Lundii Lappi 1983, 11, 35), Sámis feasted visitors generously, and various Swedish documents testify that people often shared liquor with their guests (Fellman 1910, 468; Fellman 1912, 266–268; Tornæi 1983, 64). Alcohol had the power to connect families over wide distances and keep their connections alive.

Networks constructed through the exchange of alcohol included participants who were other than human. For Sámis, the cosmos was filled with various spiritually powerful beings, including guardians of sacred sites and masters of different animal species. To survive and prosper, people needed the favor and collaboration of these other-than-human beings and actively sought to engage them in social relations. This was done through ceremonies of gift giving. Just as they gave gifts to other humans to show respect and draw them into reciprocal, mutually supportive relationships, Sámis offered gifts such as ritually butchered animals to these other-than-human beings. These powerful beings, in turn, were expected to bestow humans with gifts of their own, including health, plentiful harvests of fish or game, and success in reindeer herding (Äikäs 2011, 18; Mulk 1996, 64–65).

Liquor became a part of the reciprocal gift exchanges between Sámis and the other-than-human beings during the seventeenth century. Sámis offered alcohol especially to the female *áhkká* beings who protected the birth and well-being of babies and women in labor. During childbirth, for example, Sámis would pour alcohol on the floor of their lodge because they believed that the *áhkkás* lived underneath the floor. The guardians of fish and fishing sites also received gifts of liquor. During Christmas night, Sámi families invited Tjas-olmai, the Water Man, home to share a dinner with them. They drank a toast of alcohol in his honor and placed more liquor and meat and fish on the floor for him to eat. Gifts of liquor did not always flow from humans to other-than-human beings, however. In dreams and trance states, some Sámis were able to visit ancestral *saivo* spirits living inside sacred mountains. During these visits, the ancestors sometimes served their guests alcohol while singing and drumming with them ritually (Pulkkinen 2011, 232; Sköld 1999, 69–71).

Conclusions

Exploring how glass bottles once filled with liquor ended up in seventeenth- and eighteenth-century sites in Sápmi invites scholars to rethink the models we use to understand the spread of colonialism and capitalism in the early modern period. Following the routes of alcohol from Scandinavian towns that were increasingly linked to webs of global commerce to Sámi communities can create an impression of a powerfully expanding Eurocentric world system that inexorably shackled the continent's northern "periphery" to the growing centers of production, consumption, and capital farther south. However, while not incorrect, this image is one sided. When we concentrate on how liquor actually circulated in Sápmi and explore the cultural meanings the exchange of alcohol acquired in the Sámi homelands, a very different picture of the economic, political, and social landscape of early modern northern Europe emerges.

A pivotal feature of this emerging landscape is that it was not defined solely by networks of commerce and power radiating north from colonial and capitalist "cores" in southern Scandinavia and central Europe. Rather, such networks entangled and merged with Sámi webs of gift giving and alliance, producing a multilayered and hybrid landscape where gift exchanges, reciprocity, and trade became intimately intertwined. Furthermore, while alcohol exchange clearly assisted Swedish and other colonial merchants and officials in building expansive economic and political nets that solidified their wealth and power, it also assisted Sámis in extending their kinship webs, alliances, and reindeer-grazing areas that cut across the borders of the colonial states, maintained indigenous geographies, and challenged colonial power. Finally, the landscape liquor helped create was thoroughly intimate: exchanging alcohol did not link together abstract economic and political systems but men, women, and other-than-human beings who knew one another closely, partially because they drank together.

These findings point to three major conclusions. First, any attempt to grasp the economic and political expansion of Europe in the early modern period must take indigenous cultures seriously, for indigenous understandings of exchange, authority, and intersocietal relations shaped the forms and contours of the European expansion powerfully. Second, scholars should avoid presupposing that European networks of commerce and power were the only expansive social webs in the early modern world and should develop analytical and narrative strategies that recognize, make visible, and interrogate expanding indigenous political and economic nets. Third, and perhaps most challenging, even when dealing with large-scale systems and processes such as capitalism and colonialism, we have to be careful not to lose sight of the intimacy of lived experiences and social relations. Finding ways to connect the intimately linked women and men to the global economic and political processes framing their lives in ways that recognize the mutually constitutive character of these connections is essential for understanding the emergence of capitalism and colonialism.

Note

1. In this article, the terms Swede and Swedish are used as shorthand for all subjects of the king of Sweden. In the seventeenth and eighteenth centuries, these subjects included several hundred thousand Finns and, at times, smaller numbers of Norwegians.

References Cited

Äikäs, Tiina. 2011. *Rantakiviltä tuntureille: Pyhät paikat saamelaisten rituaalisessa maisemassa*. Rovaniemi, Finland: Pohjois-Suomen Historiallinen Yhdistys.

Aikio, Aslak. 1998. Avioliitto ja identiteetti: Saamelaisten ja suomalaisten avioituminen Utsjoella, Inarissa ja Enontekiöllä. MA thesis, Department of History, University of Oulu, Finland.

Akyeampong, Emmanuel Kwaku. 1996. *Drink, Power, and Cultural Change: A Social History of Alcohol in Ghana, c. 1800 to Recent Times*. Portsmouth, NH: Heinemann.

Brännlund, Isabelle. 2015. *Histories of Reindeer Husbandry Resilience: Land Use and Social Networks of Reindeer Husbandry in Swedish Sápmi, 1740–1920*. Umeå, Sweden: Department of Historical, Philosophical and Religious Studies and Vaartoe, Centre for Sami Research.

Diduk, Susan. 1993. European Alcohol, History, and the State in Cameroon. *African Studies Review* 36(10):1–42.

Dietler, Michael. 2006. Alcohol: Anthropological/Archaeological Perspectives. *Annual Review of Anthropology* 35:229–249.

Ervast, Johan Bartholdi. 1956. *Descriptio Lapponiae Kiemiensis eli Kemi-Lapin kuvaus vuodelta 1737*. Translated by Tuomo Itkonen. Kemi, Finland: Kemin Kotiseutu-ja Museoyhdistys.

Fellman, Isak, ed. 1910. *Handlingar och uppsatser angående finska lappmarken och lapparne I*. Helsingfors, Finland: Finska Litteratursällskapet.

———. 1912. *Handlingar och uppsatser angående finska lappmarken och lapparne II*. Helsingfors, Finland: Finska Litteratursällskapet.

———. 1915. *Handlingar och uppsatser angående finska lappmarken och lapparne IV*. Helsingfors, Finland: Finska Litteratursällskapet.

Fjellström, Phebe. 1962. *Lapskt silver: Studier över en föremålsgrupp och dess ställning inom lapskt kulturliv*. Vol. 1, *Textdel*. Stockholm, Sweden: Almqvist & Wiksell.

———. 1985. *Samernas samhälle i tradition och nutid*. Stockholm,Sweden: P. A. Norstedt & Söners Förlag.

Fur, Gunlög. 2006. *Colonialism in the Margins: Cultural Encounters in New Sweden and Lapland*. Leiden: Brill.

Graan, Olao. 1983. Relation, eller en fulkomblig beskrifning om lapparnas vrsprung, så wähl som om heela dheras lefwernes förehållande. In *Berättelser om samerna in 1600-talets Sverige*, edited by Phebe Fjellström. Umeå, Sweden: Kungl Skytteanska Samfundets handlingar 27.

Hansen, Lars Ivar. 1990. Trade and Markets in Northern Fenno-Scandinavia A.D. 1550–1750. *Acta Borealia* 1(2):47–79.

———. 2005. Spesialisert reindrift eller kombinasjonnæring? Reinholdeti Sør-Troms på 1600- og 1700-tallet. In *Fra villreinjakt til reindrift/Gåddebivdos boatsojsujttuj*, edited by Oddmund Andersen, 165–183. Drag, Norway: Árran julevsáme guovdásj.

Hansen, Lars Ivar, and Bjørnar Olsen. 2004. *Samenes historie fram til 1750*. Oslo, Norway: Cappelen Akademisk Forlag.

Harlin, Eeva-Kristiina. 2007. Suomen puoleisen Tornion Lapin markkinat. In *Peurakuopista kirkkokenttiin: Saamelaisalueen 10,000 vuotta arkeologin näkökulmasta*, edited by Eeva-Kristiina Harlin and Veli-Pekka Lehtola, 154–167. Publications of Giellagas Institute 9. Saarijärvi, Finland: Gummerus.

———. 2009. The Possibilities of Osteology in Historical Sámi Archaeology: Life and Livelihood at the 18th-Century Ohcejohka Sámi Market Site. In *Recent Perspectives on Sámi Archaeology in Fennoscandia and North-West Russia*, edited by Petri Halinen, Mika Lavento, and Mervi Suhonen, 121–132. Iskos 17. Helsinki, Finland: Finnish Antiquarian Society.

Hemminki, Tiina. 2014. *Vauraus, luotto, luottamus: Talonpoikien lainasuhteet Pohjanlahden molemmin puolin 1796–1830*. Jyväskylä, Finland: University of Jyväskylä.

Hiltunen, Mauno. 2006. *Maailma maailmojen välissä: Enontekiön asukkaat, elinkeinot ja maanhallinta 1550–1808*. Helsinki, Finland: Oikeusministeriö.

Högström, Pehr. 1747. *Beskrifning öfwer Sweriges krona lydnde lapmarker år 1747*. Stockholm, Sweden: Lars Salvii.

Itkonen, T. I. 1948. *Suomen lappalaiset vuoteen 1945, toinen osa*. Helsinki, Finland: WSOY.

Kansallisarkisto. 1796–1806. Enontekiön perukirjat 1796–1806, Lappi: 2. Arkiv av Västerbottens norra domsaga, Kansallisarkisto, Oulu, Finland.

Kvist, Roger. 1992a. Nomadic Saami and Alcohol: Jokkmokk Parish, 1760–1910. *Canadian Journal of Native Studies* 12(2):185–201.

———. 1992b. Swedish Saami Policy, 1550–1990. In *Readings in Saami History, Culture and Language III*, edited by Roger Kvist, 63–77. Umeå, Sweden: University of Umeå.

———. 2004. Myten om samerna och alkoholen. *Spiritus: Skriftserie från Vin & Spirithistoriska Museet* 6:1–13.

Kylli, Ritva. 2005. *Kirkon ja saamelaisten kohtaaminen Utsjoella ja Inarissa 1742–1886*. Rovaniemi, Finland: Pohjois-Suomen Historiallinen Yhdistys.

———. 2012. *Saamelaisten kaksi kääntymystä: Uskonnon muuttuminen Utsjoen ja Enontekiön lapinmailla, 1602–1905*. Helsinki, Finland: SKS.

Laestadius, Petrus. 1831. *Journal af P. L⊠stadius för första året af hans tjenstgöring såsom missionaire i Lappmarken*. Stockholm, Sweden: Zacharias H⊠ggström.

Lakomäki, Sami, Ritva Kylli, and Timo Ylimaunu. 2017. Drinking Colonialism: Alcohol, Indigenous Status, and Native Space on Shawnee and Sámi Homelands, 1600–1850. *NAIS: Journal of the Native American and Indigenous Studies Association* 4(1):1–29.

Lassinantti, Ragnar. 1969. Förord. In *Utkast till beskrifning öfver Enontekis sokn I Torneå Lappmark af Er. J. Grape*, i–vi. Kalix, Sweden: S. Nordströms tryckeri AB.

Lundii Lappi, Nicolai. 1983. Descriptio Lapponiæ. In *Berättelser om samerna in 1600-ta-*

lets Sverige, edited by Phebe Fjellström. Umeå, Sweden: Kungl. Skytteanska Samfundets handlingar 27.

Mäntylä, Ilkka. 1971. *Tornion kaupungin historia, 1. osa, 1621–1809*. Tornio, Finland: Tornion kaupunki.

Mulk, Inga Maria. 1996. The Role of the Sámi in Fur Trading during the Late Iron Age and Nordic Medieval Period in the Light of the Sámi Sacrificial Sites in Lapland, Northern Sweden. *Acta Borelia* 13(1):47–80.

Orser, Charles E., Jr. 1996. *A Historical Archaeology of the Modern World*. New York: Plenum Press.

Pulkkinen, Risto. 2011. Saamelaisten etninen uskonto. In *Saamentutkimus tänään*, edited by Irja Seurujärvi-Kari, Petri Halinen, and Risto Pulkkinen, 208–270. Helsinki, Finland: SKS.

Rasmussen, Siv. 2011. Prester og prestefruer i Kautokeino pastorat. *Ottar* 3:62–69.

Rheen, Samuele. 1983. En kortt Relation om Lapparnes Lefwarne och Sedher, wijd-Skiepellsser, sampt in manga Stycken Grofwe wildfarellsser. In *Berättelser om samerna in 1600-talets Sverige*, edited by Phebe Fjellström. Umeå, Sweden: Kungl. Skytteanska Samfundets handlingar 27.

Riksarkivet. 1695. *Tinget i Enontekis 1695. Svea Hovrätts arkiv, Domböcker för 1695: Västerbottens län*. Vol. 6. Riksarkivet, Stockholm, Sweden.

———. 1713. *Tinget i Koutokeino 1713. Svea Hovrätts arkiv, Domböcker för 1713–1716: Västerbottens län*. Vol. 15. Stockholm, Sweden: Riksarkivet.

Scaramelli, Franz, and Kay Tarble de Scaramelli. 2005. The Roles of Material Culture in the Colonization of the Orinoco, Venezuela. *Journal of Social Archaeology* 5(1):135–168.

Sköld, Peter. 1999. Seime staembe: Brännvinet i den samiska religionen. *Oknytt* 20(1–4):63–83.

Smith, Frederick H. 2008. *The Archaeology of Alcohol and Drinking*. Gainesville: University Press of Florida.

Söderberg, Johan. 2006. Den förindustriella tiden feam till 1720. In *Sverige: En social och economisk historia*, edited by Susanna Hedenborg and Mats Morell, 29–64. Lund, Sweden: Studentlitteratur.

Tamelander, Eino. 1941. *Tornion kaupungin pesäluetteloja 1666–1800*. Tornio, Finland: Peräpohjolan ja Lapin kotiseutuyhdistys.

Tornæi, Johannis. 1983. Berättelse om Lapmarckerna och Deras Tillstånd. In *Berättelser om samerna in 1600-talets Sverige*, edited by Phebe Fjellström. Umeå, Sweden: Kungl. Skytteanska Samfundets handlingar 27.

Tudero, Gabriele. 1983. En kort underrättelse om the österbothniske lappar, some under Kiemi Gebiet lyda. In *Berättelser om samerna in 1600-talets Sverige*, edited by Phebe Fjellström. Umeå, Sweden: Kungl. Skytteanska Samfundets handlingar 27.

Willis, Justin. 2002. *Potent Brews: A Social History of Alcohol in East Africa, 1850–1999*. London: British Institute in Eastern Africa.

4

A Round for All My Friends

Understanding the Economic Impact of Moonshine Production

KIRK D. FRENCH

Archaeological investigations of the illicit production of unregulated liquor (moonshine) provides an opportunity to discuss the emotional and intimate components that are intrinsic in economic exchange. Although the term intimate economies has generally been used by sociocultural anthropologists in reference to prostitution or physical intimacy (see Lyttleton 2014; Wilson 2004), the concept is also applicable in an archaeological context, as Nyman and Fogle have outlined in the introduction to this volume. The archaeological signatures (i.e., still furnaces, pot stills, barrel hoops, canning jars, etc.) of clandestine whiskey production can provide insights into intimate economic transactions of the past. Quantifying the number of illegal production sites in remote areas provides data that is vital for understanding the social and economic impacts that illegal alcohol had on a community.

The importance of alcohol in American culture cannot be disputed. Just five years into his presidency, George Washington sent troops to suppress an insurrection by farmers in western Pennsylvania who opposed a new tax on grain alcohol. This event, known as the Whiskey Rebellion of 1794, was the first major battle after the American Revolution. Before a true income tax was established in 1916, 71 percent of internal revenue came from taxes on alcohol (Okrent 2010). After a federal income tax was established, that new source of revenue made possible the passage of the Eighteenth Amendment of the United States Constitution. On October 28, 1919, the U.S. government declared that the production, transport, and

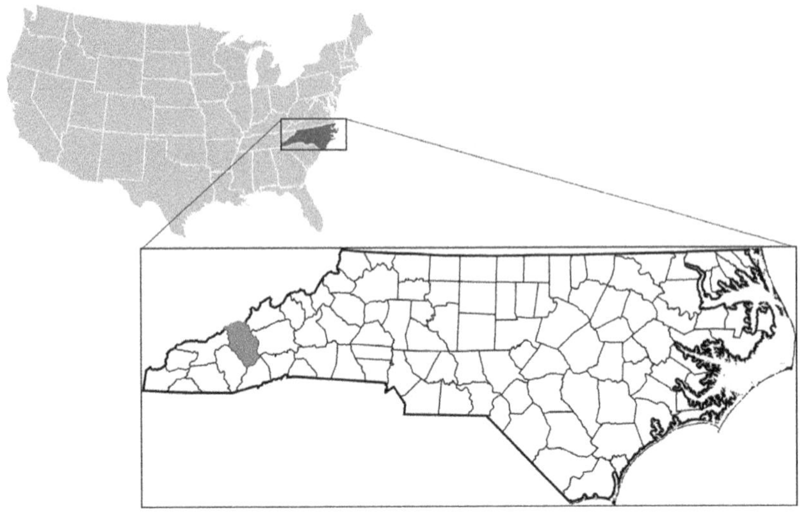

Figure 4.1. Location map of North Carolina. The Great Smoky Mountains National Park and Cataloochee Valley are located in Haywood County. Source: WorldAtlas.com.

sale of alcohol was illegal (Curtis 2007). This was the first and only time in its history that the U.S. government used a constitutional amendment to limit the rights of its people, essentially turning normal law-abiding citizens into criminals and legal exchanges into intimate trafficking (see Casias 2015, 30–34). Thirteen years later, the amendment was repealed when the Twenty-First Amendment was ratified. This is the only instance when an amendment to United States Constitution was repealed (Curtis 2007).

Illegal production of alcohol in southern Appalachia has a long and complicated history. The first federal tax on alcohol was used to pay for the Revolutionary War. Thomas Jefferson repealed it in 1802. It was reinstated from 1814 to help pay off debts incurred during the War of 1812. Three years later, in 1817, it was repealed again, only to be reinstated in 1862 to fund the Civil War. These economic burdens forced many alcohol producers to seek remote distilling locations. After the repeal of prohibition in 1932, heavy regulations coupled with successful propaganda about the dangers of locally produced whiskey kept moonshiners in the shadows. Recently there has been a surge of public interest in moonshine production and an appreciation of the area's vibrant and eclectic cultural history.

This chapter provides background on illegal moonshine production, information about methods for detecting it archaeologically, and a discussion of moonshine's social and economic impact in western North Carolina. For more than 150 years, the vast majority of local whiskey production has been unregulated, illegal, and in many regards illicit (e.g., forbidden by religious customs). The production and distribution of illegal liquor takes place in tight-knit communities where knowledge is usually passed down within a family (Miller 1991, 46), a common component of intimate economies (Bridge and Smith 2003; Hartnett and Dawdy 2013). The economic impact of craft production is difficult to measure. To better understand the intimate economies of moonshine production, the Moonshine Archaeology Project (MAP) aims to quantify whiskey production in the Cataloochee Valley of western North Carolina (Figure 4.1) before, during, and after prohibition.

Historical Background of Western North Carolina

When European settlers first arrived in western North Carolina in the late 1700s, the lands were occupied by the Cherokee (Sink 2011; Ross and Beadle 2009). The area has a much longer history of human occupation, however, that begins around 8000 BCE. Later, around 500 CE, the well-developed Hopewellian civilization lived in western North Carolina, followed by the Pisgah Phase of the South Appalachian Mississippian culture. These groups erected both villages and three earthen structures, known as the Garden Creek Mounds (31HW1-3), in Haywood County, North Carolina (Ross and Beadle 2009). Evidence suggests a continuum of cultural development in the area that eventually led to the emergence of the historic Cherokee (Sullivan and Prezzano 2001, 241–242).

North Carolina opened its western lands in 1783, and within seven months absentee speculators had purchased four million acres for approximately fifty shillings per 100 acres. The Holston Treaty of 1791 and the Treaty of Tellico in 1798 pushed the Cherokee west and opened up land near the Pigeon River for speculation and settlement (Ross and Beadle 2009, 21). In 1796, John Gray Blount purchased 176,000 acres that included the present-day Cataloochee region. The people who migrated into the region between 1798 and 1810 purchased small tracts of land for approximately $50 per 100 acres (a ~10,000 percent increase in less than twenty years). Many of the settlers were Scots-Irish whose families originated in Scotland and migrated to Ireland, then later to Philadelphia. From Pennsylvania they followed the Great Wagon Road that extended south to Georgia (Ross and Beadle 2009, 25). The Haywood County census taken in 1810 reveals that one-third of the families living there were Scots-Irish. From quilt making to housing design to whiskey production, the Scots-Irish had a huge influence on mountain culture and a lasting impact on the southern United States (Ross and Beadle 2009, 26).

The geography of western North Carolina meant that life until the 1930s was very isolated, a feature many cherished. Like most of the communities in the area, the people of the Cataloochee Valley were self-sufficient, close-knit, and often distrusting of outsiders, especially government authority. Their history explains why: King James I had "encouraged" their ancestors to leave Scotland for Ireland, where they faced religious discrimination and unfair land rents from the Irish. That is what motivated them to emigrate to the United States.

Once settled in the mountains of western North Carolina, the early immigrants enjoyed approximately fifty years of virtual solitude, with little intervention from outsiders or the government (Davis 1997, 47). Then, in 1860, the saber-rattling of the American Civil War began to affect the people of this region. Much like the residents of the mountainous territory of eastern Tennessee, many western North Carolinians were uncertain about whether to join the Confederacy, as the vast majority were not slave owners and viewed the war as unnecessary. Nevertheless, on May 20, 1861, North Carolina seceded from the United States. The region was impacted adversely for decades.

In 1865, in a successful attempt to recoup money spent on the Civil War, the U.S. government instituted an excise tax on alcohol, forcing many whiskey producers to hide their operations from officers of the Internal Revenue Service. The Volstead Act that began the prohibition era, which went into effect on January 16, 1920, increased the number of illicit whiskey producers known as moonshiners. Many household producers of whiskey for personal consumption, medicine, or small-scale trade were now criminals.

In the 1920s, representatives of the federal government informed people living in the Cataloochee Valley that they could either sell their land or be forced out via eminent domain for the purpose of creating a national park (Davis 1997, 187). The families of this region, many of whom were of Scots-Irish descent, were forced to move once again (Davis 1997, 189).

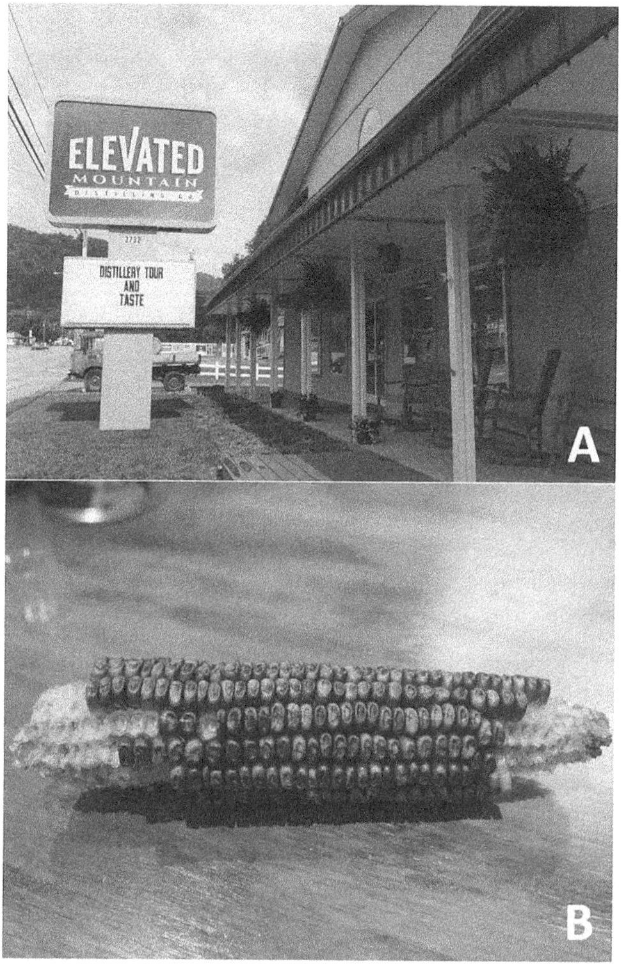

Figure 4.2. Elevated Mountain Distilling Company, the first legal distillery in the area (*a*); Bloody Butcher, a heritage breed of corn prized for making whiskey in the Cataloochee Valley (*b*). Photos by Kirk French.

After prohibition was repealed in 1933, the taxes on alcohol were high and it was illegal to produce unlicensed spirits. After World War II, it became common for federal, state, and local governments to launch expensive anti-moonshining campaigns. It was not until the late 1990s that the area's long history of whiskey production became a celebrated component at events such as local cultural heritage festivals. Recent changes in the liquor laws in North Carolina (and many other states) have allowed for the opening of many small licensed distilleries. For example, the Elevated Mountain Distilling Company (Figure 4.2a) opened in 2017 on the border of the Cataloochee Valley. The owner, Dave Angel, relies on as many local ingredients as possible, such as Bloody Butcher (Figure 4.2b) a heritage breed of corn that has been continuously grown by the Woody family, descendants of the Scots-Irish who were forced to vacate their land in the Cataloochee Valley in the 1930s during the creation of the Great Smoky Mountains National Park (Davis 1997, 189).

Whiskey Production in Western North Carolina

The technological knowledge of making whiskey came with the Scots-Irish when they emigrated to the United States. This specialized craft dates to circa AD 1100 in both Ireland and Scotland (Kosar 2010, 32). Instead of the malted barley used across the Atlantic, the immigrants in North America relied on corn (Horning 2002, 141). Liquor in Haywood County, North Carolina, like most of Appalachia, was produced from a surplus of this New World grain. The most important resource for whiskey production, however, is fresh flowing water, something the mountains of western North Carolina have in abundance (Pierce 2013, 11). In the early nineteenth century, household production of alcohol on small farms was not illegal and residents were allowed to produce their own whiskey with county permits. According to the census of 1820, twenty-one licensed stills in Haywood County produced an estimated 4,300 gallons of liquor per year (Willis 2009, 254).

During the Civil War there was such a high demand for grain to feed the military that the state of North Carolina passed two state laws that prohibited the production of corn whiskey. To generate revenue, in 1864, the state instituted a $2.00 per gallon tax on all distilled liquors. North Carolina did not repeal that tax after the war, a fact that "[was] the grievance of the mountaineer" (Blackmun 1977, 369). The high tax made legal distilling much less profitable than moonshining. As a result, many mountain farmers set up stills in remote locations to hide their clandestine operation from federal revenue officers. According to historian Wilbur Miller (1989, 197–198), a farmer could get about $10 for a full wagonload of about twenty bushels of corn. If he converted that same corn into 60 gallons of whiskey he could net $75 at market. A wagon could hold 120 gallons of liquor, so the farmer could make $150 per wagonload. With the new tax, a legal distiller could make a profit of only fifty cents by distilling two bushels of corn, while the moonshiner could make $7.50 from the same amount.

Aside from the dramatic tax increase on liquor, advances in railroad technology had an unexpected impact on the alcohol industry in western North Carolina. Capital-wealthy businesses like the W. M. Ritter Lumber Company and the Little River Railroad and Lumber Company began buying up cheap forested land and laying steep tracks in the mountains (Willis 2009, 242). They would then construct huge mills adjacent to their company towns. Young men by the thousands flocked to the area from North Carolina, across the nation, and even from Europe for a steady paycheck. These were hard-working, hard-drinking men who were living in remote locations away from their families. Logging camps such as this created an easily accessible market for moonshiners. Foremen of the logging company towns went to great lengths to discourage their workers from consuming moonshine. They wanted the workmen to stay productive and to spend their hard-earned money at the company store, not on illegal liquor. Some loggers supplemented their income by making moonshine on the side (Willis 2009, 241).

The last major change that helped bolster the illegal liquor industry in the region was the strengthening of the temperance movement (Pierce 2013, 42). As support for prohibition grew, workers in legal distilleries increasingly saw the potential profits of taking their talents to the black market. Many slowly took their skills for making whiskey into the coves and hollers of western North Carolina. After full prohibition reached the region in 1920, it was rumored that there was more whiskey being produced than at any other time in the past. In *Mountain Spirits*, author Joe Dabney (1984, 73) refers to a *New York Times* reporter who once jokingly commented on a western Carolina town that was "'dry[,]' so dry in fact that 100 gallons of illegal whiskey serves a small town of 150 inhabitants of all ages and both sexes for a week's consumption . . . and 50 gallons provide for the festivities of the Fourth of July. The prevailing thirst due to the 'dryness' of the town is amazing."

Similar quotes are rampant during this time period. There were many "moonshine capitals" in America, including Cocke County, Tennessee; Franklin County, Virginia; and Buffalo City, North Carolina. Data (e.g., court records) used to justify these claims are generally unreliable. The project described below is an attempt to find better ways of measuring the extent and impact of this illicit production and the intimate economy in which it is embedded.

The Moonshine Archaeology Project

Generally, the inception of most projects have an interesting story. The Moonshine Archaeology Project (MAP) began when I saw the 2008 documentary *The Last One* by Neal Hutcheson. The film records in detail how the moonshiner Marvin "Popcorn" Sutton builds a mountain still. After the whiskey is made and the Ball jars are full, he removes the copper pot still and coil (worm) along with the thump keg and other valuable/transportable items (Figure 4.3a). All that remains is the horseshoe-shaped still furnace made of stone (Figure 4.3b). I used scenes from the film in an Introduction to Archaeology class at The Pennsylvania State University so they could see someone modifying the landscape in order to build a still.

A few years later, a colleague suggested that the 2012 film *Lawless* starring Shia LaBeouf and Tom Hardy, a major motion picture based on Matt Bondurant's 2008 historical novel *The Wettest County in the World*, might also be relevant to the project. The narrated introduction to the film states that "during prohibition, in Franklin County, Virginia there was more liquor being made than anywhere else in the world." It is a movie, so of course there is artistic embellishment, but I began to ponder. If one wanted to, how could the statement that Franklin was the wettest county in the world be proven?

With funds from the Institute for Field Research, my wife and I traveled to western North Carolina in December 2013 to spend a few days conducting pedestrian surveys near streams in the Pisgah National Forest with the goal of testing the feasibility of a larger project. Within three days, we had located and recorded three previously unrecorded still sites.

Over the next several years, a more definitive plan was developed to empirically estimate the quantity of liquor produced in the Cataloochee area of Haywood County, North Carolina, before, during, and after prohibition. Understanding the quantity of alcohol produced is useful for understanding the impacts moonshine production had on the local economy, organized crime, volume of consumption, success rates of revenue agents seizing stills, as well as for fostering appreciation and protection of our cultural heritage.

To address these questions, in June 2017, I directed a crew of four students, who spent two weeks in Haywood County recording oral histories, conducting archival research, and performing pedestrian surveys. The most important aspect of the project was to establish a working

Figure 4.3. Typical moonshine still. The pot still is on the left, the thump keg (or doubler) is in the middle, and the worm (condenser) is on the far right (*a*); still furnace discovered on private property near Pisgah National Forest in 2013 (*b*). Photos by Kirk French.

relationship with local residents that we hoped would lead to interviews in which we could record oral histories and information about the locations of still sites in the Cataloochee Valley. Next we wanted to begin amassing historical information from archival research at the Haywood County Public Library. Lastly, we sought to determine the density of whiskey production sites along the southern section of the Caldwell Fork in the Cataloochee Valley through pedestrian survey.

Pedestrian Survey

Systematic pedestrian survey of the Cataloochee Valley (Figure 4.4a) is the most effective way to quantify whiskey production. As with most production sites, moonshiners leave behind signature artifacts such as still pots, still furnaces, and hastily made structures. Large production sites would have also required modifications to the land, for instance leveling. Illegal whiskey production sites will invariably be in remote and hard-to-reach locations (generally in rough mountainous terrain) and in close proximity (~100 meters) to the flowing water needed to cool the condenser, referred to as the "worm" (Wigginton 1972, 307). The quantity of whiskey produced at a particular site could be estimated by recording the size of the still furnace and the still pot or possibly the remnants of wooden barrels (i.e., metal barrel hoops). For her master's thesis, Medeiros (2016) developed a still typology in Alabama that could be used to estimate the quantity of distilled alcohol produced at each site.

The pedestrian survey began at the Cataloochee Campground, where the Caldwell Fork joins the Cataloochee Creek (Figure 4.4b). Moving south, the team planned to investigate Den Branch. Because of dense summer vegetation, this effort soon proved futile. The thick ferns, shrubs, and foliage created an environment with extremely poor visibility.

The second day of survey began at the high elevation of the Cataloochee Divide and focused on McKee Branch (Figure 4.4c). Starting at the spring, the crew attempted to survey both sides of the branch. Thick rhododendron made this area equally impossible. This area is a high priority for MAP because of Horace Kephart's (1922) vivid description of the typical location of illegal stills in the Smokies and the lengths moonshiners went to make sure they did not leave any sign of their activities.

> Some little side-branch is chosen that runs through a gully chocked with laurel, briers, and rhododendron as to be quite impassable, save by such worming and crawling as must make a great noise. Doubtless a faint cattle-trail follows the backbone of the ridge above it, and this is the workers' ordinary highway in going to and fro; but the descent from ridge to gully is seldom made twice over the same course, lest a trail be printed direct to the still-house.

The MAP crew spent only two days conducting pedestrian survey, as any more time spent would have yielded similarly disappointing results. We

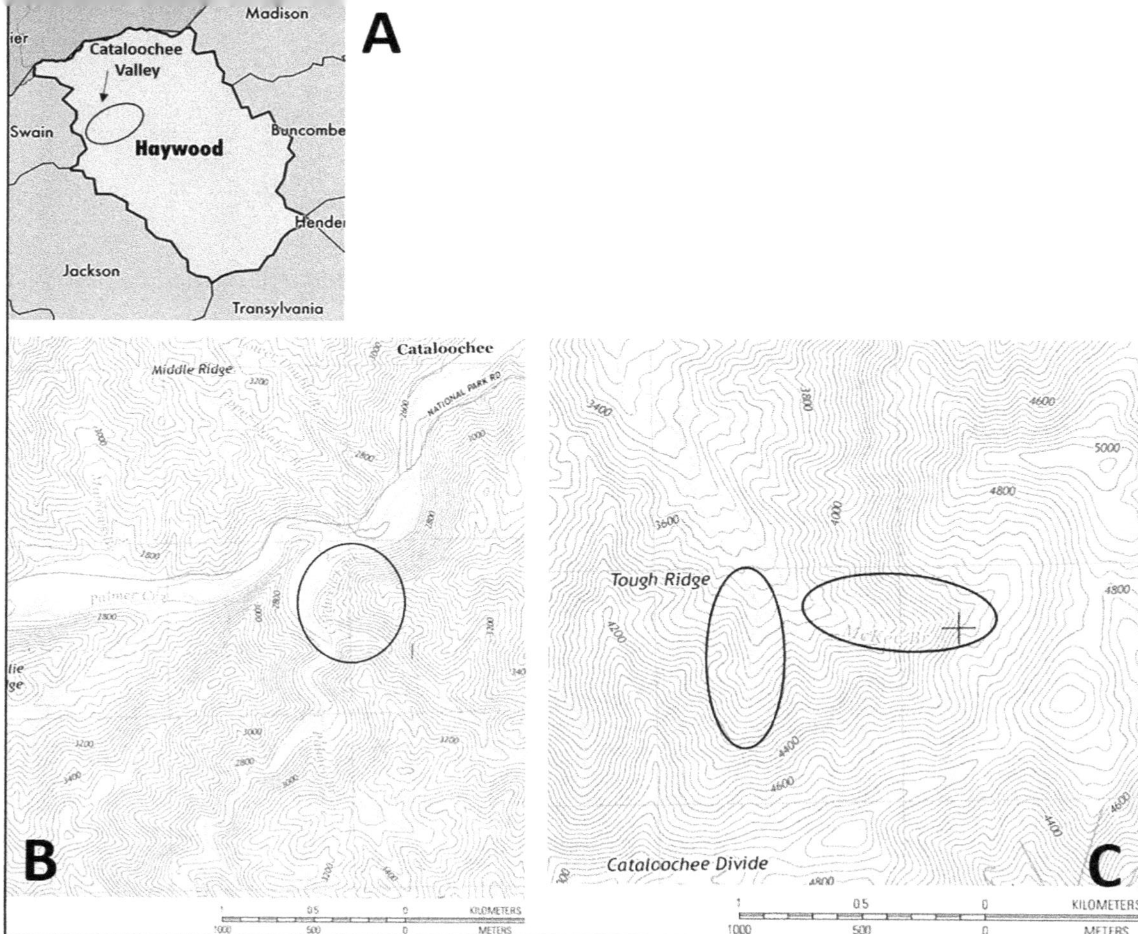

Figure 4.4. Map of Haywood County with the approximate boundary of the Cataloochee Valley delineated (*a*); the northern section of Caldwell Fork and Den's Branch, where a pedestrian survey was conducted (*b*); the southern sections of McKee Branch where pedestrian surveys were conducted (*c*). Source: United States Geological Survey.

conducted the original pedestrian survey to test the feasibility of the project in mid-December, when visibility was greater. The inaccessibility of the area was disappointing but informative. Future pedestrian surveys will have to be conducted during a narrow time frame of November, December, and possibly March. The high elevation of the Cataloochee Valley produces measurable levels of snow and ice throughout much of the winter months. By early April, vegetation has returned that limits visibility until late October.

Oral Histories

Many people from the area have a vast knowledge of the history of whiskey production in Haywood County. Conversations with local residents revealed useful information about moonshine production, distribution, and consumption. Many older citizens remember the locations of still sites from when they were kids. Recording these stories was both useful to this project and invaluable as an archive for future generations. This component of the project was by far the most productive. It also enabled MAP workers to make new connections and friendships in the area. Establishing a rapport and gaining trust when researching illegal activity is highly beneficial.

Members of MAP conducted seventeen interviews with local residents. These subjects ranged in age from 18 to 92 and included mechanics, musicians, writers, artists, farmers, students, health workers, a retired police officer, legal distillers, and moonshiners. One of the questions we asked of each subject was "What does whiskey mean to you and to the community?" Over 75 percent of the answers were remarkably similar to statements such as "it's a part of life" and "it's our cultural heritage." These interviews were also filmed and will be edited into five- to seven-minute documentaries that will be used for educational purposes at The Pennsylvania State University. They will highlight the importance of collecting ethnographic interviews in tandem with archaeological research (when applicable) and protecting our shared cultural heritage.

Intimate Economies

The secrecy involved in producing illicit liquor provides an ideal platform for discussing intimate economies in an archaeological context.

Community relationships in moonshining areas often became stronger and relied more heavily on the link between human agents and the illegal product (Hartnett and Dawdy 2013, 38), in this case whiskey. The archival research and interviews concerning illegal whiskey production MAP members conducted revealed serval examples of indebtedness, a condition that requires reciprocation in the form of payment or a favor (Watkins et al. 2006, 218; Graeber 2011, 131–133) (i.e., a driver transporting liquor, equipment, or any other tangible commodity). Several of those who were interviewed also discussed the intangible commodities present in moonshining, such as the nonmaterial value of whiskey-making knowledge (i.e., how to construct a pot still, how to distill whiskey, the locations of still sites). These are intangible commodities (Wadsworth 1911, 5).

As with most black markets, there is a need to transport the contraband, which is often a high-risk undertaking (e.g., Hartnett 2004; Tobias 1982; Wiegand 1993). Transporting moonshine requires clever methods for concealing the products—putting false bottoms in car trunks, for example (see Carter 1969, 50). Members of MAP interviewed several individuals who described earning money driving cars for moonshiners in the 1940 and 1950s. Others told stories of unknowingly participating in transporting illegal liquor, at times even across the state line into Tennessee. Some simply hauled the raw materials needed for whiskey production, for example copper sheets or sugar.

From the earliest days of whiskey production in the United States, whiskey was a tangible commodity. It was often used in lieu of cash, traded for services, given as a gift, and used to buy votes in local, state, and federal elections (Miller 1989; Pierce 2013). Whiskey production also generates intangible commodities. Intimate economic exchanges can rely on knowledge, skills, and information (Bridge and Smith 2003; Hartnett and Dawdy 2013). The awareness of friends, family, and/or neighbors of the location of a still would be one example. The knowledge and skill needed to successfully produce whiskey is also an intangible commodity. Sharing this knowledge through an apprenticeship has an unquantifiable value. An example that has recently been revealed is the acknowledgment by the Jack Daniel's Distillery that an African American slave named Nathan Nearest Green taught Jack Daniel how to make whiskey in the 1850s (Risen 2017).

Conclusions

Formal and informal economies regularly depend on one another (Halperin 1994). Informal markets often occur in secrecy and lack reliable textual evidence (Hartnett and Dawdy 2013, 38). Although a minority of archaeologists have the benefit of textual evidence (e.g., historical archaeologists and classicists), the vast majority spend their time inferring meaning solely from the material remains they uncover. Understanding illegal economic activity of the past can be difficult, but it is not impossible. Archaeologists can and have uncovered these intimate economies through analyzing the material remains from clandestine activities. Over the next several years, MAP will continue to investigate the intimate economies of whiskey production in western North Carolina with the goal of providing a clearer picture of the past.

Acknowledgments

This project would not have been possible without the assistance of Laurel Pearson, Ran Boytner from the Institute for Field Research, Neal Hutcheson, the late Ernestine Upchurch, the late Popcorn Sutton, the late Johnny Burress, archaeologists Rodney Snedeker and Linda Hall from the United States Forest Service, Ranger Nicholas Larson from the Pisgah National Forest, archaeologist Heath Bailey from the Great Smoky Mountains National Park, archaeologist Chris Espenshade from Skelly and Loy, Inc., Cookie Woods, Dave Angel and the crew at the Elevated Mountain Distilling Company, Troy Cagle, Raymond Fairchild, Mike and Shannon Woody, and the Department of Anthropology at The Pennsylvania State University. In addition, the first season of the project would not have been as productive or as fun without the energy and entertainment provided by my students, Elijah Hermitt, Carly Hunter, Cayt Holzman, and Caitlin Donahue.

References Cited

Blackmun, Ora. 1977. *Western North Carolina: Its Mountains and Its People to 1880*. Boone, NC: Appalachian Consortium Press.

Bridge, Gavin, and Adrian Smith. 2003. Intimate Encounters: Culture-Economy-Commodity. *Environment and Planning D: Society and Space* 21:257–268.

Carter, James A., III. 1969. Florida and Rumrunning During National Prohibition. *Florida History Quarterly* 48(1):47–56.

Casias, Kelli M. 2015. The Drunken Path: Discerning Women's Voices and Participation in the Informal Economy of Illegal Manufacturing of Prohibition Alcohol in the Historical and Archaeological Record. MA thesis, University of Montana.

Curtis, Wayne. 2007. Bootleg Paradise. *American Heritage* 58(2). Accessed October 1, 2017. http://www.americanheritage.com/content/bootleg-paradise.

Dabney, Joseph Earl. 1984. *Mountain Spirits: A Chronicle of Corn Whiskey*. Asheville, NC: Bright Mountain Books.

Davis, Hattie Caldwell. 1997. *Reflections of Cataloochee Valley and Its Vanished People from the Great Smoky Mountains*. Maggie Valley, NC: Self-published.

Graeber, David. 2011. *Debt: The First 5,000 Years*. NY: Melville House.

Halperin, Rhoda. 1994. *Cultural Economies Past and Present*. Austin: University of Texas Press.

Hartnett, Alexandra. 2004. The Politics of the Pipe: Clay Pipes and Tobacco Consumption in Galway, Ireland. *International Journal of Historical Archaeology* 8(2):133–147.

Hartnett, Alexandra, and Shannon L. Dawdy. 2013. The Archaeology of Illegal and Illicit Economies. *Annual Review of Anthropology* 42:37–51.

Horning, Audrey. 2002. Myth, Migration, and Material Culture: Archaeology and the Ulster Influence on Appalachia. *Historical Archaeology* 36(4):129–149.

Kephart, Horace. 1922. *Our Southern Highlanders: A Narrative of Adventure in the Southern Appalachians and a Study of Life Among the Mountaineers*. London: Macmillan.

Kosar, Kevin R. 2010. *Whiskey: A Global History*. London: Reaktion Books.

Lyttleton, Chris. 2014. *Intimate Economies of Development: Mobility, Sexuality and Health in Asia*. New York: Routledge.

Madeiros, Cassandra Ann. 2016. Lost Lightnin': Moonshine in Alabama as Represented in the Archaeological Record. MA thesis, Department of Anthropology, University of Alabama.

Miller, Wilbur R. 1989. The Revenue: Federal Law Enforcement in the Mountain South, 1870–1900. *Journal of Southern History* 55(2):195–216.

———. 1991. *Revenuers and Moonshiners*. Chapel Hill: University of North Carolina Press.

Okrent, Daniel. 2010. *Last Call: The Rise and Fall of Prohibition*. New York: Scribner.

Pierce, Daniel S. 2013. *Corn from a Jar: Moonshining in the Great Smoky Mountains*. Gatlinburg, TN: Great Smoky Mountain Association.

Risen, Clay. 2017. When Jack Daniel's Failed to Honor a Slave, an Author Rewrote History. *New York Times*, August 15.

Ross, Kathy N., and Beadle, Michael. 2009. Cherokee and Pioneers in Pre-Haywood County Territory. In *Haywood County: Portrait of a Mountain Community*, edited by Curtis W. Wood Jr., 14–31. Waynesville, NC: Historical Society of Haywood County.

Sink, Alice. 2011. *The Hidden History of the Western North Carolina Mountains*. Charleston, SC: History Press.

Sullivan, Lynne P., and Susan C. Prezzano. 2001. *Archaeology of the Appalachian Highlands*. Knoxville: University of Tennessee Press.

Tobias, Peter M. 1982. The Socioeconomic Context of Grenadian Smuggling. *Journal of Anthropological Research* 38(4):383–400.

Wadsworth, Gerald Bertram. 1911. *Principles and Practice of Advertising*. New York: Gerald B. Wadsworth.

Watkins, Philip, Jason Scheer, Melinda Ovnicek, and Russell Kolts. 2006. The Debt of Gratitude: Dissociating Gratitude and Indebtedness. *Cognition and Emotion* 20(2):217–241.

Wiegand, Bruce. 1993. Petty Smuggling as "Social Justice": Research Findings from the Belize-Mexico Border. *Social and Economic Studies* 42(1):171–193.

Wigginton, Eliot. 1972. *The Foxfire Book: Hog Dressing, Log Cabin Building, Mountain Crafts and Foods, Planting by the Signs, Snake Lore, Hunting Tales, Faith Healing, Moonshining, and Other Affairs of Plain Living*. Garden City, NY: Anchor Press.

Willis, Patrick. 2009. Industry and Commerce. In *Haywood County: Portrait of a Mountain Community*, edited by Curtis W. Wood Jr., 230–259. Waynesville, NC: Historical Society of Haywood County.

Wilson, Ara. 2004. *The Intimate Economies of Bangkok: Tomboys, Tycoons, and Avon Ladies in the Global City*. Los Angeles: University of California Press.

5

The Pitch Mill

The Material Memory of a Specialized Production Site in the Town of Oulu, Finland

MARIKA HYTTINEN, TIMO YLIMAUNU, TITTA KALLIO-SEPPÄ, MARKKU KUORILEHTO, AND PAUL R. MULLINS

"If tar, spirit or sauna will not help, the disease is fatal." This old Finnish proverb emphasizes the significance of tar in folk medicine. Tar and its derivatives pitch and pitch oil were widely used medications for diseases and different kind of conditions in early modern Finland (Juvelius [1747] 1986; Paulaharju 1958, 217, 221; Vuorela 1998, 713).[1] In everyday life, all three substances were used in multiple ways, including such diverse uses as a preservative for wooden utensils and boats and as a mosquito repellant for livestock. Globally, they were vital commodities in building and maintaining wooden sailing ships (Björklund 2001; Kaukiainen 2008, 76; Outland 2004, 5–6; Turpeinen 2010, 7; for the global trade in tar and pitch, see Hautala 1956, 1963; and Åström 1988).

During the seventeenth century, Sweden ruled the global tar markets, exporting famous "Stockholm tar" of superior quality via Stockholm to European great naval powers (Figure 5.1). Finland, which was part of Swedish kingdom until 1809, became a key supplier of tar and pitch for Sweden, which controlled and taxed Finland's tar trade (e.g., Kaila 1931, 64–65; Hautala 1963, 8–9). After 1809, when Finland was joined to Russia and became an autonomous grand duchy, tar production and trade increased further, yielding more profits to Finland's "tar burghers."

Tar was produced in tar-burning pits in forested inland regions by peasants and transported along the waterways to the coastal towns, like Oulu, along Finland's Gulf of Bothnia. In so-called tar courts, usually situated near a town's harbor, tar inspectors determined the quality of tar. Tar of high quality was stored in the tar courts and shipped to global markets, but low-quality tar was sent to the local pitch mill to be boiled into pitch. In the eighteenth and nineteenth centuries, the tar and pitch industry became increasingly important to the town of Oulu, located some 200 kilometers from the Arctic Circle in northern Finland. For instance, in 1781 Oulu exported over 14,000 barrels of tar and nearly 2,000 barrels of pitch (Halila 1953, 273).[2] By 1840, the amount of exported tar had increased to 45,720 barrels while the amount of pitch had doubled to approximately 4,700 barrels (Halila 1953, 216).

In consequence of the continuous need of the great sea powers for pitch, several pitch mills were established in Finland's coastal towns during the seventeenth century. One of those newly founded pitch mills was the pitch cookery of Oulu located on an offshore island, Pikisaari, just across the water from the inhabited urban area (distance between mainland and Pikisaari Island was approximately 400 meters). Before the town of Oulu was founded in 1605, the Pikisaari was a seasonal market place where foreign traders from the Baltic Sea and England traded goods with locals (Snellmann [1737] 2000, 85).

Pikisaari Island was the home of pitch burners and their families, who formed a small and close-knit community around the mill. Because of its spatial isolation, the community lived in seclusion and operated independently from the town of Oulu. The pitch mill was an intimate part of the inhabitants' daily lives. Their livelihoods depended on their ability to produce pitch successfully so the mill owner could get the maximum profit from it; it was important to ensure lucrative pitch production. However, boiling tar into pitch with fire was an extremely hazardous process because both tar and pitch are highly combustible substances. The high risk of fire must have made the mill workers feel insecure. Thus, pitch production was a distinctive factor that dictated the daily routines of the people who lived around the pitch mill.

From our modern and rational point of view, the pitch-boiling process was a purely economic activity in which producing and selling pitch were the most important factors in the lives of the families that burned pitch. Indeed, the archaeological record indicates that the production of pitch was a sensitive and dangerous process that affected everyday life. Excavations conducted from 2002 to 2012 in the Pikisaari pitch mill area recovered remains of the pitch boilery, a worker's house, and an adjacent

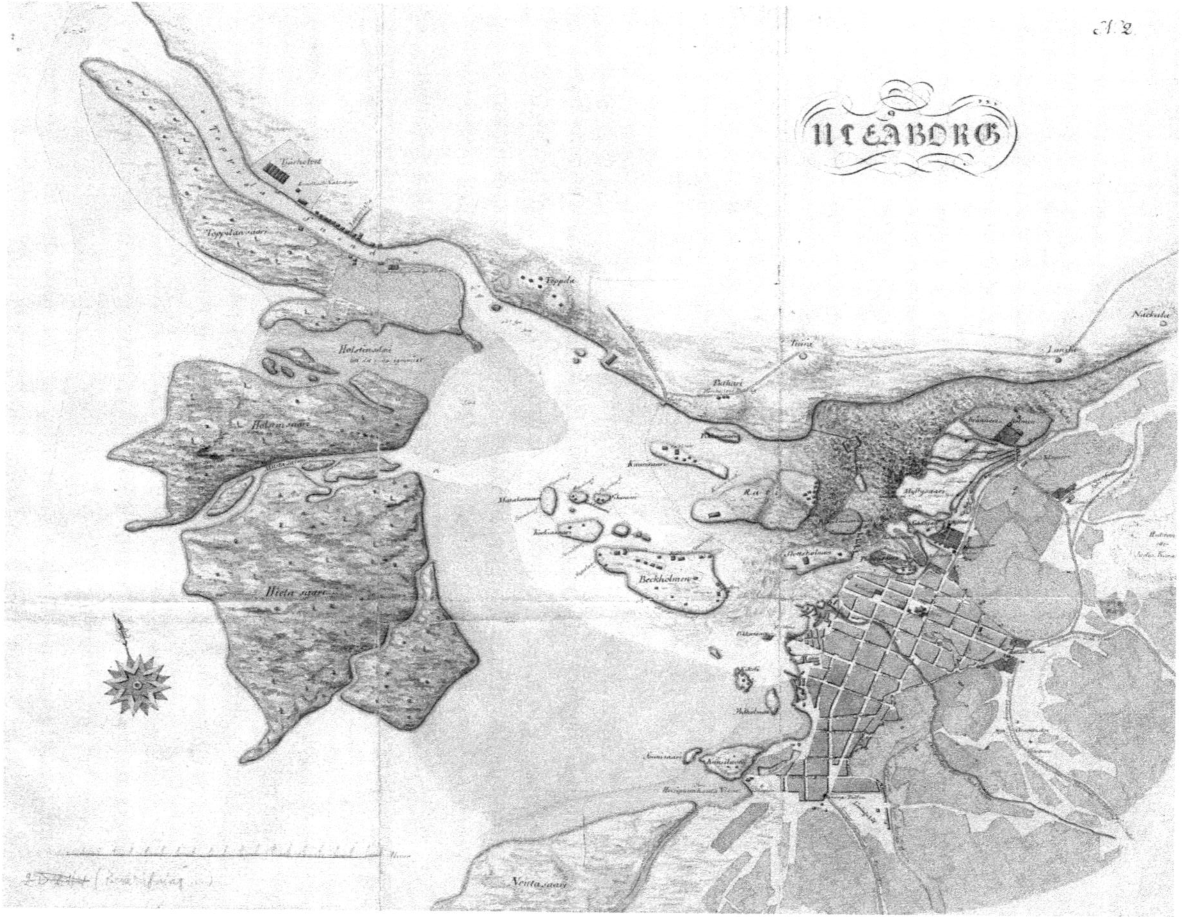

Figure 5.1. The town of Oulu (Uleåborg in Swedish) at the beginning of the nineteenth century. Pikisaari Island (Beckholmen in Swedish) is shown in the center of the map. The National Archives of Finland, Helsinki, Nymanssonin kokoelma (The Nymansson Collection).

household midden. However, some of the objects recovered suggest that activities associated with pitch burning also set the boundaries for the lived worlds of the pitch-burning families. Some features and artifacts from the household context suggest that pitch-burning families used rituals and other magical practices in their daily lives.

This chapter considers the early modern Pikisaari pitch mill in the town of Oulu from the 1640s to the end of the Crimean War in 1856. We use archaeological material and folklore to propose that in the early modern period, members of the pitch-burning community engaged in intimate interactions and exchanged esoteric information to ensure a successful and safe pitch-cooking process. We suggest that early modern pitch boiling was a rather intimate affair and not merely an economically rational process. We also suggest that through material clues, artifacts, and structures—what we call material memories—it is possible to recall "unseen" cultural aspects of everyday life and production such as folk beliefs and rituals; that is, evidence of intimate activities beyond the economic activity. These rites and rituals the pitch mill community members engaged in formed the basis for their pitch production.

Material Memory of Intimate Knowledge

Laurent Olivier (2015, 31) has stated that memory is like archaeological material: fragmented and incomplete. However, material remains have the capacity to reveal the unfamiliar or unrecorded past, and thus archaeology "deals with the material memory of the past that escapes historical consciousness" (Olivier 2015, 34). That is to say, long-vanished memories can be recalled through materiality. People unconsciously preserve information about their lives and actions in everyday material things: every memory practice has material dimensions (Mills and Walker 2008, 16; Nurmi 2009, 123). Thus, as Mills and Walker state, "memory practices have materialized through practice" (2008, 16).

Memory in general and material memory in particular are partly related to rituals and bodily practices (Connerton 1989; Forty 1999, 2; Buchli and Lucas 2001, 80; Delle 2008; Jones 2007; Meskell 2004, 64–66; Van Dyke and Alcock 2003; Warnier 2009). Williams notes that material culture is "an important medium for memory work" in ritual performances and practices; thus, material memories can be regarded as "outcomes of . . . social remembering and forgetting" (Williams 2011, 13). Memory can also be seen as traditional behavior that is linked to the social, ritual, and material worlds (e.g., Buchli and Lucas 2001, 80; Connerton 1989; Delle 2008; Forty 1999; Meskell 2004, 64–66; Van Dyke and Alcock 2003; Warnier 2009). Connerton (1989, 22–23) has defined three different forms of social memories. First, we each have individual memories. Our experiences have shaped our individuality and identity. However, this individual memory dies with each person (Sontag 2003, 86). The second is "cognitive memory claims," or how we have learned to see and understand the world's values, beliefs, and histories and ourselves as part of the world in which we are living. The third form of memory remembers our rituals or bodily performances. Connerton has used riding a bicycle as an example of bodily remembering; our body learns to remember how to do things (Connerton 1989, 22–23). Jean-Pierre Warnier (2009) has also highlighted the importance of bodily techniques in rituals for creating desired effects. In past societies, rituals were understood as a powerful way to create and maintain memories (e.g., Connerton 1989; Forty 1999, 2; Meskell 2004, 64–66; Van Dyke and Alcock 2003).

During the early modern period, folk beliefs and customs related to rites and rituals flourished throughout Europe. It was a well-known "fact" that supernatural powers and beings existed that could cause harm and misfortune to people, houses, and cattle. We propose that the use of ancient technology and rites was an essential part of pitch production on Pikisaari Island, that the community had intimate knowledge about how to protect individuals, the place, and the production process from the dangers of pitch boiling. If our theory is correct, we may assume that the archaeological data involves artifacts and structures that are related to the folk beliefs and rituals that were practiced at the site.

Historical Background of the Pikisaari Pitch Mill

Pitch cooking had begun by the 1640s in Oulu. During the Great Northern War of 1700–1721 and its aftermath, pitch production ceased. It did not resume until merchant Zacharias Wacklin, a wealthy townsman, was granted a privilege to establish a new pitch cookery on Pikisaari island in 1746 (Beckholmen in Swedish, Pitch Island in English). The mill was apparently in operation in the 1750s, as the pitch mill community and its members are mentioned for the first time in the census registers in 1754.[3] The Wacklin family held the privilege of boiling pitch in Pikisaari until

1850, when the then mill owner, Fredrik Wacklin, the grandson of the founder of the Pikisaari pitch mill, Zacharias Wacklin, died precipitously at age 42.

The island's name, Pikisaari, refers to pitch production, though several shipyards and a marine customs house were also located on the island in the eighteenth century. During the nineteenth century, a spirit distillery, a wood industry, and a mechanical industry were established on the island (Outakoski 1949; Halila 1953, 395; Hautala 1975, 139–144; Hautala 1976, 196–197, 405–408). Pitch boiling must have been the most distinctive activity of the island for the townspeople because of the name they gave to the island. That name remains the same although the pitch cookery has long vanished from the landscape of Pikisaari.

The Pikisaari pitch mill was located at the northernmost boilery in the Gulf of Bothnia. According to the census lists (*henkikirjat* in Finnish), during the mill's heyday from the late eighteenth to the early nineteenth centuries, approximately half of the people living on Pikisaari Island were mill workers and their families. For example, of the 32 inhabitants of Pikisaari in 1798, 17 were mill workers and their wives.[4] However, that total number does not include all the inhabitants of Pikisaari. There are gaps in the census registers because some people, for example children, the elderly, or the sick, were not usually entered in the records (Kuorilehto 2008, 54–55). Census registers of 1805 reveal that there was a large number of children living on the Island. According to records, there were 63 persons living in the island, including 37 children, of which 26 were the offspring of pitch mill workers.[5] Besides mill workers Pikisaari was inhabited by Crown officials, such as maritime customs officers, sailors and shipbuilders.

Women and daughters seem to have been important to the continuity of the pitch mill community and its labor system. It appears that female children were more likely to stay as a member of the pitch mill community than male children. According to historical records in the late eighteenth and early nineteenth centuries, none of the Pikisaari pitch burners' sons chose to pursue. Instead, they left the community and chose other occupations, usually seafaring. It seems that daughters married incoming pitch burners (who often had previously been seamen) and spent their entire lives as a part of the Pikisaari pitch mill community. So far, eight examples of the Pikisaari pitch burners' daughters marrying incoming pitch mill workers have been traced in historical records in the same period (Hyttinen and Kallio-Seppä in press). This is highly exceptional considering the small size of the pitch mill community and compared to the patterns in other early modern Finnish industrial communities, for example ironworks, where most iron workers' sons followed in their father's footsteps and were more critical to the direct production of iron than daughters (e.g., Haggrén 2001, 179–181; Vilkuna 1996, 53–57).

In the first quarter of the eighteenth century, the pitch mill area was probably at its largest extent. The pitch boilery was composed of the copper pitch pan in which pitch was boiled and the condenser basin made of brick (in which pitch was cooled). It was located in the middle of the mill area. Workers lived in houses situated around the mill; the distance between the pitch pan and the workers' housing was forty to sixty meters (130–200 feet). According to an 1834 fire insurance map, there were also several workshops, warehouses, and a cowshed at the site (figure 5.2). In 1841, the Finnish newspaper *Borgå tidning*, which was published in the town of Borgå (Porvoo in Finnish), reported that in Oulu, pitch production period started in May and ended on the 29th of September, which is Michaelmas Day (Mikkelinpäivä in Finnish).[6] In traditional Finnish agrarian society, Michaelmas marked the end of cattle grazing and the harvest; it was the end of the old year. Various beliefs and magical thinking were related to this day (Paulaharju 1958, 185; Pulkkinen 2014). The fact that pitch boiling ceased on Michaelmas suggest that the protoindustrial pitch community followed traditional agrarian annual rhythms.

There were several practical reasons why the pitch mill was located on the remote island. The island was located along the shipping route between Oulu and the harbor and thus it was easy to transport tar there. In addition, building regulations ordered that flammable mills had to be located on the outskirts of towns because of the high risk of fire (Kirjakka 1982, 44). Boiling pitch was always hazardous. The pitch mill (in other words the pitch pan and the condenser building, docks and storehouse) was destroyed by fire in 1773, 1805, 1853 and 1880.[7] In 1854, during the Crimean War, the British navy destroyed the shipping and marine stores of Oulu and burned down the Pikisaari pitch mill and its tar and pitch stocks and the shipyards on the island (Greenhill and Giffard 1988, 185–187; Hautala 1975, 448). However, in each case they managed to prevent the spread of fire to the workers' houses. Despite these incidents, the

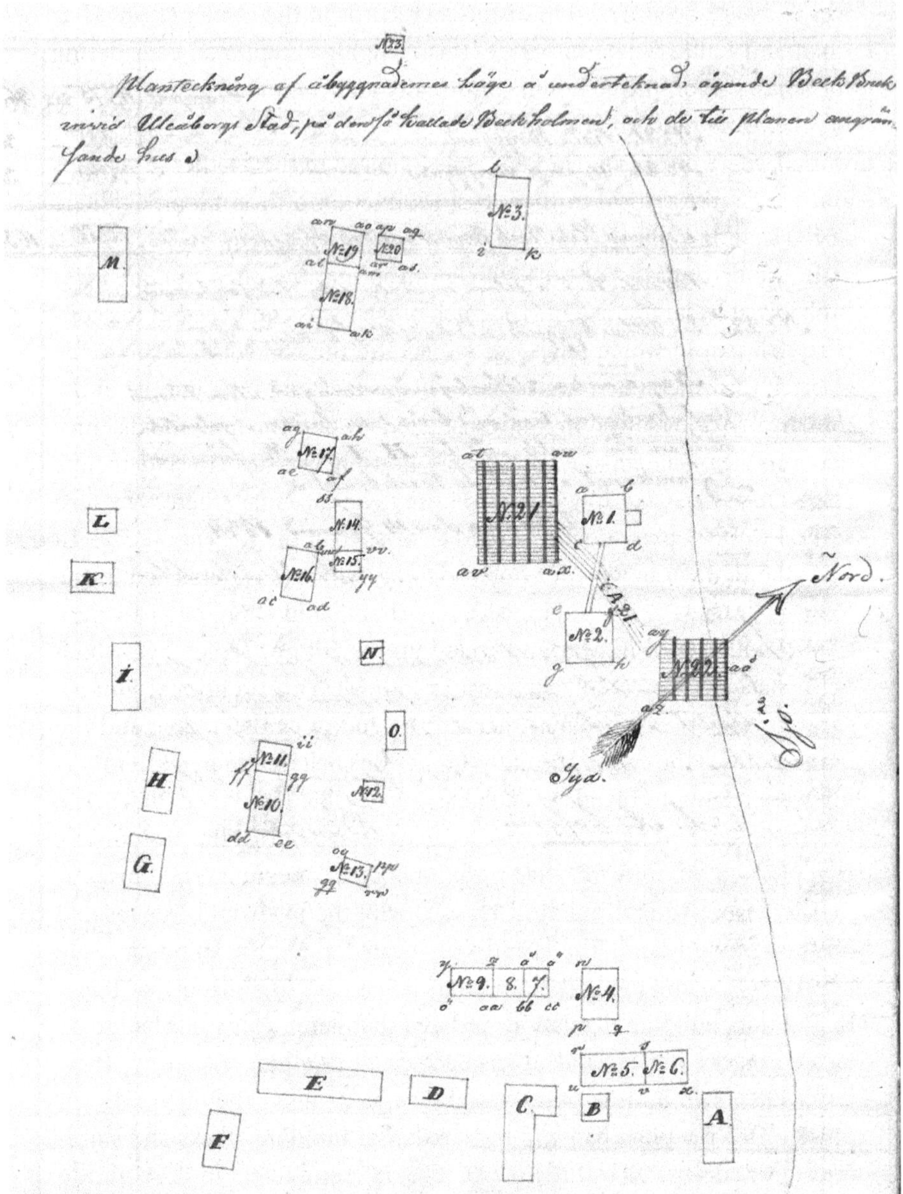

Figure 5.2. An 1834 fire insurance map illustrating the Pikisaari pitch mill area. The pitch mill (Nos. 1–2) and docks (Nos. 21–22) were situated on the shoreline. Housing and workshops (Nos. 4–6, 10–11, 14–16, 18–19) for mill workers and their families were built beside the mill, as were warehouses (Nos. 3, 7–9, 12, 17, 20) and a cowshed (No. 13). Buildings marked with letters A–M are outside the pitch mill area. Keskinäisen Vakuutusyhtiö Tarmon Arkisto (The Mutual Insurance Company Tarmo's archives), The National Archives of Finland, Helsinki.

Pikisaari pitch mill was always rebuilt and operated until the turn of the twentieth century, when production ceased and the mill was demolished along with workers' housing.

The Liminal Character of Pikisaari Island

In addition to functional factors, there might have been other reasons that influenced the location of the mill. In the northern Baltic Sea region, islands were viewed in distinctive ways. Coastal islands were associated with otherness and were seen as special places that had unique meanings. Archaeological evidence indicates that there was a relationship between islands and specific activities and beliefs. For example, metal works and burials were located on islands in prehistoric times. In premodern times, islands were perceived as liminal places between this world and the afterworld and were thus regarded as suitable places for "dangerous" activities that involved magical practices and otherworldly dimensions (Herva and Ylimaunu 2014).

Scholars have suggested that premodern smiths were perceived to be engaged with nonhuman powers because of the transformative nature of the metalwork they did. In Nordic mythology, the "magical and otherworldly dimensions" of metal working (Herva and Ylimaunu 2014, 194) were connected to shamanistic rituals by fire (Broadbent 2010; Herva and Ylimaunu 2009, 238; Herva and Ylimaunu 2014, 193–194; Sarmela 1994, 128–132). Fire was considered to be a way of conveying offerings into the otherworld. Because of this, metalsmiths were believed to have shamanistic skills and the ability to heal. In addition, according to Finnish folklore, it was important to cast spells for protection when lighting a fire for burning tar or charcoal (Sarmela 1994, 130, 132).

Because Pikisaari was physically separated from the town of Oulu, pyrotechnology could be used at the site. Several shipyards were located on the island that had smithies (metal-working sites). Both metal working and pitch burning involved using fire in transformative technologies that can be connected to both shamanistic rituals and alchemy. Alchemy was an attempt to manipulate and transmute the workings of nature through mechanical and magical arts with the help of the natural and the supernatural (Herva et al. 2010; Williams 2012). Finnish historian Zachris Topelius (1818–1898) wrote in *Helsingfors Tidningar* in 1854 about a pitch burner who made an alliance with the devil to gain wealth via alchemy. He was betrayed and killed, of course.[8] This story based on a folktale implies that the pitch-burning process was perceived as an activity that engaged with magic and the otherworld. All of this suggests that Pikisaari was an economically liminal place associated with a living tradition of rites and spells related to production processes.

Pikisaari might also have been liminal in a sociocultural sense. Medieval and early modern marketplaces were often located on islands in river estuaries because of the liminal nature of fairs. Such events provided a break from everyday routines and the freedom to behave differently than one did in "normal" everyday life and to violate commonly accepted social norms (Herva and Ylimaunu 2014, 14–15; Ylimaunu 2007, 28; Ylimaunu et al. 2017). It is important for our analysis to remember that Pikisaari was a marketplace before the founding of the town of Oulu. During the eighteenth and the nineteenth centuries, when ship building was at its height, occasional special events were organized on Pikisaari Island. When a ship was completed in the island's shipyard, a ceremonial launching was performed. The ritual was followed by festivals that included a feast provided by the ship owner that included heavy drinking. Finnish educator and writer Sara Wacklin (1790–1846), who was related to Zacharias Ephraimsson Wacklin, the then owner of the pitch mill, described ceremonies so lively that it could take several days to recover from the fun and drinking (Wacklin [1844–1845] 1989). These feasts might been occasions when deviant behavior was allowed. Thus, Pikisaari might have been a socioculturally liminal space where people were able to break away from conventional social roles and behave differently than they did in their "normal" everyday life.

Archaeologies of the Pitch Mill Site

Excavation revealed the remains of the foundations of the pitch pan on the north shore of Pikisaari Island. The foundation was partly unearthed in order to learn how it was constructed and how it functioned. The stepped brick foundation was circular. The remains of the vaulted passage to the furnace were situated in the middle of the foundation. The huge copper pitch pan that sat above the brick footings was not found during the excavations, but according to fire insurance records from 1834 it had a capacity of 45 barrels, or 5,625 liters (21,375 gallons).[9] In addition, a few wooden gutters were discovered close to the pitch cookery that were

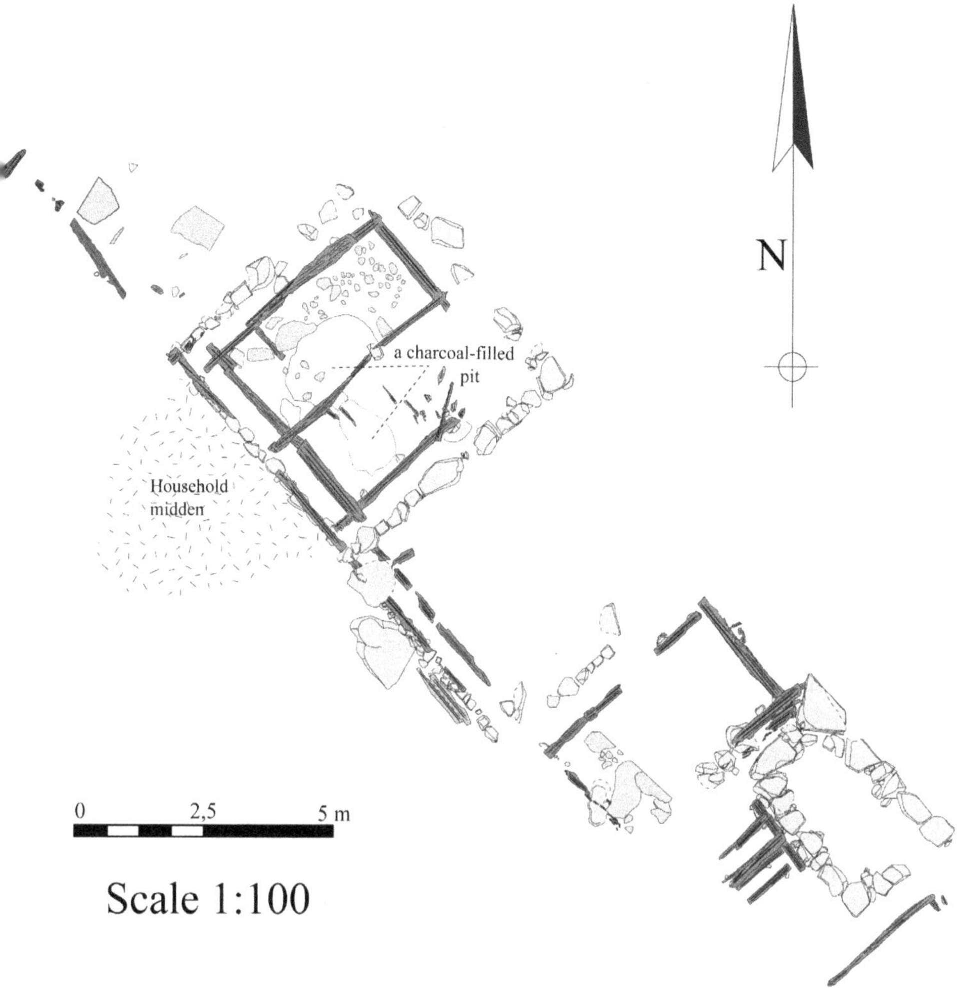

Figure 5.3. The excavated workers' house and adjacent household midden. Drawing by M. Hyttinen based on the maps by T. Ikonen/the Finnish Heritage Agency, Helsinki, and M. Suuronen, K. Mutka, T. Keski and T. Sipola/Laboratory of Archaeology, University of Oulu. Photo by M. Hyttinen.

probably originally used to run liquid pitch to the condenser basin for cooling (Rossi 2005, 197–198).

Besides the pitch cookery, an elongated house was uncovered sixty meters (200 feet) southeast of the mill (Figure 5.3). Excavation suggested that the size of the house was at least 134.5 square meters, or 1,421 square feet, but historical maps indicate that when the house was first built during the eighteenth century it was much larger.[10] A fire insurance map drawn in 1834 reveals that the building was likely partly demolished in the early nineteenth century. The fact that the stone foundation had a heat insulation soil bench indicates that people lived year-round in the building, although no fireplace was discovered. Some scattered bricks found beyond the walls of the house, however, suggested an internal furnace or furnaces (Hyttinen and Ikonen 2016, 111–112) that were likely demolished when the house was torn down around the turn of the twentieth century, when the Pikisaari pitch mill went out of business.

The house included at least four rooms, each with a different function: a kitchen, a space that was used as living quarters and a workspace, a hall, and a possible storage room. A household waste midden was adjacent to the house. The pit was filled with household refuse such as animal bones, broken ceramic vessels, household glass, and fragments of tobacco clay pipe (Hyttinen 2012; Hyttinen and Ikonen 2016; Hyttinen et al. 2016). The significant number of finds in the house and the waste midden related to attire distinguish the archaeological assemblage. These finds included nearly 170 buttons (Hyttinen 2012; Salmi and Kuokkanen 2014, 191–193). In addition, tools including gimlet blades, a punching tool, chisels, parts of measuring tools, and a button cast made of sandstone were uncovered. Considering the impressive number of buttons and the presence of several hand tools, it is conceivable that small-scale metal working occurred alongside pitch burning at the Pikisaari pitch mill area. Perhaps the pitch burners or their wives had the expertise needed for small-scale metalworking.

The house, interpreted as a worker's family dwelling, was erected above a pit filled with charcoal and red burned sand that was, according to finds, contemporary with the building or slightly older. In early modern Europe, dwellings were often protected with ritual concealments, like witch bottles, spiritual middens, hidden footwear, and other objects associated with special powers that were located both inside and outside domestic buildings (Easton 2014; Manning 2014). Similar practices accompanied European colonists who migrated to North America (Costello 2014; Manning 2014; Springate 2014). In early modern Finland, various mundane metal objects, especially coins and edged iron tools, were considered to be powerful and were used for protective purposes in everyday environments, as in dwellings (e.g., Herva and Ylimaunu 2009; Hukantaival 2016, 76–77, 125; Sarmela 1994, 133; Søvsø 2017; Talve 1980, 212).

Another folk practice common in both Finland and Sweden associated with the protection of the house was the inauguration of the building site of a house or barn with fire. This ritual was done because the "little folk"—gnomes, elves, or other guardian spirits who inhabited the inverted underground world—had to be warned and asked to move away with fire (Andersson et al. 2011, 20–21; Korhonen 2009, 264; Talve 1980, 207). Alternatively, permission to live on a site could be sought by placing a coin under the cornerstone of the house (Korhonen 2009, 264–265; Pulkkinen 2014, 117–118). Living alongside the gnomes required everyday politeness and neighborly relations. When good rapport was established, gnomes could warn people of danger or misfortune (Koskinen 1986, 9; Paulaharju 1958, 238; Pulkkinen 2014, 117–118; Sarmela 1974, 343–348). The elves who were believed to dwell in the houses were kept satisfied with various offerings, such as metal or alcohol. Their protection against evil, misery, or accidents was also desired. Metal offerings to elves were made by casting tin, especially at the end of the old year (Sarmela 1994, 160). This was a powerful rite to keep guardian spirits happy and willing to protect a dwelling and its inhabitants. It seems plausible that the charcoal pit was related to rituals that sought protection for the house and its inhabitants. The protection gnomes offered would have been highly desirable in the context of the constant danger of fire related to pitch boiling. Pewter buttons, castings of melted lead, and molten chunks of lead suggest that pewter casting was practiced at the pitch mill site, possibly to create offerings to keep elves and gnomes satisfied and obliging.

The Cultural Economy of Artifacts: Beliefs and Rituals

Several artifacts found at the pitch mill site were part of the contemporary economic world but were also possibly related to beliefs and rituals practiced at the site. These were three altered Swedish coins and one counting token (jetton) excavated from the house and the adjacent trash heap. In addition to these artifacts, a brick with a motif featuring female genitalia was also unearthed.

The three coins in the Pikisaari archaeological assemblage all have post-manufacture alterations. These coins and the jetton may have been related to supernatural powers and used as magical objects (Figure 5.4). The first coin is a one öre *kopparmynt* (copper coin) minted in the 1720s. The second is a one öre *silvermynt* (silver coin) minted in 1749. Both

Figure 5.4. Four altered coins from the Pikisaari pitch mill area. *Upper left*: 1 Öre *kopparmynt*. *Upper right*: silver ½ öre minted in 1578. *Lower left*: Nuremberg counting token. *Lower right*: 1 Öre *silvermynt*. Photo by M. Hyttinen.

coins are pierced, the copper öre near the edge and the silver öre through the middle, and the reverse is rubbed down. The third and oldest coin is a slightly broken silver ½ öre minted in 1578, nearly three decades before Oulu was founded. The silver coin was fractured from its edge and it is possible that bending caused the breakage of the coin. The reckoning counter, which was minted in Nuremberg in the eighteenth century, is pierced. A similar pierced Nuremburg counter was found in an early modern context in Tornio (Herva et al. 2012, 299–300). One side of the token displays a bust of Louis XV and the other a three-masted ship and the words "Durch Glück und Kunst" (by luck and skill).

In many medieval and early modern cultures, modified coins and tokens were associated with special or magical powers and spiritual functions. Perforated or bent coins were used as charms, talismans, or amulets that were believed to provide protection against illnesses or evil or for good luck throughout Europe (Hall 2012, 77–82; Herva et al. 2012) and North America, especially in contexts where African American slaves were present (Cofield 2014; Davidson 2004; Lee 2011; Lucas 2014; Wilkie 1997, 86–87). The key attributes that might have imbued certain coins with magical powers were material type, such as silver; particular images or elements, such as crosses and depictions of monarch; alterations, like piercing or bending of the coin, and certain numbers associated with the value of the coin (Cofield 2014, 85; Davidson 2004; Hall 2012; Lee 2011, 113–114; Linn 2014, 144–146). Coins and tokens perforated near the edge were likely worn as pendants or around the ankle as "apotropaic badges" (Davidson 2004, 38–40; Hall 2012, 76–77, 82; Herva et. al. 2012, 299–300). According to Hall (2012, 82), coins pierced in the center were not worn around neck but may have been tied around some other body part, to garments, or to pieces of furniture or walls. In these cases, protection might have been needed in a domestic setting or a workspace.

Coins were an important part of the exchange economy, since Finland was part of late-medieval Sweden. However, coins were also used for magic in the early modern Nordic world (Herva et al. 2012, 301–302). Belief in the power of silver and copper coins was widespread in early modern Finland, and people used their magical powers for a variety of purposes (Herva et al. 2012; Hukantaival 2016, 75–77, 127–128). Archaeological material suggests that coins were deliberately concealed in buildings throughout Finland (Hukantaival 2016, 66–69, 75–85). According to folklore, concealed coins were offerings to guardian spirits whose protection was desired. During childbirth, a silver coin was put with other charms in a "magic belt" that was tied around the waist of the mother to provide relief from pain (Sihvo 1986, 52–53).

Silver coins were also used in traditional tar burning which took place forested inland regions by peasants. Silver coins were powerful objects because they were believed to provide magical aid that ensured a successful burning process (Paulaharju 1958, 155–156). Traditional tar burning in pits had strong connections to the supernatural; the process included multiple rituals associated with superstitions. A tar-burning pit was regarded as a living thing that could become offended by inappropriate speech. Some words, such as tar and fire, were dangerous and had to be replaced by euphemisms during the burning process. Whistling around the pit was avoided because it was thought to raise winds or storms that would have ill effects on the burning process. The tar master who superintended the process had to circle the pit with a magic pouch containing a silver coin, the head of a snake, and a lizard plus a scythe under his arm while casting his spells. Quicksilver, milk, and pointed iron objects were also used to bring good luck during tar burning (Juvelius [1747] 1986, 18; Paulaharju 1958, 155–156; Skantsi et al. 2005; Turpeinen 2010, 30–31). It seems plausible that the magical powers of silver coins were put into effect in the Pikisaari pitch mill, perhaps during the hazardous pitch-boiling process.

The altered coins from the Pikisaari pitch mill area indicate that the Pikisaari pitch burners and their families practiced similar kinds of magical precautions in their everyday lives and during pitch boiling. One of the three coins and the Nuremberg counter were pierced and were used as lucky charms or amulets. The broken silver ½ öre and the silver one öre coin, which was perforated in the center, might have functioned as talismans in a household context or a workspace environment, as Hall (2012, 82) has described. Rituals performed with the help of silver coins may have been related to a successful boiling process. Alternatively, modified coins may have provided protection against evil or misfortunes to the families of the pitch burners and their livestock. As magical objects, the reshaped coins are material evidence of intimacy between the mill community and production site and between the mill community and pitch production process. Altered coins also emphasize that the premodern mill society still engaged with traditional, animistic ways of life and fused early modern conceptions of the world with economic, modern ones.

A brick with a coarse carving (Figure 5.5) found in the worker's household depicts female genitalia. In early modern Finland, female genitalia were seen as a route to the other world, a boundary between this world and the other world through which "transit traffic" with mythical meanings was transmitted (Apo 1995, 29–34). Exposing female genitalia put into effect powerful magical aid or protection from harm for both cattle and people. A woman could perform this in multiple ways, for instance, by jumping over a person or animal, standing over the target that needed supernatural aid, lifting one's skirt or/and by bending over, or letting the object in need of protection go through her legs. Cattle tending, which

Figure 5.5. Brick with pictorial motif. Photo by M. Hyttinen.

was traditionally women's chore, also involved magical practices. For instance, in the spring when livestock was let out from shelters to meadows, cattle had to be protected against beasts living in the forest. This was carried out by herdswoman or peasant's wife who stood on the tar barrels or tubs at the door of the cowshed, letting the cattle pass between her spread legs (Korhonen 1997, 16–17). Mothers performed magical rituals for their children and for their daughters who were getting married by jumping over them. This provided protection against evil outside the household or brought luck in marriage (Apo 1995, 22–28; Stark-Arola 1998, 163–178).

The brick bearing a carved image of female genitalia was found in the space interpreted as a possible storage room. It could have provided protection to the house from the dangers of the pitch-boiling process or other harms in the surrounding world. In the early modern Finland, carved magical symbols were used as protective motifs on dishes, tools, and buildings (Paulaharju 1958, 236; see also Talve 1980, 212). Maybe the motif in the brick was believed to protected livestock and buildings from harm and misfortunes. Instead of being concealed in or outside the building, the brick was probably built into a wall in a visible place because female genitalia were most powerful when exposed. The brick was not found in situ, and thus it is not possible to determine whether the pictorial motif of the brick faced inside or outside the house. However, the brick might indicate the importance of women in the Pikisaari pitch mill community. It seems that some pitch burners' daughters wanted to stay in the Pikisaari pitch mill community after marriage, in contrast to some sons, who left the community when they reach adulthood. This may suggest that daughters communicated intimate, esoteric knowledge that was important for the successful production of pitch. In other words, they might have had an important role in protecting the community from occupational hazards and other harms and misfortunes.

Recalled Memories from the Specialized Production Site

The economic activities and the production processes on Pikisaari Island should be understood through the premodern Nordic world view. The local traditions transmitted from one generation to the next (Søvsø 2017, 339) played a part in the production processes of the pitch mill community. In this case, apparently, esoteric traditions and knowledge were passed on to pitch burners' daughters and their incoming spouses, who became the new pitch burners in the Pikisaari pitch mill area. Passing on traditions was memory work in action that brought the past into the present through material objects. These traditions driven by objects and narratives provided cultural continuity. Object-driven cultural continuity reveals different temporalities from our contemporary western world view (e.g., Silliman 2009; Herva and Ylimaunu 2009; Symonds et al. 2015; also Ylimaunu et al. 2017).

This does not mean that transmitted memories and beliefs in the early modern world did not change over time. However, it suggests that memories and traditions most likely changed slowly. The original narratives may have been concealed and diminished across the generations and new meanings may have been added to memories of past actions and rituals. Memory work was an ongoing process, and the people on Pikisaari pitch mill site, pitch boilers and especially pitch burners' daughters, transmitted their world view, cultural practices and beliefs, and knowledge of production processes related to pitch through folklore and bodily practices. Boiling pitch, working metal in smithies, and burning tar in pits were all based on centuries-old technologies that people had passed from generation to generation. Similarly, the rites and spells used in these production processes were passed from generation to generation as active memory (see Silliman 2009, 233). In other words, the past, as a memory, was present in the contemporary present (see Silliman 2009; Mrozowski et al. 2015; Ylimaunu et al. 2017).

Pikisaari pitch mill families used material culture related to rituals to protect them from the uncertainties of life, the real or imagined dangers of the surrounding world, and the dangerous pitch production environment. The material world—altered coins, a pictorial motif on a brick and a charcoal filled pit—and rites and rituals connected the past with the present in pitch boiling activities at the pitch mill area. It is possible that the memory of how to protect the community was transmitted from the past into the present through learned rituals and the material world among female members of the pitch mill community. These memories connected the world that had passed out of existence with the living (cf., Meskell 2004, 61–62). These memories were invoked by using things such as altered coins and pictorial motifs in social practices and production practices, and meanings and memories were produced and reproduced by the interactions between Pikisaari residents and material culture. Different things were used as mnemonic indexes into the past activities and beliefs at the contemporary present in Pikisaari (see Jones 2007, 21–36).

Materialized practices transmitted memories within the Pikisaari pitch mill community across time. Bodily performances among the pitch mill community, like how to cook pitch safely and how to acquire protection from evil and misfortunes, can be understood as rituals. These rituals produced and reproduced bodily memories to achieve desired effects in a process that Connerton (1989, 35) calls "habit-memory": "the habit-memory—more precisely, the social habit-memory—of the subject is not identical with that subject's cognitive memory of rules and codes;

nor is it simply an additional or supplementary aspect; it is an essential ingredient in the successful and convincing performance of codes and rules" (Connerton 1989, 36). Thus, different kind of social habit-memories among the pitch community can be linked to everyday physical and spatial materialities.

Memory is an ongoing process that confirms how we comprehend the past and the present of the surrounding world. It also suggests how we will face the possible future (Connerton 1989; Buchli and Lucas 2001, 79–81; Van Dyke and Alcock 2003; Shackel and Palus 2006; West 2014, 177). Through the act of remembering and through material memories such as archaeological material we are able to acquire, retain, and retrieve information. Our knowledge and memories of the past strongly influence our experience of the present. In other words, past events and objects are causally connected with our experiences of the present world and this affects our present behavior and our interpretations of the world (Connerton 1989, 2). It is reasonable to say that material culture operates as a link between past, present, and future through the "life histories" of objects (Kopytoff 1986; Rowlands 1993). As Jones (2007, 224–225) has argued, things are materialized actions and memories of past activities. Material culture enables people to be connected with the past actions and to transmit those actions, rituals, and beliefs into their contemporary and future practices. Thus, things affect people "as a kind of material 'echo' from the past" (Jones 2007, 46, 57).

Summary

In this study, we have argued that Pikisaari Island and the Pikisaari pitch mill site was in many ways a distinctive place with special activities and meanings. The pitch production site provides insight into the parallel worlds of the supernatural and economic production in which a particular kind of intimacy with both the site and the process was needed. The archaeological material found on the pitch mill site and folklore suggest that pitch producers engaged in both magical and rational economic behavior. It seems that they combined beliefs and rituals, or intimate knowledge of the production process, with rational economic actions. It also seems likely that the female members of the community transmitted esoteric traditions such as rites and rituals that were embedded in everyday material culture as material memories from generation to generation.

Notes

1. Even though these substances were used as medicine, all three were as deadly as poison when abused. For instance, in 1842 a workman named Epfraim Kandola committed suicide in the town of Oulu by ingesting an excessive amount of pitch oil. National Archives of Finland, Oulu, Oulun seurakunnan arkisto (Parish registers of the town of Oulu), Kuolleiden luettelo 1792–1855 (Lists of deceased 1792–1855), IF:1, http://digi.narc.fi/digi/view.ka?kuid=5737505.

2. The capacity of the barrel was 125 liters of tar.

3. National Archives of Finland, Pohjanmaan läänin tilit [Records of the province of Ostrobothnia], Henkikirjat 1754–1754 (Census Registers 1754–1754), 9397, 269, https://astia.narc.fi/astiaUi/digiview.php?imageId=12211183&aytun=1978784.KA&j=141.

4. National Archives of Finland, Oulun läänin henkikirjat (Census registers of the county of Oulu), Oulun kaupunki (Town of Oulu), henkikirjat (Census registers 1798–1798), 9565, 510–511, http://digi.narc.fi/digi/view.ka?kuid=12689471.

5. National Archives of Finland, Oulun läänin henkikirjat (Census registers of the County of Oulu), Oulun kaupunki (Town of Oulu), henkikirjat 1805–1805 (Census Registers 1805–1805), 9616, 862–865, http://digi.narc.fi/digi/view.ka?kuid=13180200.

6. "About the Town of Oulu," *Borgå tidning*, December 1, 1841.

7. Halila (1953, 102); Hautala (1975, 280–281); "The Fire of the Pitch Mill at Pikisaari," *Morgonbladet*, August 7, 1880; The National Archives of Finland, Oulu, A. H. Virkkusen kokoelma (The collection of A. H. Virkkunen), G:2: Muistiinpanot (1774–1808) (G:2: Notes about ship building, 1774–1808; "The Fire of the Pikisaari Pitch Mill," *Oulun Wiikko-Sanomia*, July 2, 1953, http://digi.kansalliskirjasto.fi/sanomalehti/binding/411399.

8. Zachris Topelius, "Den gamle beckbrännaren," *Helsingfors Tidningar*, September 6, 1845, https://digi.kansalliskirjasto.fi/sanomalehti/binding/385766?page=1.

9. The National Archives of Finland, Keskinäisen Vakuutusyhtiö Tarmon arkisto (Archives of the Mutual Insurance Company Tarmo), Pikisaaren pikiruukin palovakuutus No. 1161 (The fire insurance of the Pikisaari pitch mill, No. 1161). Submitted in 1834, granted in 1835.

10. According to a map drawn in 1784–1786, the total size of the house was initially 268 square meters, or 2,793 square feet, and thus it seems that approximately half of the house has been excavated.

References Cited

Andersson, Josefina, Magnus Elfewdahl, Gunvor Gustafson, Britt-Marie Hägerman, Rolf Lundqvist, Ulrika Stenbeck Lönnquist, Johanna Ulfsdotter, and Stig Welinder. 2011. Visible Men and Elusive Women. *International Journal of Historical Archaeology* 15:10–29.

Apo, Satu. 1995. *Naisen väki. Tutkimuksia suomalaisten kansanomaisesta kulttuurista ja ajattelusta*. Helsinki: Hanki ja jää.

Åström, Sven-Erik. 1988. *From Tar to Timber. Studies in Northeast European Forest Exploitation and Foreign Trade 1660–1860*. Helskinki: Societas Scientiarum Fennica, Helsinki.

Björklund, Guy. 2001. Beckbruket i Jakobstad. In *Bottnisk kontakt X: maritimhistorisk konferens, Österbottens museum i Vasa 4–5 februari 2000: tjära och beck på alla möjliga sätt,* edited by Jessica Morney, 64–70. Vaasa: Österbottens museum.

Broadbent, Noel D. 2010. *Lapps and Labyrinths: Saami Prehistory, Colonization and Cultural Resilience*. Washington, DC: Smithsonian Institution Scholarly Press.

Buchli, Victor, and Gavin Lucas. 2001. *Archaeologies of the Contemporary Past*. London: Routledge.

Cofield, Sara Rivers. 2014. Keeping a Crooked Sixpence: Coin Magic and Religion in the Colonial Chesapeake. *Historical Archaeology* 48(3):84–105.

Connerton, Paul. 1989. *How Societies Remember*. Cambridge: Cambridge University Press.

Costello, Jessica. 2014. Tracing the Footsteps of Ritual: Concealed Footwear in America. *Historical Archaeology* 38(2):35–51.

Davidson, James M. 2004. Ritual Captured in Context and Time: Charm Use in North Dallas Freedman's Town (1869–1907), Dallas, Texas. *Historical Archaeology* 38(2):22–54.

Delle, James A. 2008. A Tale of Two Tunnels. Memory, Archaeology, and the Underground Railroad. *Journal of Social Archaeology* 8(1):63–93.

Easton, Timothy. 2014. Four Spiritual Middens in Mid Suffolk, England, ca. 1650 to 1850. *Historical Archaeology* 48(3):10–34.

Forty, Adrian. 1999. Introduction. In *The Art of Forgetting*, edited by Adrian Forty and Susanne Küchler, 1–18. Oxford: Berg.

Greenhill, Basil, and Ann Giffard. 1988. *The British Assault on Finland, 1854–1855: A Forgotten Naval War*. London: Conway.

Haggrén, Georg. 2001. *Hammarsmeder, masugnsfolk och kolare: Tidigindustriella yrkesarbete vid provinsbruk i 1600-talets Sverige*. Jernkontorets bergshistoriska skrifter. Stockholm: Jänrkontoret.

Halila, Aimo. 1953. *Oulun kaupungin historia II 1721–1809*. Oulu: Oulun kaupunki.

Hall, Mark A. 2012. Money Isn't Everything: The Cultural Life of Coins in the Medieval Burgh of Perth, Scotland. *Journal of Social Archaeology* 12(1):72–91.

Hautala, Kustaa. 1956. Suomen tervakauppa 1856–1913 sen viimeinen kukoistus ja häviö sekä niihin vaikuttaneet syyt. Taloushistoriallinen tutkimus. Doctoral dissertation, Helsingin yliopisto, Forssa.

———. 1963. *European and American Tar in the English Market during the Eighteen and Early Nineteenth Centuries*. Helsinki: Suomalaisen tiedeakatemia toimituksia B130.

———. 1975. *Oulun kaupungin historia III, 1809–1856*. Oulu: Oulun kaupunki.

———. 1976. *Oulun kaupungin historia IV, 1856–1918*. Oulu: Oulun kaupunki.

Herva, Vesa-Pekka, Kerkko Nordqvist, Anu Herva, and Janne Ikäheimo. 2010. Daughters of Magic: Esoteric Traditions, Relational Ontology and the Archaeology of the Post-Medieval Past. *World Archaeology* 42(4):609–621.

Herva, Vesa-Pekka, Risto Nurmi, and James J. Symonds. 2012. Engaging with Money in Northern Periphery of Early Modern Europe. *Journal of Social Archaeology* 12(3):287–309.

Herva, Vesa-Pekka, and Timo Ylimaunu. 2009. Folk Beliefs, Special Deposits, and Engagement with the Environment in Early Modern Northern Finland. *Journal of Anthropological Archaeology*. 28(2):234–243.

———. 2014. Coastal Cosmologies: Long-Term Perspectives on the Perception and Understanding of Dynamic Coastal Landscapes in the Northern Baltic Sea Region. *Time and Mind: The Journal of Archaeology, Consciousness and Culture* 7(2):1–19.

Hukantaival, Sonja. 2016. For a Witch Cannot Cross Such a Threshold. Building Concealment Traditions in Finland c. 1200–1950. PhD diss., University of Turku.

Hyttinen, Marika. 2012. Oulu, Pikisaari, Pikisaarentie 12, tontit 7–11. Teollisuusarkeologinen kaivaus 12.9.–4.11.2011 ja arkeologinen valvonta 18.6.–29.6.2012. National board of Antiquities, Helsinki. Unpublished excavation report.

Hyttinen, Marika, and Tiia Ikonen. 2016. 1600-luvun kaupunkikeskustasta 1700-luvun lopun kaupungin reunamille-poimintoja Oulun kaupunkiarkeologiasta. In *Monttu auki—Arkeologisia kenttätutkimuksia 1*, edited by Marianna Niukkanen, Petro Pesonen, and Riikka Alvik, 102–115. Helsinki: Museovirasto.

Hyttinen, Marika, and Titta Kallio-Seppä. In press. They Were Here Too—Women and Children in Industrial Communities. In *Oxford Handbook of Industrial Archaeology*. Oxford: Oxford University Press.

Hyttinen, Marika, Timo Ylimaunu, Titta Kallio-Seppä, and Paul R. Mullins. 2016. Pien polttoa ja käsityöläisyyttä-materiaaliset muistot Oulun Pikisaaren pikiruukkiyhteisöstä. In *Arkeologipäivät 2015: Teollisuusperintö & Teknologian ja niiden tutkimus*, edited by Piritta Häkälä, 27–41. Accessed June 27, 2017. http://www.sarks.fi/ap/ap2015/ap2015.pdf.

Jones, Andrew. 2007. *Memory and Material Culture*. Cambridge: Cambridge University Press.

Juvelius, Eric. (1747). 1986. *De arte picem destillandi in Ostrobotnia*. Åbo 1747. 1986 facsimile edited and translated by Meri Utrio. Somero: Amanita.

Kaila, E. E. 1931. Pohjanmaa ja meri 1600- ja 1700-luvuilla: talousmaantieteellis-historiallinen tutkimus. Suomen Historiallinen Seura: Helsinki.

Kaukiainen, Yrjö. 2008. *Ulos maailmaan! Suomalaisen merenkulun historia*. Hämeenlinna: Suomalaisen Kirjallisuuden Seura.

Kirjakka, Marjut. 1982. *Kaupunkirakentaminen Suomessa vuoteen 1875. Asemakaavoituksen sekä rakentamista ohjanneiden määräysten ja päätösten vaikutus kaupunkirakenteeseen*. Espoo: Teknillinen korkeakoulu.

Kopytoff, Igor. 1986. The Cultural Biography of Things: Commoditization as Process. In *The Social Life of Things: Commodities in Cultural Perspective*, edited by Arjun Appadurai, 63–91. New York: Cambridge University Press.

Korhonen, Teppo. 1996. Anasyrma in the Finnish Tradition. In *Ethnologia Fennica: Finnish Studies in Ethnology* 1996(24):13–30.

———. 2009. Rakennuspaikan valinta ja valtaus sekä kodin turvaaminen. In *Maasta, kivestä ja hengestä Markus Hiekkanen Festschrift*, edited by Hanna-Maria Pellinen, 262–271. Turku: Kulttuurien tutkimuksen laitos, arkeologia.

Koskinen, Juha. 1986. *Muinaisusko ja kansanusko Suomessa*. Helsinki: Sirius.

Kuorilehto, Markku. 2008. *Sukututkimuksen jatko-opas*. Helsinki: Suomen sukututkimusseura.

Lee, Lori. 2011. Beads, Coins, and Charms at a Poplar Forest Slave Cabin (1833–1858). *Northern Historical Archaeology* 40(1):103–122.

Linn, Meredith. B. 2014. Irish Immigrant Healing Magic in Nineteenth-Century New York City. *Historical Archaeology* 48(3):144–165.

Lucas, Michael T. 2014. Empowered Objects: Material Expressions of Spiritual Beliefs in the Colonial Chesapeake Region. *Historical Archaeology* 48(3):106–124.

Manning, M. Chris. 2014. The Material Culture of Ritual Concealments in the United States. *Historical Archaeology* 48(3):52–83.

Meskell, Lynn. 2004. *Object Worlds in Ancient Egypt. Material Biographies Past and Present*. Oxford: Berg.

Mills, Barbara J., and William H. Walker. 2008. Introduction: Memory, Materiality and Depositional Practice. In *Memory Work. Archaeologies of Material Practices*, edited by Barbara J. Mills and William H. Walker, 3–24. Santa Fe, NM: School for Advanced Research Press.

Mrozowski, Stephen A., D. Rae Gould and Heather Law Pezzarossi. 2015. Rethinking Colonialism. Indigenous Innovation and Colonial Inevitability. In *Rethinking Colonialism. Comparative Archaeological Approaches*, edited by Craig N. Cipolla and Katherine Howlett Hayes, 121–142. Gainesville: University Press of Florida.

Nurmi, Risto. 2009. (The) Memory Remains: The Immaterial Remnants of the Toll Fence in Tornio Town. *Interarchaeologia* 3:121–134.

Olivier, Laurent. 2015. *The Dark Abyss of Time: Archaeology and Memory*. Translated by Arthur Greenspan. Lanham, Md: Rowman & Littlefield.

Outakoski, Aslak. 1949. *Oulun konepaja osakeyhtiö 1873–1948. Raskaan teollisuuden aloittaminen Pohjois-Suomessa ja piirteitä sen kehittämisestä kolmen neljännesvuosisadan aikana*. Oulu: N.p.

Outland, Robert B. 2004. *Tapping the Pines: The Naval Stores Industry in the American South*. Baton Rouge: Louisiana State University Press.

Paulaharju, Samuli. 1958. *Kainuun mailta. Kansantietoutta Kajaanin kulmilta*. Porvoo: WSOY.

Pulkkinen, Risto. 2014. *Suomalainen kansanusko: samaaneista saunatonttuihin*. Helsinki: Gaudeamus.

Rossi, Aki. 2005. Pikisaaren pikiruukki, pien valmistus osana tervan menetystarinaa? In *Historiaa kaupungin alla. kaupunkiarkeologisia tutkimuksia Oulussa*, edited by Titta Kallio and Sanna Lipponen, 197–200. Oulu: Pohjois-Pohjanmaan museon julkaisuja 16.

Rowlands, Michael. 1993. The Role of Memory in the Transmission of Culture. *World Archaeology: Conceptions of Time and Ancient Society* 25(2):141–151.

Salmi, Anna-Kaisa, and Tiina Kuokkanen. 2014. Bones, Buttons and Buckles: Negotiating Class and Bodily Practices in Early Modern Oulu. *Post-Medieval Archaeology* 48(1):182–206.

Sarmela, Martti. 1974. Talonhaltiat sosiaalisessa kilpailussa. Suomalaisen haltiaperinteen alueellisista eroista. In *Sampo ei sanoja puutu. Matti Kuusen juhlakirja*, edited by Pertti Virtaranta, 340–59. Kalevalaseuran Vuosikirja 54. Helsinki: WSOY.

———. 1994. *Suomen kansankulttuurin kartasto, 2: Suomen perinneatlas*. Helsinki: Finnish Literature. Society.

Shackel, Paul A., and Matthew Palus. 2006. Remembering an Industrial Landscape. *International Journal of Historical Archaeology* 10(1):49–71.

Sihvo, Pirkko. 1986. *Mull on kourat kontiolta. Loitsuja ja taikoja*. Helsinki: Suomalaisen Kirjallisuuden seura.

Silliman, Stephen W. 2009. Change and Continuity, Practice and Memory: Native American Persistence in Colonial New England. *American Antiquity* 74(2):211–320.

Skantsi, Lauri, Nina Axelqvist, Merja Passoja, and Satu Vuorio. 2005. *Terva ABC-kirja*. Kokkola: K. H. Renlund's Museum.

Snellmann, Johannes. (1737) 2000. *De Urbe Uloa, Oulun kaupungista*. Translated by Sari Kivistö and Arto Kirri. Scripta Historica 28. Oulu: Oulu-Seura.

Sontag, Susan. 2003. *Regarding the Pain of Others*. New York: Farrar, Straus and Giroux.

Søvsø, Morten. 2017. Votive Offerings in Buildings from Rural Settlements: Folk Beliefs with Deeper Roots. In *Religion, Cult & Rituals in the Medieval Rural Environment*, edited by Christianne Bis-Worch and Claudia Theune, 337–345. Ruralia XI. Leiden: Sidestone Press.

Springate, Megan E. 2014. Double Consciousness and the Intersections of Beliefs in an African American Home in Northern Jersey. *Historical Archaeology* 48(3):125–143.

Stark-Arola, Laura. 1998. *Magic, Body and Social Order: The Construction of Gender through Women's Private Rituals in Traditional Finland*. Studia Fennica, Folkloristica 5. Helsinki: Finnish Literature Society.

Talve, Ilmar. 1980. *Suomen kansankulttuuri. Historiallisia päälinjoja*. Helsinki: Suomalaisen Kirjallisuuden Seura.

Turpeinen, Oiva. 2010. *Mustan kullan maa-tervan matka maailmalle*. Somero: Amanita.

Van Dyke, Ruth M., and Susan E. Alcock. 2003. Archaeologies of Memory: An Introduction. In *Archaeologies of Memory*, edited by Ruth M. Van Dyke, and Susan E. Alcock, 1–13. Malden, MA: Blackwell.

Vilkuna, Kustaa H. J. 1996. *Arkielämää patriarkaalisessa työmiesyhteisössä: Rautaruukkilaiset suurvalta-ajan Suomessa*. Historiallisia tutkimuksia 196. Helsinki: Suomen Historiallinen Seura.

Vuorela, Toivo. 1998. *Suomalainen kansankulttuuri*. Porvoo: WSOY.

Wacklin, Sara. (1844–1845) 1989. *Satanen muistelmia Pohjanmaalta/Hundrade minnen från Österbotten*. Translated by Katri Palola-Ingman. Oulu: Oulun historiaseura.

Warnier, Jean-Pierre. 2009. Technology as Efficacious Action on Objects . . . and Subjects. *Journal of Material Culture* 14(4):459–470.

West, Tamara. 2014. Remembering Displacement: Photography and the Interactive Space of Memory. *Memory Studies* (7)2:176–190.

Wilkie, Laurie A. 1997. Secret and Sacred: Contextualizing the Artifacts of African-American Magic and Religion. *Historical Archaeology* 31(4):81–106.

Williams, Gwilym. 2012. Alchemy in Archaeology. *IfA Diggers' Forum* 9. Newsletter

Williams, Howard. 2011. Remembering Elites. Early Medieval Stone Crosses as Commemorative Technologies. *In Arkæologi i Slesvig. Archäologie in Schleswig,* edited by Linda Boye, Per Ethelberg, Lene Heidemann Lutz, Sunhild Keingärtner, Pernille Kruse, Lilian Matthes and Anne Brigitte Sørensen, 13–31. Neumünster: Museum Søderjylland.

Ylimaunu, Timo. 2007. Aittakylästä kaupungiksi-arkeologinen tutkimus Tornion kaupungistumisesta 18. vuosisadan loppuun mennessä. PhD diss., University of Oulu.

Ylimaunu, Timo, Georg Haggrén, Risto Nurmi, and Paul R. Mullins. 2017. Medieval and Early Modern Marketplaces-Sites of Contacts, Trade and Religious Activities. In *New Visits to Old Churches-Sacred Monuments and Practices in the Baltic Sea Region,* edited by Janne Harjula, Sonja Hukantaival, Visa Immonen, Anneli Randla and Tanja Ratilainen, 262–282. Cambridge: Cambridge Scholars Publishing.

6

Caribbean Contradictions

Entangled Networks, Slavery, and the French West Indies

HEATHER GIBSON AND KENNETH G. KELLY

Over the past several decades, historical archaeologists have made important contributions to the comparative study of slavery in the Caribbean. They have excavated domestic contexts in the villages where enslaved laborers lived, explored informal economies and the local production of low-fired earthenware, and shed light on the conditions of daily life of enslaved people (Armstrong 1990, 2003; Bates et al. 2016; Brunache 2011; Delle 1998; Gibson 2007; Handler and Lange 1978; Hauser 2008; Hicks 2007; Higman 1998; Kelly 2011, 2014a, 2014b; Kelly and Bérard 2014; Pulsipher and Goodwin 2001; Tomadini et al. 2014; Wallman 2014; Wilkie and Farnsworth 2005 to name a few). Given the ubiquity of slavery in the Caribbean, researchers have tended to make a number of assumptions about social relations, living conditions, and power. On one level, these assumptions involve the conception that fixed categories adequately capture lived experience. Yet the tendency to dichotomize powerful and powerless, colonizer and colonized, or slave owner and enslaved fails to account for the dynamic ways these different social positions were lived, challenged, and manipulated in colonial settings. The multiple identities and loyalties that a person might simultaneously have struggled with become clearer when we change these fixed categories into lines of inquiry rather than assumed universals. The negotiations implicit in these struggles lie at the heart of the intimate economies that are the focus of this volume. A second fallacy is the assumption that what has been learned about the practices of slavery and colonialism in North America and the English-speaking islands, by far the most thoroughly studied contexts, can be taken as representative of how these systems worked throughout the Americas (see Kelly 2014a, 23 for a discussion of this). The more we learn about the everyday lives of enslaved people in different settings, however, the more apparent the need for comparative contextual studies becomes. Our work explores the French Caribbean context, focusing on the Lesser Antilles colonies of Martinique and Guadeloupe, where we have been conducting multisited archaeological research since 2001 (Figure 6.1). In this chapter, we focus on the relations of exchange and production that emerged within the plantation setting and that contributed to the creation of communities among the enslaved, where people developed a range of affective relationships. These intimate economies—the strategies of getting by, including own-account production, food sharing, shared labor in building houses, and participation in local market economies—have been theorized to be a—if not the—locus of shared identity construction within enslaved communities (Armstrong 2003; Hauser 2008; Howson 1995; Mintz 1974, 1983, 1985; Mintz and Hall 1960; Price 1966; Tomich 1990).

The sugar plantations of Guadeloupe and Martinique present a fascinating case study of intimate economies, partially because of the unique historical circumstances of France's Caribbean colonies. In the eighteenth century, Martinique and Guadeloupe were overshadowed in scale and economic importance by the colony of Saint-Domingue (present-day Haiti). Saint-Domingue was home to the largest and most productive plantations in the region and counted 500,000 slaves at the time of the Revolution. Martinique and Guadeloupe, by contrast, each had about one-fifth this number. While most ships bearing supplies and human cargo headed directly for Saint-Domingue, these islands of the Lesser Antilles were supplied by contraband and by a system of cabotage, whereby goods and people made the trans-Atlantic voyage to a major port and then were later dispersed regionally by smaller vessels (Abénon 1987; Pérotin-Dumon 1990; Schnakenbourg 1980). These local adaptations—contraband and cabotage—opened up space for a dynamic interisland network of trade, a sector dominated by marginalized Europeans and Africans working on the periphery of legality. A secondary effect of this chronic undersupplying by the metropole was an increasing degree of self-sufficiency on the local level. Since French ships could not be relied on to arrive regularly with the necessary manufactured goods and provisions, local planters (and by implication, their enslaved laborers) were better served by

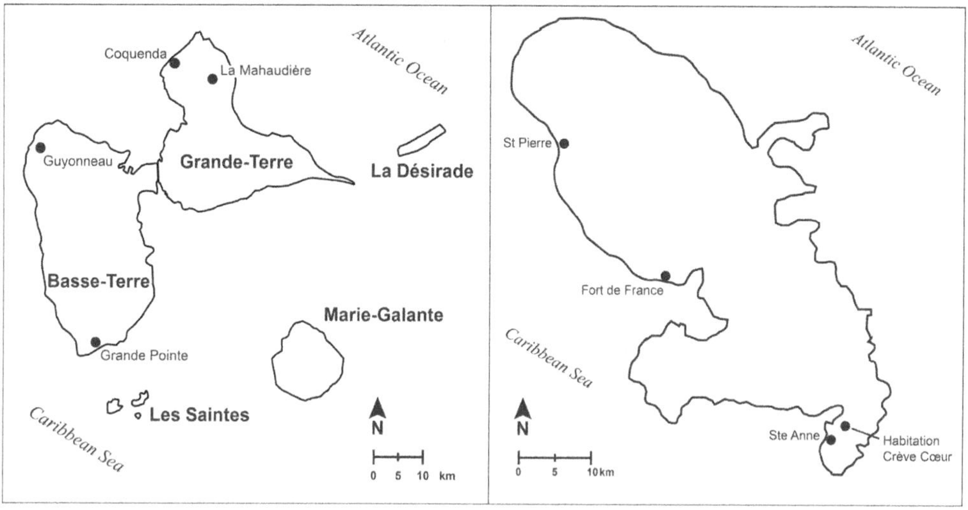

Figure 6.1. Map of the French West Indies: Martinique (*right*) and Guadeloupe (*left*).

developing local production to meet the subsistence needs of the population. The details of how this local provisioning and regional trade functioned are only gradually coming to light (see Hauser and Kelly 2011 for an example that discusses ceramics). But the material and social dimensions of these practices promise to enrich our understanding of the diversity of lived experience in the Caribbean in the eighteenth and nineteenth centuries and how these practices contributed to the creation of a shared identity that endures to this day. Key to this French West Indian identity is the notion of coping, or getting by. This strategy, known as *débrouillardism*, is a creole cultural value of resourcefulness and cunning that finds its origin in the very enslaved communities we have been studying through archaeological research. From the earliest days of the slavery system in Guadeloupe and Martinique, enslaved people were underprovisioned with the basic necessities of life, even though the Code Noir specified that planters were obligated to support their slaves. This privation forced enslaved people on plantations to seek to augment the *ordinaire* (the rations received from the planter) with food they raised, acquired through purchase or subterfuge, or gathered from the wild. These strategies for "getting by" were originally about survival, but over time a cultural value on *débrouillard* emerged that conferred status on and gave respect to individuals who asserted their autonomy and cunning by operating outside the formal economy (Browne 2004). In this chapter we argue that the roots of this strategy can be explored through archaeology and that the historical contexts of Guadeloupe and Martinique enable us to investigate how this strategy was manifest on the two island colonies.

In addition to their unique position within the French colonial sphere, Guadeloupe and Martinique are also of interest because of their unusual histories through the revolutionary period and into the nineteenth century. Although the enslaved people of the French colonies were declared free in 1794, slavery was reestablished by Napoleonic decree in 1802. While Martinique was occupied by the British in this period, Guadeloupe was not, and technically the laborers there experienced an eight-year period of "freedom" before being declared the property of their former owners once again. The particularities of how these transitions were carried out—from slavery to freedom and back to slavery again—are not always clear. Some former slaves joined the army and some moved to cities and towns when they could find work. Some mobility does seem to have been possible during this first emancipation on Guadeloupe, but many laborers stayed on plantations and engaged in subsistence agriculture and perhaps the production of sugar. Even if the promises of freedom were not realized for many in this period, there do seem to have been important changes to living conditions and social and economic networks in nineteenth-century Guadeloupe that may relate to these times of instability and challenge to the status quo.

Our insights into intimate economies in Guadeloupe and Martinique draw from three sugar plantations where Kenneth Kelly directed excavations from 2001 to 2010. Excavations were conducted in the slave villages of three estates: in Guadeloupe at Habitation Grande Pointe in southern Basse-Terre, in Habitation La Mahaudière in northern Grande-Terre, and in Habitation Crève Cœur in southern Martinique. These estates are broadly comparable—they were all sugar estates of approximately the same size and had populations of 150 to 200 enslaved workers. Habitations La Mahaudière and Crève Cœur were both active from at least the mid-eighteenth century through the late nineteenth century, whereas Habitation Grande Pointe appears to have been established somewhat later, around the beginning of the nineteenth century. Archaeological research at each plantation involved developing a base map of visible archaeological features (building foundations, house platforms, retaining walls, and areas of high artifact density) and excavating a sample of loci within each village. In addition to recovering a range of artifacts (local and imported ceramics, bottle and other glass, food remains, personal items, etc.), excavations revealed architectural features including post holes, foundations, masonry walls, and trash middens. Our analyses in the following sections are based on the spatial data from the site maps, the specifics of the architectural features, and the artifact and faunal assemblages recovered from pre- and postrevolutionary era contexts.

In our work at the laborers' village of La Mahaudière plantation in Guadeloupe, we found that assemblages from the postrevolutionary period showed increased access to imported manufactured goods. This increased quantity and diversity of imported goods over time suggests an amelioration of their living conditions and may suggest increased own-account economic activity. Despite the continued discourse decrying the lack of European manufactured goods available to the islands of Guadeloupe and Martinique, which was said to promote a robust trade in contraband, the majority of material culture recovered from all plantations that could be identified to nation was of French origin. This suggests that what contraband trade there was either concentrated on perishable materials (food, clothing, alcohol, etc.) or that cabotage, a quasi-legal transshipment (itself a form of getting by), from other French islands was the source of the French material. It is also possible that given the particular socioeconomic position of the village population as enslaved laborers on a sugar estate, such illicit imported goods were less attainable because they were difficult or expensive to acquire and thus were more likely to end up in the homes and on the tables of the wealthier classes.

It is clear that during the earliest period of occupation at La Mahaudière, material assemblages were much smaller and less diverse. This could have several different explanations. It could be that trash disposal during the early period was accomplished in a different way than it was later and that the excavation strategy employed did not identify the densest zones of midden deposit, although this appears unlikely. Another explanation for the paucity of early material despite the clear evidence that the village was occupied in the mid- to late eighteenth century, is that consumer goods became cheaper and more widely available over the course of the eighteenth and nineteenth centuries. Compounding this is the fact that during the second half of the eighteenth century, the northern part of the eastern half of Guadeloupe island, known as Grande-Terre, was establishing itself as an important sugar producing region, plantations were expanding, and the enslaved population was increasing. It seems reasonable to expect that artifact assemblages would be both larger and more diverse in a village that had been occupied for 100 years compared with one where the inhabitants were new arrivals in a new region of settlement. During the later phase of occupation, village inhabitants were likely better connected to social and economic networks beyond the plantation, both because of their free status and because these networks would have had generations to develop. Another likely explanation is that the flirtations with the revolutionary emancipation in the period 1794–1802 would have compelled formerly enslaved people who left the plantation to participate in the internal economies of the island in ways that they may not have done previously, given that they were now responsible for their entire well-being. The new skills they would have developed to get by, such as raising livestock and engaging in task work such as sewing, wage labor, and producing surplus foodstuffs would have compelled the temporarily free to seek to satisfy their needs for material culture through access to the local marketing system. Ceramics and other goods available through these markets would likely have been acquired in small lots of one or two items, not in sets, leading to a greater diversity of varieties present. Furthermore, if marketing was done on an individual basis, some of the variety in possessions may have been due to consumer choice on the part of the purchaser.

Many allusions are made in ethnohistorical texts, particularly those from the nineteenth century, to the propensity of enslaved people in the French Antilles to spend a large portion of profit gained from independent economic activity on their *toilette*, or grooming and dress. According to the sources, these special clothes, jewelry, and accessories were reserved for Sundays or feast days. Peytraud (1897) summarizes the statements of multiple visitors to the islands who noted the trend toward acquiring items of adornment. "In short, there were diverse ways for slaves to succeed at acquiring things; and the money that they did procure was devoted particularly to their grooming and their dress. . . . When they are rich enough to have silver buttons or decorated in some colored stone, they put it on their wrists or on the collar of their shirts."[1] The archaeological record at La Mahaudière reveals traces of these styles of adornment, including buttons and beads made of metal, glass, ceramic, bone, and shell. In addition, metal closures such as buckles and clasps were recovered, as were pieces of jewelry including bracelets, pendants, and earrings. Other materials related to personal adornment, such as the cloth

Table 6.1. Jewelry and fasteners recovered from La Mahaudière Village by locus

	L.18	L.19	L.27	L.32	L.33
Beads	101	9	3	8	1
Earring	1	0	0	0	0
Bracelet	2	0	0	1	0
Medallion	6	0	1	0	0
Clasp or chain	2	0	0	0	0
Buttons	99	16	25	23	5
Belt buckle	0	1	0	0	0
Buckle or clasp	4	2	1	1	0
Purse clasp	2	3	0	1	0

garments themselves or material from which shoes were made, are generally not preserved in the conditions at this site. The evidence with regard to adornment is partial, then, with a bias toward elements of dress that were aimed at embellishment.

While examples of these types of objects were recovered for all time periods of occupation at La Mahaudière, they are rarer in the early periods. In fact, most of the artifacts related to adornment—beads, bracelets, earrings, medallions—were found in a house-yard complex known as Locus 18; more specifically, in the latest contexts at Locus 18 (Table 6.1). This household contains not only several unique adornment-related artifacts but also the greatest variety within this category of materials. These objects include a crucifix pendant and a religious medallion portraying a saint that has three attachments for chains or beads, as for the central piece of a rosary. Locus 18 also yielded a twisted-copper cuff-style bracelet, a braided chain made of a copper alloy that was likely part of a necklace, and a pendant depicting a cross, a heart, and an anchor, a common combination that symbolized the Christian virtues of faith, hope, and charity (Figure 6.2). It seems that the members of this household had access to a range of goods during the second half of the nineteenth century. Finds are not limited to utilitarian objects but include a range of artifacts that may be considered display or luxury goods.

Historical and archaeological research has shown that enslaved laborers on Caribbean plantations were often afforded a certain degree of economic "freedom" through the system of own-account cultivation and through their access to the internal economy. However, it was only because adopting this system of provisioning lifted enormous economic

Figure 6.2. Artifacts from Locus 18. *Clockwise from top left*: religious medallion (LM-241), shell buttons (LM-021), crucifix (LM-194), and pendant (LM-657).

burdens from the shoulders of planters that the practice persisted at all. This is likely what Anse Bertrand planter Douillard Grandfond, the uncle of the proprietor of La Mahaudière plantation, was commenting on in an 1818 letter to Lieutenant Governor Lardenoy, who had recently issued an ordinance reiterating the need for planters to distribute the rations the Code Noir stipulated and forbidding the granting of free Saturdays. In his letter, Douillard Grandfond argued that the planters of Anse Bertrand agreed that the best arrangement for feeding the enslaved population was to give them plots of land and free time to cultivate them. He explained that during the harvest and in periods of drought, planters distributed the rations the Code Noir stipulated, but that outside of this, the most beneficial arrangement for both the planter and the slave was to substitute time and land for provisions. This arrangement was seen to strengthen the enslaved class's attachment to the land and consequently to quell rebellion or pacify desires for autonomy.[2] Though not necessarily a desirable arrangement for the enslaved at the outset, this practice did open up time and space for developing social and economic ties that formed an essential part of their strategies for "getting by."

While the archaeological evidence of diet is limited at La Mahaudière, it indicates a greater reliance on domesticated animals than on wild fauna. Planters in Guadeloupe, especially in northern Grande-Terre, repeatedly emphasized the limited nature of their provisioning to the enslaved. So while domesticated species may be interpreted as evidence of planter provisioning in some contexts, here it may actually reflect the increased ability of enslaved people to acquire and tend to their own livestock in the later periods. Because there is little or no evidence to suggest that planters increased rations of protein to their enslaved workers, we suggest that the archaeological evidence reflects greater own-account production of small and medium-sized fauna, such as chickens, goats, sheep, and pigs. This own-account production would have served two purposes—it would have potentially increased the amount and parts of animals available to the enslaved community and it would have potentially generated revenue through sale at local markets. This income could then be spent on other kinds of foods or on a wide range of goods, from ceramics to jewelry.

The architecture of enslaved housing underwent significant changes in Guadeloupe in the early nineteenth century. They had partial walls of masonry construction and prepared limestone floors that contrast sharply with the evidence for wattle-and-daub style construction from the earliest period of the La Mahaudière village. Housing in the pre-revolutionary period was characterized by lightly built wattle-and-daub structures, the *kaz en gaulettes* that can still be occasionally seen in parts of the Caribbean. These structures, which were built with wooden posts sunk into the ground and woven wattled walls, were typical of slave villages in the eighteenth century. They are represented at La Mahaudière by arrays of postholes dug through the shallow soil and into the limestone bedrock of the hillside setting of the village. We know that these postholes date to the eighteenth century because eighteenth-century artifacts are sometimes found in the fill of a hole and because some of them are covered by later construction that dates to the early nineteenth century. The posthole evidence indicates that these houses were distributed across the La Mahaudière slave village area in an irregular pattern, suggesting that the village grew organically in its early years. Beginning in the early nineteenth century, the village underwent major changes. The layout shifted to a rigidly organized grid pattern in which the houses were uniformly constructed with masonry half-walls, finished floors, and identical dimensions. At Habitation Grande Pointe, on the southern tip of Basse-Terre, our archaeological survey identified a series of houses constructed of locally cut basalt blocks that conforms to the pattern seen at La Mahaudière, where the village was established on a regular grid of similar houses. The Grande Pointe village, which dates to the early nineteenth century, does not have evidence of an earlier village but demonstrates that by the early nineteenth century, this village pattern was found from the northern tip of Grande-Terre to the southern extremity of Basse-Terre. This process of village transformation, which seems to also have occurred at Habitation Grande Pointe, is similar to a series of transformations Chapman described (1991) in the Danish Virgin Islands, which he associates with discourses of improvement of slave life in the face of increasing critiques of slavery and political pressure from abolitionists. However, this transformation at La Mahaudière and Grande Pointe took place several decades earlier than the evidence of amelioration in the Danish Virgin Islands. Based on close chronological control, we argue that these transformations in Guadeloupe occurred not because of pressure from abolitionists but as a result of what Régent calls the "negotiations" that took place during the reestablishment of slavery in Guadeloupe (Régent 2003, 294).

This argument is strengthened by evidence from elsewhere in Guadeloupe and from Habitation Crève Cœur in Martinique. Habitation Guyonneau in northern Basse-Terre is associated with two slave village sites. The eighteenth-century village site is located about two kilometers away from the industrial center of the plantation. Surface archaeological evidence indicates that it was not occupied beyond the end of the eighteenth century (Kelly 2014b, 206). Archaeological work by the Institut National de Recherches Archéologiques Préventatif (INRAP) at a location close to the industrial center identified a second slave village site with masonry houses of uniform size arranged in a regular grid pattern that dates to the very early nineteenth century, much like the pattern at La Mahaudière (Casagrande and Serrand 2008). This indicates that at least two plantations on Guadeloupe underwent the same kind of transformation at approximately the same time. Yet another slave village on a Guadeloupean plantation underwent significant change in the early nineteenth century. Although Habitation Coquenda is not the subject of archaeological excavation, Kelly visited it in 2002 as part of his reconnaissance survey. He noted that the village site indicated on the eighteenth-century Carte des Ingénieurs du Roi (1762–1764) had been subjected to plowing but that a nineteenth-century village site was still extant at an adjacent location, indicating a village relocation similar to that at Guyonneau (Kelly 2014b, 206–207).[3] We argue that these transformations are linked to the reestablishment of slavery and have a direct bearing on the intimate economies of the enslaved community. The provision of new housing in a dense, orderly village would have had implications for the increased surveillance of enslaved people and would potentially have constrained their ability to engage in own-account production of space-intensive activities, whether of livestock or agriculture, adjacent to their houses.

Another useful source of information for exploring the theme of intimate economies at La Mahaudière is the documents associated with an 1840 court case against the plantation owner, who was charged with excessive abuse of a female slave he had imprisoned for twenty-two months in a prison on the estate.[4] Douillard-Mahaudière justified this treatment by explaining his suspicions that Lucile had carried out numerous episodes of poisoning on the estate. He held her responsible for his wife's death. The accounts of the trial are packed with information about Lucile's strategies for enduring this harsh treatment and about the material dimensions of life on the plantation. Testimony revealed, for example, that Lucile did sewing work so she could earn money while she was imprisoned; her daughter and friends smuggled the supplies she needed into the prison. Lucile reported that Douillard-Mahaudière's daughter Virginie brought her money, "un demi-franc."[5] Douillard-Mahaudière provided food for Lucile while she was imprisoned but it was very minimal and consisted of a ration of water, manioc, and salted cod. But firsthand accounts relay that Lucile received supplementary food—boiled meat, marinated fish, bread, jam, sausage, cheese, wine—which were sent by Célina, her oldest daughter, who lived on another estate, and brought directly by her daughter Félicité and by Douillard-Mahaudière's daughters (Cour d'Assises 1841, 23).

Lucile's story is complicated, and her special position on the estate as a domestic who worked closely with the planter's family may have afforded her and her daughter more access to these sorts of comforts. But the subversion of authority that is suggested by regular episodes of sneaking extra food, money, and even independent work to an individual enduring a severe punishment calls into question a number of assumptions about relations of power. It is also suggestive of social ties that extended across boundaries of race and status. We learn that Lucile's family members who lived elsewhere in Grande-Terre attempted to intervene on her behalf. Her mother tried to convince the parish priest to speak with Douillard-Mahaudière.[6] Her brother, who was a free person of color living in Anse Bertrand and owned slaves himself, sold two of his slaves to raise the money to purchase Lucile so that she might be spared the harsh treatment.[7] Douillard-Mahaudière refused to sell her, and it was not until the case was brought to trial that a ruling was entered transferring Lucile off the estate and ending her imprisonment. In Lucile's case, it is clear that her social networks both within and beyond the plantation borders were essential to enduring a particularly harsh time. Prior to this episode, Lucile seems to have occupied a relatively high status on the estate because of her position as a domestic, but accounts suggest that she was sexually exploited, and in fact, Douillard-Mahaudière may have been the father of her daughter. This example brings to light complicated interpersonal relationships on the plantation. Lines were constantly being blurred and authority was being challenged.

Martinique

In Martinique, the archaeological record from Habitation Crève Cœur demonstrates a different manifestation of many of the same general processes observed in Guadeloupe. It should be noted that comparatively little archaeological work has been done on slave villages in Martinique and to date the work at Crève Cœur is the only project where the slave village was expressly targeted with questions of longitudinal change in mind. Whereas in Guadeloupe, the postrevolutionary period is characterized by an apparent amelioration of some of the conditions of slavery (elimination of night work, the greater autonomy of own-account production, larger and more durable housing, etc.), in Martinique little difference is seen between the pre- and postrevolutionary periods. Archaeological evidence from Habitation Crève Cœur demonstrates that housing in the slave village remained the lightly built wattled structures similar to those seen in Guadeloupe throughout the period of slavery, seemingly haphazardly scattered across the very steep village site (Kelly 2017, 229). Evidence of mid-nineteenth century houses suggests that they remain wattled, and small, exhibiting characteristics that had not been seen in Guadeloupe for nearly fifty years. It was not until after the abolition of slavery throughout all French colonies in 1848 that worker housing on Martinique began to resemble that seen in Guadeloupe in the early nineteenth century (Kelly 2014b, 208). Only then did a large-scale shift to masonry construction appear to occur, and even then not at Habitation Crève Cœur.

Although the Code Noir, which dated in its earliest form to 1685, stipulated the amount and kinds of rations plantation owners were to provide for enslaved people, by the late eighteenth and nineteenth centuries, practice departed from this legal obligation. Many planters substituted "free" time to work in provision grounds instead of distributing actual food. In a report published in 1763, Thibault de Chanvalon, a Martinique-born government official, noted that most planters had already moved to a system that relied on the labor of enslaved people to provide their own sustenance, which included gardening, raising livestock, and obtaining wild resources from the sea (Thibault de Chanvalon 1763, 108). While Thibault de Chanvalon did not speak specifically to the participation of enslaved people in markets, Alexandre Soleau, who visited both Martinique and Guadeloupe in the 1830s, observed flourishing markets that relied on the surplus produce and small livestock produced by enslaved people (Soleau 1835, 93). Interestingly, archaeological data show very little in the way of avian fauna remains (chickens, guinea fowl, and pigeons or doves), such as are mentioned in the accounts above. It may be that the animals were too valuable as trade items to be consumed. However, the presence of eggshell suggest that eggs may have been consumed. Although most accounts of own-account food production by enslaved people discuss garden produce, plant remains have not been archaeologically recovered in our work. Fortunately, well-preserved faunal remains recovered from Habitation Crève Cœur demonstrate that enslaved people were compelled to augment what must have been inadequate rations through acquiring wild foods, such as shellfish and other marine resources obtained from the not-too-distant coast, and small mammals such as opossum and agouti that were trapped throughout the duration of village occupation (Kelly and Wallman 2014). Given this level of dietary supplementation with wild foods and the likelihood that the rugged terrain in the vicinity of Crève Cœur provided ample locations for small gardens, it is probable that enslaved residents of the village were substantially engaged in own-account gardening (Wallman and Kelly in press). While the production or acquisition of supplemental food resources potentially enabled slaves to participate in the local marketing system, evidence from other categories of material culture that would have been purchased remains relatively limited.

Compared to La Mahaudière, the residents of Crève Cœur suffered a much reduced access to the material accoutrements that add variety and color to daily life (beads, buttons, personal items). Evidence from several households excavated at Crève Cœur shows that bone buttons, the most common type recovered on the site (albeit in much lower frequencies than in Guadeloupe), were being produced in the village by its residents. Despite careful excavation and water screening of a sample of all excavated contexts, very few beads were recovered from the site.

Yet another line of evidence that demonstrates significant distinctions between the two island colonies can be found in the low-fired coarse earthenwares called *coco-nèg* in Martinique. These culinary ceramics, analogous to colonowares in the United States, are unknown in Guadeloupe yet have been identified from several plantation sites in Martinique. At Crève Cœur the forms identified are all hollowware, associated with either cooking over an open fire or consuming liquid-based foods. This important class of artifacts is present from the earliest slave contexts at Crève Cœur and remains common through time until the abolition of slavery in 1848. Even in the years immediately following the end of slavery, when *coco-nèg* declined in usage, a government official noted that now-free workers on plantations used Friday to make pottery, among other tasks (Perrinon 1848 in Tomich 2004, 181–182).[8] Although there was a slight increase in the presence of imported ceramics of European manufacture after 1848, particularly lead-glazed earthenware cooking pots in the Vallauris style, this pattern of having to supply their own pottery needs stands in stark contrast to that seen in Guadeloupe, where *coco-nèg* does not exist, or in the southern United States, where colonowares drop out of the archaeological record during the nineteenth century. Thus, multiple lines of evidence suggest that because they were able to avoid the first revolutionary emancipation, Martiniquan planters were able to maintain a model of slavery that had more in common with its eighteenth-century manifestations elsewhere in the French colonies.

Taken together, this archaeological evidence from Habitation Crève Cœur suggests that while the enslaved laborers of this estate may have been engaged in subsistence agriculture to provision themselves, may have participated in the local production of items like bone buttons, and may have produced or traded for other locally produced items like handmade *coco-nèg*, they likely had less access to imported goods through market exchange than their counterparts at Habitation La Mahaudière in Guadeloupe.

Conclusion

The multisited archaeological evidence from our work on plantations in Martinique and Guadeloupe paints a picture of a Caribbean world that is different in significant ways from the image arrived at through the study of exclusively British colonies. We see trajectories of dramatically different experiences of the "ameliorative" effects of the gradual abolitionist tendencies of the nineteenth century, although these trajectories were within the same colonial system. We also see that even though some strict economic regulations existed that were designed to preserve the French mercantile system, local elite residents in Guadeloupe and Martinique actively subverted the policy that mandated that French colonies trade only with French merchants in order to acquire the materials they needed to pursue the sugar production that was the basis of the economy of the two islands. Furthermore, despite tremendous hardships, the enslaved residents of these islands exercised a wide variety of strategies to "get by," including independent economic activity that helped forge social relationships and build community within and beyond the boundaries of the plantation. One of the most important ways that enslaved laborers in the French Caribbean managed to adjust to, resist, and actively redefine their situations—to *se débrouiller*—was through the social networks they established both within and beyond plantation borders.

As the case of Lucile demonstrates, these ties were important both for the day-to-day functioning of households and for mediating more difficult or trying circumstances. The accounts of Lucile's daughters sneaking food and sewing work to their mother during her imprisonment, of the planter Douillard-Mahaudière's own daughter Virginie bringing Lucile money while she was imprisoned, and of her brother Alexandre selling two slaves to raise funds to purchase his sister all elucidate the degree to which intimate economies were at work within Habitation La Mahaudière. These were the means by which individuals in a variety of social positions expressed concern for a person in need within their family or social network. Independent economic activity was fundamental to establishing and reifying social relationships that transcended the strict dichotomies imagined by the colonial project.

Notes

1. "*Bref, il y avait pour les esclaves divers moyens de parvenir à avoir quelque chose; et, l'argent qu'ils se procuraient c'était particulièrement à leur toilette qu'ils le consacraient. . . . Quand ils sont assez riches pour avoir des boutons d'argent, ou garnis de quelque pierre en couleur, ils en mettent aux poignets et au col de leurs chemises*" (Peytraud 1897, 228–229).

2. Carte des Ingénieurs du Roi, 1762–1764, Archives Départementales de la Guadeloupe, Gourbeyre, Guadeloupe.

3. "*Il est bien prouvé que s'il était possible de donner toujours une journée aux nègres par semaine, et le maître et l'esclave s'en trouveraient mieux. Les plus beaux ateliers sont ceux qui reçoivent le moins d'ordinaire, et par conséquent, plus de journées, alors ils ne s'y attendent pas, ils cultivent leurs terres et s'attachent d'avantage au sol qui les nourrit, il n'y a pas un seul habitant qui ne soit pas de cet avis.*" Bernard Douillard Grandfond to Monsieur le Comte de Lardenoy, Lieutenant General et Gouverneur, September 28, 1818, Dossier 753, Carton 107, Séries Géographique Guadeloupe, Fonds Ministériel, Centre des Archives d'Outre-Mer, Aix-en-Provence, France.

4. Cour d'Assises (1841); *Gazette des Tribunaux*, February 16, 1841, 379–380; *Gazette des Tribunaux*, February 17, 1841, 384; Jollivet (1841); Schoelcher (1976).

5. Cour d'Assises (1841, 19, 26); *Gazette des Tribunaux*, February 17, 1841, 384.

6. *Gazette des Tribunaux*, February 17, 1841, 384.

7. Cour d'Assises (1841, 30); *Gazette des Tribunaux*, February 17, 1841, 384.

8. François Perrinon to Ministre de la Marine et des Colonies, Trou-au-Chat, October 8, 1848, in Tomich (2004, 181–182).

References Cited

Abénon, Lucien. 1987. *La Guadeloupe de 1671 à 1759*. Paris: Harmattan.

Armstrong, Douglas V. 1990. *The Old Village and the Great House: An Archaeological and Historical Examination of Drax Hall Plantation, St. Ann's Bay, Jamaica*. Urbana: University of Illinois Press.

———. 2003. *Creole Transformation from Slavery to Freedom: Historical Archaeology of the East End Community, St. John, Virgin Islands*. Gainesville: University Press of Florida.

Bates, Lynsey A., John M. Chenoweth and James A. Delle, eds. 2016. *Archaeologies of Slavery and Freedom in the Caribbean*. Gainesville: University of Florida Press.

Browne, Katherine E. 2004. *Creole Economics: Caribbean Cunning under the French Flag.* Austin: University of Texas Press.
Brunache, Peggy Lucienne. 2011. Enslaved Women, Foodways, and Identity Formation: The Archaeology of Habitation La Mahaudière, Guadeloupe, circa Late-18th Century to Mid-19th Century. PhD diss., University of Texas at Austin.
Casagrande, Fabrice and Nathalie Serrand. 2008. Deshaies "Guyonneau, Rivière Forban" (Guadeloupe—971). Rapport de Diagnostic 2008. Institut National de Recherches Archéologiques Préventatif (INRAP). Submitted to Service Régional d'archéologie, Guadeloupe. On file at Service Régional d'archéologie, Basse-Terre, Guadeloupe.
Chapman, William. 1991. Slave Villages in the Danish West Indies: Changes of the Late Eighteenth and Early Nineteenth Centuries. In *Perspectives in Vernacular Architecture, IV*, edited by T. Carter and B. L. Herman, 108–120. Columbia: University of Missouri Press.
Cour d'Assises de la Pointe-à-Pitre (île Guadeloupe). 1841. *Session d'Octobre 1840.* Paris: Imprimerie Blondeau.
Delle, James A. 1998. *An Archaeology of Social Space: Analyzing Coffee Plantations in Jamaica's Blue Mountains.* New York: Plenum Press.
Gibson, Heather. 2007. Daily Practice and Domestic Economies in Guadeloupe: An Archaeological and Historical Study. PhD diss., Syracuse University, Syracuse, NY.
Handler, Jerome S., and Frederick Lange. 1978. *Plantation Slavery in Barbados: An Archaeological and Historical Investigation.* Cambridge, MA: Harvard University Press.
Hauser, Mark W. 2008. *An Archaeology of Black Markets: Local Ceramics and Economies in Eighteenth Century Jamaica.* Gainesville: University Press of Florida.
Hauser, Mark W., and Kenneth G. Kelly. 2011. Colonies without Frontiers: Inter-Island Trade in the Eighteenth and Nineteenth Century Caribbean. In *Islands at the Crossroads: Migration, Seafaring, and Interaction in the Caribbean*, edited by L. A. Curet and M. W. Hauser, 41–56. Tuscaloosa: University of Alabama Press.
Hicks, Dan. 2007. *"The Garden of the World:" An Historical Archaeology of Sugar Landscapes in the Eastern Caribbean.* Studies in Contemporary and Historical Archaeology 3. Oxford: Archaeopress.
Higman, Barry W. 1998. *Montpelier, Jamaica: A Plantation Community in Slavery and Freedom, 1739–1912.* Kingston, Jamaica: University Press of the West Indies.
Howson, Jean. 1995. Colonial Goods and the Plantation Village: Consumption and the Internal Economy of Montserrat from Slavery to Freedom. PhD diss., New York University.
Jollivet. 1841. *Précis de l'Affaire Douillard-Mahaudière, Adressé à la Chambre des Députés.* Paris: Imprimerie de Cosse et G. LaGuionie.
Kelly, Kenneth G. 2011. La Vie Quotidienne: Historical Archaeological Approaches to the Plantation Era in Guadeloupe, French West Indies. In *French Colonial Archaeology in the Southeast and Caribbean*, edited by K. G. Kelly and M. D. Hardy, 189–205. Gainesville: University Press of Florida.
———. 2014a. Archaeology, Plantations, and Slavery in the French West Indies. In *Bitasion: Archéologie des Habitations-Plantations des Petites Antilles/Lesser Antilles Plantation Archaeology*, edited by K. G. Kelly and B. Bérard, 17–31. Leiden: Sidestone Press.

———. 2014b. *Les 'Rues Cases Nègres:' Archéology de la Vie des Esclaves dans les Antilles Françaises. In Archéologie de l'Esclavage Colonial*, edited by A. Delpuech and J.-P. Jacob, 199–213. Paris: La Découverte.

———. 2017. Sugar Plantations in the French West Indies: Archaeological Perspectives from Guadeloupe and Martinique. In *Archaeological Perspectives on the French in the New World*, edited by E. M. Scott, 219–239. Gainesville: University Press of Florida.

Kelly, Kenneth G., and Diane Wallman. 2014. Foodways of Enslaved Laborers on French West Indian Plantations (18th–19th century). Afriques 5. Accessed October 8, 2018. https://journals.openedition.org/afriques/1608.

Kelly, Kenneth G., and Benoît Bérard, eds. 2014. *Bitasion: Archéologie des Habitations-Plantations des Petites Antilles/Lesser Antilles Plantation Archaeology*. Leiden: Sidestone Press.

Mintz, Sidney W. 1974. *Caribbean Transformations*. Baltimore, MD: Johns Hopkins University Press.

———. 1983. Caribbean Marketplaces and Caribbean History. *Radical History Review* 27:110–120.

———. 1985. From Plantations to Peasantries in the Caribbean. In *Caribbean Contours*, edited by S. W. Mintz and S. Price, 127–153. Baltimore, MD: Johns Hopkins University Press.

Mintz, Sidney, and Douglas Hall. 1960. The Origins of the Jamaican Internal Marketing System. In *Papers in Caribbean Anthropology*, edited by I. Rouse, 1–26. New Haven, CT: Yale University Publications.

Pérotin-Dumon, Anne. 1990. Cabotage, Contraband, and Corsairs: The Port Cities of Guadeloupe and Their Inhabitants, 1650–1800. In *Atlantic Port Cities: Economy, Culture, and Society in the Atlantic World, 1650–1800*, edited by F. W. Knight and Peggy K. Liss, 58–86. Knoxville: University of Tennessee Press.

Peytraud, Lucien P. 1897. *L'Esclavage aux Antilles Françaises avant 1789, d'après des Documents Inédit des Archives Colonials*. Paris: Hachette.

Price, Richard. 1966. Caribbean Fishing and Fishermen: A Historical Sketch. *American Anthropologist* 68(6):1363–1383.

Pulsipher, Lydia M., and Conrad "Mac" Goodwin. 2001. "Getting the Essence of It": Galways Plantation, Montserrat, West Indies. In *Island Lives: Historical Archaeologies of the Caribbean*, edited by P. Farnsworth, 165–203. Tuscaloosa: University of Alabama Press.

Régent, Frédéric. 2003. Le rétablissement de l'esclavage et du préjugé de couleur en Guadeloupe (1802–1803). In *Rétablissement de l'esclavage dans les colonies française: Aux origines de Haïti*, edited by Y. Bénot and M. Dorigny, 283–297. Paris: Maisoneuve et Larose.

Schnakenbourg, Christian. 1980. *Histoire de l'Industrie Sucriere en Guadeloupe aux XIXe et XXe siecles*. Tome 1, *La Crise du Systeme Esclavagiste (1835–1842)*. Paris: Harmattan.

Schoelcher, Victor. 1976. *Des Colonies Françaises: Abolition Immédiate de L'Esclavage*. Basse-Terre, Guadeloupe: Société d'Histoire de la Guadeloupe.

Soleau, A. 1835. *Notes sur les Guyanes Français, Hollandaise, Anglaise, et sur les Antilles*

Françaises (Cayenne, Surinam, Demerary, la Martinique, la Guadeloupe). Paris: Ministere de la Marine des Colonies.

Thibault de Chanvallon, J. B. 1763. *Voyage à la Martinique*. Paris: Bauche.

Tomadini, Noémie, Sandrine Grouard and Yann Henry. 2014. L'Alimentation dans une Plantation Guadeloupéene du XVIIIe siècle. In *Bitasion: Archéologie des Habitations-Plantations des Petites Antilles/Lesser Antilles Plantation Archaeology*, edited by K. G. Kelly and B. Bérard, 69–85. Leiden: Sidestone Press.

Tomich, Dale. 1990. *Slavery in the Circuit of Sugar: Martinique and the World Economy, 1830–1848*. Baltimore, MD: Johns Hopkins University Press.

———. 2004. *Through the Prism of Slavery: Labor, Capital, and World Economy*. Lanham, MA: Rowman and Littlefield.

Wallman, Diane. 2014. Negotiating the Plantation Structure: An Archaeological. Investigation of Slavery, Subsistence and Daily Practice at Habitation Crève Cœur, Martinique, ca. 1760–1890. PhD diss., University of South Carolina, Columbia.

Wallman, Diane, and Kenneth G. Kelly. In press. The Investigation of Daily Practice of Enslaved Laborer and Sharecropper Households on an Eighteenth to Nineteenth Century French-Caribbean Plantation. In *Out of the Ordinary: Historical Archaeologies on and beyond Caribbean Plantations*, edited by T. Ahlman. Tuscaloosa: University of Alabama Press.

Wilkie, Laurie A., and Paul Farnsworth. 2005. *Sampling Many Pots: An Archaeology of Memory and Tradition at a Bahamian Plantation*. Gainesville: University Press of Florida.

7

Blurred Boundaries

Internal and Illicit Plantation Economies

KEVIN R. FOGLE

Peter Stanton, a 42-year-old enslaved field hand living in the Pee Dee region of South Carolina, had accumulated a great deal of personal property by the close of the Civil War. According to Stanton, he owned 300 pounds of smoked pork bacon, 20 pounds of lard stored in gourds, 4 bushels of mill-ground cornmeal, 5 bushels of husked corn, 30 chickens, 5 store-bought cloth shirts, 1 pair of leather shoes, 3 bed sheets and 5 quilts made by his family, and 2 store-bought blankets valued in total at $200.50. When asked how he had obtained this property, Stanton spoke of growing cotton around his wife's house, selling the cotton harvest to buy shoats from a fellow field hand, growing corn to feed the growing pigs, and eventually butchering the adult pigs to make bacon and lard. To earn additional money, he and his family made baskets and caned chairs in the evenings or in any downtime they could secure.[1]

Like Peter Stanton, many enslaved individuals in the antebellum period were active members of their local economies, buying, selling, or producing goods and often hiring themselves out for brute labor jobs or skilled tasks after hours. As the diverse internal economies of enslaved laborers flourished and thrived in early nineteenth-century South Carolina, many slaveholders grew increasingly worried about the consequences of economic engagement by bondspeople. Planters were concerned about the sense of independence instilled in bondspeople from participation in the market and were especially frightened by the diverse economic and social relationships they were forming with merchants, poor whites, and free blacks that had the power to jeopardize their hegemonic position on the plantation and potentially undermine the entire intuition of slavery (Campbell 1993; Forret 2006; Hilliard 2014; Hudson 1994, 81). On a more pragmatic level, reform-minded slaveholders viewed the economic freedom of the enslaved laborers as a direct challenge to discipline on the plantation as they believed that it encouraged theft, gambling, and the acquisition of spirits (Breeden 1980, 250–256; Hilliard 2014, 89).

Because of these perceived threats, in the last few decades of the antebellum period, southern planters made a concerted effort to severely limit the access of bondspeople to local economies where they had been previously welcome to trade (Campbell 1993, 259). In response to new restrictions on customary rights to produce, sell, and barter goods, enslaved individuals created and expanded underground economic networks to resist slaveholder reforms and retain their ability to participate in local markets (Schweninger 1992, 125).

Instead of attempting to understand the impact of late antebellum market restrictions from a broad macrohistorical perspective, this chapter examines illicit or unapproved exchange by enslaved laborers from an intimate microhistorical perspective that considers the detailed motivations that drove individual exchange. The actual transactions involving the exchange of goods and/or currency only scratch the surface of the complex relational dealings that allowed such trade to flourish in face of restrictive legal statutes and plantation rules. For enslaved individuals, the tangible risk of breaking late antebellum economic restrictions in order to maintain their participation in local markets relied exclusively on the personal relationships they had developed with poor whites, merchants, and other individuals who were willing to trade with them. Both parties were at risk because of the illegality of most trade and the potential ire of the elite planter class. Trust and discretion were paramount in these antebellum exchanges, especially when trade involved goods that might have been stolen from planters or items that slaveholders expressly prohibited on plantations. This approach attempts to extrapolate the deeply embedded meanings and motivations that drove and maintained these vibrant intimate economies in the late antebellum period.

This chapter examines the nature of antebellum market reforms planter J. D. Witherspoon implemented and the resulting illicit and licit economies Witherspoon's bondspeople and other local enslaved communities developed in the Pee Dee region of South Carolina. Witherspoon's plantation, which was in operation from 1808 to 1862, was known as Witherspoon Island or Lowthers Lake Place and was located on the banks of the Pee Dee River in Darlington District (present-day Darlington County). An absentee owner cotton planation, Witherspoon Island was occupied by the enslaved workforce and an overseer, while J. D. Witherspoon and his wife Elizabeth Boykin Witherspoon lived in the nearby town of Society Hill. This plantation site, which was the subject of archaeological research from 2009 to 2014, is an ideal locus for examining the implementation of and resistance to antebellum economic reforms because of a remarkable documentary record and the presence of intact unplowed archaeological household contexts associated with several enslaved dwellings.

Reforming the Internal Economy

In the nineteenth century on J. D. Witherspoon's plantation and on many plantations throughout the South, a wide variety of economic reforms were conceived and implemented in an attempt to rein in the market participation of their enslaved laborers (Campbell 1993; Ravenel 1936, 748–777). Legislators in South Carolina were some of the first to address these concerns by attempting to limit the access of enslaved people to the open market with a series of laws in the late eighteenth and nineteenth centuries that severely restricted the ability of merchants and private citizens to trade with enslaved individuals and that outlawed liquor sales to bondspeople altogether (Henry 1914, 81–82; Lichtenstein 1988). Cases of trading with slaves were hard to convict in court without evidence from enslaved laborers, who were barred from testifying under South Carolina law. The proof needed for such a conviction was a reliable white witness who had to see a bondsman enter a store or house with certain items and leave without those goods (Forret 2006, 98–99). In Darlington District, the location of J. D. Witherspoon's plantation and personal residence, convictions of accused traders and liquor dealers were lower than 40 percent. Even though the penalty could range up to a year in jail and $1,000, the greatest fine issued in Darlington was six months and $250, suggesting that the maximum penalty was rare (Henry 1914, 86).

The ineffectiveness of these statues at preventing flagrant everyday trading and liquor sales became the source of strident complaints from antebellum slaveholders (Forret 2006, 103–104; Hilliard 2014, 64). Prosecution was also low because small-scale trade with enslaved individuals for eggs, chickens, or produce had become routine in many parts of South Carolina and the enforcement of existing laws at this level was lax or non-existent. The editor of a newspaper in Laurensville, South Carolina, in 1855 made the following observation about the practice:

> In our opinion there is nothing better calculated to injure the negro property than that of purchasing from them, without permits from their owners, chickens, eggs, vegetables and such things. The farmers in the country make great complaints—and we fear they have just cause for it—against the citizens of the village for encouraging such traffic. It is true, we of the village often suffer great inconveniences, for the want of such necessaries, and many attempt to excuse themselves for buying from negroes on that ground, but in our opinion, they are adopting the very plan to make the inconvenience greater. What is the reason that the farmers around us do not raise such things and supply us with them? Why, simply because our citizens will buy them from negroes, who, nine cases out of ten, steal them, either from their owners or the neighboring planters, consequently it is unprofitable business.[2]

The poor enforcement of laws regarding trade with the enslaved in South Carolina meant that slaveholders needed new means to regulate their bondspeople's access to the open marketplace (Campbell 1993; Forret 2006, 103–104). Planters responded by attempting to limit trade with a series of reforms related to internal plantation economies. Starting in the 1830s, agricultural journals and plantation management literature took up this issue with vigor, proposing a range of solutions (Campbell 1993, 253–254; Forret 2006, 97).

Reformers laid out plans that attempted to reshape the economic opportunities that were traditionally available to many enslaved communities in the eighteenth and early nineteenth centuries. Advocates framed the economic changes as benefiting the enslaved laborers through paternalistic market guidance via a patchwork of new plantation rules and localized legal reforms. They argued that reforms performed a dual role: they protected their bondspeople from unscrupulous trading partners and kept their bondspeople from spending hard-earned money on foolish trinkets and unwholesome goods such as alcohol (Breeden 1980, 266–280; Ravenel 1936, 748–777).

More extreme reform plans suggested that enslaved families should be restricted from growing personal cash crops such as corn or cotton altogether. Proponents argued that if they did not grow crops, enslaved individuals would not engage in dangerous night work and that plantation tools would be not be damaged and work animals were not stressed or injured. Perhaps most important, theft of the planter's corn or cotton was more easily detected when cash crops were disallowed on a plantation because stolen crops could not be disguised as legitimate slave-raised crops (Breeden 1980, 266–280). Many slaveholders suggested that in return for good behavior and hard work, planters could provide a reward at the end of the year in the form of extra time off, gifts of clothing or mercantile goods, or small amounts of cash (Breeden 1980, 257–265).

J. D. Witherspoon's sons-in-law William H. Evans and John N. Williams both advocated the use of cash rewards and implemented this plan on their large Darlington plantations.[3] In a report on cotton cultivation published in *The Rural Register*, a nationally distributed agricultural publication, Evans (1860, 180) argued that

> I know of nothing better than a system of rewards for extra picking—"twenty-five cents will pick five times as much cotton as twenty-five lashes." If every planter would discontinue the practice of allowing his negroes to plant a crop for themselves, and instead thereof pay them in money, at Christmas, for extra picking, we would get our crops out in better time . . . whilst we would avoid much of the punishment of our negroes, which is disagreeable to us and injurious to them, and prevents in a great measure, that fruitful source of all crimes with them—the constant traffic with every grog-shop in the country.

This plan was only sporadically implemented. Many planters were loath to restrict bondspeople from growing cash crops because they saw this practice as a social reform tool. In the minds of slaveholders, growing crops promoted industriousness and responsibility among the enslaved population and left slaves little free time to cause mischief (Breeden 1980, 266–280). South Carolina planter R. King Jr. (1828, 525) illustrated how this practice was also a covert form of social control in his contribution to the *Southern Agriculturalist*, where he suggested that "if industrious for themselves, they will be so for their masters, and no Negro, with a well-stocked poultry house, a small crop advancing, a canoe partly finished, or a few tubs unsold, all of which he calculates soon to enjoy, will ever run away." Because many slaveholders wanted their slaves to be diligent, value personal property, and remain economically tied to the plantation, they allowed them to plant cash crops on their plantations throughout the late antebellum period.

An interest in letting slaves grow their own crops or produce goods in their free time did not mean that reform-minded planters were willing to let these activities go on unsupervised. Thomas C. Law, a planter in Darlington District, developed a set of recommendations regarding slave-controlled crops. Among other things, he suggested that bondspeople "should be permitted to have a small crop that they can call their own to cultivate their little notions, which should be ploughed, by the owner's direction, as regularly as his own, & which they will find employment in hoeing, when they have finished their tasks or when time is given to them."[4] His plan helped mitigate some of the planter's concerns regarding cash crops by having slaveholders directly oversee the planting process and by giving his bondspeople time to maintain their personal crops during the day to prevent injury and overtiring.

Where slaves were allowed to grow cash crops, planters sought novel ways to insulate them from the larger free market and from unscrupulous traders on plantations. Paternalistic slaveholders claimed that such traders robbed slaves of their hard-earned income (Breeden 1980, 266–280). One of the most widely implemented plans to this effect was the creation of a plantation store. A memoir of plantation life written in 1876 by noted South Carolina botanist H. W. Ravenel, a former planter, mentioned the importance of the plantation store and the evils it helped ward off.

> The matter of trade between the negroes and the small country stores, was always a fruitful source of trouble and annoyance to the planters. Not only was the price of goods exorbitant, but whiskey, rum and other contraband articles were freely sold to them—and stolen goods (cotton, corn, and other plantation supplies) taken in exchange. To correct this evil, the custom was adopted of having a store on the plantation with such simple goods as the negroes would want most, cheap calicoes, homespuns, handkerchiefs, tinware, molasses, sugar, tobacco, etc. These goods were bought by the master at wholesale rates, and sold to the negroes at cost, simply for their accommodation and benefit, and to put a stop to the trade with the country store. It checked the evil completely, and the Plantation

> store became a successful and amelioratory [*sic*] institution, and was generally adopted. (Ravenel 1936, 748–777)

Ravenel describes the plantation store as an alternative to the open market, where slaves regularly had access to the small merchants, peddlers, and poor whites who were willing to trade with them for both licit and illicit goods. A plantation store thus acted to control slaves by limiting them to trading at the prices slaveholders were willing to pay and to buying the merchandise their little stores carried. Even if a planter did not operate a physical store on his planation, reform advocates felt that the slaveholder should be obligated to buy everything his enslaved community produced to keep slaves from trading with unprincipled individuals and to better detect theft based on detailed knowledge of personal production within their enslaved communities.[5]

Planters were urged not to pay slaves in cash for their goods. Cash was dangerous in the slaveholder's eyes because "the possession of money itself encouraged slaves to leave the plantation surreptitiously at night to spend their earnings as they desired—and thereby assert their independence" (Campbell 1993, 248). Planters regularly offered their bondspeople credit with reputable merchants where the owner had accounts. In exchange for goods or services, slaves would be given a credit order by their owner that was valid for a specific merchant. They could then visit the merchant and shop for the amount of credit the order specified among the goods the merchant thought suitable. Credit systems thus enabled masters to maintain direct control over where their slaves shopped and what they could buy with their earnings (Campbell 1993, 265–266).

Reforms and the Internal Economy on Witherspoon Island Plantation

Both archaeological evidence and the documentary record offer some clues about the specific roles J. D. Witherspoon's slaves played in the internal economy. Bondsmen on Witherspoon Island Plantation, like their counterparts in the larger Pee Dee region, would have grown crops, kept pigs and chickens, potentially labored for pay after hours in evenings or on holidays, and produced saleable goods at home such as baskets or mats.

Court documents and family correspondence strongly suggest that the enslaved families on J. D. Witherspoon's plantation were permitted to raise their own crops. The few financial accounts that survive come from a legal battle surrounding the inheritance of the plantation after J. D. Witherspoon died in 1860. Court records, which contain a detailed list of the estate's credits and expenses for the years 1860 to 1862, have two relevant entries. Both are payments made to plantation slaves in exchange for crops or by-products of their crops. The first is a payment of $17.50 on July 24, 1860, labeled "to plantation negroes for rice straw." The second is a payment of $19.03 on April 1, 1861, "to slaves for crops."[6] These transactions clearly reveal that enslaved individuals on Witherspoon Island were allowed to maintain personal plots and profit from the crops they raised. They also may indicate that the slaves were obligated to sell their harvests to the planter.

Faunal remains recovered from excavated plantation quarter sites at Witherspoon Island clearly indicate that members of enslaved households were allowed to raise chickens and possibly pigs to supplement the rations the planter provided and potentially for exchange. The preponderance of chicken remains and eggshell identified in these household assemblages strongly suggests that poultry were at least partially raised for the thriving local chicken and egg trade noted earlier in the Laurensville, South Carolina, newspaper account and in the account of Peter Stanton, who owned thirty chickens.

A surviving account for an enslaved carpenter illustrates the internal economies for skilled laborers in the Pee Dee area. J. D. Witherspoon regularly hired out Albert, a respected carpenter in the Darlington region, for construction-related projects from the 1830s until Albert's death sometime around 1855.[7] The profits Albert earned benefited Witherspoon directly. Albert also earned income by taking on jobs in his down time or by paying J. D. Witherspoon to allow him to take on individual projects during workdays.

Account books from E. W. Charles, a merchant in the town of Darlington, include an account for Albert. It shows that Albert received $30 of store credit in 1834 for completing a project for H. W. Charles. Throughout the year Albert bought a range of goods with the credit. He purchased both consumables such as flour, sugar, candy, and tobacco and fine clothing articles for himself, including a silk hat and an expensive $12 cloth coat.[8] Albert had advantages that most Witherspoon bondspeople did not: he had the ability to earn money or credit and some freedom to travel. After Albert's untimely death from illness, Elizabeth B. Witherspoon reflected on the impact of hiring out Albert when she wrote about his replacement, a young slave named Jesse, who was being apprenticed by Mr. Woolard, a local carpenter. She wrote that her husband regretted allowing Jesse to work with Mr. Woolard for such a long period because Jesse "will only be a plantation carpenter. . . . Mr. Witherspoon will not spoil another by hiring him out."[9] In this quote, "another" almost certainly refers obliquely to Albert, the only other known Witherspoon carpenter. The "spoiling" Elizabeth Witherspoon wrote of likely referred to Albert's accumulation of property and his expectation of certain rights or privileges as a steady income earner for Witherspoon that went well beyond the rights and expectations of Witherspoon's field hands and household servants.

It appears that J. D. Witherspoon implemented certain elements of economic reforms on his cotton plantation in an attempt to regulate the access his bondspeople had to local markets. While we know that Witherspoon allowed his slaves to grow personal crops and did not pay annual premiums to his slaves, it is unclear if Witherspoon slaves were allowed to grow personal cotton patches. It seems likely that the plantation slaves were granted this privilege, as many of the neighboring planters in the Pee Dee region regarded slave cotton crops as a customary practice.[10] Also, as an absentee planter, is it is unlikely that Witherspoon operated a regular plantation store during his weekly or bi-monthly visits to the island.

The best evidence of economic reforms J. D. Witherspoon implemented comes from merchants located in the town of Society Hill. Their accounts show that John and Boykin Witherspoon, the two sons of planter J. D. Witherspoon, regularly gave a large number of credit orders to their enslaved laborers throughout the 1840s and 1850s, likely as payment for extra work or private crops.[11]

The accounts for J. D. Witherspoon show only a few credit orders per year, nowhere near the number that would be needed to support the two to three hundred bondspeople he controlled during this period. In 1850, Witherspoon gave credit orders to only ten enslaved individuals. One example is the credit order Witherspoon gave Jim, who purchased a padlock, shoes, an overcoat, and a fur hat between January 10th and 12th of that year.[12] A close examination of slave inventories and family correspondence reveals that the slaves who were given credit orders were all Witherspoon household servants or skilled tradesmen who were housed at the planter's residence in Society Hill, not the plantation laborers who lived at Witherspoon Island. The low number of credit orders on J. D.

Witherspoon's account, then, is likely due to the remote location of the Witherspoon plantation, which was nearly twenty miles away from the village of Society Hill. In contrast, the plantations the two Witherspoon sons owned were significantly closer to Society Hill, and their slaves would have had more convenient access to the merchants in town. Unfortunately, no records survive for the stores that would have been closest to J. D. Witherspoon's plantation.

In the tens of thousands of artifacts recovered from Cabin Sites 1 and 2 on Witherspoon Island, only one coin was found, an 1896 Indian head penny associated with occupants from the tenant farming era. The absolute absence of coins from the antebellum contexts on Witherspoon Island strongly suggests that Witherspoon used credit-based economic controls and that cash was rare on the plantation.

The Response of Enslaved People to Economic Reforms

The economic reforms Witherspoon and others implemented attempted to impede slave autonomy in the marketplace while at the same time creating an environment of increased dependence on the planter. By denying their bondspeople crops, limiting slaves to plantation stores, or using credit-only systems with approved merchants, planters denied their bondspeople access to the local marketplace. The only unfettered economic access available to enslaved individuals was an underground economy based on illicit and illegal trade (Schweninger 1992, 125).

Most underground exchange in the Darlington region was between slaves and poor whites living close to cotton plantations. Slave narratives and legal filings suggest that most trade occurred at night at the residence of poor whites or at prearranged locations far from patrols or other witnesses. Slaves primarily traded crops and foodstuffs in exchange for goods such as coffee, sugar, molasses, cloth, finished clothing, liquor, and firearms (Forret 2006, 79–89). Sallie Paul, a former slave from nearby Marion District, recalled a prolific trade with poor whites during slavery. "You see, all de white folks wasn' equal. Some was poor en de colored people sell dem things dey white folks never want. Oh, dey take anything you carry dem" (Federal Writers' Project 1941d). The greatest volume of trade involved slaves exchanging corn and pork for liquor (Forret 2006, 79–89).

Legal cases of trading with slaves that went to trial offer some important clues to the type of trade that occurred between bondspeople and established merchants or individuals. In the 1859 case of South Carolina *v.* Peggy Elrod, the "defendant was convicted of trading with a slave. The trading took place three years ago last March, and consisted in her letting the slave have a half gallon of whiskey in exchange for a bushel of corn." Elrod was also accused of selling a "teacup full of whiskey to a slave named Randall, the property of Major Simpson, for which he paid her ten cents" (Richardson 1860, 662–663). The details of the transaction reveal that bondspeople were paying Peggy Elrod in both cash and goods for varying amounts of liquor.

In South Carolina *v.* William Rollins, a poor white storekeeper located near Society Hill was convicted of trading with slaves (Forret 2006, 104). The proof in the 1859 case was that a white witness said that a "slave went into defendant's shop with five pounds of bacon and an empty bottle and came out without the bacon and with a bottle of whiskey." The slave in the case was reported as saying "he had five pounds of bacon and would have brought more if he had known that the defendant would have taken it." The defendant replied that "you might have brought five, ten, fifteen, twenty, or fifty pounds and I would have taken it" (Richardson 1860, 297–298). Peggy Elrod, William Rollins, and their enslaved trading partners were active participants in an established intimate economy that thrived outside the law and the surveillance of slaveholders.

Two of J. D. Witherspoon's household slaves were known to frequent the house of a poor white in the town of Society Hill. Elizabeth B. Witherspoon wrote that she would "be glad when Moore leaves the neighborhood. Hamlet & Alick frequent his house & it is said he is a retailer of liquor. Someone will supply his place but perhaps not in so retired a situation."[13] Her casual mention of a grog shop in Society Hill supports a suspicion that at least one individual in every neighborhood was willing to break the law and provide liquor to slaves in exchange for stolen or personally produced goods. Records citing drunkenness among enslaved Witherspoon members of Welsh Neck Baptist Church during the 1840s and 1850s corroborate that Witherspoon household servants had regular access to intoxicating spirits.[14]

To buy from Moore and others like him, Witherspoon slaves like Alick had to be creative in their attempts to earn money or goods that could be exchanged for illicit merchandise like liquor. Elizabeth Witherspoon discovered some of Alick's illicit entrepreneurial activities in 1859. Apparently Alick had been earning cash by selling cakes to his fellow slaves and others. He had been covertly baking them at night in the Witherspoon's kitchen using their ingredients and supplies. More troubling perhaps to his owners was the fact that Alick had been had badgering and threatening other Witherspoon household slaves to leave the kitchen door unlocked at night. Alick went as far to threaten Emma, a temporary cook, with a conjured illness if she did not let him into the exterior kitchen. In his threat to Emma, Alick claimed that he was responsible for causing other illnesses among the Witherspoon slaves, including a debilitating sickness that had laid up the lead cook for over a year. When his threats were discovered, Alick fled Society Hill and was gone for three months.[15] He was eventually caught working in Charleston and was then sold for running away and for other crimes, especially his treatment of the other household slaves.[16] The saga of Witherspoon's footman Alick shows the lengths that certain bondspeople would go to in order to participate in the varied and vibrant intimate economies of the Pee Dee region.

Even in a rural setting, Witherspoon plantation slaves would have had opportunities for exchange with poor white neighbors, members of nearby enslaved communities, and the traveling peddlers who were the frequent source of planter complaints (Berlin and Morgan 1993, 33). For Witherspoon Island, an additional center of trade was the private boat landing on the Pee Dee River. The river was a highway of commerce. Small steamboats carried cotton bales downriver to Georgetown and delivered supplies to large plantations on the return trip. The boat crews were frequently made up of hired slaves, and many flats, canoes, and smaller boats were entirely run by slaves. This provided ample opportunities for trade.[17] Charles Ball's well-known early nineteenth-century narrative from central South Carolina mentions an arrangement he made with a river boat captain to secretly trade fish and plantation goods for bacon and other items. Ball observed that the risk of trading with enslaved individual created an unbalanced exchange relationship. The white boat captain was able to offer "a hundred pounds of bacon for three hundred shad," which according to Ball "was at least twice as much [shad] as the bacon was worth." The captain was able to set these highly unfavorable terms of trade due the "hazard of being prosecuted for dealing with slaves, which is a very high offence in Carolina" and because the captain knew he was purchasing shad and other goods that "in point of law, did not belong to" Charles Ball (Ball 1859, 221).

Similarly, Hector Smith, a former slave from the Darlington region recalled that "my Massa whip my gran'mammy wid a leather strap. . . . You see she had a knack of gwine off for some cause or another en meetin de boat what run up en down dat big Pee Dee River en bring fertilizer en all kind of goods to de peoples." Her master "told her not to go nowhe' bout dat boat," but she went "off anyhow no matter bout de whip" (Federal Writers' Project 1941c). What exactly Hector's grandmother was doing at the boat landing is unknown, although some form of illicit trade like Charles Ball described is certainly a strong possibility.

According to the Witherspoons, by 1856, Society Hill and the entire Darlington region had become "so notorious for negro trading that the gentlemen have at last resolved to try to check it." Elizabeth Witherspoon told a story about Smoot's store in Society Hill, which had been selling whiskey to a poor white named Kelly, who was suspected of providing liquor to slaves in exchange for corn:

> They have run off one man, Kelly, who lived at Sparrows & have a stricter police. Smoot's clerk said Kelly's trade was worth from thirty to fifty dollars a week to Smoot. A gentleman saw a number of small bags of corn in Smoot's store & heard the clerk tell Smoot it was Kelly's corn. Kelly got whiskey in exchange for the negroes corn, even Mr. McIntosh's old man Peter has been sent to the plantation for drunkenness & pilfering, he has been thought highly of by his master.[18]

It appears that Kelly was acting as a factor for slaves, taking certain risks from slaves by selling their goods for them in exchange for a portion of the money or corn. If the amount of trade done by Kelly is accurate, it represents a significant level of exchange with bondspeople in the Society Hill area.

Because of the forbidden nature of the exchange and the potential need to dispose of stolen goods quickly, historians have suggested that slaves were willing to take a financial loss on most trades, as Charles Ball mentioned in his account. That meant that trade with slaves could be very profitable for individuals who were willing to risk the legal consequences and the ire of their neighbors if they should be found out. Kelly was promptly driven out of Society Hill when his white neighbors discovered he had been trading with slaves, for example (Forret 2006, 93). Of course, there is no guarantee that the corn Kelly was taking from slaves was stolen; the corn may have been part of a repurposed weekly ration or the slaves may have grown it in a planter-allowed patch. Or it could have been pilfered, as the "gentlemen" of Society Hill presumed.

In addition to concerns about the vast quantities of liquor and other prohibited items that entered slave quarters, planters believed that the slaves' illicit trade was driven by theft of their crops, livestock, and supplies. The historical record of planters and travelers in the antebellum south suggests that theft was commonplace on plantations (Lichtenstein 1988). Many planters were of the racist opinion that all slaves are prone to theft and rascality, which they believed was an inherent racial trait (Hilliard 2014, 26–28). The Witherspoons appear to have adhered to a similar view. When Boykin Witherspoon wanted to purchase a house servant for his new home near Shreveport, he wrote to his mother to see if any of their acquaintances in Society Hill had any suitable enslaved individuals for sale. She replied about a possible candidate named Robert who had recently been accused of stealing from his master. Elizabeth Witherspoon wrote that "none of us think his appropriating money he picked up was at all surprising, tho it was very wrong, few of that class of people could resist the temptation." She believed that "most of our yards would be without servants if we kept none but honest ones. I am not sure I would have one left."[19]

Historians who have examined theft by enslaved laborers suggest it was driven by a complex series of factors that included need, customary rights, material gain, procuring items for trade, and as a form of active resistance (Forret 2006; Hilliard 2014; Lichtenstein 1988). All of these motivations are highly plausible; every act of theft is connected to the mindset, living conditions, needs, and wants of that specific individual. Historical sources have shown that many slaves in the nineteenth century considered pilfering from their planter not theft but justified "taking." Frederick Law Olmsted reported from his travels that it was a near-universal belief in slave quarters that "the result of labor belongs of right to the laborer, and on this ground, even the religious feel justified in using 'Massa's' property for their own temporal benefit. This they term 'taking,' and it is never admitted to be a reproach to a man among them that he is charged with it, though 'stealing,' or taking from another than their master, and particularly from one another, is so" (Olmsted 1953, 82–83). Historians have framed this belief as an element of a moral economy whereby slaves challenged the hegemony of planters by appropriating goods that their labor created both for their immediate needs and for comfort (Lichtenstein 1988, 415–418).

The moral economy of "taking" seems to have been prevalent among slaves in the Pee Dee cotton region. At Salem Baptist, a church across the river from Witherspoon Island, the white leadership was shocked to learn in the early 1850s of "certain doctrines partially believed and taught by Negroes who profess Christ," including "a general and very common belief that it is not a sin to pilfer their Master's property." The church formed a committee to look into this belief and reported "after making extensive inquiries" that their slaves "do not hold that it is wrong to steal from their Masters. This seems to be a general sentiment among them as well in the church as out of it. We have ascertained that some of our own members hold it."[20] This justification of "taking" by enslaved individuals was a critical source of goods that drove intimate economies in the antebellum south.

The cases of theft among the enslaved members of Darlington area churches likely typify the common thefts perpetrated in the Pee Dee region. Church discipline cases regularly include charges of stealing hogs and corn and pilfering other foodstuffs. At Welsh Neck Baptist Church in Society Hill, enslaved members Daniel and Rose were charged in 1836 for their involvement in the theft of hogs. Daniel was accused of conspiring with Rose's husband to steal hogs and was excluded from the congregation "by unanimous vote." The church censured Rose, who supposedly knew about her husband's conduct and "had reproved him" but had not alerted the congregation and her planter to her husband's illicit acts.[21] In 1839, Billey and Evelina, also members of Welsh Neck, were charged with pilfering corn from the plantation. The church found that Billey was "guilty of stealing corn from the plantation crib" and his wife Evelina was found "guilty of partaking of the corn stolen by Billey, knowing it to be stolen" and "of carrying home corn from the field, after replanting, contrary to the rule of the plantation." Both were excluded from the church.[22]

An enslaved member named Paul at Salem Baptist Church was accused of theft and found guilty "for milking his masters cattle unbeknowing to his master . . . and denying of it." Paul was found to be guilty and was excommunicated for the crime in 1831.[23] While the case of Paul milking cows was likely for personal consumption, there is no way of knowing if the hogs or corn in the other cases from these local churches were taken to supplement a hungry family's diet or were intended for barter in the underground economy or both.

While being excommunicated from church was one result of participating in or being accused of theft, planters exacted more serious punishments. Aaron Ford, a former slave from the Pee Dee region, recalled his "grandfather tell bout whippin slaves for stealin." The grandfather told young Aaron to avoid taking things that were not his at all costs. "If a pile of corn was left at night," Aaron was told "not to bother it" because while "breakin corn, sometimes people would make a pile of corn in de grass en leave it en den come back en get it in de night." Aaron's Grandfather sternly warned him "not to never bother nothin bout people's things" to avoid becoming involved with the theft of stolen goods (Federal Writers' Project 1941b, 75–76).

When George, an enslaved man who belonged to a local Darlington planter, was found with pork that supposedly came from several missing hogs that belonged to his owner, he was quickly sold off to a local slave-trading firm.[24] Although slave narratives reveal that the theft of pigs was a very common crime in the region, George was separated from his friends and family for his supposed larceny.

An 1858 letter from Elizabeth B. Witherspoon to her son relays a complex story of theft and blame between a Witherspoon household servant, Rhoda, and her husband, Hercules, who belonged to a neighbor, Capt. Edwards:

> Dr. Presley came to see me several weeks since & said he had been robbed of fifty dollars, that Hercules had changed twenty dollars at Carrigan's [a local merchant], Hercules confessed he had taken money from the Dr. & described the place & time when he got it. Three days after, he changed his story & said Rhoda had given him twenty dollars. Upon hearing that your father counted his money & said he had lost $20. I told him he probably was mistaken that he often had panics about money. Unfortunately a few days after he went to Mr. Coker's [another merchant] to get money to pay his taxes & there met the Capt. & told him he had lost twenty dollars. It was a great relief to the Capt. He said he had never known Hercules to steal anything except bacon. When your father came home & told me I was much annoyed at his mentioning the money. I soon recollected that I had paid Mrs. Josey five dollars for weaving. Your father

then recollected he had taken ten dollars to the plantation & William Evans reminded me that I had paid him 3 dollars for a sack of flour & I had the two dollar bill, so the twenty dollars was accounted for but still the stigma rests on Rhoda. She is very indignant. Capt. brought H. [Hercules] here to confront Rhoda. He could not raise his eyes when he accused her & Mr. Kiroin who was present said he was mad enough to give him fifty lashes. Col. Wilson advises Capt. to put him in his pocket, but he thinks him innocent. Rhoda says he shall never come here again unless he clears her of that charge & others equally unfounded. I was so astonished at Hercules' charges against Rhoda & so distressed that I never spoke to her about it. She waited two or three days & finding I said nothing she told me she wanted to talk to me that I might tell Miss Betsey [J. D. Witherspoon's daughter Elizabeth] before she went away what I thought of her. I told her I had nothing to say to her that I had trusted her & she had deceived me. She protested she had not taken from me the cloth which Hercules told his Master Rhoda had given him. Capt. saw cotton cloth which H. said Rhoda had given to make sheets. Capt. did not say how many yards he had & I have not seen the cloth, but if he had sent it I could not probably identify it. Rhoda has abundant opportunities to pilfer from me. I am not very watchful of the cloth. I give her everything she asks me for anything I always give her & more than she asks & this made me think she would not rob me. I wish I could know the truth. I am not disposed to give much credit to H. statements, but it is so base an act for a man to accuse his wife wrongfully that I am staggered & know not what to think. H. was asked if Rhoda had given him any other cloth he said she had given drawers. Rhoda says he has no drawers except his master's old ones. He made other charges but it is too tedious to go into all particulars. A lady told me she felt very sorry for me, that she heard Hercules was cleared & Rhoda convicted & she knew I thought so much of Rhoda. I am not fully persuaded of Rhoda's innocence but I have no doubt of Hercules' guilt. I was so shocked at the idea of her perfidy that I could say nothing to her. Nothing that I would say could be harsh enough if she was guilty. My silence hurt her I dare say she would have preferred my scolding her to my total silence. This affair has troubled me but not half so much as it would have done had I not gone through far greater.[25]

There is no clear answer in the letter about who stole the money that began the incident. As the investigation into the crime continued, Hercules threw suspicion on his wife for taking the money and committing other crimes of opportunity. The obfuscation in this case may have been intentional and appears to have stymied any punishment for Hercules or Rhoda aside from the silent treatment Rhoda endured from her mistress. The fact that Capt. Edwards said that it was a "great relief" to find that Hercules was innocent of the initial theft because he had been known to steal only bacon in the past indicates that for Edwards, the theft of food by slaves was customary and that small losses were to be expected or even accepted.

Slaves also found ways to circumvent the credit system J. D. Witherspoon and his sons implemented by intentionally purchasing more goods than they were allowed or by forging credit orders (Campbell 1993, 266–267). In 1852, a posse of local planters that included members of the Witherspoon and Williams families broke up a slave maroon camp in the Pee Dee swamplands near Society Hill. A northern tutor named Ruth Hastings who lived with Sally Witherspoon Williams, the eldest daughter of J. D. Witherspoon, recorded the hunt in a letter to her parents, who lived in New York.

> A camp had been discovered on the swamp very near here, they suppose it had been there two or three years they, the Negroes, had guns etc. and they had found pens and paper there. Someone had taught many of them to write and read—that one of Mr. W's Negroes presented a forged order at the store as they found several had done before on Saturday night and when they inquired about it, he went away—they found he had left the plantation, and supposed he was in this camp which they mean to break up.[26]

The enslaved individual who belonged to Mr. W. was likely owned by either J. D. Witherspoon or his son John Witherspoon based on the shorthand code Hastings used in her letters. The account by Hastings is important because it details a case in which literate slaves were able to successfully forge orders for credit at local stores. They could purchase anything they wanted as long as the forgery was good and the requested amount was small enough and thus would not raise the suspicion of the merchant.

When reforms at the plantation level and the existing legal code failed to curb the wave of slave theft and illicit trade, local planters in Darlington took the law into their own hands, as Kelly, the poor white who was trading slave goods at Smoot's store in Society Hill, learned. The problem was so prevalent that in 1857 planters in Darlington formed a Vigilance Society to augment the neighborhood patrol. The stated goal of the Vigilance Society was the "detection and punishment of negro traders" and pushing for increased legal punishments for those convicted. The *Darlington Family Friend* newspaper, which published a notice of the formation of the Vigilance Society, made an editorial comment: "We are led to believe that, until the law provides a sufficient punishment, it will not be asked to interfere between the public and the negro trader in this district."[27]

The Vigilance Society made national news in 1858 for making a raid on a small store near Darlington that was rumored to be a supplier of liquor to slaves. When three barrels of whiskey were delivered to the store, the society members attempted to shut the store down and dispose of the liquor. They were rebuffed by friends of the retailer. The next day, when a large group of armed Vigilance Society members gathered to storm the store, a bloody conflict ensued. Shots were fired on both sides, a melee broke out, and Vigilance Society members killed two individuals inside the store. Many were wounded on both sides. More than fifty members of the society, including several Witherspoon acquaintances, were tried for the murder of the merchants accused of trading with bondspeople, but the jury quickly acquitted all of them.[28] This deadly incident highlights the level of concern of planters regarding trade with their slaves and also the profitability of such exchange for merchants. Both groups were willing to shed blood for what was important to them.

Resistance on Witherspoon Island

The hundreds of plantation slaves on Witherspoon Island left no documentary trail regarding their involvement in cases of theft or illicit trade. It seems highly probable that plantation bondspeople, like their counterparts in the Witherspoon household, were involved in some aspects of the underground economy, by growing crops, raising chickens, disposing of legitimate property in unauthorized ways, or stealing plantation goods or livestock for trade. Enslaved laborers at Witherspoon Island likely found ways to exercise some amount of control over their economic interactions.

In the absence of historical documentation, archaeological analysis of houseyard landscapes on Witherspoon Island may provide some evidence of slave participation in the underground economy. One of the main challenges is that the archaeological record is often silent regarding items that were stolen or purchased with pilfered goods. In most cases, it is impossible to distinguish between the belongings of slaves that were supplies received from the planter as part of their allotment or that were purchased legitimately from those that were stolen or traded for in the underground economy (McKee 1999, 232). Good context is essential for making these types of interpretations. Examples might include unusual caches of intact goods, animal remains where the carcass of a consumed pig or chicken appears to have been intentionally concealed, or cases where traditionally prohibited items like liquor or firearms were disposed of or hidden. Historical archaeologists examining slave habitations must consider the possibility that a portion of the household assemblage may have been obtained by theft or purchased through the underground economy that thrived wherever restrictions on access to the market existed.

Liquor, one of the most common items slaves purchased illicitly in the Darlington region, may provide the best evidence for access to an underground market at the Witherspoon Island plantation. Liquor was commonly prohibited on plantations in the late antebellum period because planters believed that it led to unruly behavior and sleepless nights, encouraged further theft, and generally challenged the plantation order (Breeden 1980, 250–256). This was almost certainly true at Witherspoon Island based on the planter's negative regard for excess liquor in society at large.[29]

For the archaeologist, liquor bottles may occasionally be indicators of underground economic activity when found in certain antebellum slave contexts. A major challenge is that bottles originally created for alcohol likely made up a very small proportion of the liquor trade with slaves. As court cases document, slaves often bought small irregular volumes of alcohol that would have been put in bottles or vessels provided by the slaves themselves. Such vessels would have included tinware coffeepots, ceramic jugs or mugs, waterproof bags, glass tumblers, and even teacups, as noted in the case of South Carolina *v.* Peggy Elrod (Richardson 1860, 662–663).

The use and reuse of such vessels certainly made it less likely that planters would detect slaves' access to liquor and made hiding liquor a much simpler task. Also, many merchants who traded with slaves, as seen in the case of the Darlington Vigilance Society, bought liquor in bulk barrels instead of selling it in bottles marked whiskey. According to planters, selling bulk liquor gave traders the ability to make additional profit by selling "poisonous" adulterated liquors or watered-down spirits (Hilliard 2014, 24).

Analysis of the antebellum bottle glass assemblage from slave dwellings on Witherspoon Island was made difficult because of the highly fragmented condition of the glass recovered from yard contexts around the cabins. A study of bottle function (both form and color) suggests that nearly 29 percent (n = 377) of the total bottle remains (n = 1,309) from one cabin were originally associated with storage of alcohol. That being said, a very large proportion of all bottles manufactured in the early to mid-nineteenth centuries were manufactured purposely to hold some form of alcohol (beer, wine, liquor, champagne), so it is hardly surprising that nearly a third of the antebellum glass bottles at Witherspoon Island were related to alcohol.

Bottles in this yard context do not necessarily represent a high level of liquor consumption by Witherspoon slaves but may instead show a pattern of moderate alcohol consumption with significant bottle reuse. Many of the bottles in the assemblage show extensive wear and scratching on the interior walls that is indicative of extended reuse for various household purposes. Additionally, it is likely that nonalcohol bottles in this assemblage may have stored illicit spirits at some point and that certain medicinal products, like bitters, may have been consumed not for their curative properties but for their high alcohol content instead.

The unplowed yard context surrounding the cabin sites is pockmarked with hundreds of features that represent everything from posts and planting holes to rodent tunnels and small pits. Among the sheet middens, yard deposits, and a multitude of features, there is only one context that may be considered a very likely candidate for illicit activity. The evidence comes from a small pit feature (MT102.F54.A) in a yard area that contained only a single crushed bottle (Figure 7.1). The stratigraphic context of the pit feature strongly suggests that it was dug in the late antebellum period. Based on the form of the bottle, manufacture techniques, and the embossed "Patent" decoration, it was determined to be a quart-sized liquor bottle that was likely produced in the 1850s. Similar pit features in the yard area all contained a variety of material culture rather than a single item, suggesting that concealment of the bottle may have been the intended purpose. The bottle showed no obvious evidence of reuse and was broken soon before it was buried, as the majority of the fragments

Figure 7.1. Archaeologist excavating small pit feature with concealed liquor bottle (MT102.F54.B). Photo by Kevin R. Fogle.

were found within the feature. In the context of regular inspections from overseers or drivers, it would have been essential to hide and dispose of true liquor bottles in covert locations like this shallow pit. The clear function of this "patent" liquor bottle suggests that it may originally have been acquired in a trade of opportunity, perhaps associated with river traffic, rather than a purchase from an illicit grog shops that typically sold bulk liquor. It should also be noted that the placement of the bottle in the landscape, the orientation of the bottle, and the feature contents do not lead me to argue for any spiritual interpretation of this feature. The enslaved individual who hid this bottle was likely attempting to conceal his involvement in the illicit intimate economies that developed between Witherspoon bondspeople and Darlington residents despite the restrictions Witherspoon and other local planters put in place.

Ancillary evidence of the underground economy on Witherspoon Island may include the seven locks recovered from both cabin sites. These were probably purchased by slaves themselves. The presence of so many locks and padlocks associated with antebellum contexts at both cabin sites may suggest that Witherspoon bondspeople were concerned about the possibility of theft by fellow slaves. Alternatively, locks on doors or on boxes and chests would have provided a small degree of protection from search and seizure of illicit or prohibited goods by overseers or drivers. The limited archaeological examples from Witherspoon Island show the challenges that all archaeologists face when attempting to identify specific features or items as evidence of contraband that may have been stolen or purchased in the underground economy.

Discussion

The more planters in the Pee Dee region and elsewhere in the Southeast "sought to establish controls over slaves—with regulations, laws, judicial decisions—the more it became apparent that the cultural and economic constraints working against such controls were simply too strong to overcome" (Schweninger 1992, 119). With actions such as forging credit orders, baking cakes at night in slaveowner's kitchen for personal gain, and taking plantation livestock or crops to sell to passing riverboats, enslaved individuals actively worked to resist antebellum economic reforms where they were implemented. Even with a restrictive credit-based system in place, Witherspoon bondspeople found many creative ways to access the wider marketplace to acquire the commodities they needed and wanted. Instead of quelling illicit trade and making the planter the center of the economic world for slaves, market reforms in the late antebellum period pushed trade networks further out of sight to the back doors of willing merchants and the dwellings of poor whites, where slaves forged and strengthened new relationships (Forret 2006).

Squire Dowd, a former slave, made the following observation regarding the relationships between slaves and poor whites that slaveholders feared most. "The white folks rode to church and the darkies walked, as many of the poor white folks did. We looked upon the poor white folks as our equals. They mixed with us and helped us to envy our masters. They looked upon our masters as we did" (Federal Writers' Project 1941a). Dowd's words ring true when one considers the efforts J. D. Witherspoon and other large slaveholders undertook to prevent the formation of intimate economies among parties who shared a mistrust of the elite planter class.

Notes

1. Claim of Peter Stanton, Marlboro County, SC, December 5, 1877, Claim File #892, Southern Claims Commission Approved Claims, 1871–1880, microfilm roll RG217-SC-Bx243, National Archives and Records Administration, Washington, DC.

2. "Trading with Negroes," *Edgefield Advertiser*, September 5, 1855, 4.

3. "Letter from a Delaware Farmer Traveling in the South," *American Farmer* 11 (1853):370–372; Evans (1860).

4. Thomas Cassels Law, "Report on Management of Slaves: Duty of Overseers and Employers," August 10, 1852, Thomas Cassels Law Papers, South Caroliniana Library, University of South Carolina.

5. Law, "Report on Management of Slaves."

6. Equity Case #484, Darlington County Historical Commission, Darlington, South Carolina.

7. J. D. Witherspoon to B. Witherspoon, undated letter fragment [1856], Witherspoon family papers.

8. E. W. Charles Accounts, South Caroliniana Library, University of South Carolina.

9. E. B. Witherspoon to B. Witherspoon, December 12, 1856, Witherspoon family papers.

10. Campbell (1993); "Letter from a Delaware Farmer Traveling in the South," 371.

11. W. C. Coker and Company Records, 1842–1907, Society Hill, S.C., South Caroliniana Library.

12. W. C. Coker and Company Records.

13. E. B. Witherspoon to B. Witherspoon, June 14, 1859, Witherspoon family papers.

14. Minutes of Welsh Neck Baptist Church (Darlington County, S.C.), 1737–2010, South Caroliniana Library, University of South Carolina, Columbia.

15. E. B Witherspoon to B. Witherspoon, May 20, 1859, Witherspoon family papers.

16. E. B. Witherspoon to E. Witherspoon, August 5, 1859, Witherspoon family papers.

17. Charles & Company Papers, South Caroliniana Library.

18. E. B. Witherspoon to E. Witherspoon, December 22, 1856, Witherspoon family papers.

19. E. B. Witherspoon to B. Witherspoon, January 30, 1858, Witherspoon family papers.

20. Minutes of Salem Baptist Church, 1797–1930, (Marlboro County, S.C.), South Caroliniana Library, University of South Carolina, Columbia, 102.

21. Minutes of Welsh Neck Baptist Church, 171.

22. Minutes of Welsh Neck Baptist Church, 220.

23. Minutes of Salem Baptist Church, 100.

24. B. W. Edwards to W. Edwards, April 28, 1857, B. W. Edwards Biographic File, Darlington County Historical Commission.

25. E. B. Witherspoon to B. Witherspoon, April 26, 1858, Witherspoon family papers.

26. R. Hastings to R. N. Hastings, June 16, 1852, Ruth Hastings Papers, William L. Clements Library, University of Michigan.

27. Reprinted in "Negro Trading," *Charleston Mercury*, August 7, 1857, 2.

28. "Extraordinary Trial," *Brooklyn Daily Eagle*, April 8, 1858, 2.

29. E. B. Witherspoon to E. Witherspoon, December 22, 1856.

References Cited

Ball, Charles. 1859. *Fifty Years in Chains; or, The Life of an American Slave*. New York: H. Dayton Publishers.

Berlin, Ira, and Philip D. Morgan, eds. 1993. *Cultivation and Culture: Labor and the Shaping of Slave Life in the Americas*. Charlottesville: University Press of Virginia.

Breeden, James O. 1980. *Advice among Masters: The Ideal of Slave Management in the Old South*. Westport, CT: Greenwood Press.

Campbell, John. 1993. As "A Kind of Freeman": Slaves' Market-related Activities in the South Carolina Up Country, 1800–1860. In *Cultivation and Culture: Labor and the Shaping of Slave Life in the Americas*, edited by Ira Berlin and Philip D. Morgan, pp. 243–274. University Press of Virginia, Charlottesville.

Evans, William H. 1860. Report of the Committee on Cotton: Read before the Darlington (S.C.) Agricultural Society. *The Rural Register* II:180.

Federal Writers' Project. 1941a. *Slave Narratives: A Folk History of Slavery in the United States from Interviews with Former Slaves*. Vol. 11, North Carolina Narratives, Part 1. Washington, D.C.

———. 1941b. *Slave Narratives: A Folk History of Slavery in the United States from Interviews with Former Slaves*. Vol. 14, *South Carolina Narratives*, Part 2. Washington, D.C.

———. 1941c. *Slave Narratives: A Folk History of Slavery in the United States from Interviews with Former Slaves*. Vol. 14, *South Carolina Narratives*, Part 4. Washington, D.C.

———. 1941d. *Slave Narratives: A Folk History of Slavery in the United States from Interviews with Former Slaves*. Vol. 14, *South Carolina Narratives*, Part 3. Washington, D.C.

Forret, Jeff. 2006. *Race Relations at the Margins: Slaves and Poor Whites in the Antebellum Southern Countryside*. Baton Rouge: Louisiana State University Press.

Henry, H. M. 1914. *The Police Control of the Slave in South Carolina*. Emory, VA: Privately published. https://archive.org/details/policecontrolofs00henr.

Hilliard, Kathleen. 2014. *Masters, Slaves, and Exchange: Power's Purchase in the Old South*. Cambridge: Cambridge University Press.

Hudson, Larry E. 1994. All that Cash: Work and Status in the Slave Quarter. In *Working Toward Freedom: Slave Society and Domestic Economy in the American South*, edited by Larry Hudson, 77–94. Rochester, NY: University of Rochester Press.

King, Rufus, Jr. 1828. On the Management of the Butler Estate, and the Cultivation of the Sugar Cane. *Southern Agriculturist & Register of Rural Affairs* 1:525.

Lichtenstein, Alex. 1988. "That Disposition to Theft, With Which They Have Been Branded": Moral Economy, Slave Management, and the Law. *Journal of Social History* 21:413–440.

McKee, Larry. 1999. Food Supply and Plantation Social Order: An Archaeological. Perspective. In *"I, Too, Am America": Archaeological Studies of African-American Life*, edited by Theresa Singleton, 218–239. Charlottesville: University of Virginia Press.

Olmsted, F. L. 1953. *The Cotton Kingdom: A Traveler's Observations on Cotton and Slavery in the American Slave States*. New York: Knopf.

Ravenel, Henry W. 1936. Recollections of Southern Plantation Life. *Yale Review* 25:748–777.

Richardson, J. 1860. *Reports of Cases at Law, Argued and Determined In the Court of Appeals and Court of Errors, of South Carolina*. Vol. 12, *From January 1859 to May 1860*. Charleston, SC: McCarter & Co.

Schweninger, Loren. 1992. Slave Independence and Enterprise in South Carolina, 1782–1865. *South Carolina Historical Magazine* 93:101–125.

8

Intimacies and Attachments

Households and Hucksters on a Barbadian Plantation

MATTHEW C. REILLY

Economic activities and networks operate on multiple scales, from the local to the global. This not only challenges archaeologists to think about the multiple and linked instantiations of economic activity but to also consider how the economic is tethered to other dimensions of social life, including, but not limited to, the political, the environment, family life, sexuality, material culture, and experience. In colonial contexts, economic factors may have been the underlying factor that motivated and guided such endeavors, but they were never completely separate from the practices and politics that shaped everyday life. This chapter explores how the intimate and the global are intertwined in the material record from a plantation tenantry in Barbados occupied by poor whites during and after the period of slavery.[1] Capitalism and slavery were certainly alienating forces. On the plantation, however, these divisions were blurred by local circumstances.

Archaeological materials and historical documents associated with a poor white tenantry known as Below Cliff reveal the points of intersection of global, island-based, and local economic networks and the community-based intimacies that transcend materialist approaches to the archaeological record. For example, a domestic space that doubled as a shop suggests that an analysis based on the neat separation of spheres may overlook holistic interpretations of how spaces on the plantation were experienced. Hucksters and shopkeepers who were active on the plantation were vital members of the community who facilitated the intersections of the economic and the social. In what follows I explore subtle yet significant interpretative shifts that seek to push analyses away from the geographic scale and from materialist approaches to economics and toward a framework that prioritizes intimacies and attachments. Far from being strictly reflections of alienation, exchanges in plantation networks that are visible in the archaeological and historical record indicate the links between the economic and the intimate.

Scale and Scope of Analysis

Production of sugar in the Caribbean involved the trade in human beings from Africa, goods to and from North America, colonial commodities to Europe, and luxury goods from East Asia. These colonial activities were thus global. The macroeconomic networks of the colonial system have long captivated historians and archaeologists, especially those inspired by Immanuel Wallerstein's world systems theory, but growing emphasis on how these global processes affected life on the local level has inspired a shift in orientation. While not entirely opposed to macroscale analyses, supporters of microhistory have voiced their "dissatisfaction with global perspectives and meta-narratives" and have "urged a return to narrative, detailed analysis on a small scale, and the search for unforeseen meanings embedded in cases" (Walton et al. 2008, 4). Through this oscillation of scale, "microhistorians always look for the answers for 'great historical questions' . . . when studying small objects" (Magnússon and Szijártó 2013, 5) or for "large lessons discovered in small worlds" (Walton et al. 2008, 5; for a recent critique of grand narratives and a call for a "singularlized archaeology," see Mímisson and Magnússon 2014).

Advocates of microhistory acknowledge the intersections of these various scales and that "*small* and *large*, *micro* and *macro* are comparative terms that have meaning only in relation to one another" (Walton et al. 2008, 6, italics in original). Seeing these terms as dichotomous may blind us to ways small and large scales may intersect and affect one another, how they work *through* and *with* one another. For these reasons, geographer Geraldine Pratt and literary scholar Victoria Rosner (2006, 2012) suggest a feminist-inspired approach that replaces the local with the intimate. They explain their perspective: "In shifting from the idea of the local to that of the intimate, we are employing terms that are not defined *against* one another but rather draw their meaning from more elliptically related domains." They seek to "show how the intimate and the global intertwine, to try to intervene in grand narratives of global relations by focusing on the specific, the quotidian, the affective, and the eccentric" (Pratt and Rosner 2012, 2). The goals of this approach align with those of microhistory, but what may appear to be a semantic shift is of consequence for archaeological studies of the intimate and the global.

The intimate, like the local, is partially concerned with space—it has to do with a closeness between people, places, and things. Intimacy, however, extends beyond the domain of the local with reference to Pratt and Rosner's use of attachment, which they describe as attachments: "relationships to others and to objects; [relationships to] sensory data and experiences of contact; bonds of family, desire, or affinity" (2012, 7). These attachments operate on internal and personal levels, providing meaning and context to the quotidian and material dimensions of everyday life. Like analyses of microhistory, studies of intimate attachments can be grounded in an artifact, a household, an individual, a family, or a community. The divergence in analytical perspective prioritizes how the intimate and the global act through and with one another rather than a primary concern of how to get from one to the other.

Personal and intimate attachments can operate at the local level while simultaneously being operational on a global scale. The life history of a thing, therefore, can allow for approaches that span the economic and cultural processes that characterize the production, use, and discard of commodities (Kopytoff 1986). Artifact biographies can be useful for analyzing global and local markets when viewed through a lens of consumption, including functionality and social meaning (Herva and Nurmi 2009). When the intimate is emphasized, however, the research questions shift from market considerations or "great historical questions" to a focus on what can be gleaned about attachments. What elements of the relationship between community members and the plantation economy enabled tenants to participate in global economic networks? What choices did residents make about what goods they consumed and about who they engaged with in the marketplace? Finally, what do domestic goods tell us about the relationships between residents, their neighbors, the physical environment of objects, and local, island, and global socioeconomics?

The relationships and attachments evoked in these questions are of the utmost consequence in a highly racialized society like Barbados. Many of the quotidian dimensions of life on the plantation landscape were dependent on the master-slave relationship (Singleton 2015, 5–7), but in

Barbados, thousands of poor whites complicated the relationship between race and class. In such a setting, the nature of interactions, exchanges, and attachments between poor whites and enslaved or free Afro-Barbadians takes on added significance. My emphasis on networks composed of racially diverse individuals does not imply that these plantation residents were immune to the structural dimensions of racial oppression or that they actively resisted racial hierarchies. Rather, I suggest that these networks and relationships demand careful analysis of how intimacies and attachments affected and were affected by broader systems and structures of plantation society. This type of analysis begins with a consideration of the economic character of plantation production.

From the Alien to the Intimate

Tensions permeate discussions of the local and global beyond the realm of economics (see Gosden 2012), but in considering global and intimate networks in the context of Barbados, macroscale economics and plantation capitalism need to be carefully considered in order to expose the dynamic relationship between these broad processes and the intimacies of everyday life. In contrast to assumptions that plantation production occupied the "borderlands" of capitalism (Croucher and Weiss 2011, 7), scholars of the Caribbean have expressed little hesitance about asserting that plantation production in the region was capitalistic and industrial in the seventeenth century and, to a lesser degree, in the sixteenth century (see for instance Mintz 1974, 1985; Williams 1994; Tomich 2004; Solow and Engerman 1987; Beckles 1997). This scholarship shifts the focus from industrial transformations in the metropole to the burgeoning capitalist infrastructure in plantation colonies.

A pairing of capitalism and plantation production lends itself to materialist approaches to analyses of plantation spaces and labor. James Delle (1998, 2014) has championed such an approach in his analyses of Jamaican coffee plantations (see also Meniketti 2015; Armstrong and Reilly 2014; Hauser 2011a; Cossin and Hauser 2015). His strictly Marxist analysis of plantation slave labor is a significant step in explicating the capitalistic character of plantation production using the labor of the enslaved. What I challenge below, however, is the view that provision modes of production and, by extension, other informal economies and markets were diametrically opposed to broader economic networks of capitalism.

Modes of production that challenged the capitalist infrastructure are similarly relevant to Daniel Sayers's (2014) discussion of alienation. Suggesting that the concept has been largely neglected by archaeologists, Sayers brings Marx's notion of alienation to the fore in his analysis of maroons in the Great Dismal Swamp on the border of Virginia and North Carolina. As Sayers notes, alienation is the foundational concept of Marx's analysis of the experience of modern life. For Marx, alienation "saturates all aspects of human existence and has real social and political-economic power throughout modern history" (2014, 27). Under the capitalist mode of production or the capitalistic enslavement mode of production, a distinction Sayers makes (2014, 55), this involves very specific and totalizing forms of alienation, including alienation of the individual from other human beings.

A focus on alienation provides critical insights into the diverse ways that capitalism dehumanizes social relations. Directly relating to the discussion of intimacy and attachment, in an early manuscript, Marx comments that alienation is also manifest in the relationship between individuals and materials, noting that an individual's "labour becomes an object, an *external* existence . . . it exists *outside him*, independently, as something alien to him" (Marx quoted in Tucker 1978, 72, italics in original). A growing body of literature on materiality and actor-network theory that draws on wide-ranging readings of philosophers such as Heidegger and Latour would certainly take exception to such a claim. The crux of the argument is deeply rooted in the context of the experience of capitalism; labor's external existence partially explains the alienation of plantation laborers from the commodities produced on plantations like sugar, cotton, rice, tobacco, indigo, coffee, or rum.

However, those who were impacted most negatively by the capitalist mode of production or the capitalist enslavement mode of production actively challenged alienating forces. As Sayers points out, it is possible that for the enslaved, the "alienating diasporic exile fostered resistance and defiance on a regular basis" (2014, 77; see also Weik 2012). In addition to explicit resistance, laborers were able to circumvent alienating forces through their involvement in alternative economic activity. While port towns, provision grounds (Delle 2014), slave villages, and inconspicuous locales at plantation peripheries are not necessarily evidence of escapes from capitalism or its associated ideologies (see Leone 2005), markets (Hauser 2008) offered plantation residents an opportunity to socially and economically engage with other residents in intimate and informal ways. Marx hinted at such encounters in *Capital Vol. 1* (1967, 77–78) when he suggested that "since the producers do not come into social contact with each other until they exchange their products, the specific social character of each producer's labour does not show itself except in the act of exchange." In a rather dismissive manner, Marx allowed his critique of the alienating character of labor under capitalism to obscure the importance of these market exchanges as they relate to more intimate economic networks.

These related yet contentious forms of economic activity were able to operate in tandem and often functioned through one another rather than in direct opposition to each other. From the perspective of planters, provisioning plantation laborers with the necessary rations and goods could be costly. Relying on alternative economies such as Sunday markets or local production and exchange enabled laborers to acquire goods not provided by planters. From the perspective of laborers—enslaved, free, black, white, male, and female—plantation production often failed to meet daily needs and desires in terms of subsistence, shelter, clothing, sociability, and recreation. Although they were tethered to global capitalism through their roles on sugar plantations and their consumption of mass-produced European goods, plantation residents developed intimate networks and attachments that have been underexplored in the Barbadian context. The alienation workers experienced in relation to agroindustrial production demanded alternative means through which residents could find sources of intimacy in the context of an alienating mode of production.

Productive Spaces and "Useless" Populations at Clifton Hall Plantation

In Barbados, plantations were settings where the global and the intimate intertwined. Plantations were also where the allocation and organization of space reflected the coalescence of economic and racial strategies. Extracting profit on the plantation was partially dependent on how space was organized, which was ultimately determined by planters and managers, who implemented specific strategies designed to develop the most efficient method of production. This entailed "the planter's control over enslaved labor and the physical location of the plantation's various components, including fields, sugar works and mills, the planter's house, workers' housing, and provision grounds" (Armstrong and Kelly 2000,

375; see also Handler 2002; Hicks 2007; Lenik 2012; Delle 2014). Following published guides that described the ideal way to construct and manage a plantation (Bates 2015; Hauser 2015), planters and managers adhered to a colonial and capitalist logic when organizing plantation space.

This model of plantation operation was put into effect in Barbados in the mid-seventeenth century. Prior to and during its implementation, thousands of Europeans worked on the island. Most served as indentured servants, laboring for a master for a set amount of time (three to seven years) in exchange for food, clothing, shelter, passage across the Atlantic, and goods or currency at the end of their term Others were small farmers who planted a variety of cash crops on small plots of land (see Beckles 1989). Their descendants who remained on the island would come to be pejoratively referred to as poor whites or "Redlegs." These Barbadians lived in urban Bridgetown and in the rural districts of the island, where they lived as tenants on marginal plantation land. Historian Jill Sheppard (1977, 34) estimates that throughout the era of slavery (1627–1834), the number of "Redlegs" on the island fluctuated between 8,000 and 12,000, encompassing roughly three-quarters of the white population on an island that reached over 80,000 inhabitants by 1834.

Poor whites occupied a rather precarious position in Barbadian society. Following the shift in labor on the plantations from indentured servants to enslaved Africans by the end of the seventeenth century, many laboring Europeans and their descendants had difficulty finding gainful employment. Many males served as militia tenants on plantations, residing on marginal acreage in exchange for their service in case of slave uprisings. Other tenants paid rent to landowners and practiced small farming, fished, or participated in cottage industries. The precariousness of poor whites was connected to their socioeconomic and racial status. From the perspective of planters, poor whites contributed little to the success of the island's sugar industry. While some poor whites worked on plantations as overseers, boilers, gardeners, distillers, domestics, laundresses, and laborers, enslaved Afro-Barbadians did the overwhelming majority of work on plantations.

At Clifton Hall Plantation in the eastern parish of St. John, 260 enslaved Afro-Barbadians toiled to maintain production operations at the sugar estate at the time of emancipation. As evidenced by a deed from 1653,[2] the plantation had been in operation for the sole purpose of growing sugar since at least the early 1650s, relatively early for a plantation located near the island's east coast. At the time of emancipation in 1834, Clifton Hall and its 260 enslaved laborers were owned by Robert Haynes Jr. Male members of the Haynes family held nine sugar plantations with ninety-five or more enslaved people, seven of which had over 200. They received thousands of pounds in compensation for their "loss of property" after emancipation (Centre for the Study of the Legacies of British Slave-Ownership 2017). By that time, the Haynes family was deeply embedded in a global capitalist economy. Their enslaved laborers, too, were part of this system, and their daily roles on the plantation afforded them degrees of alienation, among other dimensions of dehumanization.

In many ways, Clifton Hall was an archetypal sugar plantation. The longevity of these agricultural factories across the Barbadian landscape is testament to their economic efficiency and global profitability, despite ebbs and flows in return on investment based on fluctuating markets. Upon closer examination, however, the intricacies of daily life at Clifton Hall reveal the limitations of analyzing the plantation through a purely macroeconomic or materialist perspective. In the northeastern region of the plantation, the sugar fields come to an end at the edge of Hackleton's Cliff. This limestone feature spans much of the east coast and separates the flat, fertile valley atop the cliff from the rough, rolling topography below. Despite its unsuitability for large-scale agricultural production or even inhabitation, the land below the cliff is listed as leased on the 1653 deed. While archaeological evidence has yet to confirm occupation for this early date, it is likely that tenants inhabited this land in the seventeenth century. From that time, poor whites made this tenantry, known as Below Cliff, their home until it was fully abandoned in the early 1960s.

Parish registries and oral traditions gathered from former residents confirm that Below Cliff was a predominantly poor white community, signaling its distinction from the village for the enslaved atop the cliff and the tenantry established for the formerly enslaved following emancipation. The racial divide between these communities was spatial and visual. Observers even commented on the drastically different landscapes above and below the cliff. Of the panoramic view offered below the cliff, Griffith Hughes, the author of *The Natural History of Barbados,* (1750, 23–24) observed that

> the high impending rocks yield a dreary rueful appearance: the several deep chasms below, over which they project, are imbrowned

> with the thick foliage of lofty trees. The adjacent steep declivity is crowded with irregular precipices, and broken rocks; the whole view terminating in the tempestuous sea, over whole craggy shores the foaming waves incessantly break—All solemnly awful, if not horrifying scenes! Except when the eye is relieved by a glimpse, or sometimes a full sight, of the neighbouring plantations.

Hughes contrasts the economic order and efficiency of the plantation with the unruly state of nature and disorder below the cliff. At the time Hughes visited, the area below the cliff was far from a state of wilderness. His account of the area as devoid of human activity may be part attributed to his interest in the island's geology, geography, flora, and fauna, but it can also be attributed to elite perceptions of the "Redlegs" as irrelevant in colonial production schemes. John Williamson, an English doctor who visited the island on his way to Jamaica in 1798, succinctly expressed such sentiments when he described poor whites as "a degenerate and useless race as can be imagined" (1817, 27). During his travels throughout the West Indies in 1825, Henry Nelson Coleridge (1826, 315) similarly observed that the "lowest whites" were "without exception the most degraded, worthless, hopeless race I have ever met with in my life."

If we consider the global economic processes of which sugar plantations were a part, the context of his condemnation of poor whites as being "useless" or "worthless" becomes clear. The uselessness and redundancy of poor whites was a common trope among eighteenth- and nineteenth-century observers. To an extent, such castigations were correct. This is not to suggest that I support the derisive attitudes expressed by island and visiting elites. Rather, poor white plantation residents did little to ensure the global profitability of plantations. Select members of the Below Cliff community were employed as plantation employees and some tenants across the island served in the island's militia to protect planters from the threat of rebellion. But most residents of Below Cliff took part in the workings of the plantation at their own discretion and on a limited basis. Barbados experienced only one instance of legitimate rebellion in 1816, although there were several conspiracies in the seventeenth century (see Handler 1982), so the tenants who served as militia members minimally benefited the plantation owner in terms of labor performed.

From a materialist perspective, it is evident that the global and the local counteracted one another at this Barbadian plantation. At the local level, those living below the cliff engaged in a way of life that was out of sync with broader economic processes. Unlike enslaved people, poor whites could make choices about the nature of their involvement in the plantation system. After slavery ended, the colonial government attempted to have them sent to other islands because of the high unemployment among tenants (Watson 2000). Many archaeological and historical analyses of plantation economies have focused on how enslaved people developed strategies to circumvent planter control and "ameliorate the poverty of their material and economic lives" (Handler and Wallman 2014, 443). In some cases, these strategies worked to the advantage of planters, who were able to reduce provisioning costs, while in other cases provisioning modes of production directly combated plantation production (Delle 2014). In most cases, though, local economic networks were juxtaposed with the global spheres of exchange that created the conditions on the plantation and were aligned with or worked against local operations. The dynamic and sometime contentious relationship between global and local economies can be described in vivid detail. Moving beyond description, however, takes us into the realm of the intimate.

Intimacies and Attachments below the Cliff

The landscapes of plantation society as described in accounts like those of Hughes, Williamson, and Coleridge present the perspectives of individuals with particular ideas about how a colonial society should function. Working against colonialist models, "things—and their inferred circulation in these networks—provide a map of human interaction and power that is different from those drawn by imperial cartographers" (Hauser 2011b, 431). The construction of a different map, as it were, makes it possible for researchers to investigate how intimacies work through broad economic spheres that go beyond the dichotomy of global and local. These intimacies transcended the spatial and racial boundaries the plantocracy established.

Colonial logic concerning acceptable and unacceptable forms of intimate encounters was manifest in localized settings (Voss and Casella 2012; Reilly 2016a). In her study of French Louisiana, Shannon Dawdy notes that practices as mundane as the placement and spacing of houses indicate specific attempts to segregate groups, in this case French people and enslaved Africans. She suggests that French elites believed that "spaces should be segregated and designed to put a comfortable distance between the groups" (2006, 148). A similar logic is apparent in Barbados, where planters allocated specific spaces for particular groups. This pattern was also apparent in the urban capital of Bridgetown (Handler 1974, 16). In the case of Clifton Hall, the great house and the manager's residence were located west of the village for enslaved people. These residences, along with the sugar works and fields, were all located atop Hackleton's Cliff on a flat, fertile plain. The poor whites who lived at Clifton Hall were clustered in the rough plots below the cliff. Such divisions provide support for historiography that claims that poor whites "existed on the fringes of Barbadian society in total isolation" (Browne 2012, 16). Isolation, or at least perceived isolation, rendered poor whites inconsequential to colonial elites, but the intimacies seen in the material and historical record mark their incorporation in local and global networks.

Within the tenantry, individual households reveal the degree to which inhabitants engaged in diverse economic networks and how these networks speak to intra- and intercommunity intimacies. Domestic sites in the now heavily forested area were identifiable by the ruins of limestone foundations that rectangular boarded houses once sat on. This form of vernacular architecture is known as the chattel house and can still be found across the island today. It has long been attributed to the post-emancipation period, when formerly enslaved people moved from their villages to peripheral tenantries where they owned their homes but not the parcels on which they were sited (Watson and Potter 2001). The evidence from excavated domestic sites below the cliff revealed no discernible differences in architectural form between those structures and structures in twenty-first-century Barbados. Because of the dates associated with imported ceramics and glass recovered from the interior and exterior of these structures, it is likely that chattel houses were the standard architectural form below the cliff at least as early as the years leading up to emancipation. Thus, poor white tenants were constructing the same form of vernacular architecture as Afro-Barbadians in the early decades of the nineteenth century.

This type of architecture accommodated functions that went beyond the domestic. Household industries, crafts, and economies in the Caribbean have received some archaeological attention (see, for example, Handler and Wallman 2014; Gibson 2009). The plantation landscape offers a contrast to trends in urban contexts in the early nineteenth century, where a more rigid separation of space along lines of labor and gender was unfolding as a result of expanding capitalistic practices (see Wall 1994). In Below Cliff, one of the households under investigation in this study doubled as a shop. A former resident of the Below Cliff community recalls a modest shop his aunt operated below the family home he shared with his parents and siblings. Materials excavated from the former two-story, wood-boarded structure are thus representative of the intersections of global economic networks and the intimacies of daily household life. While artifacts from this household have been discussed elsewhere (see Reilly 2015, 2016a, 2016b), here I focus on the dual function of this space to highlight the intersections of the alien and the intimate.

Through hucksters and shopkeepers, residents of Below Cliff had access to mass-produced wares arriving from the British Isles and locally produced goods. The shop was part of the island's internal marketing system, a socioeconomic network that began in the mid-seventeenth century and involved enslaved people, free people of color, and white Barbadians of all economic statuses. The goods exchanged included ground provisions, fish, meat, fruit, cottage industry goods (jams, arrowroot, earthenware pottery, etc.), and imported goods like refined earthenwares. Hucksters were mobile vendors who often sold goods at the "great market" in Bridgetown, but others serviced the rural areas, purchasing and providing goods for plantation residents. During the period of slavery, some free people of color and white Barbadians had served as shopkeepers or merchants in the rural districts. After emancipation, the formerly enslaved who had enough capital also could fill these roles. The nineteenth-century huckster has a twenty-first-century correlate in the "Coolie man" who purchases preordered goods in Bridgetown and delivers them by van to residents in the rural districts of the island.

In an effort to regulate such ventures, parish vestries were collected and recorded the taxes individual vendors paid. Minutes (BDA D279) from meetings in the parish of St. John indicate that several residents of Below Cliff were tax-paying shopkeepers. For instance, in 1896, the vestry taxed sixty-one shopkeepers in the parish of St. John (the parish home of Below Cliff). According to local baptism registries, five of these shopkeepers (George Goddard, William King, Edward Marshall, Lucretia Mayers, and Mary Small) were residents of Below Cliff.[3] Men and women of diverse racial backgrounds acquired and sold goods in this informal economy. Despite the attempts of legislators and planters to restrict the ability of free people of color and enslaved people to participate in marketing activities, "in most cases the practices they were designed to control continued" (Handler 1974, 127). Before and after emancipation, illegally acquired goods were also commonly bought and sold, leading one plantation's attorney to note in 1741 that white hucksters were "often worse than the Negroes, by receiving all stolen goods" (Handler 1974, 125). Economic exchanges spanned the illicit and the intimate and involved racially diverse members of the plantation community.

According to a former resident, his aunt sold cooking necessities such as oil, butter, flour, and sugar and imported items such as buttons, ceramics, and textiles in her shop. During excavation of this plot, we collected ninety-six buttons. Given what we know about the dual function of the structure, this assemblage raised interpretive challenges. Were these buttons items of adornment worn by members of the resident family or were they goods that had once been for sale in the shop? Such questions would eventually be answered through collecting oral histories, which confirmed that the diverse assortment of buttons of varying shape, size, color, and material (not a single matching pair is found in the collection) was sold at the shop for local residents who needed to replace shirt buttons that were lost or broken through use (Reilly 2016b).

As items of adornment and marketable goods, the buttons need to be considered in the ambiguous context of the dual-functioning structure. Stratigraphic control was limited during excavations because of steep topography and unstable limestone deposits (the result of regular land slippages and rockslides in the area; see Reilly 2016a). The fact that the structure had a boarded floor also raises questions about the archaeological deposits. Is it possible to separate deposits from the shop from those of the domestic portion of the structure? While the shop was only in operation for a portion of the structure's existence, it left a durable material signature. Local residents recall the careful process of lowering the house to a single-story structure after the shop was closed. The foundational support that was deemed superfluous after the closing of the shop now lies in disarray in the form of jumbled limestone blocks to the northeast of the remaining articulated foundation (Figure 8.1). Without the oral histories that provided this detailed explanation of the site, the overlapping of these spheres would be almost completely undetectable by archaeology alone. The melding of the economic and intimate spheres demands an approach

Figure 8.1. Southeastern wall of housing platform for Wilson Norris's childhood home (*left side of photograph*) and limestone rubble left from the small shop that once rested below the family's household (*right side of photograph*).

to material culture that considers how individuals navigate these intersections and attachments.

The locally made course earthenwares recovered from Below Cliff are illustrative of poor white involvement in multiracial ceramic markets (see Reilly 2016b). The majority of ceramics recovered (roughly 70 percent of the 1,055 sherds from three households), however, were imported refined earthenwares from England and Scotland; they ranged from pearlware to twentieth-century ironstone. The presence of these ceramics indicates access to imported goods in the rural districts throughout the period of slavery and into the post-emancipation era. The ubiquity of these wares across colonial contexts can certainly support approaches to the material record that focus on the global market. The presence of these wares below the cliff should come as little surprise, despite perceptions that residents of Below Cliff were isolated from the rest of the island. The ability of poor whites to consume these goods speaks to both the reach of global markets and the significance of local internal marketing networks on the island (see Handler 1974, 125–130). Scale and scope correlate to specific geographies in the movement of global goods from Britain (England and Scotland) to the rural parishes of Barbados. The accumulation of such goods is representative of both the global and the local.

The ceramic assemblage at Below Cliff is similar to materials collected during walking surveys of the Mount Plantation in the neighboring parish of St. George (Finch et al. 2013). The sites are roughly contemporaneous and the majority of artifacts date to the decades surrounding emancipation or the first half of the nineteenth century. Scottish-made sponge-decorated whiteware plates were recovered from both Below Cliff and the field that had previously been a tenantry for freedpeople at the Mount (Upper Tenantry). These popular mass-produced wares were more affordable than their English counterparts (Cruikshank 2005). This is evidence that laborers likely had less access to goods from England because of their economic status. John Finch (2015) has pointed out that choice in terms of decorative style and vessel shape could have certainly played a role in consumer behavior for enslaved and free plantation residents in Barbados, especially as imported ceramics became more accessible in the years leading up to emancipation (see also Wilkie and Farnsworth 2005). Additionally, according to Finch (2015, 204), such consumption patterns could have been the way that recently emancipated Afro-Barbadians entered the global sphere of exchange.

The agentive and self-making interpretations put forward about Afro-Barbadian consumption patterns are appealing. They capture the degree to which global markets had an impact on the daily lives of laborers, even if that impact can be associated with the alienating forces of capitalism. What is crucial, however, is a consideration of the locales of exchange that likely mitigated the often cumbersome forces of global commodity consumption. The imported earthenwares that constitute the majority of the ceramic assemblage from Below Cliff are evidence that poor whites were involved in global economic networks, but the function of more intimate markets cannot be ignored. The tax-paying shopkeepers who lived in Below Cliff sold goods like the one nestled below one of the excavated households. Instead of privileging the global, materialist, or consumption elements of these artifacts, perhaps a more emic perspective would highlight the attachments between community members such goods engendered in places of exchange and habitation.

Conclusion

Glimmers of the intimate economies of Barbados can still be found across the landscape, although large grocery and department stores are becoming more common and accessible. Humble bars known as rum shops also serve as convenient stores or restaurants, selling a host of household goods. In many cases, the owners and operators live adjacent to, behind, or even inside the shop. Different spheres of activity intersect in close proximity: as customers enjoy a drink, children do schoolwork in the adjoining room. Suggestions that these shops represent a quaint picture of bygone Barbados overlook the complexity and significance of these nuanced socioeconomic systems. Furthermore, an interpretation of such networks as being antithetical to or fully representative of broader systems of capitalism can overlook how spaces of exchange and residence become entangled, pushing beyond the more vulgar materialist renderings of consumption.

In the case of the household and shop discussed here, a single structure and its associated archaeological record reflects an intersection of spheres. Intimate, domestic space is literally on top of a site of market exchange. Buttons are thus material attachments that conjoin the economic and the intimate. Furthermore, the shopkeeper, in this case a family member of those who resided in the excavated household, and the shop are the social conduits through which these attachments are forged. Analyses of socioeconomic exchange need not be limited to designated market zones or more densely populated island locales. Rather, marginal plantation zones could host activities that countered the alienating forces of plantation capitalism and engendered intimate social attachments.

Notes

1. The label "poor white" is a pejorative that carried social stigmas in the past, as it does now. It largely refers to the descendants of seventeenth-century European indentured servants or small farmers who lived on the margins of the plantation landscape as militia members or subsistence farmers and tenants. While the term will not be closed in quotation marks in this chapter, it is nonetheless a moniker that should be used with caution. Tenantries were small plots of land on plantations leased out to free island inhabitants by planters for small fees. The tenantry system, which had existed since the earliest settlement of the island, became widespread after full emancipation in 1838, when the formerly enslaved took up residence on marginal plantation plots as tenants.

2. Book of Deeds 3/3, page 11, Barbados Department of Archives, Blackrock, Barbados.

3. Vestry Minutes, vol. 279; Baptismal Registry, 1863–1891, both of St. Margaret's Anglican Church, St. John's Parish Church, Barbados.

References Cited

Armstrong, Douglas V., and Kenneth G. Kelly. 2000. Settlement Patterns and the Origins of African Jamaican Society: Seville Plantation, St. Ann's Bay, Jamaica. *Ethnohistory* 47(2):369–397.

Armstrong, Douglas V., and Matthew C. Reilly. 2014. Recovering Evidence of Initial Settler Farms and Early Plantation Life in Barbados. *Slavery and Abolition* 35(3):399–417.

Bates, Lynsey. 2015. "The Landscape Cannot Be Said to Be Really Perfect": A Comparative Investigation of Plantation Spatial Organization on Two British Colonial Sugar Estates. In *The Archaeology of Slavery: A Comparative Approach to Captivity and Coercion*, edited by Lydia W. Marshall, 116–142. SIU Occasional Paper No. 41. Carbondale: Southern Illinois University, Center for Archaeological Investigations.

Beckles, Hilary McD. 1989. *White Servitude and Black Slavery in Barbados, 1627–1715*. Knoxville: University of Tennessee Press.

———. 1997. Capitalism, Slavery and European Modernity. *Callaloo* 20(4):777–789.

Browne, David V. C. 2012. *Race, Class, Politics and the Struggle for Empowerment in Barbados, 1914–1937*. Kingston: Ian Randle Publishers.

Centre for the Study of the Legacies of British Slave-Ownership. 2017. Legacies of British Slave-Ownership Database. University College of London Department of History. Accessed September 30, 2017. https://www.ucl.ac.uk/lbs/.

Coleridge, Henry Nelson. 1826. *Six Months in the West Indies in 1825*. London: John Murray.

Cossin, Zev A., and Mark W. Hauser. 2015. Sugar Economics: A Visual Economy of the Plantation Landscape in Colonial Dominica. In *Historical Archaeologies of Capitalism*, edited by Mark P. Leone and Jocelyn E. Knauf, 399–419. New York: Springer.

Croucher, Sarah K., and Lindsay Weiss. 2011. The Archaeology of Capitalism in Colonial Contexts, an Introduction: Provincializing Historical Archaeology. In *The Archaeology of Capitalism in Colonial Contexts: Postcolonial Historical Archaeologies*, edited by Sarah K. Croucher and Lindsay Weiss, 1–38. New York: Springer.

Cruickshank, Graeme. 2005. *Scottish Pottery*. Buckinghamshire: Shire Publications.

Dawdy, Shannon Lee. 2006. Proper Caresses and Prudent Distance: A How-To Manual from Colonial Louisiana. In *Haunted by Empire: Geographies of Intimacy in North American History*, edited by Ann Laura Stoler, 140–162. Durham, NC: Duke University Press.

Delle, James A. 1998. *An Archaeology of Social Space: Analyzing Coffee Plantations in Jamaica's Blue Mountains*. New York: Plenum.

———. 2014. *The Colonial Caribbean: Landscapes of Power in the Plantation System*. New York: Cambridge University Press.

Finch, Jonathan. 2015. Atlantic Landscapes: Connecting Place and People in the Modern World. *Journal of African Diaspora Archaeology and Heritage* 4(3):195–213.

Finch, Jonathan, Douglas V. Armstrong, Edward Blinkhorn, and David Barker. 2013. Surveying Caribbean Cultural Landscapes: Mount Plantation, Barbados, and Its Global Connections. *Internet Archaeology* 35(September).

Gibson, Heather R. 2009. Domestic Economy and Daily Practice in Guadeloupe: Historical Archaeology at La Mahaudière Plantation. *International Journal of Historical Archaeology* 13(1):27–44.

Gosden, Chris. 2012. Post-Colonial Archaeology. In *Archaeological Theory Today*, edited by Ian Hodder, 251–266. Malden, MA: Polity Press.

Handler, Jerome S. 1974. *The Unappropriated People: Freedmen in the Slave Society of Barbados*. Baltimore, MD: Johns Hopkins University Press.

———. 1982. Slave Revolts and Conspiracies in Seventeenth-Century Barbados. *New West Indian Guide* 56(1–2):5–42.

———. 2002. Plantation Slave Settlements in Barbados, 1650s to 1834. In *The Shadow of the Plantation: Caribbean History and Legacy*, edited by Alvin O. Thompson and Woodville K. Marshall, 123–161. Kingston: Ian Randle Publishers.

Handler, Jerome S., and Diane Wallman. 2014. Production Activities in the Household Economies of Plantation Slaves: Barbados and Martinique, Mid-1600s to Mid-1800s. *International Journal of Historical Archaeology* 18(3):441–466.

Hauser, Mark W. 2008. *An Archaeology of Black Markets: Local Ceramics and Economies in Eighteenth-Century Jamaica*. Gainesville: University Press of Florida.

———. 2011a. Uneven Topographies: Archaeology of Plantations and Caribbean Slave Economies. *The Archaeology of Capitalism in Colonial Contexts: Postcolonial Historical Archaeologies*, edited by Sarah K. Croucher and Lindsay Weiss, 121–142. New York: Springer.

———. 2011b. Routes and Roots of Empire: Pots, Power, and Slavery in the 18th-Century British Caribbean. *American Anthropologist* 113(3):431–437.

———. 2015. Blind Spots of Empire: Plantation Landscapes in Early Colonial Dominica (1763–1807). In *The Archaeology of Slavery: A Comparative Approach to Captivity and Coercion*, edited by Lydia W. Marshall, 143–163. SIU Occasional Paper No. 41. Carbondale: Southern Illinois University, Center for Archaeological Investigations.

Herva, Vesa-Pekka, and Risto Nurmi. 2009. Beyond Consumption: Functionality, Artifact Biography, and Early Modernity in a European Periphery. *International Journal of Historical Archaeology* 13(2):158–182.

Hicks, Dan. 2007. *The Garden of the World: An Historical Archaeology of Sugar Landscapes in the Eastern Caribbean*. London: British Archaeological Reports.

Hughes, Griffith. 1750. *The Natural History of Barbados in Ten Books*. London: Published by author.

Kopytoff, Igor. 1986. The Cultural Biography of Things: Commoditization as Process. In *The Social Life of Things: Commodities in Cultural Perspective*, edited by Arjun Appadurai, 64–91. Cambridge: Cambridge University Press.

Lenik, Stephan. 2012. Mission Plantations, Space, and Social Control: Jesuits as Planters in French Caribbean Colonies and Frontiers. *Journal of Social Archaeology* 12(1):51–71.

Leone, Mark P. 2005. *The Archaeology of Liberty in an American Capital: Excavations in Annapolis*. Berkeley: University of California Press.

Magnússon, Sigurður Gylfi, and István M. Szijártó. 2013. *What Is Microhistory? Theory and Practice*. New York: Routledge.

Marx, Karl. 1967. *Capital, Volume 1*. New York: International Publishers.

Meniketti, Marco G. 2015. *Sugar Cane Capitalism and Environmental Transformation: An Archaeology of Colonial Nevis, West Indies*. Tuscaloosa: University of Alabama Press.

Mímisson, Kristján, and Sigurður Gylfi Magnússon. 2014. Singularizing the Past: The History and Archaeology of the Small and Ordinary. *Journal of Social Archaeology* 14(2):131–156.

Mintz, Sidney W. 1974. *Caribbean Transformations*. New York: Columbia University Press.

———. 1985. *Sweetness and Power: The Place of Sugar in Modern History*. New York: Penguin Books.

Pratt, Geraldine, and Victoria Rosner. 2006. Introduction: The Global and the Intimate. *Women's Studies Quarterly* 34(1–2):13–24.

Pratt, Geraldine, and Victoria Rosner, eds. 2012. *The Global and the Intimate: Feminism in Our Time*. New York: Columbia University Press.

Reilly, Matthew C. 2015. The Politics of Work, "Poor Whites," and Plantation Capitalism in Barbados. In *Historical Archaeologies of Capitalism*, edited by Mark P. Leone and Jocelyn E. Knauf, 375–397. New York: Springer.

———. 2016a. Archaeologies of Instability: Order and Disorder in Colonial Barbados. *Journal of Social Archaeology* 16(2):216–237.

———. 2016b. "Poor White" Recollections and Artifact Reuse in Barbados: Considerations for Archaeologies of Poverty. *International Journal of Historical Archaeology* 20(2):318–340.

———. 2016c. "Poor Whites" on the Peripheries: "Poor White" and Afro-Barbadian Interaction on the Plantation. In *Roots of Empire: Archaeologies of Freedom and Slavery in the Caribbean* edited by Lynsey A. Bates, James A. Delle, and John M. Chenoweth, 49–78. Gainesville: University Press of Florida.

Sayers, Daniel O. 2014. *A Desolate Place for a Defiant People: The Archaeology of Maroons, Indigenous Americans, and Enslaved Laborers in the Great Dismal Swamp*. Gainesville: University Press of Florida.

Sheppard, Jill. 1977. *The "Redlegs" of Barbados: Their Origins and History*. New York: KTO Press.

Singleton, Theresa A. 2015. *Slavery behind the Wall: An Archaeology of a Cuban Coffee Plantation*. Gainesville: University Press of Florida.

Solow, Barbara L., and Stanley L. Engerman, eds. 1987. *British Capitalism and Caribbean Slavery: The Legacy of Eric Williams*. Cambridge: Cambridge University Press.

Tomich, Dale W. 2004. *Through the Prism of Slavery: Labor, Capital, and World Economy*. Lanham, MD: Rowman and Littlefield.

Tucker, Robert C., ed. 1978. *The Marx-Engels Reader*. New York: W. W. Norton & Company.

Voss, Barbara L., and Eleanor C. Casella, eds. 2012. *The Archaeology of Colonialism: Intimate Encounters and Sexual Effects*. Cambridge: Cambridge University Press.

Wall, Diana diZerega. 1994. *The Archaeology of Gender: Separating the Spheres in Urban America*. New York: Springer.

Walton, John, James F. Brooks, and Christopher R. N. DeCorse. 2008. Introduction. In *Small Worlds: Method, Meaning, and Narrative in Microhistory*, edited by John Walton, James F. Brooks, and Christopher R. N. DeCorse, 1–13. Santa Fe: School for Advanced Research.

Watson, Karl Stewart. 2000. "Walk and Nyam Buckras": Poor-White Emigration from Barbados, 1834–1900. *The Journal of Caribbean History* 34(1–2):130–156.

Watson, Mark R., and Robert B. Potter. 2001. *Low-Cost Housing in Barbados: Evolution or Social Revolution?* Mona: University of the West Indies Press.

Weik, Terrance M. 2012. *The Archaeology of Antislavery Resistance*. Gainesville: University Press of Florida.

Wilkie, Laurie A., and Paul Farnsworth. 2005. *Sampling Many Pots: An Archaeology of Memory and Tradition at a Bahamian Plantation*. Gainesville: University Press of Florida.

Williams, Eric. 1994. *Capitalism and Slavery*. Chapel Hill: University of North Carolina Press.

Williamson, John. 1817. *Medical and Miscellaneous Observations Relative to the West India Islands*. Edinburgh: Alex Smellie.

9

Inside and Outside Capitalism

The Life of Sealers on the South Shetland Islands, Antarctica

MELISA A. SALERNO, M. JIMENA CRUZ, AND ANDRÉS ZARANKIN

Historical archaeologists have studied capitalism as a global process intimately associated with the forces of modernity and colonialism from a variety of perspectives (Johnson 1996, 1999; Leone 1988, 1995; Orser 1996, 2000). Most researchers agree that the formal aspects of capitalism are frequently associated with practices and relationships that encourage the experience of certain degrees of distance, rupture, and exteriority with nature, things, and people, opening the way to objectification, commodification, and individualism. The interventions of capitalist businessmen and the sociospatial segmentation of practices of gathering, manufacturing, exchanging, and consuming sometimes lead to mediated and impersonal relationships, whereby commodities have no value beyond an economic one. Furthermore, differential access to commodities often emphasizes social distinction and hierarchies.

Over the last decades, several researchers have insisted that capitalism is not a homogenous process (Andrade Lima 1999, 2001; Funari et al. 1999; Funari and Zarankin 2004; Senatore and Zarankin 2002). Analyses of specific archaeological contexts have provided numerous examples of resistance and the resignification of capitalist practices and relationships. These examples have proven useful for discussions of the strengths and weaknesses of capitalism at different scales of analysis. Following the work of anthropologists (Price 1975), historical archaeologists are currently discussing the implications of peripheral economies that could have existed alongside the formal aspects of capitalism. In particular, some researchers are attempting to understand a relatively unexplored aspect of these small-scale economies: their intimate dimension.

Researchers stress that in contrast to formal capitalism, intimate economies are bound to practices and relationships that foster the encounters, intimacy, and permeable frontiers among nature, people, and things. Intimate economies frequently take place in small groups that tend to share real, perceived, or pretended trust, such as family, friends, and working groups (Casella and Voss 2011). In those cases, gathering, manufacturing, consuming, and exchanging might imply close relationships based on group identity and memory. Moreover, things may have an emotional value in addition to an economic one (Gavin and Smith 2003). Barter and sharing often play an important role in intimate economies. In particular, sharing may act as an integrative or coordinating process, making an economic system that effectively allocates goods without calculating returns (Price 1975). Thus, sharing may be a way to create solidarities and defy the hierarchies the formal aspects of capitalism produce and reproduce (Bauer and Agbe-Davies 2010; Wilson 2004).

Since 1995, we have collaborated on a research project in historical archaeology focused on the expansion of capitalism over Antarctica (Zarankin and Salerno 2015; Zarankin and Senatore 1999a, 1999b, 2005, 2007; Zarankin et al. 2011). According to official history, in 1819, sealers were the first to arrive to the South Shetland Islands, the closest Antarctic archipelago to the coasts of South America (Fitte 1962; Miers 1920; Stackpole 1955). They operated in the region in different moments of the nineteenth century, mainly looking for seal skins and elephant seal oil (Berguño 1993a, 1993b). American companies played a leading role in the exploitation (followed only by the British and some other nations) (Basberg and Headland 2008; Headland 1989; Stackpole 1955). Sealing was part of a capitalist industry; it produced huge profits and employed thousands of workers.

In this chapter we explore how sealers managed to get the food and clothes they considered necessary for survival. We will focus on two different but interrelated contexts that were part of the sealing voyages bound to the South Shetlands: life on board the vessels (through analysis of documentary sources) and life on the Antarctic hunting grounds (through analysis of archaeological evidence). Bearing in mind that sealers worked for a capitalist industry, we will discuss whether they relied solely on the practices and relationships typically associated with the formal aspects of capitalism at these micro-scale contexts. In the latter case, we will seek to answer the following questions: What were the main features of this peripheral economy? What social practices and relationships did it encourage? Did sealers participate in an intimate economy as we previously described it? Was this economy parallel, contradictory, or complementary to formal capitalist exchanges? What connections did this all have with the development of the sealing industry?

The Historical Context of Capitalist Sealing

Marine mammals have been exploited by different sociocultural groups over time. What we may call traditional forms of exploitation involve small-scale hunting to meet the needs of a particular community. Capitalist forms of exploitation have a broader (even global) scale, following a market logic that takes into account supply and demand and costs and benefits (Gillespie 2005; Motos and Wilson 2006; Stevenson et al. 1997). In the seventeenth century (and perhaps before that), the capitalist exploitation of marine mammals began to focus on whaling as a means to get different products (Francis 1990). Whale oil was essential for illuminating cities and was used as a lubricant for industrial machines. Other products, such as whalebones and ambergris were used to manufacture corsets, umbrellas, and fixatives for perfumes (Creighton 1995; Currie [1960] 2001; Verrill 1916).

At first whalers operated near the coasts, until the overexploitation of animal resources and the development of new naval technologies took them into more distant regions. Some researchers claim that as time went by whalers found opportunities to hunt other marine mammals (Clark 1887). In this chapter we will focus on the exploitation of fur seals. However, it is important to note that sealers were opportunistic and that they often took advantage of the availability of different animals (Stackpole 1955; Watson 1931). According to logbooks, some sealers hunted whales when they had a chance to do so. And when sealers could not find enough fur seals, they hunted other species such as elephant seals to complete their cargo (Mayorga 2016).

The sealing industry began to grow in the late eighteenth century as the market for sea otter skins declined, mainly because of overexploitation. The United States and Great Britain played a leading role in the industry

(Busch 1985). Seals were hunted for their skins and sometimes for their oil. Seal skins were mainly sold (or exchanged for other products) in Canton, China, and London (Smith 2002; Tapia Calisto et al. 2007). They were a symbol of status. While seal skins were used to produce coats, suitcases, and trunks in the Chinese market, they were used to manufacture clothes and hats in the United Kingdom (Berguño 1993a; Fanning 1924; Stehberg 2003). Elephant seals were hunted for their oil, a product used as a machine lubricant and a wool softener (Pearson 2016).

Sealers visited distant regions to find their prey. They began to operate in the South Seas along the coasts of Patagonia and the Malvinas/Falkland Islands in the late eighteenth century (Caviglia 2015; Mayorga 2017). Despite the secrecy surrounding the locations of hunting grounds, sealers were able to deplete an animal colony in a couple of years. Thus, sealers were constantly searching for new hunting grounds, defying the limits of the known world at the time (Richards 2003). The "discovery" of Antarctica was related to this process. Sealers first arrived to the South Shetland Islands, the closest archipelago to the coasts of South America, in 1819. There they found an abundance of animal resources (Fitte 1962; Miers 1920; Stackpole 1955). The levels of exploitation fluctuated during the nineteenth century, following changes in animal colonies and the logic of the market (Berguño 1993a, 1993b).

Sealing vessels associated with companies from different nations visited the South Shetland Islands. American vessels were most abundant, especially those from Stonington, New London, and Mystic, Connecticut (Headland 1989; Zarankin et al. 2018). The defining characteristics of U.S. sealing companies were shaped by the parameters of a capitalist enterprise, such as a distinction between capital and labor, hierarchies among workers, and specific hiring conditions, among others.

The owners of the companies or vessels made the initial investment for the voyages, while the captains represented their interests and were in charge of making decisions once the vessels set sail. Some captains were the owners of the vessels or were partners in the company they represented. Crews included officers who made the men comply with the orders of the captain. Some crew members, such as carpenters, coopers, and the cook, attended to specific duties. Seamen (who were divided into "able seamen" and "green hands," according to their experience) were the lowest in the hierarchy. They provided the labor needed to sail vessels and made up the gangs that killed and processed the animals at the rookeries, frequently under command of an officer (Salerno 2011; Stackpole 1955; Stehberg 2003).

The income a crew member received for his work was determined by his place in the hierarchy. Men were paid in lays, or shares of the final proceeds of the voyage. Captains received the highest shares and seamen received the lowest (Busch 1985, 1994; Currie [1960] 2001; Davis et al. 1997). This system was beneficial for the owners of sealing companies. Because the money each crew member received depended on the number of skins or the amount of oil taken during the voyage, it was in the interest of all men to look for and intensively exploit animal resources. However, because an owner's profit margin depended on the retail price of the products the company sold, they did not pay a fixed salary. When retail prices fell, owners held back their product and waited for a rise in prices. This could delay the payment of shares and leave crew members with no other option but to sail again immediately.

The crews of American sealing voyages were made up of Americans, Europeans, Africans, and Native Americans (Busch 1985; Salerno 2011; Shoemaker 2015; Stehberg 2003). For those who embarked from American ports, a set of rules shaped the hiring process. All crew members had to a sign the shipping articles, a sort of contract that specified the nature of the voyage, the destination, the length of the journey, and the lay or share the crew member would receive (Butts 1848; Dana 1851). Merchant shipping became increasingly better organized in the nineteenth century. As a result, new norms began defining the obligations of companies and captains to ensure better working conditions (Butts 1848; Dana 1851; Parish 1857).

Sealers, Food, and Clothing

The importance of food and clothing for sealers in Antarctica can be established by a series of references. In the context of several forms of abuse seamen suffered, a series of norms was established that stated that the owners of vessels had to provide food and clothing and that captains could not deny them to any member of the crew (Butts 1848; Parish 1857). According to sailors' journals, their sea chests were filled with clothes and eating utensils such as pots, spoons, and so forth (Holmes 1861; Jones 1861; Salerno 2011).

A sealing voyage could last from several months to one, two, or more years, depending on the location of the hunting grounds, the availability of animals, the logistics of trade, and so forth. Although sealing ships bound for Antarctica made several stops along the way to the hunting grounds, these stops were brief and sealers spent most of the time on board the vessels during the journey. Once they arrived at the sealing grounds, the crew spent most of the time on land. Thus, there was a circulation of people and things between the vessels and the hunting grounds (Salerno 2011).

For this study, we have drawn on sealers' journals and logbooks, newspapers devoted to the whaling and sealing industries, and the outfitting lists of vessels for information about sealers' lives on board the vessels. The archaeological remains of sealers' camps gave us insight into their lives on the South Shetland hunting grounds.

On Board Sealing Vessels

Sealing companies were in charge of outfitting vessels with the equipment needed for sailing, hunting, and processing the animals. They also provided food and clothes for the crew. Following accepted practices and rules, the owners of the companies had to buy enough food to meet the needs of a specific number of people for the length of a given journey. These amounts were specified in the shipping articles and in other documents. In the nineteenth century, a specialized market developed in U.S. ports to supply whaling and sealing companies with these goods. The *Whalemen's Shipping List, and Merchant's Transcript*, a journal devoted to the whaling and sealing industries, provides evidence of the types of stores that offered food and other supplies for maritime companies (Salerno 2011). Some stores even published a sort of buying guide that suggests which products all vessels should take on before beginning a journey.

The advertisements in the *Whalemen's Shipping List* indicate that there was a certain degree of standardization in the food supply for vessels (Cruz 2014). Although there was a range of types of stores and brands, the types of goods were always similar (Figure 9.1). Some food items were industrially produced in large quantities, such as salted meat and sea biscuits (Goody 1995). Some products were sold in units that were associated with particular methods of storage and transport. For instance, sea biscuits were sold in barrels and butter in tubs and firkins.

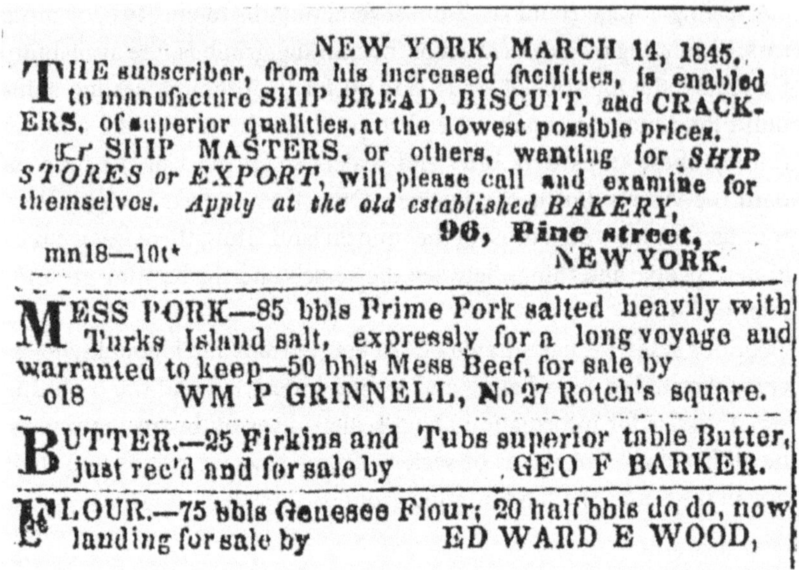

NEW YORK, MARCH 14, 1845.

THE subscriber, from his increased facilities, is enabled to manufacture SHIP BREAD, BISCUIT, and CRACKERS, of superior qualities, at the lowest possible prices.

☞ SHIP MASTERS, or others, wanting for *SHIP STORES or EXPORT*, will please call and examine for themselves. *Apply at the old established BAKERY,*

96, Pine street,

mn18—10t* NEW YORK.

MESS PORK—85 bbls Prime Pork salted heavily with Turks Island salt, expressly for a long voyage and warranted to keep—50 bbls Mess Beef, for sale by

o18 WM P GRINNELL, No 27 Rotch's square.

BUTTER.—25 Firkins and Tubs superior table Butter, just rec'd and for sale by GEO F BARKER.

FLOUR.—75 bbls Genesee Flour; 20 half bbls do do, now landing for sale by ED WARD E WOOD,

Figure 9.1. Food advertisements in the *Whalemen's Shipping List Journal*, April 1, 1845, page 15 and November 5, 1844, page 140. Courtesy of Mystic Seaport Museum.

The food that whaling and sealing companies purchased in American ports included ready-to-eat meals as well as ingredients for cooking (Cruz 2014). While most of the items in the first category were fresh, such as cheese, apples, strawberries, plums, and lemons, most of the items in the second category were nonperishables such as flour, salt, cider vinegar, beans, sugar, and rice.

Some products were obtained in intermediate ports and other less formal locations. For example, sealing vessels bound for the South Shetland Islands often visited the Azores to get fresh fruits and vegetables. They also made a series of stops in Patagonia for hunting, gathering, and exchanging food with indigenous groups. Unlike products obtained in formal ports, hunting and gathering frequently involved the participation of seamen. In this way, they became part of the system of supply. Products obtained in informal locations were not necessarily standardized as many of those obtained prior to departure or at other intermediate ports and often required preparation before they could be consumed.

The cook was in charge of food preparation on board the sealing vessels. The rest of the crew focused on sailing and preparing themselves for the hunting grounds. The cook prepared different dishes for the captain, the officers, and the rest of the crew. At least in the case of the seamen, he decided what they would eat (even though food rations were stipulated by the captain, taking into account possible setbacks). The cook worked in the kitchen, a clearly defined space, and served meals at specific times.

Eating was part of the daily routine that organized life on board the vessels. People ate in different places according to their rank. The captain and the officers ate in the captain's cabin, the seamen in the forecastle. While eating was a collective activity, it also produced and reproduced social differences. The captain, the officers and the seamen ate different types, qualities, and amounts of food (Nordhoff 1856).

Once a crew member signed his shipping articles, he was given some money in advance to buy an outfit. The *Whalemen's Shipping List* provides evidence of the fact that numerous stores in U.S. ports were devoted to filling seamen's needs (Salerno 2011, 2016). Because some of these places were owned by whaling and sealing companies, the money they gave crew members in advance rapidly found its way back to the owners of the vessels. Whalers and sealers frequently complained about the inflated prices and poor quality of the articles sold at these stores. The most frequent victims of outfitters were green hands, who did not know what kind of products were appropriate for the voyages (Davis 1874; Holmes 1861; Nordhoff 1856).

Most of the stores that advertised in the *Whalemen's Shipping List* offered similar types of clothes (Salerno 2011, 2016). Many stores sold ready-to-use garments, although some also offered custom goods (Figure 9.2). Sealers' outfits included different styles of pants, frocks, and jackets made of dark wool, canvas, waterproof fabrics; drawers, stockings, and shirts (either plain or striped in different colors) made of wool, cotton, and flax; shoes and boots; and different types of hats and caps. A seaman's outfit also included a variety of types of needles for repairing sails and clothing.

On board the vessels, hierarchical differences among the members of the crew could have been produced and reproduced through dress, as the captains, the officers, and the seamen had access to different products and probably wore them in different ways (Salerno 2011, 2016). A crew member's responsibilities determined the number and quality of the sets of clothes he had on board. As clothes got dirty or even torn, crew members would use their leisure to wash and mend them. Because of this, all seamen had to learn how to mend garments (Nordhoff 1856).

The possibilities for acquiring new clothes were limited. Some articles

SEAMENS' CLOTHING.

AT THE WHOLESALE CLOTHING WAREHOUSE,

202 *Pearl Street New York.*

THE Subscribers would respectfully inform the Agents and Fitters of Whale ships that they have and will keep constantly on hand a large stock of

HEAVY WOOLEN, CANVASS, AND DUCK

CLOTHING,

together with water proof OIL SUITS, TARPAULIN HATS, SHEATHS AND BELTS, SHEATH KNIVES, SAIL NEEDLES &c &c suitable for men engaged in the Whaling trade

also a large assortment of

INFITTING CLOTHING,

consisting of Blue Cloth Jackets, Pants, Vests, White and Fancy Shirts.

All of the above Goods are of the best quality and carefully selected by ourselves, and we feel confident in saying that we possess advantages which enable us to offer our Goods at such prices as cannot fail to give satisfaction to purchasers.

J. W, LEWIS & CO,

Corner Maiden Lane and Pearl St.

N. T. GIFFORD & CO.,

MERCHANT TAILORS AND DEALERS IN CLOTHS

OF EVERY DESCRIPTION,

GERMAN, FRENCH AND AMERICAN COATINGS, ALL COLORS, DOESKINS, CASSIMERES, VESTINGS, &c., &c.,

CUT AND MADE IN THE MOST GENTEEL STYLE.

MEN'S & BOYS'

CLOTHING.

THIS DEPARTMENT CANNOT BE SURPASSED IN THE STATE—ALL CUSTOM MADE—the most fashional e tyles, and the best materials, made expressly for City trade. Spring Overcoats, Frock and Sack Coats, Pants and Vests in endless quantities.

HATS AND CAPS.

We have a splendid stock of Silk Hats of the best make, from Bebee, Leary, Gennin & Bird's, New York. Caps of all styles made by the best manufacturers in New York and Boston. Soft Hats of all qualities.

Gent's French and American Furnishing Goods.

The best stock in the city. All styles of Neck-Ties, Stocks, Gloves, Handkerchiefs, Suspenders, Under Garments, &c. We keep the best WHITE SHIRTS made in the State, made expressly for the city trade,—for fit and style they cannot be surpassed. TRUNKS, VALISES, UMBRELLAS, &c, in great variety.

OFFICERS AND SEAMEN'S OUTFITS.

We are prepared to make up Outfits at short notice. Also on hand ALL KINDS OF OUTFITTING GOODS of the best materials on hand.

INDIA RUBBER GOODS.

We have the Agency of one of the BEST HOUSES IN THE COUNTRY, and will sell India Rubber Coats, Pants, Leggins, Bags, Caps, &c., at the Manufacturer's Prices

☞ The public are invited to call and examine this Stock of Goods before purchasing elsewhere ONE PRICE AND CASH TO ALL.

apl 1 NO. 12 1-2 UNION STREET, NEW BEDFORD. eptf

Figure 9.2. Outfitting advertisements in the *Whalemen's Shipping List Journal*, June 6, 1848, page 56 and October 7, 1862, column 5. Courtesy of the Mystic Seaport Museum.

could have been bought or exchanged in intermediate ports or in other more informal locations. In addition, seamen's journals frequently mention the "slop chest," a stock of clothes and other items such as tobacco that whaling and sealing companies purchased at the departure ports and captains sold to crew members during the journey (Olmsted 1841). As these products were sold at high prices that were later deducted from pay, seamen tried to avoid being in a position where they needed to resort to such purchases.

On the South Shetland Sealing Grounds

Once on the South Shetland grounds, sealing vessels distributed gangs of an officer and four or more men on the shores. Sealers lived and worked on the islands for days, weeks, or even months during the summer season, depending on the availability of animals and the captain's orders; sometimes captains decided to look for new animal colonies while the gangs were working on shore. The archaeological survey of the archipelago shows that most nineteenth-century sealers' camps were established on Livingston Island (Zarankin and Senatore 1999a, 1999b, 2005, 2007; Zarankin et al. 2011), particularly on the Byers Peninsula, located in the southwest of Livingston Island. Twenty-six sites were identified in this area. Here we will focus on the information obtained through the excavation and analysis of four sites, Playa Sur 1, Lima-Lima, Cerro Negro, and Punta Varadero (Figure 9.3).

Sealers took a small number of items with them when they left their ships. They had to build their own shelters and other structures devoted to work, including rooms for producing oil and storing goods. Sealers mainly used local materials to build these structures, taking advantage of natural outcrops and rocks to erect walls (Figure 9.4). They used skins and sometimes old pieces of canvas for roofs and built furniture from whale vertebrae. Sealers' shelters consisted of small enclosures that had no internal divisions. Unlike the hierarchical space of the vessels, all the members of the gang (including the officer) ate and slept in a single room (Zarankin and Senatore 1999a, 1999b, 2005, 2007; Zarankin et al. 2011). Most of the archaeological finds in sealers' shelters consist of food and clothing remains.

Analysis of food remains demonstrates that sealers living and working on the South Shetland Islands relied more on local resources than on

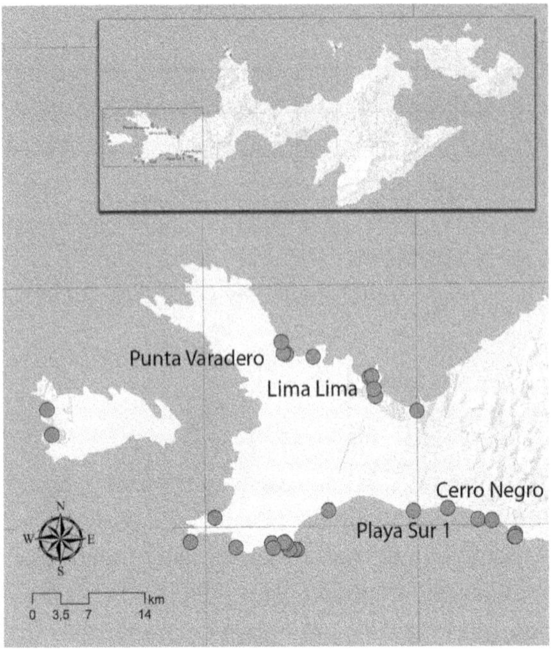

Figure 9.3. Location of sealers' camps on Byers Peninsula.

Figure 9.4. The Punta Varadero sealers' site. General photo (*a*); drawing of the main structure, where sealers probably ate and slept (*b*); drawing of the smaller structure interpreted as a storage room (*c*). Photo by Laboratório de Estudos Antárticos em Ciências Humanas.

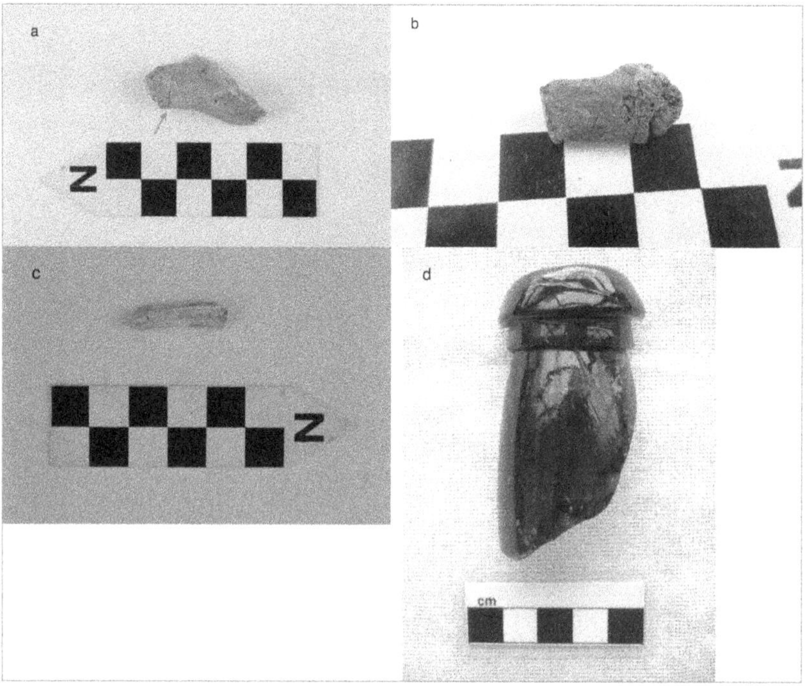

Figure 9.5. Food remains found at sealers' camps: marine mammal bones with cut marks (*a*, *b*); calcined bone (*c*); bottle fragment (*d*). Photo by Laboratório de Estudos Antárticos em Ciências Humanas.

the items from the vessels (Cruz 2011, 2014). Although captains provided the gangs with some supplies such as coffee, alcohol, and small rations of pork and beef, these provisions were probably not enough to feed all the men for the length of time they spent on the islands. Thus, sealers had to obtain their own food from hunting and gathering (Figure 9.5). The men frequently consumed the flesh and organs of the seals and elephant seals they killed. They also hunted a variety of birds and gathered eggs. The food products available locally were more varied than those crew members brought from their vessels, and eating such unfamiliar foodstuffs undoubtedly introduced the men to completely new flavors.

While what the crew ate depended on owners and captains while crews were on board, when they were on the South Shetland Islands such decisions could have been more collective. On land, sealers had a closer relationship to their food. Obtaining food from local resources required the work gang to participate in killing animals and butchering meat. In

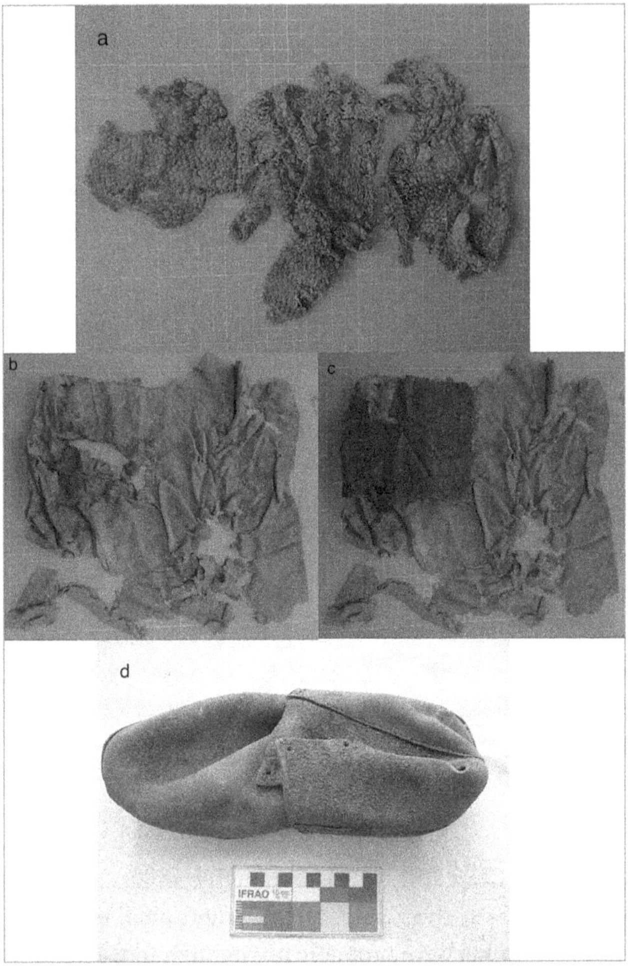

Figure 9.6. Clothing remains found at sealers' camps: knitted glove (*a*); woven fragment and associated patch (*b*, *c*); leather shoe (*d*). Source: Salerno 2011.

the absence of a cook, at least some of crew worked to prepare meals. Eating took place in the undifferentiated space of the shelters, where officers and the rest of the men gathered around a hearth. Considering that food choices were limited, everybody had equal access to the same meals.

Clothing remains found at sealers' camps include fragments of woven and knitted textiles and leather shoes (Salerno 2006, 2011, 2016) (Figure 9.6). Most of the woven pieces could have been part of jackets and pants made from woolen and linen fibers. Some of the knitted pieces could have been part of handcrafted wool sweaters or gloves that were probably produced at home or at sea, outside the formal capitalist market. The woven fragments often show signs of repair such as mending stitches and patches made out of different fabrics. The shoe remains are mostly those of nineteenth-century work shoes of a standardized appearance. Most of them show signs of damage, including holes in specific areas of the soles and possible wear and tear indicated by exposed sole stitches.

Once on shore, the men could not acquire new garments and had to make the best of the few garments they brought with them from the vessels. Environmental conditions were harsh and the men worked long hours killing and processing animals. This would have been hard on clothing, and all men likely found it necessary to mend their clothes far more often than when they were on board ship. Garments and shoes were discarded only when they could no longer be worn. Fabrics were recycled, and it would not have been strange for the men to have shared these materials with their cohorts. Sealers could also have used animal skins to manufacture some goods, as in the case of an pair of leather gaiters found at one of the sites. The shared experience of living and working together on the South Shetlands may have blurred some of the social differences in the men's appearance.

Conclusion: Formal Exchanges, Intimate Economies of Sharing, and Capitalist Sealing

Nineteenth-century sealing was part of a capitalist economy ruled by supply and demand in the global market. We have focused on how sealers managed to get food and clothes on board ships and on the Antarctic hunting grounds. We have not assumed that sailors' participation at the macro scale of the capitalist system shaped all of their practices and relationships in only one way.

On board ship, food was mainly supplied by sealing companies. The volume provided was based on the length of the voyage and the number of crew members. On some occasions, seamen gathered food in intermediate locations. Meals were prepared by specialized staff and were distributed in specific ways following the orders of the captain. Before a journey began, seamen purchased clothes using money they were given in advance for their work. This calculated, regulated, and controlled supply was intimately associated with formal capitalistic markets that produced and reproduced individualism and social hierarchies. There may have been cracks in this system, however, that included barter among seamen. Items obtained in the formal capitalist marketplace also conferred a sense of belonging to the business of sealing and of having a specific rank on board.

Circumstances were much more extreme on the South Shetland Islands. Even though sealers brought some food and their own clothes from the vessels, archaeological analysis suggests that these products were not enough or even appropriate for survival in Antarctica. On the South Shetland grounds, men seem to have been left to their own devices. Gangs had to build shelters, get their own food, and repair (or even manufacture) their clothes. Sealers had to improvise and gain access to other products in less regulated and less controlled (albeit more collective) ways. This is where the concept of intimate economies becomes an interesting tool for better understanding the relationships of sealers with things and with each other.

While hierarchies were emphasized on board, the material conditions of sealing camps could have blurred social differences. Officers and seamen lived in the same shelters. All of them participated in gathering, preparing, and consuming the same kind of food. Remnants of discarded clothes could have circulated for the repair of everybody's garments. Sealers' relationships with their food and clothing could have been much more intimate while they were in the sealing camps than they were with items provided on board or bought at outfitting stores, as the men could have perceived them as a product of their own efforts, requiring no intermediaries. Food and clothes produced or repaired on the South Shetland Islands were worth more than their economic value. In this context, sealers engaged in an intimate economy deeply rooted in sharing. Sharing could have strengthened solidarities and helped ease the tensions that arose in a harsh living and working environment. Furthermore, it could have strengthened the collective identity of sealers, well beyond differences in rank.

From our perspective, the microscale economies set in motion around eating and dressing on board the vessels and on the Antarctic sealing grounds were complementary. Both formal capitalist exchanges and the informal sharing of an intimate economy served the sealing industry at a particular moment of its development. Just as sealing companies encouraged their employees to exploit animal colonies to the maximum extent by inviting the men to participate in the profits of the voyage and by not fixing hunting dates or the number of animal skins to be taken, they also expected to get the most from workers at a low cost.

Throughout the nineteenth century, set norms regulated seamen's access to food and clothes, limiting the amount to which their employers could exploit them. These norms could have emerged as a response to the possibility that production could be increased if workers had access to better living and working conditions. There was an increasing intention to regulate the condition of the men and how the vessels were outfitted. But the provisions the company supplied at the departure port were not enough for the whole voyage, and it was always necessary to find more in other locations. Company owners and captains trusted that sealers could meet their own food and clothing needs. This was a moment of mixtures and transitions, regarding both the supply of some goods by the companies and the need of sealers to become self-sufficient.

Over the course of the nineteenth century, this situation changed on the South Shetlands grounds. First, as the number of seals and elephant seals declined, sealers may have started limiting themselves to hunt what they could and go back to the vessels without establishing camps. (We are studying this issues using logbooks from different moments of the nineteenth century.) Second, when sealing stopped being profitable, animal exploitation turned to whales. In the early twentieth century, a permanent whaling station was constructed on Deception Island, one of the South Shetland Islands. It was designed as a factory where social relationships and supplies were strictly regulated. Even though the whaling station could have brought about better material conditions for workers, it also could have eroded the practices of sharing and solidarity that sealers had traditionally produced and reproduced in Antarctica in the past.

Acknowledgments

We would like to thank Mary Beaudry, James Nyman, and Kevin Fogle for inviting us to participate in this volume. We also want to thank the members of the Landscapes in White research project for their help and support. Finally, we extend our gratitude to IMHICIHU–CONICET in Argentina and to UFMG, FAPEMIG, and CNPq (PROANTAR project) in Brazil for their financial support of our research.

References Cited

Andrade Lima, Tania. 1999. El Huevo de la Serpiente: Una Arqueología del Capitalismo Embrionario en el Río de Janeiro del Siglo XIX. In *Sed Non Satiata. Teoría Social en la Arqueología Latinoamericana Contemporánea,* edited by Andrés Zarankin and Felix Acuto, 189–238. Buenos Aires: Del Tridente.

———. 2001. Os Marcos Teóricos da Arqueología Histórica, Suas Possibilidades e Límites. In *Arqueología Uruguaya. Hacia el Fin del Milenio,* vol. 1, 11–29. Montevideo: MEC.

Basberg, B., and Robert Headland. 2008. The Nineteenth-Century Antarctic Sealing Industry: Sources, Data and Economic Significance. NHH Discussion Paper No. 21/2008, September. Accessed January 1, 2014. https://papers.ssrn.com/sol3/papers.cfm?abstract_id=1553751.

Bauer, Alexander A., and Anna S Agbe-Davies, eds. 2010. *The Social Archaeologies of Trade and Exchange: Exploring Relationships among People, Places, and Things.* New York: Routledge.

Berguño, J. 1993a. Las Shetland del Sur: El ciclo lobero. Primera parte. *Boletín Antártico Chileno* (April):5–13.

———. 1993b. Las Shetland del Sur: El ciclo lobero. Segunda parte. *Boletín Antártico Chileno* (October):2–9.

Busch, Briton Cooper. 1985. *The War against the Seals: A History of the North American Seal Fishery.* Ontario, Canada: McGill-Queen's University Press, Kingston.

———. 1994. *Whaling Will Never Do for Me: The American Whaleman in the Nineteenth Century.* Lexington: University Press of Kentucky.

Butts, I. R. 1848. *Every Sailor His Own Lawyer. The Rights of Seamen: The Coaster´s and Fishermen´s Guide, and Master's and Mate´s Manual.* Boston: I. R. Butts.

Casella, Eleanor C., and Barbara Voss. 2011. Intimate Encounters: An Archaeology of Sexualities within Colonial Worlds. In *The Archaeology of Colonialism: Intimate Encounters and Sexual Effects,* edited by Barbara Voss and Eleanor C. Casella, 1–10. Cambridge: Cambridge University Press.

Caviglia, Sergio E. 2015. *Malvinas: Soberanía, Memoria y Justicia.* Vol. 2. *Balleneros, Loberos, Misioneros, s. XVIII–XIX.* Rawson: Ministerio de Educación de la Provincia de Chubut.

Clark, A. Howard. 1887. The Antarctic Fur Seal and Sea Elephant Industries. In *The Fisheries and the Fishery Industries of the United States.* Section 4, vol. 2, edited by G. Brown Goode, 400–467. Washington, DC: U.S. Government Printing Office.

Creighton, Margaret. 1995. *Rites and Passages: The Experience of American Whaling, 1830–1870.* Cambridge: Cambridge University Press.

Cruz, M. Jimena. 2011. Aproximaciones a las Prácticas Alimentícias de los Grupos Foqueros (Islas Shetland del Sur, siglo XIX). Undergraduate thesis, University of Buenos Aires, Buenos Aires.

———. 2014. Incorporando Comidas e Contextos. A Alimentação e o Corpo Nos Grupos Foqueiros nas Shetland do Sul (Antártica, Século XIX). MA thesis, Federal University of Minas Gerais, Belo Horizonte, Brazil.

Currie, Stephen. (1960). 2001. *Thar She Blows: American Whaling in the Nineteenth Century.* Minneapolis: Lerner Publications.

Dana, R. Henry. 1851. *The Seaman's Friend.* Boston: Thomas Groom & Co.

Davis, Lance, Robert E. Gallman, and Karin Gleiter. 1997. *In Pursuit of Leviathan: Institutions, Productivity and Profits in American Whaling, 1916–1906.* Chicago: University of Chicago Press.

Davis, William. 1874. *Nimrod of the Sea; or The American Whaleman.* New York: Harper & Brothers.

Fanning, Edmund. 1924. *Voyages and Discoveries in the South Seas, 1792–1832.* Salem, MA: Marine Research Society.

Fitte, Ernesto J. 1962. *El Descubrimiento de la Antártida: Crónica de los Hombres y Barcos que Exploraron las Aguas de las Shetland del Sur.* Buenos Aires: Emecé.

Francis, Daniel. 1990. *A History of World Whaling.* Ontario, Canada: Viking.

Funari, Pedro P., Siân Jones, and Martin Hall. 1999. Introduction: Archaeology in History. In *Historical Archaeology. Back from the Edge,* edited by Pedro P. Funari, Siân Jones, and Martin Hall, 1–20. London: Routledge.

Funari, Pedro P., and Andrés Zarankin. 2004. Arqueología Histórica en América del Sur; Los Desafíos del siglo XXI. In *Arqueología Histórica en América del Sur; Los desafíos del siglo XXI,* edited by Pedro P. Funari and Andrés Zarankin, 5–10. Bogotá: Ediciones Uniandes.

Gavin, Bridge, and Adrian Smith. 2003. Intimate Encounters: Culture-Economy-Commodity. *Environment and Planning D: Society and Space,* 21:257–268.

Gillespie, Alexander. 2005. *Whaling Diplomacy. Defining Issues in International Environmental Law.* Cheltenham: Edward Elgar Publishing.

Goody, Jack. 1995. *Cocina, Cuisine y Clase. Estudio de Sociología Comaparada.* Barcelona: Gedisa.

Headland, Robert. 1989. *Chronological List of Antarctic Expeditions and Related Historical Events.* Cambridge: Cambridge University Press.

Holmes, Lewis. 1861. *The Arctic Whaleman; or, Winter in the Arctic Ocean.* Boston: Thayer & Eldridge.

Johnson, Matthew H. 1996. *An Archaeology of Capitalism.* Blackwell, Oxford.

———. 1999. Historical, Archaeology, Capitalism. In *Historical Archaeologies of Capitalism,* edited by Mark P. Leone and Parker B. Potter, 219–232. New York: Kluwer Academic Press/Plenum Publishers.

Jones, John D. 1861. *Life and Adventure in the South Pacific.* New York: Harper & Brothers.

Leone, Mark P. 1988. The Georgian Order as the Order of Merchant Capitalism in Annapolis, Maryland. In *The Recovery of Meaning: Historical Archaeology in the Eastern United States,* edited by Mark P. Leone, and Parker B. Potter Jr., 235–261. Washington, DC: Smithsonian Institution Press.

———. 1995. A Historical Archaeology of Capitalism. *American Anthropologist* 97(2):251–268.

Mayorga, Marcelo. 2016. Antecedentes Históricos Referidos a la Caza de Lobos Marinos y su Interacción con el Medio Geográfico y Humano en el Extremo Austral Americano: El Caso del Lobero Escocés William Low. *Magallania* 44(2):37–64.

———. 2017. Actividad Lobera Temprana en la Patagonia Oriental: Caza de Mamíferos Marinos. *RIVAR* 4(11):31–51.

Miers, John. 1920. Account of Discovery of New South Shetland, with Observations on its Importance in Geographical, Commercial and Political Point of View: With Two Plates. *Edinburgh Philosophical Review* 3:367–380.

Motos, Lorenzo, and Douglas Wilson. 2006. *The Knowledge Base for Fisheries Management*. Amsterdam and Oxford: Elsevier.

Nordhoff, Charles. 1856. *Whaling and Fishing*. Cincinnati: Moore, Wilstach, Keys & Co.

Olmsted, Francis A. 1841. *Incidents of a Whaling Voyage, to Which Are Added Observations on the Scenery, Manners and Customs, and Missionary Stations of the Sandwich and Society Islands*. New York: D. Appleton & Co.

Orser, Charles E., Jr. 1996. *A Historical Archaeology of the Modern World*. Plenum, New York.

———. 2000. *Introducción a la Arqueología Histórica*. Buenos Aires: AINA.

Parish, A. 1857. *The Sea Officer's Manual, Being a Compendium of the Duties of a Commander; First, Second, Third and Fourth Officer; Officer of the Watch; and Midshipman; in the Mercantile Navy*. London: Smith, Elder & Co.

Pearson, Michael. 2016. Charting the Sealing Islands of the Southern Ocean. *Journal of the Australian and New Zealand Map Society* 80:33–56.

Price, John A. 1975. Sharing: The Integration of Intimate Economies. *Anthropologica, New Series* 17(1):3–27.

Richards, Rhys. 2003. New Market Evidence on the Depletion of Southern Fur Seals, 1788–1833. *New Zealand Journal of Zoology* 30(1):1–9.

Salerno, Melisa A. 2006. *Arqueología de la Indumentaria: Prácticas e Identidad en los Confines del Mundo Moderno (Antártida, Siglo XIX)*. Del Tridente/Panorama Gráfica y Diseño, Buenos Aires.

———. 2011. Persona y Cuerpo-vestido en la Modernidad: Un Enfoque Arqueológico. PhD diss., University of Buenos Aires, Buenos Aires.

———. 2016. Persona y Cuerpo-vestido en la Modernidad. Los Loberos-balleneros de la Industria Capitalista del siglo XIX. *Vestigios. Revista Latino-Americana de Arqueología Histórica* 9(1):113–153.

Senatore, M. Ximena, and Andrés Zarankin. 2002. Leituras da Sociedade Moderna em Latinoamerica: Cultura Material, Discursos e Práticas. In *Arqueología da Sociedade Moderna na America do Sul. Cultura Material, Discursos e Praticas*, edited by Andrés Zarankin and M. Ximena Senatore, 5–18. Buenos Aires: Ediciones del Tridente.

Shoemaker, Nancy. 2015. *Native American Whalemen and the World: Indigenous Encounters and the Contingency of Race*. Chapel Hill: University of North Carolina Press.

Smith, Ian W. G. 2002. *The New Zealand Sealing Industry: History, Archaeology and Heritage Management*. Wellington: Department of Conservation.

Stackpole, Edouard. 1955. *The Voyages of the Huron and the Huntress: The American Sealers and the Discovery of the Continent of Antarctica*. Mystic, CT: Marine Historical Association.

Stehberg, Ruben. 2003. *Arqueología Histórica Antártica. Aborígenes Sudamericanos en los Mares Subantárticos en el siglo XIX*. Santiago: Centro de Investigaciones Diego Barros Arana.

Stevenson, Marc G., Andrew Madsen, and Elaine Maloney, eds. 1997. *The Anthropology of Community-Based Whaling in Greenland: A Collection of Papers Submitted to the International Whaling Commission*. [Edmonton]: Canadian Circumpolar Institute.

Tapia Calisto, C., Marcelo Mayorga, and G. Maldonado. 2007. Loberos Norteamericanos e Ingleses en Patagonia, Tierra del Fuego e Islas sub-antárticas y Antárticas, Entre Fines del. siglo XVIII y 1840. Undergraduate thesis, Universidad de Magallanes, Punta Arenas.

Verrill, A. Hyatt. 1916. *The Real Story of the Whaler. Whaling, Past and Present*. New York: D. Appleton & Company.

Watson, Arthur C. 1931. A Voyage on the Sealer *Emeline* and the Journal from Washington Fosdick's Manuscript Preserved in the Museum of the Old Dartmouth Historical Society at New Bedford. *Zoologica* 19(14):475–549.

Wilson, Ara. 2004. *The Intimate Economies of Bangkok: Tomboys, Tycoons, and Avon Ladies in the Global City*. Berkeley: University of California Press.

Zarankin, Andrés, and M. Ximena Senatore. 1999a. "Estrategias y Tácticas" en el Proceso de Ocupación de la Antártida—siglo XIX. In *Desde el País de los Gigantes. Perspectivas Arqueológicas en Patagonia*, vol. 1, 315–327. Río Gallegos: Universidad Nacional de la Patagonia Austral.

———. 1999b. Ocupación Humana en Tierras Antárticas: Una Aproximación. Arqueológica. En *Soplando en el Viento . . . Actas de las Terceras Jornadas de Arqueología de la Patagonia*, 629–644. Río Gallegos: Comité Editorial de las Terceras Jornadas de Arqueología de la Patagonia.

———. 2005. Archaeology in Antarctica: Nineteenth-Century Capitalism Expansion Strategies. *International Journal of Historical Archaeology* 9(1):43–56.

———. 2007. *Historias de un Pasado en Blanco. Arqueología Histórica Antártica*. Brazil: Argumentum, Belo Horizonte.

Zarankin, Andrés, and Melisa A. Salerno. 2015. So Far, So Close: Approaching Experience in the Study of the Encounter between Sealers and the South Shetland Islands (Antarctica, Nineteenth Century). In *Antarctica and the Humanities*, edited by Peter Roberts, Lize-Marié van der Watt, and Adrian Howkins, 79–103. London: Palgrave Macmillan.

Zarankin, Andrés, Melisa Salerno, and Adrian Howkins. Forthcoming. From Antarctica to New England: Approaching the Memory of Sealing and Sealers. In The *Proceedings of the 2016 Historical Antarctic Sealing Industry Conference, and Related Historical and Geographical Data*, edited by Robert Headland. Cambridge: Scott Polar Research Institute, University of Cambridge.

Zarankin, Andrés, Sarah Hissa, Melisa A. Salerno, Yacy-Ara. Froner, Gerusa Radicchi, Luis G. Resende de Assis, and Anderson Batista. 2011. Paisagens em Branco: Arqueologia e Antropologia ntárticas-Avanços e Desafios. *Vestígios: Revista Latino-Americana de Arqueología Histórica* 5(2):9–51.

10

Surf and Turf

Understanding Montaukett Economic Strategies during the Whaling Era

ALLISON MANFRA MCGOVERN

In the late nineteenth century at the easternmost point of Long Island, members of the great Montauk "tribe" of Indians were left, secluded and dwindled in numbers, to lose their "true" native identity to the changing capitalist world. At least, this is the story that was in place when I began my investigations into the archaeological site that is remembered as their last group habitation site. This narrative claims that the Montauketts, the indigenous people who lived there, were dispossessed of their homeland as large tracts of land in Montauk, New York, were about to be developed to accommodate the private hunting practices of wealthy New Yorkers. When the Montauketts fought back in a New York State courtroom, they were stripped of their tribal status.

This is not the whole story, obviously. Montaukett identity was not really erased with the swing of a judge's gavel. And the Montaukett people were not really isolated at the eastern end of Long Island, cut off from the changing, capitalist world that was unfolding all around them. In fact, this chapter is about the *integration* of Montaukett people into networks of economic and social activity that probably supported their own survivance but also were dependent on their contributions.[1] The data and methods presented here are from my research on the Indian Fields site, where some Montauketts lived in a small settled village for roughly 150 years in the eighteenth and nineteenth centuries before they were dispossessed of their homes. Two domestic sites at Indian Fields—the Pharaoh home and the Fowler home—provide household-level data for understanding

Montaukett economic strategies during the apex and the decline of the whaling era. As I began to research the names and lives of Indian Fields residents to connect their identities to the archaeological contexts, patterns of social, kin, and labor networks emerged that linked Montaukett people at Indian Fields to indigenous peoples, people of color and mixed heritage, and whites across the northeast region. As laborers in agricultural fields, as tenders of the livestock that grazed throughout Montauk, as fishermen and shellfish harvesters, and as whalers on ships destined for international waters, Montauketts were instrumental in the landed gentry's accumulation of wealth. These elites maintained political and economic control of the landscape of eastern Long Island throughout the period of my study and into the present time. Yet deeper connections developed in these labor networks that connected families through kin and social ties. These relationships are key to understanding the endurance and survivance of Montaukett peoples and the intimate economies in which they were engaged in the eighteenth, nineteenth, and twentieth centuries.

This case study is a project in network thinking: it involves consideration of forces that connect and potentially bind people together. Although I am influenced by the works of some social network analysis practitioners, my research is by no means a comprehensive application of that methodology. I am simply interested in the human-to-human connections that historical archaeologists can make by linking material culture, documents, cultural landscapes, and evidence of past human activity. In a sense, linking people and things together through activities that are simultaneously economic and cultural renders these connections intimate (Bridge and Smith 2003). In my work, I found that social network analysis is a useful tool for connecting the dots between individuals and/or communities and places of employment in eastern Long Island and abroad (Brughmans 2010; Knappett 2013). I am especially interested in "ties between people" and the data that can be used to investigate those ties (Bernard 2005, 377).

My work with the Indian Fields archaeological collection did not begin as a study of networks or relationships. I initially resisted reconstructions of relationships because similar research historians and archaeologists had done on eastern Long Island indigenous peoples reinforced racist notions of indigenous cultural decline. Historians and anthropological researchers who had studied these documents and archaeological collections saw the

Montauketts and their histories as "relics" of past indigenous traditions. The work of prior researchers has been used to support historical claims that the Montauketts were largely culturally extinct and that the "remnant" Montaukett individuals who existed were rendered inauthentic by marriages with non-indigenous (primarily African American) partners. The result was a political tool: a narrative that supports the dispossession of indigenous people from their homelands and erases their claims to land. In an attempt to resist these racist interpretations, I approached the Indian Fields archaeological collection (which was excavated roughly forty years before I began my investigation) with an attempt to use an objective lens to understand material culture and a documentary perspective that favored indigenous experiences over capitalist interpretations.

As I moved through the archaeological collection, I encountered material culture that crossed that great divide between prehistory and history, tradition and modernity (McGovern 2015; Scheiber and Mitchell 2010). But one particular item encouraged interpretive analysis beyond the usual typologies used in archaeology: a hand-painted glass tumbler that had been reconstructed from fragments recovered at the Pharaoh household archaeological context (Figure 10.1). This item was unique; it was not like anything seen in other Long Island historical archaeological collections. It was the kind of item that you would expect to be curated, but when I searched for similar items in local historical societies on eastern Long Island, I found no comparable examples. That prompted me to think about what sorts of activities, local and/or global, could account for its presence.

In the process of researching comparative archaeological data for indigenous sites in eastern Long Island, I encountered a reference in gray literature to an archaeological site located roughly fourteen miles west of Indian Fields that mentions a similar glass object (although the hand-painted decoration was different) (Cammisa et al. 1999). That site, the Bianco/Caroll site, was a late eighteenth- through early nineteenth-century domestic site in an area of known indigenous habitation, yet the archaeologist who investigated the site interpreted it as African American based on local assumptions of indigenous identity. The presence of this similar glass artifact in contemporary archaeological sites inhabited by people of similar backgrounds prompted me to think about how the people who inhabited these sites might have been engaged in similar activities and perhaps even in similar networks.

Figure 10.1. Hand-painted glass tumbler recovered from Jeremiah Pharaoh's home. Photo by Allison Manfra McGovern.

I put aside local arguments of contested indigenous identity and sought out the types of activities that might explain the presence of this artifact that seemed to be unique to eastern Long Island. I proceeded with the notion that investigating local contexts and connecting them to regional and global activities does not require a set of a priori assumptions about identity (Terrell 2013). Nonetheless, right about now, a brief depiction of Montaukett history is necessary for moving forward.

A Brief Depiction of Montaukett History

The indigenous Montauketts are locally remembered as one of the "thirteen tribes" of Long Island Indians, a mythicized oversimplification of indigenous identity and sociopolitical organization that has been canonized in local history books (Strong 1992). The dominant narrative in local histories depicts Montauketts as a once-powerful indigenous community that welcomed and formed an alliance with the first white colonist in coastal New York, Lion Gardiner. According to this narrative, by the nineteenth century, Montaukett culture had degraded and been replaced by Euro-American influences. The "evidence" for this "cultural loss" was the presence of Euro-American material culture (which was seen as replacing indigenous material culture in archaeological contexts), a reliance on wage-based subsistence strategies, and kin partnerships with African American and mixed-heritage people. But in these twentieth-century descriptions of nineteenth-century acculturation, there was no accounting for the oppressive colonialist policies and capitalist approaches to land and resources that heavily impacted indigenous lifeways and no consideration of indigenous persistence.

This colonialist history placed the Montaukett people in Montauk, the easternmost hamlet of Long Island, in a spatially bounded location that does not necessarily reflect multigenerational lived experiences of Montaukett people. They have always practiced what Deena Duranleau (2009) calls "flexible sedentism," using preferred locations for seasonal homes. They, and other indigenous peoples on Long Island, maintained connections to both people and places through social and kin networks that oftentimes extended far beyond modern geographic boundaries.

When whites arrived in East Hampton in the seventeenth century, they established their village roughly twenty miles west of Montauk. As the white population expanded, they enacted policies to restrict indigenous settlement to areas outside the white village. By the mid-eighteenth century, indigenous Montaukett people were dispersed in small settlements throughout the towns of East Hampton and Southampton, but a small village was present at Indian Fields in Montauk. Based on the archaeological evidence, Montaukett people settled permanently at Indian Fields around the mid-eighteenth century. Their village shrank in size and composition until the end of the nineteenth century, when they were dispossessed and relocated by white development. In the 1970s, archaeologists investigated several features at the Indian Fields settlement as a means of documenting the sites for the county parks department (which, by then, owned all the property that included Indian Fields). Archaeologists uncovered a total of twenty-three features, including five house patterns, three middens, seven storage features, two stone walls, and six additional unidentified features (Johannemann 1993).

Focusing on two households from Indian Fields, I explored indigenous economic conditions during the rise and fall of the commercial whaling industry, specifically between 1780 and 1885, when many indigenous men were employed as whaling crew. Because the two Indian Fields households provide the material traces of daily lives, I view them as loci for Montaukett identity construction, consumption, and labor. The earlier household, which the Pharaoh family inhabited, was occupied by Jeremiah Pharaoh and Aloosa Tallman Pharaoh from roughly 1780 through 1830. The later household, which William and Mary Fowler and their children occupied, was inhabited from about 1840 until 1885. Because the Indian Fields village functioned like a reservation, the households there were not counted on any federal censuses before 1870 (McGovern 2015).[2] I consulted account books, legal transactions, town records, lawsuits, lists of whaling ship crews, and Montaukett family histories to reconstruct the names and identities of families at Indian Fields.

The Home of Jeremiah Pharaoh and Aloosa Tallman Pharaoh

Jeremiah Pharaoh was part of a Montaukett family whose name is still alive in East Hampton and abroad. For centuries, the Pharaoh name has been connected to leadership in the Montaukett tribal group. Aloosa Tallman's ancestry is a bit more difficult to trace. The presence of the name Tallman in Sampson Occom's records suggests that she was Delaware. She and Jeremiah may have become acquainted through Occom's network of northeastern Indians.

The home of Jeremiah and Aloosa was a small structure fourteen feet long and fourteen feet wide built partly of fieldstone in a circular or oval floor pattern. Part of a nearby fieldstone enclosure fence was incorporated into the foundation wall of the structure. Although the Pharaoh house does not resemble a particular housing type, it is representative of the vernacular architecture recorded at Native American sites throughout southern New England (Cipolla et al. 2007; McBride 1990; Rainey 2010; Silliman and Witt 2010; Sturtevant 1975). This home combined indigenous building traditions with some Euro-American architectural features (e.g., a glass window, construction nails). A dense living surface that included faunal and fish bone mixed with crushed shell and various artifacts was found on the interior floor. Animal skins or reed mats would have lined the floor or served as raised bedding in similar structures.

Jeremiah and Aloosa were married in Nantucket in 1794.[3] In 1806, Jeremiah Pharaoh was documented as living at Indian Fields in a household of three people (Anonymous [1809] 1993). The other two members of his household were probably his wife Aloosa and their son, also Jeremiah, who was born in 1802.[4] These and other glimpses of Pharaoh family life were revealed in diary entries that Jeremiah made in the pages of a law book that Sampson Occom once owned. Although the location of the law book is currently unknown, East Hampton antiquarian Orville B. Ackerly took notes on the Pharaoh entries and subsequently published in the local newspaper *Sag Harbor Express* in 1924. From these accounts, we know that Jeremiah Pharaoh was a whaler who sailed out of Nantucket when that port gained prominence for launching deep-sea whalers. We know that he and his wife were married in the port where Jeremiah found work, we know that their son died at age six, and we have a record of Jeremiah's responses to the conditions at his homeland, Indian Fields, which he witnessed when he returned from sea: "I Jeremiah Pharaoh the Bold mariner I sailed the world all over nine long years. When I Returned home I found my relations stranded which grieved my heart ful so."[5]

While it is not known how many whaling ventures Jeremiah engaged in, what ships he sailed on or where they went, it is evident from the archaeological record that his household was economically stable. No documented economic transactions have survived for Jeremiah and Aloosa's household, although we have records of such transactions for other contemporary Indian Fields residents. Yet the archaeological record contains evidence of a rich assortment of late eighteenth- and early nineteenth-century ceramics, suggesting that whaling provided a means of acquiring these and other market goods. An interesting variety of refined earthenware ceramics from the eighteenth century includes three plates, two teapots (one Jackfield and one Astbury), a Staffordshire slipware platter and pitcher, two redware platters (one might be a milk pan), seven pearlware vessels (teacups, bowls, or small mugs), a vase or pitcher, an English stoneware mug, a Rhenish blue and gray jug, a creamware chamber pot, two hollow storage vessels (one redware and one stoneware), and an unusually chunky undecorated shallow redware dish. In addition to these items, metal utensils, metal sewing items, and the previously mentioned painted glass tumbler are among the market items recovered from the archaeological site.

The material deposits suggest that the house was inhabited continuously from the late eighteenth into the early part of the nineteenth century, including while Pharaoh was at sea. In this tiny structure, an open hearth was present near the south wall. An abundance of faunal material, including the remains of some medium-sized mammals, shellfish, fish, and turtles was recovered from inside and outside the structure. Pharaoh probably owned a cow or sheep, and in 1813, he profited by having a white East Hamptoner's cattle graze on his land.[6] The size of his structure and the reliance on locally caught foods suggest that the Pharaoh family subsisted on very modest means. Among the artifacts from this household is an unusually large quantity of sewing materials such as buttons, button molds, and pins and bone needles and awls. Based on preliminary analysis, this evidence for women's work seems to exceed household-level tasks. It seems that Aloosa and Jeremiah were sewing and making baskets for the local market to bring in additional income. During Jeremiah's absences at sea, it might have been Aloosa who was fishing, gathering oysters, and making baskets in exchange for market goods.

William and Mary Fowler's Home

The second household assemblage is from a slightly larger square-shaped house with a fieldstone foundation that measures around 15 × 24 feet. This structure, which was inhabited from the mid to the late nineteenth century, was the home of William Fowler, his wife Mary, and their children. Fowler's employment is unclear; his name in account books suggests that he was a laborer who worked in various capacities for East Hampton whites. He does not seem to be documented on any whaling voyages, even though many other Native American men from East Hampton were sailing out of Sag Harbor between 1840 and 1860. This was the golden age of whaling, and many men of color from eastern Long Island sought employment in the industry. Whaling ventures that departed from the port at Sag Harbor, which has one of the most complete records for whaling during this time, peaked in 1840 (Barsh 2002, 90).

In 1870, six households at Indian Fields were listed on the federal census. The Fowler household included William, his wife Mary, and five children ranging in age from 5 to 25 years old. He was listed as the head of household again on the 1880 federal census, when his household included only himself, his wife, and their three youngest children. By that time, his daughter Maria was married to David Pharaoh (they had their own household at Indian Fields) and at least one of his sons was employed in whaling, which explains his absence from the census.

There were far more people living in the Fowler house than in the Pharaoh home, yet in comparison there was less density and diversity of archaeological materials. There are also fewer archaeological clues about the strategies the Fowlers used to meet the daily needs of the household. One major difference between William Fowler's household and the earlier household of Jeremiah Pharaoh is a reliance on market goods. It seems that the Fowler household was relying less on locally available foods and more on what could be purchased at a store through credit or exchange. Only eight pieces of bone and ten pieces of shell were recovered from the Fowler house, compared to more than 200 shells and thousands of bone fragments from the Pharaoh house.

Account books provide a better record of Montaukett consumption for this period. William Fowler's name appears in at least two account books, which record that he bartered his services in fishing for goods such as cordwood and sundries.[7] Account books also suggest patterns of social interactions and networks. I found that it was possible to compare the economic activities related to employment in whaling and consumption of the residents of Indian Fields and other people of color in the town of East Hampton. In addition to revealing similarities in economic strategies, the data suggest that residents inevitably crossed paths in the stores where they did business and in many cases labored together for white farmers and on whaling ships.[8] These pluralistic settings—locations in the public sphere that brought people of Native American, African, and European ancestries together—provided opportunities for multicultural interaction and influence both locally and internationally (i.e., at sea).

The two household deposits, therefore, must be understood in relation to local, regional, and global contexts to expose how local and regional activities are connected to each other and to global economics. Such an approach emphasizes local responses to colonial and capitalist processes and reminds us that neither colonialism nor capitalism were monolithic, hegemonic phenomena. Beyond the household, connections between the local and the global depend on data about both location and relations between people. Intersections between the local and the global, are nodes in a network of social and economic interaction. Aletta Biersack points out that while place has a central meaning in local-global articulations, an understanding of relational space is necessary for connecting the dots between places or nodes (2006, 16).

In this study, nodes are places of settlement (i.e., households, villages, and neighborhoods), places of work or production (e.g., whaling ships, ports and destinations, and the fields and homes of whites), and places of consumption (e.g., shops). Places of consumption are indicated by account books from stores, warehouses, and perhaps the homes of white merchants, farmers, and company owners—generally, any record from places where the consumer transactions took place. These records indicate important economic ties among consumers, laborers, and merchants. The obvious links between the nodes are labor, production, and consumption. But it eventually became evident that kinship and community also linked these nodes.

Tracing Networks: Account Books, Crew Lists, and Miscellaneous Documents

In an effort to contextualize the Montaukett economic strategies at Indian Fields, I developed a comparative data source. I looked at other places in the town of East Hampton where Native American people lived and worked. These were places where African-descended people also lived and worked in East Hampton. Beginning with federal census data, I constructed a database of all people of color who were documented as residents of the town of East Hampton from 1790 to circa 1900. Then, using maps and historical accounts, I identified where the residences of people of color were located on the landscape. I learned from this process that there was a settlement north of East Hampton village whose residents were free people of color (African Americans, Native Americans, and mixed-heritage people) by the late eighteenth century. Through town records, account and day books, and ledgers, I reconstructed labor patterns for these individuals. When I compiled this information into a single database, kin networks became more evident and I was eventually able to connect people and places across space and time.

In general, the account books or ledgers were associated with well-known East Hampton whites whose homes, stores, or warehouses could be located on the historical landscape. I used whaling crew lists to located the name of the ship that employed a crew member and recorded the port from which it sailed and its intended destination. Each individual in my database can be mapped at at least one node. For instance, I located

Jeremiah Pharaoh at Indian Fields/Montauk and Nantucket. I could not identify the destination for the ships that employed him out of Nantucket. But a circa 1830–1840s Montaukett whaler named George Pharaoh, who also lived at Indian Fields, is better documented and appears at a number of nodes: Indian Fields/Montauk, Freetown, Sag Harbor (from where his ships sailed), and destinations that included the northwest coast of North America, the South Seas, and Brazil.

Native American, African-descended, and white men and women were interconnected in a web of economic exchange. In account books, daybooks, and ledger books, I found evidence that people of color (i.e., Native Americans, African Americans, and mixed-heritage people) performed a variety of types of work in exchange for goods and sometimes cash. White merchants, storekeepers, farmers, and other business owners organized and documented a system of credit. The people of color I was researching paid their debts for purchased goods by baling hay, caning chairs, cutting cordwood, and doing various other tasks. In some cases, they paid their debts in cash, and in other cases, white men who employed Native American and African American men and women paid the debts. These sources also include details about how Native American and African American men were outfitted for work on whaling ships: employers provided them with the items they would need on upcoming whaling voyages on credit with the expectation that they would return a portion of their share from the expedition to pay for the goods.

Purchases of shoes, candles, and sundries provide traces of consumption of necessities; purchases of cloth, thread, teawares, and crockery indicate traces of household activities; and purchases of meat, fish, corn, flour, molasses, liquors, tobacco, and a variety of other items provide traces of foodways and affinities. These snapshots in time encourage archaeologists and historians to imagine the daily practices involving these items and the social relations that characterized those activities.

The demographic data also shed light on how the constructed cultural landscape of color constrained cultural movement. Federal census data, land and mortgage deeds, wills, and probates provide geographic placements in the landscape that can be cross-referenced with nineteenth- and early twentieth-century maps. These sources enable us to trace the pathways from homes and neighborhoods to work, shops, the harbor, and other neighborhoods, presenting a web of travel and communication across the town of East Hampton (Figure 10.2). Settlement was

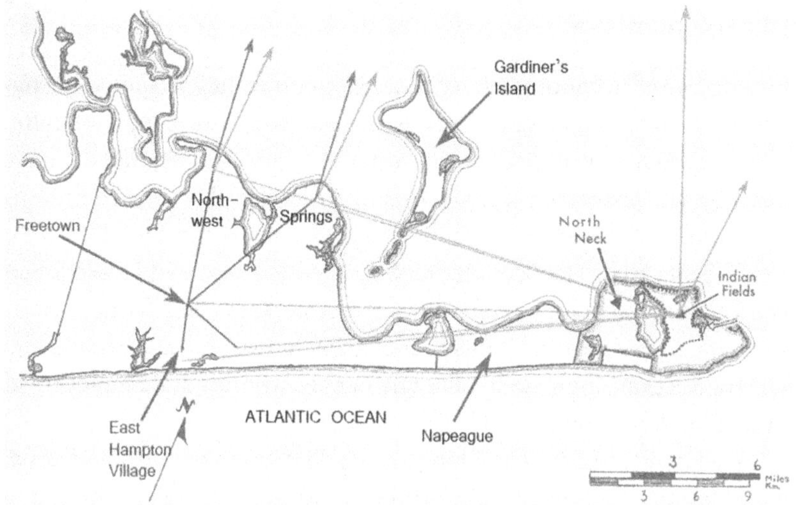

Figure 10.2. Map of local and regional nodes and pathways.

circumscribed by whites, who sold land to Native American and African American people in designated areas (often in close proximity to places of employment, which were often the homes and the fields of the whites who sold the land). While some free people of color lived along the wooded portions of the roads that connected villages (e.g., Peter and Triphenia Quaw lived on a road that connected North West Road and Hands Creek Road on the west side of Three Mile Harbor in the mid-nineteenth century), there were also neighborhoods, like Indian Fields, Freetown, Accobonack, and Springs, a section of Sag Harbor that was eventually named Eastville, an area in Bridgehampton.

These data demonstrate that Montaukett people were entangled in a web of social and economic activity that transcended local geographical boundaries. They were integrated into a complex network of labor, production, and consumption, and their participation was integral to the successes of capitalism through various flows of social and economic activity. African and Native American men and women of East Hampton often worked together for whites in their homes and fields, performing skilled and unskilled labor. The primary documents that recorded their presence and activities provide clues to social and kin networks as people crossed paths and made long-lasting connections.

Making Connections

The ledgers and account books of East Hampton whites provide information about their exchanges of goods and services with people of color. In these accounts, it is evident that when African American and Native American whalers were not at sea, they and their families worked in similar positions. A survey of sixteen account books at the East Hampton Library Long Island Collection demonstrated the repeated employment of and credit system for goods with Native American and African American people. They were residents of Freetown, Springs, and Montauk, and their transactions indicate an entanglement of laborers and employers in a system of debt peonage.

The whaling industry has a long history that began with drift whaling, which dates to the seventeenth century (and possibly before that), and ended with an expansive industry that was reliant on deep-sea ventures, which continued into the early twentieth century. The industry was impacted through the years by competition among nations, changing demands for energy sources, the desire for luxury goods, and trade regulations, all of which resulted in highs and lows in profits. Whaling drew all types of men for employment at sea, but the involvement of indigenous (Montauketts, Shinnecocks, Unkechaugs, and other Algonquians from throughout New England) and African American men in North American whaling was particularly conspicuous (Cash 1989; Strong 1989).

Each New England port rose to prominence and then declined as another New England port prospered. For instance, Nantucket rose to prominence in the eighteenth century (during Jeremiah Pharaoh's time), followed by New London in the early nineteenth century, Sag Harbor from 1820 to 1840, and finally New Bedford from the 1840s to 1892. Crew lists document that indigenous and African American men from eastern Long Island (and elsewhere) were employed on ships out of each of these ports. They went to ports where work was available and sometimes remained settled at or near those ports after whaling ended, finding work in farming and factories. The New Bedford economy, where whaling ships continued to sail after the turn of the twentieth century, was based largely on maritime commerce and agriculture even after whaling ended. Kathryn Grover notes that unlike other Massachusetts cities that turned to production of shoes and textiles, New Bedford did not become an industrial city (2001, 8). She writes that "whaling, more than any of the relatively tolerant maritime trades, . . . welcomed the participation of people of color, and as white and immigrant labor entered the factories[,] the decks and forecastles of whalers may have grown especially dependent on whalemen of color until the 1850s. Those laborers in turn viewed whaling, despite its disadvantages, as one of the only occupations available through which they might support themselves and their families" (Grover 2001, 8). This economic pattern is similar to the patterns in eastern Long Island. A few factories for processing maritime commodities were established in East Hampton, but the area did not become industrialized. East Hampton remained largely rural as a growing resort contingent developed. People of color continued to find work on whaling ships until the turn of twentieth century, and the connections they made with crew members should not be underestimated. By searching crew lists and whaling accounts, it becomes evident that African American and Native American men from Long Island sailed together, settled together, and some eventually formed kin ties among their families.

Whaling also exposed men to unfamiliar parts of the world, particularly as the voyages traveled farther in search of whales. This expanded their network involvement beyond the local and regional nodes (Figure 10.3). The men of whaling crews met people from all parts of the world and occasionally stopped in foreign lands for supplies and crew (where they also purchased or traded for personal goods). Some abandoned their ships to settle far from home (Shoemaker 2013, 2014). Contrary to contemporary local history perspectives, East Hampton's men of color were worldly; they learned about new people and cultures at sea and in foreign ports. Their experiences at sea force us to reconsider their involvement in shaping global commerce (Cohen 2008). These experiences would have been altogether different from those of the whites who employed them at home, who viewed Native Americans, for instance, as living relics of ancient cultures. At ports such as Sag Harbor and New Bedford, the presence of whalers from other lands throughout the Caribbean, the Azores, Cape Verde, and the South Pacific contributed to a sense of cosmopolitanism, as men occasionally joined whaling ships that were already at sea (Grover 2001; Shoemaker 2014). Foreign whalers who remained at Sag Harbor also formed kin relations with people of color in East Hampton town (Zaykowski 1991).

My generalizations about indigenous and African American women's work in East Hampton prior to the nineteenth century are based

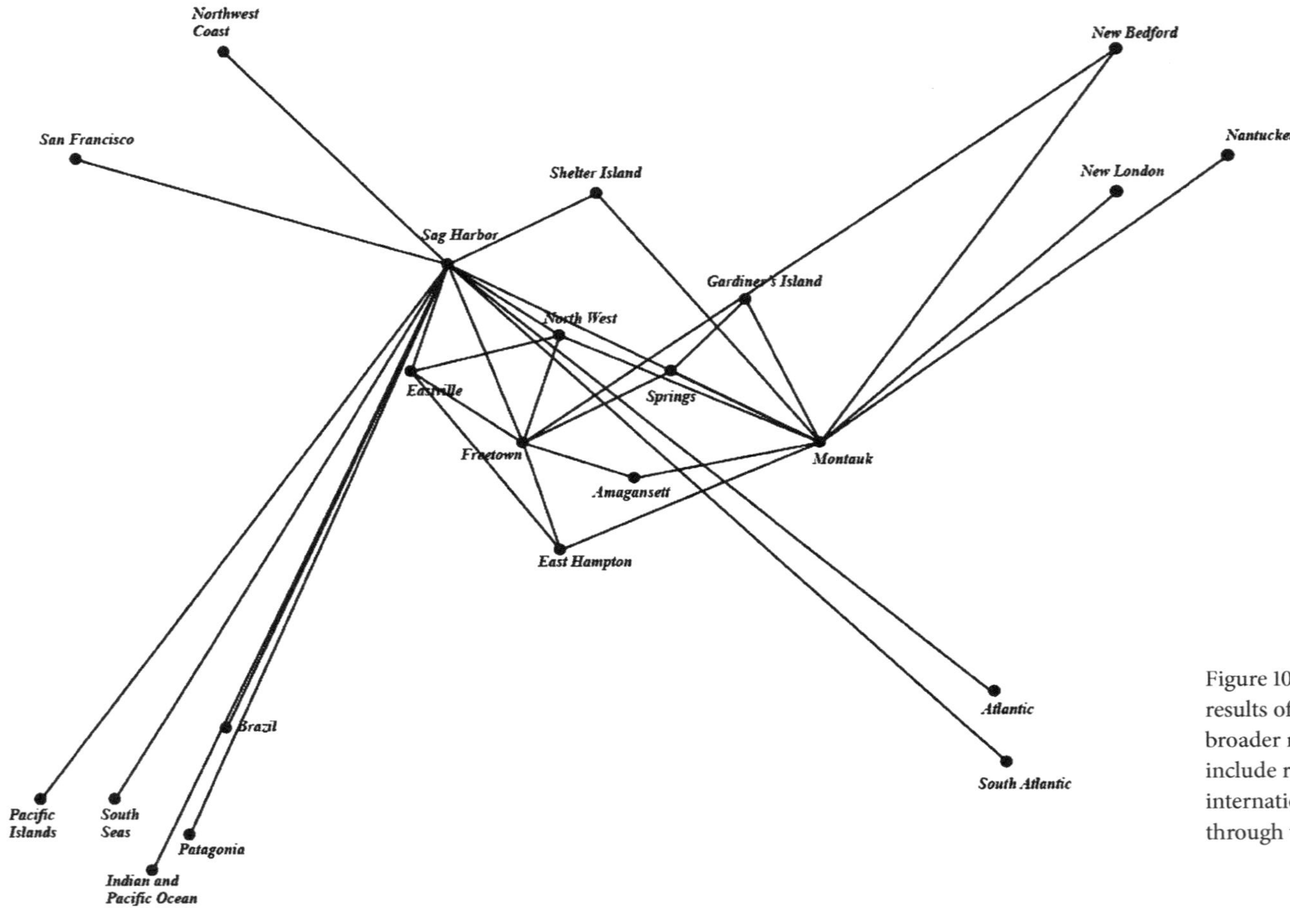

Figure 10.3. The results of mapping broader networks to include regional and international nodes through whaling.

on patterns associated with agricultural life in rural northeastern North America, as records of men's employment were better preserved. Some women worked in the homes of whites as domestics. Montaukett women of Indian Fields were also involved with men in small-scale farming activities at home and in the fields of the elites. In 1799, for instance, Stephen Pharaoh and his wife, who lived at Indian Fields, pulled two acres of flax for John Lyon Gardiner.[9]

By 1850, women of color were documented as domestic servants in white homes and as washerwomen. The federal census notes that they often took washing into their own homes. Women of color were listed as heads of household as early as 1800, and post-1850 censuses indicate that their households often included boarders and extended kin. Eliza Cooper, for example, was listed as a head of household on the 1880 federal census. Her household included Clarissa Depth, a thirteen-year-old boarder who worked as a servant, a ten-month-old boarder named Benjamin C. Coles, and the following extended kin: grandson Silas C. Fowler, grandson Samuel Quaw, granddaughter Maggie Banks, and nephew John L. Horton, who was at sea at the time. Cooper's occupation was listed as "keeping house," but her household was probably supported by income from its members.[10]

An oral history recorded in 1929 with Thomas Edwards, a white who was a lifelong resident of East Hampton, provides a vivid description of the setting and the people of Freetown (Edwards 1929). Like most Long Island histories written from local memory, the source must be considered carefully. But in this rare find, the names of Freetown residents from just fifty years earlier come to life, along with the memories of the work they performed. Edwards remembered "'Aunt Peg,' a colored soap maker," who smoked a clay pipe and baked in an old brick oven; Hannah Hannibles, a Native American woman who caned chairs; Levi Stoves, a whaleman who worked for farmers; Sylpha, who "cooked sometimes at summer boarding houses, washed and did other kinds of work for the village people"; Kate Jack, who made scrub brushes and was a domestic in several white homes; Ed Deesberry, who labored on farms, cut wood, and performed other odd jobs; his wife Dorcas Deesberry, who "had been married before, and was the mother of Israel Quaw and Mary B., who married Robert Montgomery, an ex-slave, and a very religious man"; John Horton, who worked for Norman Barnes; Isaac and Jerry Wright, who farmed and fished; and Sam Butler (1929, 254–256). Edwards's memories provide interesting details about work, craft production, and kin that are difficult to reconstruct from primary documents alone.

As I mapped labor patterns and movement, social and kin networks began to emerge, especially when I compared local twentieth-century memories with my eighteenth- and nineteenth-century database. The results demonstrated not only patterning in types of labor but also social connections that were established and maintained across geographical distances and time. Those distances included locations twenty or more miles away from Indian Fields; settlements in Freetown, Springs, and elsewhere; and years and miles at sea. The significance of tracing social and kin networks lies in our ability to understand these networks from an emic perspective. They were not simply networks that resulted from white enforcement of a conscripted labor class. In fact, indigenous systems of exchange (which functioned for trade and within social or kin networks) were well established across broad landscapes in the pre-Columbian era. Post-contact networks were therefore not new cultural constructions. These networks ensured survival that helped minimize risk while men and women sought work outside their homes (Stack 1974; see also Young 2004). It was through these relationships that Montaukett survivance and social reproduction, both on and off Indian Fields, was maintained.

Conclusions

The residents of Indian Fields experienced numerous social and economic changes that impacted their lives in various ways. These are documented locally through archaeology at the homes of Jeremiah Pharaoh and William Walter Fowler. But these households were not isolated at the eastern end of Long Island. In fact, the residents of these and other households at Indian Fields were entangled in complex social and economic relationships that transcended local and regional boundaries. Their movement through the landscape and the seascape is fundamental to understanding how they navigated changing social and economic contexts, as these factors often simultaneously provided opportunities for them to establish new social and kin relationships and to strengthen existing ones.

The hand-painted glass tumbler was a material reminder of how artifacts can encourage network thinking and connect a local site to regional and global economic activities. Network thinking enables us to consider the movements of material culture and think about the interactions of people: where people meet (in labor networks, in kin networks, in consumer networks, in neighborhoods) and what happens when people meet (they form new relationships or reinforce existing ones).

The lives of people in the past do not fit into bounded geographical boxes. By thinking about networks, we can open up interpretations to include the experiences of people both at and away from our archaeological contexts. In this case, network thinking helped me consider the internal and external forces in Montaukett networks. While labor and material culture may lead many of us to consider the dominant forces (capitalism, colonialism) that draw people together, it is important to also note that indigenous world views and indigenous network thinking were important forces for maintaining survivance by contributing to community sustainability, social reconstruction, and the persistence of identity.

Notes

1. The term "survivance" is borrowed from indigenous studies and employed here to emphasize a Native American presence that is informed simultaneously by indigenous continuity and the challenges of colonialism (Atalay 2006; McGovern 2015).

2. Prior to 1870, Native Americans who were not taxed were excluded from the census, which was used to determine the apportionment population base. This is why Native Americans who lived on reservation lands are absent from the census rolls.

3. Marriage of Jeremiah Pharoh and Lois Talmon, in *Vital Records of Nantucket, Massachusetts to the Year 1850,* vol. 4, edited by Henry Edwards Scott, editor (Boston: New England Historic Genealogical Society, 1927), 273.

4. Jeremiah's birthdate is in a copy of entries in a law book that once belonged to Samson Occum. Orville B. Ackerly wrote up the notes around 1921 the *Sag Harbor Express* published them in 1924.

5. Orville B. Ackerly, "Bits from the Book of Jeremiah Pharaoh," *Sag Harbor Express and the News and the Corrector*, July 31, 1924.

6. Common Pasture List, 1813, East Hampton Library Long Island Collection, East Hampton, New York.

7. Account Book no. 3 of Captain James Post, 1826–1900; Nathaniel Hand Daybook, 1855, Long Island Collection, East Hampton Library, East Hampton, New York.

8. Isaac Van Scoy Account Books, 1829, 1835; Nathaniel Hand Daybook, 1855, Long Island Collection, East Hampton Library.

9. John Lyon Gardiner, Account Book 2, 1801–1806, Long Island Collection, East Hampton Library.

10. The young boarders in Cooper's household may have been foster children. This pattern, though not well documented, seems to have continued into the twentieth century.

References Cited

Anonymous. (1809) 1993. "A Memorandum of the Famelyes and the Number of each Family of Natives Living and Residing on Montauk." In *History and Archaeology of the Montauk*, 2nd ed., edited by Gaynell Stone, 408–409. Readings in Long Island Archaeology and Ethnohistory, Volume 3. Mattituck, NY: Suffolk County Archaeological Association.

Atalay, Sonya. 2006. No Sense of the Struggle: Creating a Context for Survivance at the NMAI. *The American Indian Quarterly* 30(3–4):597–618.

Barsh, Russell L. 2002. "Colored" Seamen in the New England Whaling Industry: An Afro-Indian Consortium. In *Confounding the Color Line: The Indian-Black Experience in North America*, edited by James F. Brooks, 76–107. Lincoln: University of Nebraska Press.

Bernard, H. Russell. 2005. Review: Linton C. Freeman, the Development of Social Network Analysis. *Social Networks* 22:377–84.

Biersack, Aletta. 2006. Reimagining Political Ecology: Culture/Power/History/Nature. In *Reimagining Political Ecology (New Ecologies for the Twenty-First Century)*, edited by Aletta Biersack and James B. Greenberg, 3–40. Durham, NC: Duke University Press.

Bridge, Gavin, and Adrian Smith. 2003. Intimate Encounters: Culture-Economy-Commodity. *Environment and Planning D: Society and Space* 21:257–268.

Brughmans, Tom. 2010. Connecting the Dots: Towards Archaeological Network Analysis. *Oxford Journal of Archaeology* 29(3):277–303.

Cammisa, Alfred G., Thomas Amorosi, Felicia Cammisa, Diane Dallal, Joseph Diamond, William Goldsmith, Justine McKnight, and Nancy Stehling. 1999. Six Thousand Years of Land Use at Three Mile Harbor: The Bianco Estate Phase III Data Recovery of the Carroll Site, East Hampton, Suffolk County, New York. North Babylon, NY: Tracker Archaeological Services.

Cash, Floris Barnet. 1989. African American Whalers: Images and Reality. *Long Island Historical Journal* 2(1):41–52.

Cipolla, Craig N., Stephen W. Silliman, and David B. Landon. 2007. "Making Do": Nineteenth-Century Subsistence Practices on the Eastern Pequot Reservation. *Northeast Anthropology* 74:41–64.

Cohen, Paul. 2008. Was there an Amerindian Atlantic? Reflections on the Limits of a Historiographical Concept. *History of European Ideas* 34:388–410.

Duranleau, Deena Lynne. 2009. "Flexible Sedentism: The Subsistence and Settlement Strategies of the Pre-Contact Residents of Coastal New England and New York." PhD diss., Harvard University.

Edwards, Thomas M. 1929. *Reminiscences of Old East Hampton by the Sea*. East Hampton, NY: Higginson Book Company.

Grover, Kathryn. 2001. *The Fugitive's Gibraltar: Escaping Slaves and Abolitionism in New Bedford, Massachusetts*. Amherst: University of Massachusetts Press.

Johannemann, Edward. 1993. Indian Fields Site: Part 1, Montauk, Suffolk County, Long Island, New York. In *The History and Archaeology of the Montauk*, 2nd ed., edited by Gaynell Stone, 645–655. Readings in Long Island Archaeology and Ethnohistory, Volume 3. Mattituck, NY: Suffolk County Archaeological Association.

Knappett, Carl, ed. 2013. *Network Analysis in Archaeology: New Approaches to Regional Interaction*. Oxford: Oxford University Press.

McBride, Kevin. 1990. The Historical Archaeology of the Mashantucket Pequots, 1637–1900: A Preliminary Analysis. In *The Pequots in Southern New England: The Fall and Rise of an American Indian* Nation, edited by Laurence M. Hauptman and James D. Wherry, 96–116. Norman: University of Oklahoma Press.

McGovern, Allison Manfra. 2015. "Disrupting the Narrative: Labor and Survivance for the Montauketts of Eastern Long Island." PhD diss., City University of New York. Accessed January 25, 2018. http://academicworks.cuny.edu/gc_etds/1045.

Rainey, Mary Lynn. 2010. Native American Architecture on Nantucket Island. In *Nantucket and Other Native Places: The Legacy of Elizabeth Alden Little*, edited by Elizabeth S. Chilton and Mary Lynn Rainey, 25–62. Albany: State University of New York Press.

Scheiber, Laura L., and Mark D. Mitchell. 2010. *Across a Great Divide: Continuity and Change in Native North American Societies, 1400–1900*. Tucson: University of Arizona Press.

Shoemaker, Nancy. 2013. Mr. Tashtego: Native American Whalemen in Antebellum New England. *Journal of the Early Republic* 33(1):109–132.

———. 2014. *Living with Whales: Documents and Oral Histories of Native New England Whaling History*. Amherst: University of Massachusetts Press.

Silliman, Stephen W., and Thomas A. Witt. 2010. Complexities of Consumption: Eastern Pequot Cultural Economics in Eighteenth-Century New England. *Historical Archaeology* 44(4):46–68.

Stack, Carol. 1974. *All Our Kin: Strategies for Survival in a Black Community*. New York: Basic Books.

Strong, John. 1989. Shinnecock and Montauk Whalemen. *Long Island Historical Journal* 2(1):29–41.

———. 1992. The Thirteen Tribes of Long Island: The History of a Myth. *Hudson Valley Regional Review* 9(2):39–73.

Sturtevant, William C. 1975. Two 1761 Wigwams at Niantic, Connecticut. *American Antiquity* 40(4):437–444.

Terrell, John Edward. 2013. Social Network Analysis and the Practice of History. In *Network Analysis in Archaeology: New Approaches to Regional Interaction*, edited by Carl Knappett, 17–42. Oxford: Oxford University Press.

Young, Amy. 2004. Risk and Women's Roles in the Slave Family: Data from Oxmoor and Locust Grove Plantations in Kentucky. In *Engendering African American Archaeology: A Southern Perspective*, edited by Jillian E. Galle and Amy L. Young, 133–150. Knoxville: University of Tennessee Press.

Zaykowski, Dorothy Ingersoll. 1991. *Sag Harbor: The Story of an American Beauty*. Sag Harbor, NY: Sag Harbor Historical Society.

11

Intimacies of Glass in Early Eighteenth-Century Louisiana

DIANA DIPAOLO LOREN

Trade and Intimacy

Pierre LeMoyne d'Iberville's journal of his travels along the Mississippi River in the early eighteenth century is punctuated with notations of the presents he gave to Native Americans to facilitate alliances. Iberville's journal and other early colonial accounts of French and Native American interactions in the Lower Mississippi Valley often included discussions of the items needed for "trade with the Indians." Glass beads were always included as part of the gift, described as "trade goods" or "trinkets." These items were used to facilitate French colonization of the Lower Mississippi Valley. Such offhand descriptions of glass beads as trinkets conceal the social dimensions of how colonial individuals wore beads on the body in presentations and performances of identity and community.

It is perhaps not surprising that French colonists gave these shiny little objects such fleeting attention, but in some ways it is. Glass beads, along with other trade goods such as axes, iron knives, linen shirts, and wool blankets, were gifted in diplomatic interactions to create alliances with Native American chiefs. Glass beads were also traded for necessities. For example, in his interactions with a group of Bayogoula men, Iberville noted that "I gave a present of knives, glass beads, and axes to him and his comrades, whom he summoned. They gave us buccaned [smoked] buffalo meat and bear meat" (McWilliams 1991, 55). Imagine how welcome some dried buffalo meat was to the French who were navigating mosquito-filled waterways without ample provisions. Glass beads were also important after initial interactions, as the French traded them for other food and services throughout the eighteenth century. Thus, these small items were more than just trinkets; they were objects that were integral to the success of the French colonization of the Lower Mississippi Valley. In the archive, however, this importance appears to be understated and we often read it as such, focusing on the importance of glass beads for Native American communities.

How Native Americans engaged with glass beads has been a common topic in archaeological literature since the early twentieth century, when the focus was aimed at bead identification and determining European sites of production (e.g., Kidd and Kidd 1970). Recent scholarly interest has focused on how Native American peoples incorporated glass beads into adornment and embroidery practices throughout the colonial Eastern Woodlands and on the complex meanings glass beads carried in those contexts (e.g., Karklins 1992; Turgeon 2001, 2004; Blair 2017; Blair et al. 2007; Loren 2010, 2013; Panich 2014). In this chapter, I seek to make beads more intimate, an approach that is common in studies of small finds (Beaudry 2009, 2006; Loren 2010; Loren and Beaudry 2006; White and Beaudry 2009), in order to focus on how Native American and French individuals wore and used them in daily life. I consider glass beads as a bodily object—an object that was needed for tangible and intangible bodily care—to determine how they were constituted in social relationships and embodied in daily life rather than as fetishized "trade goods" in historical descriptions and contemporary interpretations.

The Trudeau Site (aka the Tunica Treasure)

The French colony of Louisiana was incorporated at the end of the seventeenth century after several decades of exploration in the Lower Mississippi Valley. When the French arrived in 1700, many Native American communities had long been established along the Mississippi River, including the Tunica, who lived in several villages on the east bank at the juncture of the Yazoo and Mississippi Rivers. Soon after, more French households, posts, and concessions (plantations) were established along the Mississippi River (Brain 1988).

French émigrés to Louisiana included French nobleman (who were often officials), Jesuit priests, soldiers from a variety of backgrounds, middle-class craftsman, lower-class laborers and servants (both male and female), freed prisoners (again both male and female), and some elite women (Usner 1992). By 1726, less than 100 French settlers and soldiers lived in the Tunica area (Usner 1992, 48). Historical accounts indicate that the Tunica allied with the French in several wars against other neighboring Native Americans, notably the Natchez in 1729. In the 1730s, the Tunica moved just a few kilometers south along the east bank of the Mississippi, a location known in the archaeological record as the Trudeau site. By the beginning of the nineteenth century, the Tunica had moved again, to Marksville Prairie on the Red River in Louisiana. Today, the Tunica-Biloxi Indian Reservation is located in Marksville, Louisiana.

The Lower Mississippi Survey of the Peabody Museum of Harvard University excavated the Tunica region in the 1970s and 1980s. This research culminated in the publication of *Tunica Treasure* (1979) and *Tunica Archaeology* (1988), which provide description and analysis of eighteenth-century material recovered from sites in the Tunica region of present-day Mississippi. *Tunica Treasure* is the evocative and perhaps somewhat controversial name for a volume that focuses on a rich collection of artifacts that a local pothunter recovered from the Trudeau site. This collection of European-manufactured material is notable for its diversity and size; it is one of the largest and most diverse collections to ever be recovered from a French colonial site in the Southeast. The second volume details archaeological excavations conducted from 1971 to 1982 at Trudeau and in some of the smaller villages, including those known in the archaeological record as the Bloodhound and Haynes Bluff sites. Funerary objects were repatriated to the Tunica-Biloxi Tribe of Louisiana before and under the Native American Graves Protection and Repatriation Act of 1990 (Brain 1979, 1988), while other nonfunerary collections are housed at the Peabody Museum of Archaeology and Ethnology at Harvard University. In my discussion, I draw from Brain's published research and from artifacts in the Peabody's collections.

Bodily Objects, Trade Goods, and Intimacy

It is difficult for me to understand glass beads that are in storage or are captured in image and archive as "trade goods." I consider glass beads to be personal objects that fall generally under the category of small finds (Beaudry 2009, 2006; Loren 2010; Loren and Beaudry 2006; White and Beaudry 2009). In that vein, I tend to think more about beads as personal items that were worn on the body, such as beads strung on a necklace or sewn onto a garment. I am drawn to interpreting the relationship between beads and bodies following the work of other scholars, including Laurier Turgeon (2001, 2004). Moreover, again following Turgeon and others, glass beads are worn on the body in a variety of ways and for various purposes, some of which go beyond adornment (Karklins 1985, 1992; Hamell 1983). Beads were worn for more complex reasons—in spiritual pursuits, to encourage fertility, to entice, and to heal. When I think about beads in this way, I understand them as bodily objects: objects used and needed for both practical purposes and intangible bodily concerns (Brown 2009). Bodily objects materialize the needs and desires of the physical and spiritual body and are embodied in different practices of presenting and performing one's body (Chaplin 2003; Joyce 2005; Lindman and Tarter 2001; Loren 2001, 2010; White 2012, 2013). They evoke questions of what it meant to be properly and fashionably dressed, how to express sexuality or religious fervor with material culture, how to treat illness, and how materially embody bodily uncertainties and ambiguities.

Seeing glass beads as objects that were needed to attend to bodily concerns is only one interpretation, as they were valued items of trade for Europeans colonizing the New World. Glass beads were at the heart of early Louisiana economy. Glass beads and other items manufactured in Europe, such as linen and wool, were traded for pelts (deer, bear, buffalo, and beaver), pitch and tar, and salt (Dawdy 2009, 107; Greenwald 2013, 113). Glass beads arrived in Louisiana in barrels that carried thousands of different colors and sizes of glass beads. Those barrels made their way to warehouses run by the French Company of the Indies (Compagnie des Indes), which during the middle of the eighteenth-century held a monopoly over Louisiana trade, including the slave trade, negotiations with Native American peoples, and the purchase and export of tobacco grown in Louisiana (Greenwald 2013; Usner 1992). From French Company warehouses, glass beads were sold to French colonists who used them in various economic and social interactions. However, it was often difficult for French immigrants to gain access to the goods and "trinkets" in French Company warehouses, because the prices of the goods in warehouses were often inflated and supplies were scarce and poorly managed.

The difficulties of obtaining glass beads made these items perhaps a little dear to both the French and the Tunica who wanted and needed them to attend to bodily concerns. Commodity is a familiar term to archaeologists, who have used the concept to explore labor, reciprocity, and consumption or, put another way, the ways material culture becomes social (Appadurai 1986; Bridge and Smith 2003; Cipolla 2017; Dietler 2010; Dillian and White 2009; Gosden 2005; Heath et al. 2017; Mullins 2011; Silliman and Witt 2010). Intimate engagements are part of these discussions but discussions of this concept have largely been connected to sexuality and physical intimacy (e.g., Voss and Casella 2011). However, intimate engagements can be conceptualized more broadly to explore how commodities operated laterally rather than vertically between individuals. Vertical approaches to commodity use, an approach political economists often espouse, explores how "value and knowledge are distributed socially and geographically up and down the chain" from empire to colonist and colonized (Bridge and Smith 2003, 259). This approach contrasts with those that explore lateral connections—the connections between individuals—to illuminate how economic activity creates, maintain, and renegotiates intimate ties (Zelizer 2005, 3). Intimate transactions are not trivial; they facilitate and complicate social relationships and refine our understanding of self and other in relationship to things (Zelizer 2005). These intimacies are materialized in objects that have biographies that were constituted in the context of social relations (Bridge and Smith 2003, 258).

Glass beads have long been placed in the category of "trade goods" in historical description and contemporary classification. Yet a larger concern is at play here. When glass beads are considered a "trade good," they are interpreted and fetishized as such. They are removed from the realm of social relationships and their object biography is boiled down to the moment of exchange. Such considerations do not examine how they were constituted in and constituted bodily concerns. However, bodily concerns were often an important aspect of these interactions that needs to be factored into interpretations. Europeans traded beads for body work and for food for their bodies. Native Americans used beads in different ways: to place them on their bodies, to bury with a loved one, and as payment for sexual and household work. These were intimate transactions. The fact that glass beads could become intimate with the body—could materialize identity, create desire, heal self—is another way to consider them. To do this, I'd like to start with what was written and unwritten in the historical record.

The Intimacy of Glass Beads and What Is Unwritten

Evidence of the importance of glass beads as a cornerstone of the Louisiana colony's economy can be found in many historical sources. Mentions of glass beads are found in d'Iberville's journal from the early years of the colony and in the works of other authors, notably Jean-François-Benjamin Dumont de Montigny's *Mémoires historiques de la Louisiane* (1747) and Antoine-Simone Le Page du Pratz's *Histoire de la Louisiane* (1758). In the later accounts more information is shared about glass beads and how French and Native American communities used them, including the Tunica. I am interested in using these accounts to understand how glass beads were used for physical and metaphysical bodily care and in intimate, social relationships.

As I read through these sources to understand the intimate aspects of glass beads in the Louisiana colony, I drew inspiration from Stoler (2009, 3–4), who emphasizes the importance of the unwritten in the archive, not only hidden transcripts or subversive messages but also what went without saying about colonial life that people at the time understood in context. What is "unwritten" illuminates uncertainties and anxieties; such silences are telling regarding emergent ontologies and understandings of being. What is not said pertains to aspects of daily life that relied on presumed common sense (Stoler 2009). In reference to the colonial world, I am most interested in how how bodily work was recognized, defined, and described, particularly what was unwritten in the intimate connections between trade goods and bodily concerns.

What did eighteenth-century French missionaries, settlers, and government officials know about colonial bodies? How were social relationships and bodily concerns constituted through material goods, such as glass beads? In French texts, the bodies of Europeans, Native Americans, and Africans were differentiated by skin color, attire (or the lack thereof), types of adornment, how an individual comported him or herself, what religion an individual practiced, the social or economic status of the individual, gender, and occupation (Loren 2001, 2010, 2011, 2017; Sayre 1997; White 2013). French writers exhibit uncertainty in these texts, but not about Native American bodies. They seem uncertain about their own bodies, their clothing, how they should comport themselves in relationship to the bodies that surrounded them (White 2013). How the body was constituted through clothing and adornment signaled where an

Figure 11.1. Illustration of "Indian Woman Chief; Indian Woman; Young Woman" by Dumont de Montigny (1747). Source: Newberry Library, Chicago, VAULT Ayer MS 257, figure no. 4.

individual fit (or did not fit) into different categories (Loren 2001, 2011; White 2013). Artifacts of clothing and adornment were also related to other bodily concerns such as notions of belonging, health, and spirituality that were written and unwritten in historical texts.

Louisiana government officials and settlers requested supplies and the trade goods they needed. A compilation of requests made in 1701–1703 indicates that settlers and officials requested nearly 500 pounds of glass beads "for presents to be made to the Indians of said country" and "to give to persons dispatched to friendly nations" (Brain 1979, 289–295). The requests specified large and very small beads and requests 200 pounds of large violet and white beads (Brain 1979, 294). In 1734, an official requested nearly 2,500 pounds of beads, including "1500 lbs. white glass beads of the finest sort from Holland and 1000 [ibid] sky-blue and black" (Brain 1979, 298–299). Requests for specific sizes, colors, and qualities of beads, suggest what was unwritten: that French colonists and Native Americans needed certain colors and qualities of glass beads for the social interactions that were constituted in the exchange and use of these small objects.

More specific information about beads and bodily concerns is found in the accounts of Dumont de Montigny. In his *Mémoires historiques*, a watercolor illustrates how dark blue or black glass beads were worn around the neck of a female chief and a young woman (Figure 11.1). In the accompanying narrative, Dumont outlined the movement of glass beads in the colony. He wrote of a calumet ceremony: "At each phrase or each pause, the chief who is being honored expresses his thanks with the sound '*houis, houis*,' spoken from deep down in his belly. When this oration, or harangue, is finished, the chief is presented with his gifts: perhaps tanned deerskins, skins filled with oil; guns; shirts; glass beads; vermillion; knives; or sometimes even slaves" (quoted in Sayre and Zecher 2012, 342–343). Here, the exchange of glass beads was between chiefs, suggesting the importance of this item within and between neighboring communities. The items in this exchange were largely related to bodily care and work, such as shirts to cover bodies, guns to protect bodies, and vermillion to paint bodies, and even bodies themselves, in the case of slaves.

While this example provides some information about the interactions between bodies, economies, and objects, other sections of the narrative provide more specific information on intimate economies. In his discussion of women, Dumont noted:

> There were even some Indian women who came to offer themselves to the soldiers or habitants, to the officers and the sergeants, and this at a very cheap rate. But if you paid them a little more generously, such as with an *alconand* [petticoat] that cost eight livres at the king's storehouse, then the Indian woman served as your wife and your slave at once. She looked after the cooking, made the flour and the bread, both fluffed up the bed and helped to flatten it. Others hire themselves out for one or two days like field slaves, to pound the corn and make flour from it, and for this, very little, perhaps a handful of salt, a yard of ribbon, or an assortment of green, blue, red, white, or black beads such as on a rosary. (quoted in Sayre and Zecher 2012, 350)

Dumont's narrative suggests that the exchange of beads were not only payment for caring for bodies of others—preparing food, making beds, engaging in sexual acts—but were also used to attend to the bodily concerns of the individual who received them as payment. In the image, a chief and a young girl wear them around their necks as indications of status and age. But glass beads were also used in other intimate ways, some of which can be inferred from what was unwritten.

French descriptions of dances, healing ceremonies, and sexual comportment suggest other aspects of how glass beads attended to bodily concerns. Dumont detailed several dances and ceremonies in his narrative, distinguishing between different kinds of dances that were performed at funerals and at hunting, healing, and seasonal renewal ceremonies and festivals (Sayre and Zecher 2012, 340–344, 358–366). The sound of bodies in dance, movement, and song were as notable as the small items adorned with beads, bells, and claws that clinked during movement (Sayre and Zecher 2012, 341–342). For example, here is how Dumont described the movement of bodies during a calumet ceremony:

> The envoys are dressed up like real harlequins in their best outfits, most often with rattles hanging all around them and occasionally small bells, with feathers on their heads and faces painted red. . . . They walk altogether in a rhythm, dancing and holding the calumet aloft, keeping time with arm gestures, with their bodies and their feet, following the sound of one who beats the drum. . . . Thus they arrive singing and dancing. (Sayre and Zecher 2012, 342)

Bodies adorned with such items, such as glass beads, similarly clinked during dances, or any other kind of movement (Turgeon 2004, 37). What is unwritten in such accounts is the difference between Native American and French bodies in those moments. Schooled in Catholicism, French settlers, soldiers, and priests were taught to cover the flesh (and their shame), to move quietly through the landscape, and to hold their bodies in restraint (Loren 2001; Sayre 1997). French colonialists who left those conventions behind—such as the *coureurs des bois*—joined the ranks of the unclean; their French counterparts saw them as decidedly uncivilized and viewed them with fear and disdain (White 2012). But female Native American bodies adorned with beads and unrestrained by excess clothing suggested sexual freedom to the French and became the objects of their desire (White 2013, 82–84).

Similarly unwritten is the desire of the Tunica and other Native Americans to wear beads upon their bodies. In Dumont's narrative, he discussed how beads were payment for caring for other bodies. Objects received for bodily work were often worn on the bodies of indigenous peoples, becoming part of the embodiment of colonial selves. They materialized new social interactions and engagements, new ways of understanding their bodies in a colonial context. It is not coincidence that Native Americans chose glass beads so frequently when they could have chosen other kinds of European-manufactured items that included other items of clothing and adornment. Glass beads were entirely novel. Although they resembled beads Native Americans had long fashioned from marine shell, they had a particular power that came from their virtual indestructability and their translucent colors, particularly the blues that evoked the other-than-human realms of water and sky (Richter 2011, 122). Turgeon (2004, 35–36) has argued that glass beads were a particularly important aspect of dressing and adorning one's body with material culture because of the associations between beads and bodies, particularly as beads were often likened to eyes or light. The nuances of intimacy that are written and unwritten in historical accounts suggests an interpretation of glass beads far beyond that of trade good. They were a form of payment that was desired in intimate transactions and were worn on the body to create sound. These intimacies are found as residue in the material record and should be interpreted as such.

Glass Beads Recovered from the Trudeau Site

Among the eighteenth-century objects recovered from the Trudeau site, beads are notable. Over 190,000 were recovered (190,186 in total) (Brain 1979, 1988). Of these, 99.7 percent (189,676) are glass beads and the remaining 510 are made from shell, jet, fossil, carnelian, quartz, or cowry. Brain devised a new glass bead typology because he encountered varieties not accounted for in Kidd and Kidd's (1970) classic glass bead typology. Brain documented that nearly 100 different varieties of beads were recovered from Trudeau as part of a project to discuss distribution and place of manufacture (Brain 1979, 96–133; Brain 1988, 405).

If the intimacy of glass beads is to be considered, however, this assemblage needs to be examined through a different lens that pays particular attention to size, shape and color. Most of the glass beads (96 percent) were small to medium-sized (3–12 mm). Less than 1 percent were large to very large (12–20 mm). The predominant shape was rounded oval (62

Figure 11.2. White glass beads, Kidd and Kidd variety IVa13, Brain variety IVA1, PM 971-28-20/23933. Copyright 2018 President and Fellows of Harvard College, Peabody Museum of Archaeology and Ethnology, PM# 971-28-20/23933.

percent), but other shapes included donut, faceted, round, and raspberry. The most popular color was white, as the majority of the beads (just over 115,00) were a small compound rounded bead with an opaque white layer surrounding a clear core (Kidd and Kidd variety IVa13, Brain variety IVA1; Figure 11.2). Blue beads, including light and dark blue and turquoise, accounted for 24 percent of the assemblage, and burgundy beads accounted for 8 percent.

Glass beads were part of variety of clothing and adornment artifacts that have been recovered from the Trudeau site. The assemblage included shoe buckles, tinkler cones and janglers, brass bells, religious and secular jewelry, shell ear pins, and coat and sleeve buttons (Brain 1979, 1988). Tools used for making and mending clothing such as needles, thimbles, scissors, and pins were also part of the collection. The artifacts of clothing and adornment recovered from domestic and midden contexts suggest a mixing of different fashions in practice, while those recovered from burials suggest more purposeful combinations of different fashions.

Although glass beads were just one aspect of dress, the diversity of beads found at the site is striking; nearly 100 different varieties have been recovered. These beads are many colors, shapes, and sizes. This diversity underscores the importance of glass beads for the Tunica and suggests that different kinds of beads were likely needed for different bodies and activities, including spirituality and healing. The Tunica clearly preferred small, rounded white glass beads. The 1734 requests underscores this: it specified "1500 lbs. white glass beads of the finest sort from Holland" (Brain 1979, 298–299). What can be made of the importance placed on the color white?

Waselkov et al. (2015) have noted the resemblance of small white glass beads to pearls and shell. Only 120 beads made from marine shell exist in the Trudeau assemblage. While obtaining glass beads may have relieved some individuals of the labor associated with producing this material, there are other reasons why white beads were meaningful. Waselkov et al. (2015, 10) refer to the Bead Spitter myth recorded in nineteenth-century ethnographies of southeastern Native American mythologies (Lankford 2011). The Bead Spitter myth is the story of a being who had the ability to produce supernaturally powerful shell beads, sometimes by transforming water into shell (Lankford 2011, 189–191; see also Swanton 1929). People, notably women, would go to the Bead Spitter because they wanted white beads and often needed to perform to obtain them. That myth has resonance here in that while the intimacies of giving beads are different from intimacies of use, they are never considered trinkets or separate from the body.

Final Thoughts

Glass beads were essential material goods in economic and diplomatic relationships in the eighteenth century. More important for this discussion, however, glass beads were bodily objects that were used in intimate social entanglements. One could argue that glass beads were just objects of adornment, baubles the Tunica acquired so they could incorporate them into their dressing practices. As a bodily object, however, glass beads attended to tangible and intangible bodily concerns. They were given as payment for bodily work. They were worn in the hair and around wrists, ankles, and necks and were embroidered on clothing. In the archaeological record of the Tunica, they were recovered from middens, where they were lost or displaced, and from burials, where they accompanied a loved one. In this complicated colonial mess, glass beads embodied nuanced intimacies that went far beyond the realm of a trade good. Glass beads were worn to embody allegiance, wealth, age and status; to honor the living and the dead; and to promote health and cure sickness. They enabled the wearer to capture lightness and whiteness next to the body, using items that were not so easily or neutrally obtained as we have often interpreted when placing them in the category of trade.

There is still quite a bit left unwritten in this discussion. When we discuss the embodiment of material culture, we are still far from truly understanding lived experience in the eighteenth century. Our lived experience is a different kind of reality and we miss much when we try to understand the nuances of the past. We live with the residue of past archaeological interpretations and the legacies of typological categories. Even so, what is written and unwritten in historical sources and archaeological assemblages provides us with a greater understanding of how beads as a bodily object constituted intimate relationships in eighteenth-century Louisiana.

References Cited

Appadurai, Arjun, ed. 1986. *The Social Life of Things: Commodities in Cultural Perspective.* Cambridge: Cambridge University Press.

Beaudry, Mary C. 2006. *Findings: The Material Culture of Needlework and Sewing.* New Haven, CT: Yale University Press.

———. 2009. Bodkin Biographies. In *The Materiality of Individuality: Archaeological Studies of Individual Lives*, edited by Carolyn L. White, 95–108. New York: Springer.

Blair, Elliot H. 2017. Modeling Consumption: A Social Network Analysis of Mission Santa Catalina de Guale. In *Material Worlds: Archaeology, Consumption and the Road to Modernity*, edited by Barbara J. Heath, Eleanor E. Breen, and Lori A. Lee, 9–34. New York: Routledge.

Blair, Elliot H., Lorann S. A. Pendleton, and Peter Francis. 2007. *The Beads of St. Catherine's Island.* American Museum of Natural History Papers 89. New York: North American Archaeology Fund, American Museum of Natural History.

Brain, Jeffrey P. 1979. *Tunica Treasure.* Papers of the Peabody Museum of Archaeology and Ethnography 71. Cambridge, MA: Harvard University Press.

———. 1988. *Tunica Archaeology.* Papers of the Peabody Museum of Archaeology and Ethnography 78, Cambridge, MA: Harvard University Press.

Bridge, Gavin, and Adrian Smith. 2003. Intimate Encounters: Culture-Economy-Commodity. *Environment and Planning D: Society and Space* 21:257–268.

Brown, Kathleen M. 2009. *Foul Bodies: Cleanliness in Early America.* New Haven, CT: Yale University Press.

Chaplin, Joyce E. 2003. *Subject Matter: Technology, the Body, and Science on the Anglo-American Frontier, 1500–1676.* Cambridge, MA: Harvard University Press.

Cipolla, Craig N., ed. 2017. *Foreign Objects: Rethinking Indigenous Consumption in American Archaeology.* Tucson: University of Arizona Press.

Dawdy, Shannon Lee. 2009. *Building the Devil's Empire: French Colonial New Orleans.* Chicago: University of Chicago Press.

Dietler, Michael. 2010. *Archaeologies of Colonialism: Consumption, Entanglement, and Violence in Ancient Mediterranean France.* Berkeley: University of California Press.

Dillian, Carolyn D., and Carolyn L. White. 2009. *Trade and Exchange: Archaeological Studies from History and Prehistory.* New York: Springer.

Dumont de Montigny, Jean-François-Benjamin. 1747 *Mémoires historiques de la Louisiane contenant ce qui y est arrivé de plus mémorable depuis l'année 1687 jusqu'à present.* Paris: Claude Jean Baptiste Bauche.

Gosden, Chris. 2005. What Do Objects Want? *Journal of Archaeological Method and Theory* 12(3):183–211.

Greenwald, Erin M. 2013. *A Company Man: The Remarkable French-Atlantic Voyage of a Clerk for the Company of the Indies.* New Orleans: The Historic New Orleans Collection.

Hamell, George R. 1983. Trading and Metaphors: The Magic of Beads. In *Proceedings of the 1982 Glass Trade Bead Conference*, edited by Charles F. Hayes III, 5–28. Rochester, NY: Rochester Museum and Science Center Research Record.

Heath, Barbara, Eleanor E. Breen, and Lori A. Lee, eds. 2017. *Material Worlds: Archaeology, Consumption and the Road to Modernity.* New York: Routledge.

Joyce, Rosemary A. 2005. Archaeology of the Body. *Annual Review of Anthropology* 34(1):139–158.

Karklins, Karlis. 1985. *Glass Beads: The Nineteenth-Century Levin Catalogue and Venetian Bead Book and Guide to Description of Glass Beads.* Studies in Archaeology, Architecture, and History. Ottawa, Ontario: Environment Parks Canada.

———. 1992. *Trade Ornament Usage among the Native Peoples of Canada: A Source Book.* Ottawa, Ontario: Environment Parks Canada.

Kidd, Kenneth A., and Martha A. Kidd. 1970. A Classification System for Glass Beads for the Use of Field Archaeologists. *Canadian Historic Sites: Occasional Papers in Archaeology and History* 1:45–89.

Lankford, George E. 2011. *Native American Legends of the Southeast: Tales from the Natchez, Caddo, Biloxi, Chickasaw, and Other Nations.* Tuscaloosa: University of Alabama Press.

Le Page du Pratz, Antoine-Simone. 1758. *Histoire de la Louisiane.* Paris: Du Bure.

Lindman, Janet Moore, and Michele Lise Tarter. 2001. The Earthly Frame, a Minute Fabrick, a Centre of Wonders. In *A Centre of Wonders: The Body in Early America*, edited by Janet M. Lindman and Michele L. Tarter, 1–9. Ithaca: Cornell University Press.

Loren, Diana DiPaolo. 2001. Social Skins: Orthodoxies and Practices of Dressing in the Early Colonial Lower Mississippi Valley. *Journal of Social Archaeology* 1(2):172–189.

———. 2010. *The Archaeology of Clothing and Bodily Adornment in Colonial America.* Gainesville: University of Florida Press.

———. 2011. Fear, Desire, and Material Strategies in Colonial Louisiana. In *The Archaeology of Colonialism: Intimate Encounters and Sexual Effects*, edited by Barbara L. Voss and Eleanor Conlin Casella, 105–121. Cambridge: Cambridge University Press.

———. 2013. Considering Mimicry and Hybridity in Early Colonial New England: Health, Sin and the Body "Behung with Beades." *Archaeological Review from Cambridge* 28(1):151–168.

———. 2017. Christian Symbols in Native Lives: Medals and Crucifixes in the Tunica Region of French Colonial Louisiana. In *Foreign Objects: Rethinking Indigenous Consumption in American Archaeology*, edited by Craig N. Cipolla, 94–109. Tucson: University of Arizona Press.

Loren, Diana DiPaolo, and Mary C. Beaudry. 2006. Becoming American: Small Things Remembered. In *Historical Archaeology*, edited by Martin Hall and Stephen W. Silliman, 251–271. Oxford: Blackwell.

McWilliams, Richebourg Gaillard, ed. 1991. *Iberville's Gulf Journals.* Translated by Richebourg Gaillard McWilliams. Tuscaloosa: University of Alabama Press.

Mullins, Paul. 2011. The Archaeology of Consumption. *Annual Review of Anthropology* 40:133–144.

Panich, Lee M. 2014. Native American Consumption of Shell and Glass Beads at Mission Santa Clara de Asís. *American Antiquity* 79(4):730–748.

Richter, Daniel. 2011. *Before the Revolution: America's Ancient Pasts.* Cambridge, MA: Belknap Press of Harvard University Press.

Sayre, George M. 1997. *Les Sauvages Américains: Representations of Native Americans in French and English Colonial Literature.* Chapel Hill: University of North Carolina Press.

Sayre, George M., and Carla Zecher, eds. 2012. *The Memoir of Lieutenant Dumont, 1715–1747: A Sojourner in the French Atlantic.* Chapel Hill: University of North Carolina Press.

Silliman, Stephen W., and Thomas A. Witt. 2010. The Complexities of Consumption: Eastern Pequot Cultural Economics in Eighteenth-Century New England. *Historical Archaeology* 44(4):46–68.

Stoler, Laura Ann. 2009. *Along the Archival Grain: Epistemic Anxieties and Colonial Common Sense.* Princeton, NJ: Princeton University Press.

Swanton, John R. 1929. *Myths and Tales of the Southeastern Indians.* Bureau of American Ethnology Bulletin 88. Washington, DC: Smithsonian Institution.

Turgeon, Laurier. 2001. French Beads in France and Northeastern North America during the Sixteenth Century. *Historical Archaeology* 35(4):58–82.

———. 2004. Beads, Bodies and Regimes of Value: From France to North America, c. 1500–c. 1650. In *The Archaeology of Contact in Settler Societies*, edited by Tim Murray, 19–47. Cambridge: Cambridge University Press.

Usner, Daniel H. 1992. *Indians, Settlers and Slaves in a Frontier Exchange Economy: The Lower Mississippi Valley before 1783.* Chapel Hill: University of North Carolina Press.

Waselkov, Gregory A., David W. Morgan, and Billie Coleman. 2015. Ceramics and Glass Beads as Symbolic Mixed Media in Colonial Native North America. *BEADS: Journal of the Society of Bead Researchers* 27:3–15.

Voss, Barbara L., and Eleanor Conlin Casella, eds. 2011. *The Archaeology of Colonialism: Intimate Encounters and Sexual Effects.* Cambridge: Cambridge University Press.

White, Carolyn L., and Mary C. Beaudry. 2009. Artifacts and Personal Identity. In *International Handbook of Historical Archaeology*, edited by Teresita Majewski and David Gaimster, 209–225. New York: Springer.

White, Sophie. 2012. "To Ensure that He Not Give Himself Over to the Indians": Cleanliness, Frenchification, and Whiteness. *Journal of Early American History* 2 (2012):111–149.

———. 2013. *Wild Frenchmen and Frenchified Indians: Material Culture and Race in Colonial Louisiana.* Philadelphia: University of Pennsylvania Press.

Zelizer, Viviana A. 2005. *The Purchase of Intimacy.* Princeton, NJ: Princeton University Press.

12

Clandestine, Ephemeral, Anonymous?

Myths and Realities of the Intimate Economy of a Nineteenth-Century Boston Brothel

JADE LUIZ

Prostitution was illegal in nineteenth-century Boston, but that does not mean it did not thrive there, nor does it mean that brothels operated in secret or left little trace in the archaeological and documentary records. Analysis of archival and archaeological evidence pertaining to the 27–29 Endicott Street brothel in Boston's North End suggests that the residents of the brothel developed strategies for coping with the reality of being purchased for ostensibly intimate acts. Even though the brothel was advertised in a widely disseminated "sporting guide," the women who worked in and ran it used aliases to mask their true identities. Clients were provided with a wide array of ancillary services, such as special meals, wine, and drink that they consumed in an ersatz middle-class setting. These supplementary offerings suggest the clients purchase a particular style of fantasy experience in addition to intimate sexual acts. In such an intimate setting, it is perhaps unsurprising that presentation of self was key to the intimate economy of the brothel.

The anthropological concept of "intimate economies" concerns several factors regarding types of labor that are typically not included in a capitalist system. When one is intimate with someone, this closeness can be understood in physical, emotional, and cognitive ways (Hoffman and Moreno 2016, 1). While intimacy can be seen as private, inalienable, and noncommercialized, many scholars have identified the numerous ways that certain intimate exchanges can result in marketable "products," even if those products are nonmaterial. The opponents of the commercialization of intimacy claim that when intimacy is exchanged for money, the integrity between the body and the self is disrupted and that this disruption has psychological consequences (Hoffman and Moreno 2016). Many types of intimate labor, however, such as child care, housework, and nonmarket exchanges were vital to the precapitalist and preindustrial economy and continue to be as so economic systems shift.

Michael Hardt (1999) refers to intimate labor as "affective" or "caring labor," or acts that are traditionally seen as immaterial. Hardt notes that while "caring labor" is immersed in the corporeal, or experienced bodily, its production is still largely immaterial. He argues that the "products" of this affective labor are largely social networks and forms of community (Hardt 1999, 96). Hardt, however, is mostly focused on the labors performed predominantly by women within the traditional household. In many instances, "the intimate" has operated as shorthand for "the household." However, there is a potential for any intimate relations to become intertwined with the economic system.

In her discussion of migrant workers operating within an intimate economy, Nicole Constable defines intimate relations as "social relationships that are—or give the impression of being—physically and/or emotionally close, personal, sexually intimate, private, caring, or loving" (2009, 50). The caveat that these relationships may "give the impression" of being close in some way is significant to a study of the intimate economy of sex work. The relationship between sex workers and their clients can be viewed as a "performance" in which a sex worker might feign love to mask the economic exchange and the benefits they receive. Some scholars further define this relationship in terms of "bounded authenticity," or constructions of romantic intimacy based on historical expectations (Constable 2009, 55).

In viewing current intimate economies, Ara Wilson notes that intimate identities and relationships have been and continue to be centrally involved in the operations of modernizing markets (Wilson 2004, 6). In this sense, the "features of people's daily lives" (such as social identities and relationships) which, through their practice, have come to seem non-economic, are economically crucial. By calling them "intimate economies," Wilson proposes that the deeply felt orientations and entrenched practices that make up personal and private lives and individual selves are not separate from economic systems (Wilson 2004, 6).

Despite the apparently intimate nature of sex work, historical archaeologists often frame discussions of sites where formal prostitution took place in terms of how they are distinct from other intimate spaces, such as working- or middle-class, private, domestic homes. As early researchers discovered, many of the archaeological assemblages that make up sites of organized prostitution (such as brothels) share most (if not all) of their material record with contemporary domestic households (i.e., Seifert 1991; Meyer et al. 2005; Foster et al. 2005). Understanding this, earlier archaeologists distinguished brothel sites from surrounding domestic deposits based on the numbers of fine or expensive dining wares and fixtures (i.e., Foster et. al. 2005; Seifert 1991; Seifert et al. 2000; Spude 2005; Yamin 2005), exotic food types (Costello 2003; Dixon 2005), and increased quantities of medical bottles (i.e., Costello 2003; Ketz et al. 2005; Seifert 1991).

Researchers in the archaeology of prostitution have largely moved away from this basic classification and have been more generally interested in questions related to how people used these spaces. One of the most challenging elements that archaeologists have encountered, however, deals with the difficulties inherent in determining the artifacts that relate to public, "front-stage" brothel space and behind-the-scenes, "backstage" brothel space (Burnette 2014; Fisher and Loren 2003; Gallagher 2014; Keim 2013; Ketz et al. 2005; Meyer et al. 2005; Spude 2005; Yamin 2005). In some research, the distinction between the two is more achievable, such as the difference between the presentation of self outside and inside the brothel space (Keim 2013). Additional research has been done to try to distinguish artifacts related to the "front-stage" brothel patrons, and the "backstage" life of prostitutes by isolating artifacts related only to women and those related only to men (Ketz et al. 2005). Gendering objects is problematic for several reasons (Dawdy and Weyhing 2008). However, it is even more difficult to determine what would be used only in "front-stage" space and what only "behind-the-scenes" when objects are recovered from mixed contexts such as privies because of the way that brothel economy is structured.

The distinction between which artifacts are used privately and which are used in the semi-public brothel parlor also concerns archaeologists interested in exploring how prostitution reflected social issues contemporary to when a brothel was in operation. Problems such as the perception of the morality of impoverished women have been examined through the analysis of infanticide in the nineteenth century and its association with promiscuity (Crist 2005). Public discomfort with prostitution can be reflected through zoning laws throughout the urban landscape in order to control prostitution within "red-light" districts (Charles 2014) or in legislation that limited the public visibility of prostitutes (Graham 1998).

Archaeologists have also worked to change common perceptions about different social groups through their analysis of brothel space and how it was manipulated. For example, cultural stereotypes, such as the association of the French with heightened sexuality (Dawdy and Weyhing 2008) led some researchers to assume that associated spaces are brothels even when they are not. Additionally, in spaces African Americans owned in the nineteenth century, expensive décor and middle-class organization of a social space was used to challenge contemporary, racist assumptions about black business owners (Dixon 2005). In Jamie Arjona's piece on *jook* houses in the rural South, she proposes that the concept of "crookedness" in early twentieth-century black parlance can be used interchangeably with queerness (or, in the queer theory sense of the word, the disruption of the heteronormative). While *jook* houses were not always synonymous with prostitution, in some circumstances, they were casual centers that provided food, beverages, gambling, music, prostitution, and "a general good time" (Arjona 2017, 50). The commonness of *jook* houses in private homes obfuscates what constituted domestic contexts and "further disintegrated the foundation of home as the core of nuclear family" in the rural African American experience (Arjona 2017, 51).

While the above concepts can seem intimate and private, the nature of the spaces being explored were often characterized by a lack of privacy and a monetization of intimate experiences, or Constable's concept of "bounded authenticity." It is unlikely that any visitor to a nineteenth-century brothel would have felt they were entering a purely private environment, especially in "parlor" houses, where guests would congregate while waiting for their turn or choosing prostitutes, and because of the economic negotiation that they would need to make with the madam upon entering the space. At the same time, the madam kept tight control over the fantasy environment of the brothel through how the space was organized, through the presentation of the women who worked for her, and through her relationship with the world outside the brothel walls. The brothel at 27–29 Endicott Street was not unusual for a nineteenth-century urban brothel in this regard.

The Brothel Privy at 27–29 Endicott Street

In 1993, archaeologists excavated the remains of a double-chambered, brick-lined privy associated with the lot in Boston's North End where 27–29 Endicott Street once stood. This excavation was carried out as archaeological cultural resources management mitigation for the Big Dig project that placed Boston's central artery highway underground in the late 1990s (Cheek and Balicki 2000). Although the focus of the excavation was the eighteenth-century Mill Pond site (Figure 12.1), a privy dating to the middle of the nineteenth century was exposed and voluntarily excavated as a salvage effort. Researchers later discovered that the privy fill dated to the period 1853 to 1867, when the building at 27–29 Endicott Street housed a brothel run by three subsequent madams (Table 12.1). Of the over 8,000 individual artifacts recovered, researchers identified a minimum of 343 ceramic vessels, 290 glass vessels, and numerous other artifact types related to décor, dress, dining, and entertainment.

While the data collected on the artifacts recovered from the privy at 27–29 Endicott Street are very detailed, analyzing sub-assemblages of

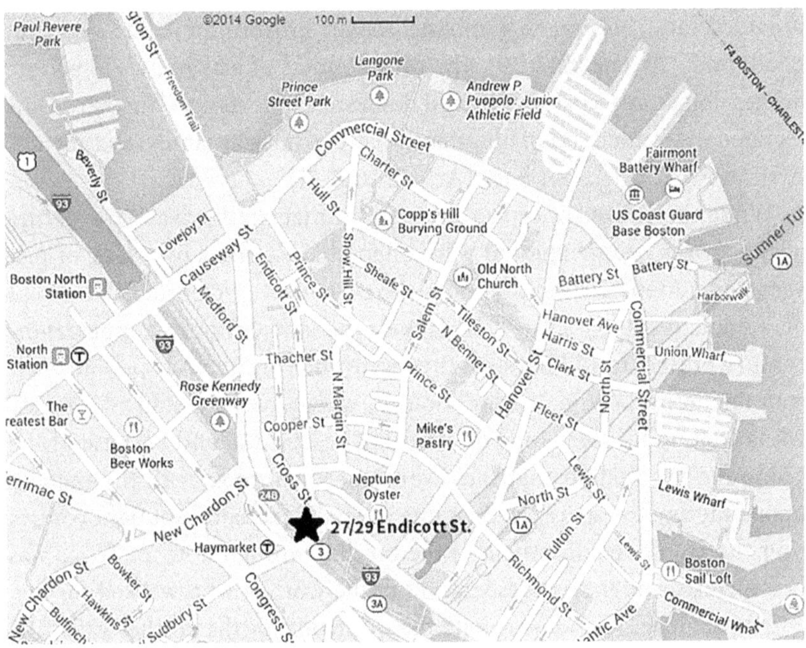

Figure 12.1. Location of 27–29 Endicott Street indicated by star on modern map of Boston. Source: Google Maps.

Table 12.1. Women employed at 27–29 Endicott Street during its use as a brothel

Name	Age	Occupation	Place of birth
1855			
[Mary] A. Adams	35	None	Vermont
Mary Colby	20	None	Ireland
Margaret Sullivan	28	None	Ireland
Eliza McMohan	22	None	Vermont
Catherine Manlin	18	None	New Hampshire
J. Ordinay	17	None	Maine
Ellen Pinkham	22	None	New Hampshire
Jane Clark	19	None	Massachusetts
J. Morton	20	None	Massachusetts
Eliza Thompson	21	None	Rhode Island
1860			
Louisa Cline [Cowen]	31	None	Massachusetts
Anna Hamilton	24	None	New Hampshire
Fannie Roberts	19	Milliner	Massachusetts
Eva Clark	17	None	Massachusetts
Eba Heath	22	Dressmaker	Maine
Anna Heath	19	Dressmaker	Maine
Adeline Jones	25	Domestic	Massachusetts
Sarah Hill	24	Domestic	Massachusetts
1865			
Louisa L. Cowen	35	None	Vermont
Dora Adams	23	None	England
Emma Healy	20	None	Ireland
Carrie Allen	23	None	Nova Scotia
Jennie Franklin	19	None	New York
Lottie Forrest	21	None	Vermont
Mary Lake[1]	24	None	Maine
Esther Cameron	20	None	Maine
Margaret Hobo	28	Servant	Nova Scotia

Sources: Massachusetts state census, 1855, Suffolk County, Massachusetts, population schedule, Boston, Ward 3, vol. 33, dwelling 1075, family 2187, A Adams. Microform, reel 24, New England Historic Genealogical Society, Boston, Massachusetts; U.S. federal census, 1860, Washington County, Maine, population schedule, Perry, page 49, dwelling 367, family 342, John Doyle, NARA microfilm publication M653, roll 454; Massachusetts state census, 1865, Suffolk County, Massachusetts, population schedule, Boston, Ward 3, vol. 31, dwelling 128, family 197, Louisa Cowen, microfilm reel 28, New England Historic Genealogical Society, Boston, Massachusetts.

Note: 1. Mary Lake is listed the following year in the Boston tax valuation as the primary resident associated with the property. Her occupation was recorded as "prostitution." She married William Padelford in 1867 and continued to reside at 27–29 for several more years.

items related to practices of everyday life, as Mary Beaudry has proposed (2013), has the potential to lead to greater depth of interpretation of the daily lived experience of people who occupied brothel spaces. Studying objects with an eye toward how they were habitually used together in everyday life not only provides a practical examination of object use-life but also contributes a possible way of exploring the "synesthesia" of sensory experience or the reality that many senses are used together in perceiving and may not be restricted to the Aristotelian five-sense schema of sight, sound, taste, touch, and smell (Beaudry 2013, 187; Day 2013; Hamilakis 2013). When artifacts are classified into appropriate sub-assemblages (e.g., dining, entertainment, personal hygiene), those sub-assemblages can be examined in relation to contemporary literature and considerations of where types of space fall on a spectrum of private to public. Because most of the goods used and consumed at the brothel would have figured in the brothel's economy, these sub-assemblages can be used to interpret the types of activities related to dining, drinking, and other forms of consumption at the Endicott Street brothel and to begin to understand how recovered objects contributed to the experience of visiting the brothel.

The artifacts associated with the embodied acts and practices of the women involved in the sex trade at 27–29 Endicott most significantly intersect with an archaeology of the senses as defined by Yannis Hamilakis (2013) and Jo Day (2013). Sensory data (such as information about textures, colors, and fragrances) has the potential to strengthen our understanding of why certain objects might have been acquired and used in the brothel. Decisions made because of factors such as what was socially fashionable, what was representative of prevailing health knowledge, and so forth, contributed to efforts the madam made in order to establish a successful brothel economy. Additionally, because the women who lived and worked at the Endicott Street brothel constructed their identities through everyday practices and through negotiating a variety of social rules and resources (Conkey and Gero 1997; Silliman 2001), artifacts related to the presentation of self can have multiple meanings and interpretations. Artifacts such as perfume, cosmetics, vaginal syringes, medicine and treatments, and breast shields used during nursing can be read as charged markers that indicate ideas about health (or the lack thereof), maternity, morality, and domesticity carried by Boston's white middle class. Even artifacts related to clothing and attire, such as the bone corset grommets recovered from the privy, can give us a great deal of information about the relationship of an individual's body to her clothes and how she was projecting herself within the brothel space and, more generally, within Boston's urban landscape.

We cannot cleanly separate material into front of house spaces (spaces dedicated to erotic performance) and back of house spaces (spaces for preparing for work and for nonwork activities). The fact that we have little historical information about how brothel spaces were used means that we do not know whether certain brothel users (clients, madams, prostitutes, etc.) would have encountered certain objects, let alone whole sub-assemblages, during their movement through the brothel environment. Instead, it is more useful to focus on how women might have used sub-assemblages or objects for the purpose of satisfying customers and creating fantasies.

Bostonians have never had a static relationship with prostitution. As social movements rose and fell in strength, perceptions of vice changed. Boston's relationship with sex work, however, might be different from that of other urban centers because the founding principles of Puritanism shaped much of Boston society, even after the Puritans lost much of their social and political power at the end of the seventeenth century (Hobson 1990, 15). The extreme repression of sexual activity outside marriage (it could be punished in Puritan Boston with public whippings) influenced the creation of anti-fornication laws and the election of a series of mayors who were either vocal in support of the eradication of prostitution or looked the other way when rioters attacked red light districts. Because of fluctuations in public sensibilities about prostitution, managers of brothels needed to be able to read where the boundaries of social respectability lay and navigate them while carrying out their illegal trade. Houses that catered to middle-class and wealthier men needed to provide an atmosphere of safety and anonymity that did not attract the attention of reform activists and law enforcement.

In the nineteenth century, prostitution operated on a spectrum that reflected the cost and environment of services offered. William Sanger's 1859 report on prostitution in New York identified five classes of prostitution (Sanger 1972, 549): expensive, first-class parlor houses; second-class houses; "public" third-grade houses with a saloon at the entrance; fourth-class houses; and streetwalkers. Although Sanger described "houses of assignation," where unmarried couples might rent a room together or a prostitute and her client might meet, he did not describe kept mistresses, the highest class of sex workers, or the "crib" prostitutes who rented a room that they might have shared in shifts with another prostitute and would have occupied a position just above streetwalkers. Sanger distinguished the different classes of prostitution based on the cost of the house's furnishings, the refinement and cleanliness of the women who worked in a house, and the degree of privacy and discreetness a house provided to visitors.

There is evidence that Boston sex workers moved fluidly from brothel to brothel throughout the city and among brothels in major East Coast cities. Kate Austin, who in 1870 was the madam of a second-class house at 121 Crosby Street in New York (Anonymous 1870, 24), ranged widely along the eastern seaboard. Her biography in an 1865 "sporting guide" indicates that she began her career under Madame Philip Emerald of Boston, then moved to Mary Ann Hall's house in Washington, DC, for a year, then went to 197 Greene Street in New York, then returned to Boston, where she worked for the madam "Mitty Cowen, in Endicott Street" (likely Louisa Cowen, the second madam at 27–29 Endicott Street). By 1865, she had returned to New York and was living at 618 Broadway Street (Anonymous 1865, 57). Five years later, she was running her own house in Boston.

"A First Class House, Handsomely Furnished": The Material Fantasy of a Brothel Economy

A brothel economy is predicated as much on the creation of fantasy as it is on the sale and purchase of sexual favors. The number of ancillary services (such as food, drinks, and entertainment) a brothel offers is directly tied to its ranking. Cribs offered only basic sexual favors without any amenities. At the other end of the spectrum, the highest-class parlor houses were opulent and well appointed. They often had differently themed rooms, they sold expensive alcohol to the patrons, and they may have had hired entertainment, such as the piano "professors" in New Orleans (Rose 1974, 103). This type of house would have had the highest ranking in the prostitution hierarchy. Several different threads of evidence suggest that the brothel at 27–29 Endicott Street was in the middle range of that hierarchy, perhaps a second-class house in Sanger's ranking. It was neither as cheap as one of the raucous brothels on North Street just a few blocks east that the police frequently raided nor as expensive and elite as some of the contemporary parlor houses recorded in the guidebooks of cities such as New York and Washington, DC.

In *The Gentleman's Directory*, most of the "first-class houses" are described as "exquisitely furnished." For example, the entry for "Miss Jennie Creagh" at 17 Amity Street describes the furnishings, noting that it was splendid "from top to bottom, sparing neither expense nor labor to render it a palace of beauty forever, with it's [*sic*] French mirrors, English and Brussels carpets, rosewood furniture, superb bedding and everything in character" (Anonymous 1870, 28). Neither Jennie Creagh nor the women she employed were mentioned. Entries such as this are common in this guide. It is as though the sexual services on offer were inconsequential in comparison to the sumptuous surroundings. In the rare instances in which an author mentioned the women who worked in these spaces, he referred to them as "cheerful," "lovely," or "full of wit."

The fantasies madams and brothel employees created could be far more subtle. In their 2001 discussion of interpretive archaeology, Adrian and Mary Praetzellis describe an 1890s brothel deposit in Los Angeles that exhibits evidence of the less fashionable heavy ostentation of high-Victorian decoration. The gaudy parlor decorations, formal and highly decorated tablewares, and ornate oil lamps suggested to Praetzellis and Praetzellis (2001, 652) that the house was purposefully decorated in an exaggerated Victorian style. Praetzellis and Praetzellis hypothesized that the management of this brothel created an atmosphere of familiarity for its patrons. Although the brothel's primary business was selling sex, the atmosphere of leisure and Victorian familiarity provided the illusion that the men visiting the brothel were not engaged in a business transaction. A fantasy of domestic comfort was created for the men who visited.

The brothel at 27–29 Endicott Street also appears to have created a fantasy atmosphere of comfortable mid-nineteenth century domesticity. The objects recovered from the 27–29 Endicott Street privy include highly decorated teawares and dinner wares and cut and pressed table glass and lighting glass. The three most common types of ceramics recovered from the Endicott Street privy are ironstone, transfer-printed whiteware or pearlware, and blue shell-edged pearlware. Of these, a minimum of sixty-nine vessels are decorated teawares, many of which match others in the deposit, suggesting sets rather than individual purchases. The largest recovered set bears the Charles Meigh blue transfer-printed pattern called

Figure 12.2. Tivoli pattern tea bowl and saucer produced by Charles Meigh in the period 1843 to 1855. Note the serious imperfections in the transfer, especially around the rim of the tea bowl. Photo by Jade Luiz.

Tivoli. Eight nearly intact tea bowls and four saucers in this pattern were identified (Figure 12.2). Because this pattern was produced only from 1843 to 1855, it was likely purchased during the early years of the brothel, although it might have been purchased second-hand or at a discount later. However, most of the transfer-printed vessels have flaws in the transfer, such as spots of blurring or wrinkles in the pattern. In Penny Crook's examination of ceramic quality and consumer decision making, she notes that consumers in 1770 could save as much as 50 percent on imperfect ceramics (Crook 2011, 585). The "seconds market," or the sale of substandard crockery and other goods, thrived into the middle of the nineteenth century. Being able to evaluate and choose ceramics prudently from the selection of flawed goods had a certain social cachet in the communities that took advantage of the seconds market (Crook 2011, 584). While transfer-decorated wares are hardly high-cost goods, the presence of so many flawed vessels suggests that the brothel manager likely purchased cheaper versions in quantity.

Despite the prevalence of flawed transfer-printed wares, it appears as though distinctions were made in the brothel between sets for tea or coffee and sets for dining. Of the ninety-eight plates, soup plates, and serving dishes, the largest number are blue transfer-printed like the teawares

Table 12.2. Minimum number of plate forms by type (measurements from Miller 1980)

	Dinner (10")	Soup (9")	Lunch (8")	Twiffler (4–7")	Muffin (> 4")	Saucer types	Total
UNDECORATED							
Whiteware/pearlware	5	1	5	1	0	27	39
WHITE MOLDED							
Whiteware/pearlware	0	0	1	0	0	1	2
TRANSFER PRINTED							
Whiteware/pearlware	2	1	8	5	11	16	43
Ironstone	6	3	1	0	5	15	30
Porcelain	0	0	0	0	4	0	4
Yellow ware	0	0	0	1	0	0	1
HANDPAINTED							
Whiteware/pearlware	0	0	1	0	0	3	4
Shell-edged	1	1	6	3	0	0	11
Total plate forms	14	6	22	10	20	62	134

discussed above. Only eleven of the thirty-one transfer-printed plates are dinner plates, however (Table 12.2). With the exception of two dinner plates and a soup plate, all transfer-printed plates are luncheon-sized plates and smaller. In contrast, most of the eleven blue shell-edged plates are luncheon-sized or larger; this assemblage includes only three smaller, twiffler-sized plates.[1] The ironstone and undecorated whiteware recovered from the privy was a mix of all sizes. It is likely that the smaller transfer-printed plates were used to serve small snacks or desserts with tea. The quantity of both teawares and small plates suggests that visitors to the brothel were served tea with dishes that would not have been out of place in a contemporary middle-class household. The plainer blue shell-edged pearlware, undecorated whiteware, and ironstone might be what the women who lived and worked at the brothel used when their clients were not around.

Although the minimum number of alcohol bottles is surprisingly small, whiskey flasks predominated in the bottles that were recovered, suggesting a preference for whiskey over ale and wine. Of the sixteen confirmed alcohol bottles, five were wine or champagne bottles (at least two are likely champagne, as two champagne corks were recovered), ten were figured whiskey flasks, and one was a case gin bottle. Considering the minimum of forty-three colorless glass tumblers identified (twenty-five of which are fluted and appear to match each other) alongside the numerous teawares identified, it is likely that much of the brothel space must have represented the typical parlor of the period, a place where visitors and prostitutes socialized, and perhaps while being entertained with music, gambling, or erotic performances and games.

Historical descriptions of brothel spaces suggest that they were an alternate site of homosocial male bonding, similar to gentlemen's clubs. In his analysis of prostitution in New York City, Thomas Gilfoyle suggests that the emergence of male "sporting culture" in the 1830s promoted male aggressiveness and promiscuity. This culture was organized around various forms of gaming such as gambling and pugilism and other blood sports. Gilfoyle argues that for sporting men, respectable heterosexuality was associated with femininity and female control, whereas prostitution, sexual display, and entertainment signified the masculinity of youthful bachelorhood (Gilfoyle 1992, 99). The institutions that supported commercial sex promoted male camaraderie and sexual fraternity. The domestic parlors of the 27–29 Endicott Street brothel would have allowed for conversation and jovial competition (both recreationally and sexually) among the men who visited there. The presence of teawares and a limited access to alcohol suggests that the madams who managed the brothel sought to establish an atmosphere of civility.

Unfortunately, only a few of the purely decorative elements of the brothel space were recovered: two vases and a figurine of an 1830s couple walking arm in arm. However, other means of interpreting the ambiance of the space can be inferred from the objects recovered. An important element of the sensory experience of any space, but one that is often overlooked, is the effect of the quality of light in a room. The quality, brightness, and color of light can better illuminate something or make blemishes less visible. It can affect the mood and overall comfort of the room's occupants. Many sources of light were important at the Endicott Street brothel. Fragments of lamp bases, chimneys, and shades are well represented in the assemblage, as are numerous smaller finger lamps, or small portable oil lamps with chimneys and sometimes shades (Figure 12.3). In addition to these obvious light sources, mirror fragments were also recovered and many of the other glass artifacts (such as bowls, dishes, and drinking glasses) are cut or pressed glass that would have reflected the light in different ways than unadorned glass vessels.

Figure 12.3. Font of glass finger lamp. Photo by Jade Luiz.

Unexpectedly, of the thirteen identified lamp fonts, seven belong to finger lamps. This provides an evocative image of what it must have been like to move through the brothel. It is possible that the madam and the prostitutes who worked in the brothel used light to control the spaces where clients were allowed to enter. In a dark hallway, before the ubiquity of gas lighting, a visitor unfamiliar with the space would have to rely on access to light as he moved through the halls. The presence of the lamps also serves as a reminder of the dangers women faced who traditionally worked in darkness. On January 1855, a newly laid gas line at a brothel at 176 Endicott Street caused an explosion so severe that it blew out one wall of the structure as well as numerous doors and windows. Contemporary newspaper accounts vary widely, but the most common explanation appears to be that one of the women working at the brothel, Frances Craig, entered a room with a lit lamp, igniting trapped gas from a leaky gas line.

She suffered severe burns, and another woman, Matilda Pinteaux, injured her arm when the blast knocked her down the stairs.[2] One of the articles reporting on the explosion reminded its readers of another mishap with a lamp that had occurred at the same location. In May 1851, during an altercation, Martin Waldron assaulted a prostitute named Medora Webster with an oil lamp. When the lamp broke, much of Medora's face, chest, and arms were severely burned. She later succumbed to her injuries.[3]

"Very Pretty [and Clean] Girls": Economic Considerations of the Body

The bodily presentation of women in the brothel would have been just as vital to the creation of fantasy the brothel economy relied on. Because of this, the women at the 27–29 Endicott Street brothel daily embodied the practices of prostitution and presented their bodies as desirable commodities (Figure 12.4). These women likely used several strategies to cope with being viewed primarily as sexual objects to be bought and sold. One of the more materially present strategies is through choices in dress. It is highly probable that the prostitutes at 27–29 Endicott Street came from working-class backgrounds. Two of the three madams, Louisa Cowen and Mary Lake, came from low-income farming families. Several gold and gold-filled pieces of jewelry were recovered from the privy deposit, as were a black glass and copper alloy crucifix and faceted glass beads that likely would have been used in jewelry or to decorate items of clothing. Louisa Cowen made several bequests of clothing and jewelry in a will she wrote in 1865. She left her "plaid gown, cloak, and bonnet" to her sister-in-law and stipulated that her other clothes were "to be equally divided" between her two sisters. She left all of her "black jewelry" to one of her sisters and bracelets and a neck chain to a niece.[4] Most interesting for this analysis is the fact that she bequeathed a gold crucifix to Mary Lake, the madam who succeeded her and apparently had worked for Louisa for a short time before Louisa's death.[5] This bequest is intriguing because it speaks to Mary's religious affiliation (she was buried in a Catholic cemetery in Malden, Massachusetts) and because the transfer of an item of great personal significance illustrates a meaningful relationship between two women.

The authors of sporting guides for men often noted that the women who worked in brothels dressed tastefully and elegantly. Women who worked in higher-end brothels such as the one at 27–29 Endicott likely used dress to justify their choice of profession to other working-class women. Nell

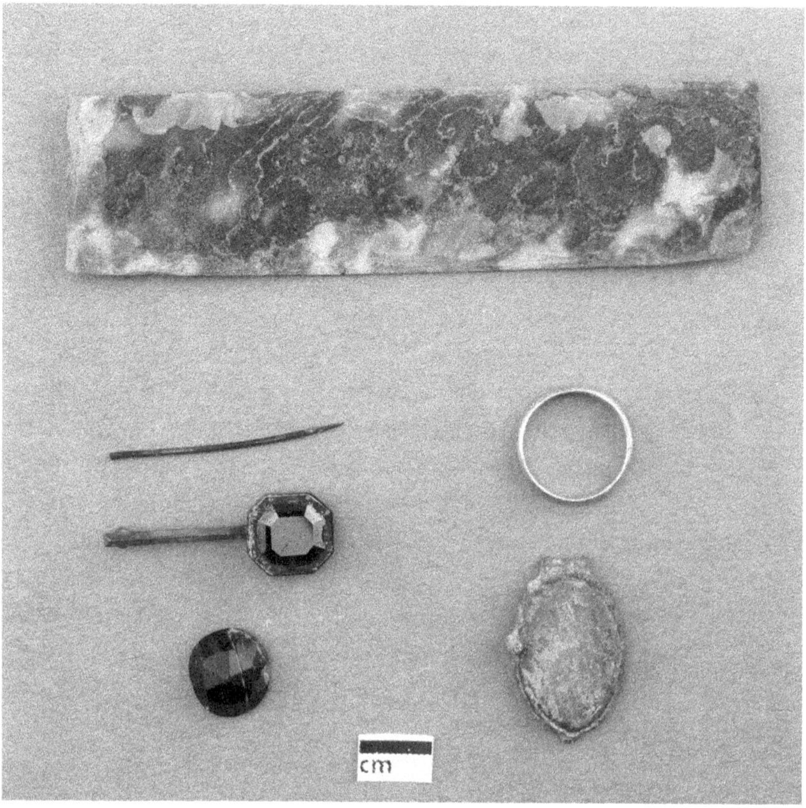

Figure 12.4. Various elements of personal adornment: (*top*) tortoise-shell hair ornament, (*clockwise from bottom left*) faceted jet bead, gold-filled pin with faceted glass gem, gold ring, glass-fronted locket fragment. Photo by Jade Luiz.

Kimball remarked in *Nell Kimball: Her Life as an American Madam* that much of a prostitute's income in a high-class house would be spent on the latest fashion in dress. She claimed that the women who worked at the most elite brothels often popularized certain fashions (Kimball 1970, 89). Sadly, little detail could be determined about the garments the women of 27–29 Endicott Street wore. Although precedent exists for good textile preservation in Boston privies (see Heck and Balicki 1998), textile preservation at 27–29 Endicott was poor. Leather was present, however, in the form of women's indoor shoes (Stevens and Ordoñez 2005). Sixty-one buttons were recovered, of which thirty-eight were undecorated white porcelain, bone, or shell and were one centimeter in diameter or smaller. This suggests a high loss of underwear buttons, which is unsurprising in a privy deposit. Many of the remaining buttons were made of colored glass and or were ceramic or cuprous with molded designs. These buttons would have added a decorative element to a garment.

The bodies of the prostitutes who worked in reputable houses were expected to be clean and free from disease. The prevention or treatment of venereal disease would have been of primary importance for both the women sex workers and the patrons who purchased sexual favors. The recovery of bottles containing treatments for venereal diseases and abortifacients such as copaiba oil and thirty-nine body and plunger pieces of vaginal syringes provides evidence that the women at 27–29 Endicott were actively coping with the dangers of disease and pregnancy. Medicine bottles are also present in the assemblage, including twelve patent medicine bottles and five apothecary bottles. Like the alcohol bottles at this site, patent medicine is remarkably underrepresented. Those that are present vary widely. Some of the patent medicine bottles contained Doctor Marshall's Snuff, a product aimed at combating congestion. Other products were for external use, such as Doctor Tobias's Venetian Liniment. Although it is important to remember that the privy provides only a limited sample, it seems unlikely that the women of 27–29 Endicott were self-medicating with "cure-all" patent medicines containing mostly alcohol and narcotics such as opium and cocaine.

There is evidence that the women working at 27–29 Endicott Street were expected to have sweet-smelling breath and skin. Researchers have identified many different artifact types in the collection related to personal hygiene. Even though concern with oral hygiene was low in the mid-nineteenth century, researchers identified several fragments of bone toothbrushes and at least three bottles of Van Buskin's Fragrant Sozodont, an early tooth powder (Figure 12.5). Other cosmetic items such as French and American perfume bottles were recovered from the site, as were items that might have been perfumed such as powders or skin tonics. These products would have contributed to the non-visible narrative of the woman who used them. Which perfume a woman chose contributed to how brothel clients and her co-workers perceived her. As the perfume warmed and evaporated during the wearing, the scent would transform. It was often customary for regular patrons of brothels to present gifts of perfume to their favorite prostitutes (Kimball 1970, 78). In such cases, the prostitute would wear the intimate sexual expectations of the patron on her skin for hours.

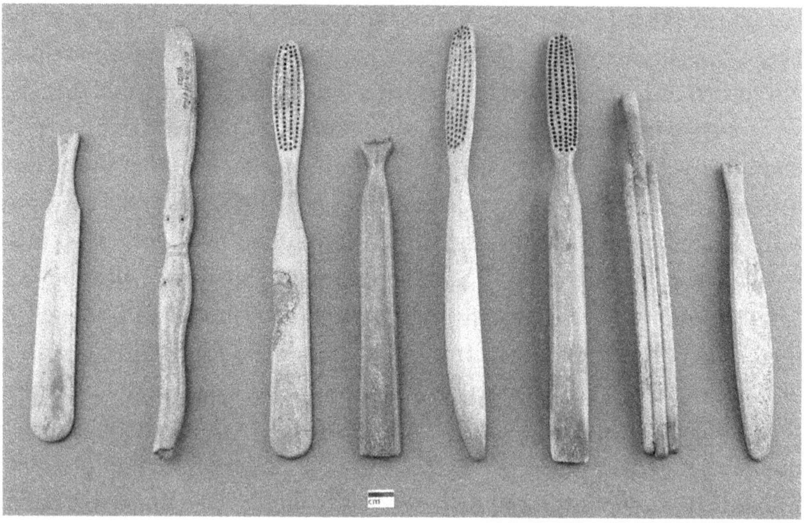

Figure 12.5. Bone toothbrush fragments. Photo by Jade Luiz.

Cleanliness and the appearance of cleanliness was clearly important to the women of 27–29 Endicott Street. The ceramic assemblage includes nine wash basins and nineteen pitchers or water jugs. Other items for preparing the *toilette* include combs for removing lice and for dressing the hair.

"Real People—Not Objects": Obfuscation and the Economy of Sex Work

Women engaged in sex work would often adopt aliases and reported different names, ages, or places of birth to government officials. For example, the longest-serving madam at the house, Louisa Cowen, would variably report her name as "Louisa Cowan," "Cowant," and "Cline" in tax records, to census takers, and to compilers of city directories. Her will gives some clues to her history; it reveals that she was the youngest daughter of farmers in Wells, Vermont. While she died young (at the age of 27 according to her grave marker), in contrast to what many nineteenth-century morality narratives about prostitution forewarned, she did not die friendless.[6] Cowen returned to her home shortly before she died and was buried in the family plot in Wells. In 1856, the year after she took on the running of the brothel at 27–29 Endicott Street, Cowen purchased her parents' farm but allowed them to continue living and working on it for the cost of the taxes; her parents were able to keep any profit that the farm generated.[7] No record of Louisa's marriage has been found, but it is possible that she was married to the painter Henry Cowen sometime before 1855. His death from heart disease was reported at 27 Endicott Street in that year.[8] It is unclear whether the two were actually married or if Louisa merely adopted his surname as a convenience to legitimize their relationship—if they had any relationship at all. It is entirely possible that in fabricating her "madam" name, Louisa took inspiration from the young man who died at the brothel (for examples of name fabrication, see Abbott 2007, 43).

An even more complicated example is the four different surnames the last madam, Mary Lake, used. According to her death certificate, her maiden name was Mary Doyle, but in earlier records such as the 1860 Maine census, she was listed with her family under the name Mary Lake. As there is no record of her marriage, it is possible that she was attempting to conceal the illegitimate birth of her son George, who was reported as George Doyle in Maine in the 1860 federal census[9] and as George Lake ten years later, when he joined his mother at Endicott Street.[10] Mary Lake was first recorded at 27–29 Endicott as a prostitute under Louisa Cowen in the 1865 Massachusetts census, but tax records and a city directory for the next year indicate that she had taken over as madam following Cowen's death.[11] In 1867 she married a homeopathic doctor named William Padelford and took his last name.[12] They continued to live at the property (which appears to have been operated as a boardinghouse instead of a brothel because of the presence of two other families with children[13] and a police officer[14]) until around 1876, when they moved a few blocks away to Portland Street. The following year, Mary began reporting her last name as Brown to census takers, in city directories, and on tax documents. William Padelford died at the Portland Street address in 1888.[15] There is no indication that Mary and William had divorced or that she had remarried, so it is likely that she was using an alias during this time. When Mary died in Cambridge in 1903, both her death certificate and the burial record in Holy Cross Cemetery in Malden, Massachusetts, listed her name as Mary Padelford.[16] She likely returned to her married name sometime after she moved from 88 Portland Street.

Records of women at 27–29 Endicott indicate that women in sex work intentionally reported their ages falsely. While one might assume that prostitutes would have said they were younger than they were, the madams of 27–29 Endicott Street did just the opposite. Mary Lake provides a good example. When she was first recorded at the property in 1865, she was recorded as age 24.[17] Two years later, when she was the madam of the brothel and was married to William Padelford, the age on the marriage certificate was 34. By 1870, when she had theoretically turned to a life of respectable domesticity, the census reported her age as 29. Despite the issues associated with age reporting in the historical record, Mary's 1865 and 1870 recorded ages more closely match those given on earlier and later documents than the age reported on her marriage record. Louisa Cowen's age was reported as 31 in the 1860 census and as 35 five years later (even though she was only 27 when she died).[18] It appears that for the madams at 27–29 Endicott Street, that the goal age was in the low- to mid-thirties. Perhaps this was old enough to be experienced but not too old to be unattractive to the men who frequented the brothel.

Discussion

Although copious documents were produced in the nineteenth century about prostitution, very few of them were written by women engaged in sex work. None of these accounts portrayed the everyday realities of life in a brothel. While sex work was undoubtedly titillating to some, in fact much of the time of the prostitutes at 27–29 Endicott Street appears to have involved the day-to-day practices that benefited the brothel economy. It is probable that brothel life for prostitutes was tedious and was broken only occasionally by excitement. Undoubtedly the reason that archaeologists have such difficulty identifying sites of prostitution through the material culture alone (see Siefert et al. 2000) has to do with this reality of quiet repetition of brothel practices. Although the women who lived in the house had agency within their private lives, evidence suggests that everything about the daily brothel space, from the table settings to health and grooming practices, was carefully constructed with the explicit purpose of promoting the economic success of the brothel.

Despite the dangers of prostitution and the psychological strain women who were viewed as commodities likely experienced, the brothel economy relied as much on the coping strategies of the women who lived and worked there as it did on the setting designed to enhance male fantasy experiences. These strategies transcended material culture and were manifest in the creation of dual identities: each woman in the house had a private identity and a public identity. In manipulating their ages and places of origins and creating aliases for themselves, these women created a separation between their working lives and their personal lives.

At the same time, the expectations of the male patrons also shaped the economy of the 27–29 Endicott Street brothel. Conclusive records about the male patrons of this brothel do not exist, the way that the brothel space was arranged and decorated leaves traces of their presence. Because the brothel likely provided entertainment and meals, patrons could use its parlor atmosphere as a space for homosocial bonding. It appears that at 27–29 Endicott Street, purchasing sex was not the only function of the brothel.

On its surface, the transactions between sex workers and their clients appear to be private and intimate; they are sexual, often conducted behind closed doors, involving specific acts negotiated between two individuals. In reality the entire exchange is predicated on the manipulation of fantasy by the brothel's madam and her control of the space, of the ancillary offerings available, and of the transactional nature of the sexual encounter. At the same time, the male clients who patronized a nineteenth-century brothel would have been conscious of being seen by other men in attendance. They would have needed to negotiate the semi-public homosocial, masculine environment of the brothel "parlor" before and after their private sexual needs were met.

While the relationship between client and sex worker might not have been private or particularly intimate, sex workers still had rich and complex private lives. The women working at 27–29 Endicott Street sought love, or at least marriage, as in the case of Louisa Cowen and Mary Lake. Their relationships with their children appear to have been strong as well, as evidenced by Mary Lake's continued connection to her son George. The idea of husbands or children living in the brothel, perhaps being supported by the sex work of their wives or mothers, appears antithetical to the popular image of the solitary and independent prostitute or madam. At the same time, Louisa Cowen appears to have been accepted, even cherished, by her family, even though she was a brothel madam and may have started her career as a prostitute. These relationships contradict the prevailing moralizing literature of the time that suggested that sex workers would be denied all meaningful, intimate relationships because of their chosen profession.

Despite appearing so from the outside, the nineteenth-century brothel environment was neither ephemeral nor anonymous. The fantasy of transgressive sex and women who were sexually available for the right price was in fact tightly controlled and directed by the madam. If the madam wished to be successful, she had to be constantly vigilant about changing public perceptions of prostitution and about what her male customers considered comfortable and genteel. The madam's economic control played out materially though the food served to brothel workers and the objects related to dress and hygiene that were either provided to or expected of brothel employees.

Notes

1. A twiffler is an intermediate-sized plate, somewhere between a dinner plate and a side or luncheon plate. George Miller (1980) gives its diameter as four to seven inches.

2. "Gas Explosion," *Boston Traveler*, January 18, 1855, 2; "Gas Explosion," *Daily Atlas*, January 18, 1855, 2; "Serious Gas Explosion," *Boston Courier*, January 17, 1855, 2.

3. "Serious Results of a Quarrel," *The Congregationalist*, May 16, 1851.

4. Will of Louisa Cowen, June 24, 1865, Probate Records, vol. 163, Suffolk County Probate Court, Boston, Massachusetts.

5. Louisa wrote her will on June 24, 1865. It was presented to the probate court on August 4, 1865, with the note that she had died.

6. The grave marker of "Louisa wife of Henry Cowen," gives her date of birth as 1838 and the death year as 1865. East Wells Cemetery, Rutland County, Vermont.

7. Asa Clemons, sale of property to Louisa Cowen, December 7, 1857, Vermont Land Records, Town Clerk, Wells, Vermont, Microfilm #29226. Family History Library, Salt Lake City, Utah.

8. Death record for Henry Cowen, July 2, 1956, Deaths in Boston, Massachusetts Vital and Town Records, Massachusetts Vital and Town Records, 1856, Holbrook Research Institute, Provo, Utah.

9. U.S. Federal Census. 1860. Washington County, Maine, population schedule, Perry, p. 49, dwelling 367, family 342, John Doyle; NARA microfilm publication M653, roll 454.

10. U.S. federal census, 1870, Suffolk County, Massachusetts, population schedule, Boston, Ward 2, page 204, dwelling 778, family 1656, Wm. Padelford, NARA microfilm publication M593, roll 641.

11. Massachusetts state census, 1865, Suffolk County, Massachusetts, population schedule, Boston, Ward 3, vol. 31, dwelling 128, family 197, Louisa Cowen, microfilm reel 28, New England Historic Genealogical Society, Boston, Massachusetts; tax valuation, personal estate, "house by Mrs. Lake," Boston Street Book, 1866, 27+29 Endicott, City of Boston Archives, West Roxbury.

12. Marriage record for William Padelford and Mary Lake, March 6, 1867, Massachusetts Vital and Town Records, Marriages reported in Boston, Town and City Clerks of Massachusetts, Holbrook Research institute, Provo, Utah.

13. U.S. federal census, 1870, Suffolk County, Massachusetts, population schedule,

Boston, Ward 2, page 204, dwelling 778, family 1656, Wm. Padelford; NARA microfilm publication M593, roll 641.

14. Tax valuation, personal estate, "house by Mrs. Lake," 27+29 Endicott, Boston Street Book, 1867, City of Boston Archives, West Roxbury.

15. Death record, William Padelford, May 28, 1888, Massachusetts Vital and Town Records, Holbrook Research Institute, Provo, Utah.

16. Death record, Mary F. Paddleford, November 30, 1903, Massachusetts Vital and Town Records, Holbrook Research Institute, Provo, Utah.

17. Massachusetts State Census, 1855, Suffolk County, Massachusetts, population schedule, Boston, Ward 3, vol. 31, dwelling 128, family 197, Louisa Cowen, microfilm reel 28, New England Historic Genealogical Society, Boston, Massachusetts.

18. Entry for Louisa Cline [Cowen], U.S. federal census, 1860, Suffolk County, Massachusetts, population schedule, Boston, Ward 3, page 181, dwelling 689, family 1545, NARA microfilm publication M653, roll 521.

References Cited

Abbot, Karen. 2007. *Sin in the Second City: Madams, Ministers, Playboys, and the Battle for America's Soul*. New York: Random House.

Anonymous. 1865. *Rogues and Rogueries of New York*. New York: J. C. Haney.

Anonymous. 1870. *The Gentleman's Directory*. Carlisle, PA: Applewood Press.

Arjona, Jamie M. 2017. Homesick Blues: Excavating Crooked Intimacies in Late Nineteenth- and Early Twentieth-Century Jook Joints. *Historical Archaeology* 51(1):43–59.

Beaudry, Mary C. 2013. Feasting on Broken Glass: Making a Meal of Seeds, Bones, and Sherds. *Northeast Historical Archaeology* 42:184–200.

Burnette, Richard T. 2014. Masculinity in a Nineteenth Century Western Mining Town : Gendered Relations of Power in a Red-Light District, The Vanoli Sporting Complex (5OR30), Ouray, Colorado. Colorado State University. PhD diss., Colorado State University.

Cheek, Charles D., and Joseph Balicki. 2000. *Archaeological Data Recovery: The Mill Pond Site (Bos-HA-14) Boston, Massachusetts*. Boston: Massachusetts Historical Commission.

Charles, Theodore P. 2014. The Landscape Archaeology of Saloons in Wallace, Idaho. MA thesis, University of Idaho.

Conkey, Margaret W., and Joan M. Gero. 1997. Programme to Practice: Gender and Feminism in Archaeology. *Annual Review of Anthropology* 26(1):411–437.

Constable, Nicole. 2009. The Commodification of Intimacy: Marriage, Sex, and Reproductive Labor. *Annual Review of Anthropology* 38:49–64.

Costello, Julia G. 2003. "A Night with Venus, A Moon with Mercury": The Archaeology of Prostitution in Historic Los Angeles. In *Restoring Women's History through Historic Preservation*, edited by Gail Lee and Jennifer B. Goodman Dubrow, 177–196. Baltimore, MD: Johns Hopkins University Press.

Crist, Thomas A. 2005. Babies in the Privy : Prostitution, Infanticide, and Abortion in New York City's Five Points District. *Historical Archaeology* 39(1):19–46.

Crook, Penny. 2011. Rethinking Assemblage Analysis: New Approaches to the Archaeology of Working-Class Neighborhoods. *International Journal of Historical Archaeology* 15:582–593.

Dawdy, Shannon Lee, and Richard Weyhing. 2008. Beneath the Rising Sun: "Frenchness" and the Archaeology of Desire. *International Journal of Historical Archaeology* 12(4):370–387.

Day, Jo. 2013. Introduction. In *Making Senses of the Past: Toward a Sensory Archaeology*, edited by Jo Day, 1–31. Center for Archaeological Investigations Occasional Paper 40. Carbondale: Southern Illinois University Press.

Dixon, Kelly. 2005. *Boomtown Saloons: Archaeology and History in Virginia City*. Reno: University of Nevada Press.

Fisher, Genevieve, and Diana DiPaolo Loren. 2003. Introduction: Embodying Identity in Archaeology. *Cambridge Archaeological Journal* 13(2):225–230.

Foster, Michael S., John M. Lindly, and Ronald F. Ryden. 2013. The Soiled Doves of South Granite Street: The History and Archaeology of a Prescott, Arizona Brothel. *Kiva* 70(4):349–374.

Gallagher, Diana Smith. 2014. "Cleanly in Their Persons and Cleanly in Their Dwellings": An Archaeological Investigation of Health, Hygiene, and Sanitation in Eighteenth Century New England. PhD diss., Boston University.

Gilfoyle, Timothy J. 1992. *City of Eros: New York City, Prostitution, and the Commercialization of Sex, 1790–1920*. New York: Norton & Company.

Graham, A. J. 1998. The Woman at the Window: Observations on the "Stele from the Harbour" of Thasos. *The Journal of Hellenic Studies* 118:22–40.

Hamilakis, Yannis. 2013. *Archaeology and the Senses: Human Experience, Memory, and Affect*. Cambridge: Cambridge University Press.

Hardt, Michael. 1999. Affective Labor. *Boundary 2* 26(2):89–100.

Heck, Dana B., and Joseph F. Balicki. 1998. Katherine Naylor's "House of Office": A Seventeenth-Century Privy. *Historical Archaeology* 32(3):24–37.

Hobson, Barbara Meil. 1990. *Uneasy Virtue: The Politics of Prostitution and the American Reform Tradition*. 2nd ed. Chicago: University of Chicago Press.

Hoffman, Susanne, and Adi Moreno. 2016. Introduction: Global Intimate Economies: Discontents and Debates. In *Intimate Economies: Bodies, Emotions, and Sexualities on the Global Market*, edited by Susanne Hoffman and Adi Moreno, 1–30. New York: Palgrave Macmillan.

Keim, Alexander. 2013. In the Street: Personal Adornment and Movement in the Urban Landscapes of Boston. In *Archaeologies of Mobility and Movement*, edited by Mary C. Beaudry and Travis Parno, 237–253. New York: Springer New York.

Ketz, K. Anne, Elizabeth J. Abel, and Andrew J. Schmidt. 2005. Public Image and Private Reality: An Analysis of Differentiation in a Nineteenth-Century St. Paul Bordello. *Historical Archaeology* 39(1):74–88.

Kimball, Nell. 1970. *Nell Kimball: Her Life as an American Madam by Herself*. Edited by Stephen Longstreet. New York: MacMillan.

Meyer, Michael D., Erica S. Gibson, and Julia G. Costello. 2005. City of Angels, City of Sin: Archaeology in the Los Angeles Red-Light District ca. 1900. *Historical Archaeology* 39(1):107–125.

Miller, George L. 1980. Classification and Economic Scaling of 19th Century Ceramics. *Historical Archaeology* 14:1–40.

Praetzellis, Adrian, and Mary Praetzellis. 2001. Mangling Symbols of Gentility in the Wild West: Case Studies in Interpretive Archaeology. *American Anthropologist* 103(3):645–654.

Rose, Al. 1974. *Storyville, New Orleans: Being an Authentic, Illustrated Account of the Notorious Red-light District.* Tuscaloosa: University of Alabama Press.

Sanger, William W. 1972. *The History of Prostitution.* New York: Arno Press.

Seifert, Donna J. 1991. Within Site of the White House: The Archaeology of Working Women. *Historical Archaeology* 25(4):82–108.

Seifert, Donna J., Elizabeth Barthold O'Brien, and Joseph Balicki. 2000. Mary Ann Hall's First-Class House: The Archaeology of a Capital Brothel. In *Archaeologies of Sexuality*, edited by Robert A. Schmidt and Barbara L. Voss, 117–128. London: Routledge.

Silliman, Stephen. 2001. Agency, Practical Politics and the Archaeology of Culture Contact. *Journal of Social Archaeology* 1(2):190–209.

Spude, Catherine Holder. 2005. Brothels and Saloons : An Archaeology of Gender in the American West. *Historical Archaeology* 39(1):89–106.

Stevens, Sarah C., and Margaret T. Ordoñez. 2005. Fashionable and Work Shoes from a Nineteenth-Century Boston Privy. *Historical Archaeology* 3(4):9–25.

Wilson, Ara. 2004. *The Intimate Economies of Bangok: Tomboys, Tycoons, and Avon Ladies in the Global City.* Berkeley, CA: University of California Press.

Yamin, Rebecca. 2005. Wealthy, Free, and Female: Prostitution in Nineteenth-Century New York. *Historical Archaeology* 39(1):4–18.

13

Uncovering an Early Seventeenth-Century Token Currency Scheme at Jamestown, Virginia

BEVERLY A. STRAUBE

Sometimes historical evidence hides for centuries in plain sight until tightly dated archaeological findings from relevant contexts suggest interesting new interpretations of the documentary record. Such is the case with a 1609 scheme by the Virginia Company of London to provide a token coinage for its nascent colony in Jamestown, Virginia. Mention of this scheme is found not in the few surviving pages of official company records but in a 1610 promotional tract written in lines of verse by Robert Rich, one of the company's investors. Historians have paid scant attention to the tract's monetary plan that, without any supporting proof, appears to be nothing more than optimistic hyperbole intended to counteract negative reports about conditions in Jamestown. But over the past twenty-three years, support for the token coinage plan has been coming out of the ground through archaeological excavations of James Fort, the first area of settlement on Jamestown Island for the English colony that began in 1607. Within sealed early fort features, an unusual assemblage of 110 obsolete Irish pennies and halfpennies has been found (Figure 13.1). Standing in sharp contrast to the nineteen coins in contemporary circulation found in the same contexts, these numismatic coppers minted in England in 1601 and 1602 represent the largest single archaeological assemblage of this emission. Even archaeological excavations at Carrickfergus, one of the Irish exchanges for the coinage while it was current, did not yield as many (Robert Heslip, personal communication 2004).

Figure 13.1. Obverse (*left*) and reverse (*right*) of Irish copper penny from James Fort, dated 1601. Courtesy of Preservation Virginia.

While it would be easy to ascribe uncommon portable objects like these to the initial robust trade for food the English had with the Powhatan Indians (Kelso 2006, 178–179; Noël Hume 1972, 171; Noël Hume 2008, 267; Potter 1989; Straube and Luccketti 1996, 46–49), the concentration of large numbers of the obsolete coinage in discrete fort contexts dating to the early summer of 1610 suggests otherwise. I am proposing that there was a plan to introduce a token currency to the Jamestown colony in 1609 as an experiment by the Virginia Company to satisfy the needs of a labor force accustomed to the exchange of money for goods and services. Instead of minting a new coinage, as the charters of settlement allowed, the Virginia Company chose a cheaper alternative that recycled decried Irish coinage for that purpose.[1] This discrete reuse would ensure that the company could maintain control of monetary arrangements in the colony because the coins would hold no value for outsiders. Illegal trade with mariners on supply ships to Jamestown had surfaced as a problem for the colony: sailors sold food and drink at four times their value to desperate settlers. Sometimes these victuals were goods that ships' crews had purloined from the company's shipments intended for the colonists (Strachey 1973, 72). By creating an intimate closed economy for its colony, the Virginia Company hoped to prevent illegal transactions to the extent that it could.

Archaeological evidence also discloses that the coins were scrapped before the plan was enacted. This change, a response to a near-collapse of the colony, probably accounts for the lacuna in the Virginia Company records concerning token coinage for Jamestown. Undocumented and unrealized, the scheme suggested by archaeology reveals the Virginia Company's intention to place value on the day-to-day efforts of the men it had sent to extract resources from its colony. At the same time, the company's plan was ultimately meant to benefit itself. Localized exchange for goods the company supplied at prices it set for rates of pay the company set could have meant constant indebtedness for the colonists.

This study explores the biography of the Irish coinage and how it may have been supplied to meet the perceived emotional need for exchange in the early Virginia colony. A parallel adaptive measure of token money taken six years later in Jamestown's sister colony Bermuda further supports the idea. In addition, a later plan that resulted in sending unpopular and obsolete English coinage to cash-poor Virginia in the second quarter of the seventeenth century suggests that this may have also been a fiscal solution that had been considered earlier. But first, I will present the verse of Robert Rich that provided the key to understanding the unusual assemblage of base metal coins found in the early James Fort contexts.

Robert Rich's Promotional Tract

In July 1609, Robert Rich was sailing to Jamestown aboard the *Sea Venture* with Sir Thomas Gates, Jamestown's new governor, and several other newly appointed leaders of the Virginia colony when a hurricane caught the ship and cast it upon the reefs of Bermuda. Over nine months, the castaways built two ships that they finally sailed to Virginia. During that time, Rich, who was a part of the gentry, was in the company of Gates and his coterie and would have been privy to the organizational changes Gates planned to enact when he reached Jamestown.

The shipwreck survivors finally arrived in Virginia in May 1610, but Rich appears to have continued on to England at his first opportunity. His poetic promotional tract, rather lengthily entitled *Newes from Virginia. The Lost Flocke Triumphant: With the happy Arrival of that famous and worthy knight Sr. Thomas Gates: and the well reputed & valiant Captaine Mr. Christopher Newporte, and others, into England*, was published in London on October 1, 1610. Rich probably rushed his piece to press at the behest of the Virginia Company as an attempt at damage control. Erstwhile colonists who had recently returned from Virginia were circulating negative reports about "the Country itselfe, & of the Carriage of the business there" (Virginia Company 1890, 355). The promised riches had not been forthcoming and the Virginia Company was desperate to attract new investors and settlers to its struggling colony.

The pertinent part of Rich's verse to this study is as follows (Rich [1610] 1890, 425–426):

> To such as to Virginia
> Do purpose to repaire;
> And when that they shall hither come
> Each man shall have his share,
>
> Day wages for the laborer
> And for his more content,
> A house and garden plot shall have
> Besides 'tis further ment
>
> That every man shall have a part
> And not therof denied
> Of general profit, as if that he
> Twelve pounds, ten shillings paid;
> And he that in Virginia
> Shall copper coyne receive,
> For hyer, or commodities,
> And will the country leave
>
> Upon delivery of such coyne
> Unto the Governour,
> Shall by exchange, at his returne
> Be by their Treasurer
> Paid him in London, at first sight

Rich describes an economic system whereby colonists shared in the profits generated in Virginia whether or not they owned shares in the joint-stock company. In addition, individuals would be paid wages for their labor or for the commodities they produced while in the colony. But the detail that particularly caught my eye was that the payment would be in "copper coyne" that individuals could exchange for a bill of credit before leaving Virginia. The credit would then be redeemed in London by the treasurer of the Virginia Company. What was this copper coin? While the 1606 charter of settlement from King James I granted the Virginia Company the right to mint coinage, it never did. In addition, there was no contemporary regal issue of base metal coinage in England. The poem's statement that recipients would be able to exchange coinage as they left Virginia indicates that this was token money and of no value outside the Jamestown community.

Nuremberg Jettons

Numismatist Louis Jordan (2009, 194–195) also noticed Rich's reference to copper coin and speculated that he was referring to Nuremberg jettons, also known as casting counters (Figure 13.2). These coin-like calamine brass objects originated in medieval Europe as mathematical aids for working with Roman numerals. Used in conjunction with a gridded counting board or cloth representing decimal units, the objects permitted manual tracking of calculations that otherwise would be quite onerous. Although F. P. Barnard's seminal study of casting counters claimed that they were sometimes distributed in the Low Countries in medieval times as tokens for work and were "exchangeable for coin" (Barnard 1916, 78), archaeologists John Schofield and Alan Vince (2003, 160) could find no evidence "that jettons were ever intended to be used for exchange" in Britain. Some researchers, however, continue to assert that jettons were used as token money in America without citing proof for their beliefs (Jordan 2009, 191; Berry 2002, 22–23). It appears to be one of those ideas that has been repeated so often that it has become reified as the truth without questioning the supporting data. A recently published guide to

Figure 13.2. Brass Nuremberg jetton of Hans Krauwinckel II, ca. 1586–1635, from James Fort. Courtesy of Preservation Virginia.

North American numismatic archaeology, for example, stated that jettons "were formally tolerated as aids to accountancy but often circulated as half-farthings, farthings, and halfpence when they were not being used as gaming tokens signifying much larger sums in games of cards or dice" (Akin et al. 2016, 84).

Jettons may have served as money substitutes and as tokens in gaming later in the colonial period once their accountancy function became redundant, but it is very unlikely that these mass-produced metal objects were used in James Fort as token currency. Numerical skills were unevenly distributed in early modern English society with the result that throughout the seventeenth century counters and counting boards using Roman numerals continued to be used side by side with the written methods of computing Arabic numbers (Thomas 1987). Although Arabic numbers were employed in commercial transactions by the mid-sixteenth century in England, the early calculating methodologies for the new arithmetic were unwieldy and were not universally taught. Even an accountant of the Lord of Northumberland, the brother of Jamestown colonist George Percy, is recorded in 1607 as having to learn "the art of arithmetic" (Thomas 1987, 120). Fifty years later, when English diarist Samuel Pepys was 30 years old, he wrote that he was learning his multiplication tables for the first time (Wallis 1978, 2). Some individuals, especially those who still counted on their fingers, distrusted calculations by pen because they did not completely understand the arithmetic and could not check for errors. It was not until the late seventeenth century that "Arabic numerals had come to be known as 'English figures' and the Roman numbers seemed archaic" (Thomas 1987, 121).

In sum, the scores of jettons found in the early fort contexts would have been inappropriate devices for the token money scheme. Not only were they needed at Jamestown for accountancy, they were also in current use in England for the same function, so they were far too widespread and accessible. Nuremberg jettons were commonly used in the sixteenth and seventeenth centuries, as is reflected by the fact that they are found in almost every archaeological excavation of English sites dating to that period (Mernick and Mernick 2017). Anyone venturing to Virginia at that time could easily have filled his pockets with casting counters purchased from a dealer before undertaking the voyage and thus could have upset the colony's fiscal system.

If not jettons, then what could Robert Rich's "copper coyne" be? Excavations of early James Fort contexts have strongly suggested that at least some of the token money consisted of pennies and halfpennies the London Mint issued in 1601 and 1602 for use in Ireland. By the time of Jamestown's founding, these copper coins had been decried; they were no longer circulating in Ireland and had no value in England. These were the perfect tools to use for a token currency in Virginia. They embodied the physical attributes familiar to individuals accustomed to using coins and tokens, they were less expensive to produce than a new emission, and they were worthless outside the Jamestown community, thereby providing the Virginia Company with a means of control over an intimate closed economy. In previous research on the topic I have conjectured that other obsolete tokens recovered from the early fort contexts were also part of the monetary scheme, perhaps representing different denominations of coin (Straube 2014; Straube 2016, 183–208). These include sixteenth-century brass beer tokens from a northern Dutch city, copper tickets to a royal healing ceremony of King James I, and lead tokens bearing iconography relating to Queen Elizabeth I. Here I focus on the Irish coinage that has the strongest case for being part of this undocumented fiscal plan.

Pennies and Halfpennies for Ireland

Queen Elizabeth I instituted the program of coinage for Ireland to finance her government in that country during Tyrone's Rebellion. Secretary of State Sir Robert Cecil and lord-Treasurer Thomas Sackville had convinced Elizabeth that the scheme would be a lucrative venture for the Crown. Equally important, by creating a new coinage with little intrinsic value that at the same time demonetized all other moneys circulating in Ireland, the plan hoped to keep English sterling out of the hands of the rebels. Elizabeth faced mounting costs to support her army in the war that had begun in 1593, and some of the "great summes of money" had found its way into the hands of Tyrone's rebels, who used it to support their cause. As Elizabeth stated in her 1601 proclamation instituting the coinage, Tyrone's forces were able to purchase from the continent "such warlike provisions as they need, as with pouder lead, match, armes, and weapons of all sorts, and with wines, cloth and other necessaries" (Nelson 1905, 59). It was therefore considered that decrying all moneys circulating in Ireland, "whether Irish, English, or foreign," and replacing it with a token coinage that was only current in Ireland and had a face value that was much higher than its intrinsic worth, would deny the rebels access to the supplies from foreign countries they were buying with silver coinage (Symonds 1917, 122).

While serving to hamstring the rebels, it was also considered that the billon shillings, sixpences, and threepences and the copper pennies and halfpennies were an economical way to support Elizabeth's fighting forces. The money would only circulate in Ireland and would be the only officially sanctioned currency for that country. Individuals entering or leaving Ireland swapped their money at one of seven official exchanges: London, Bristol, and Chester in England and Dublin, Cork, Galway, and Carrickfergus in Ireland. By the Crown's 1601 proclamation, the Irish exchanges would issue bills for the tendered money redeemable at the English exchanges at the rate of nineteen shillings in English coins for every twenty shillings of new Irish coins. The same exchange rate would apply for travelers to Ireland, who were no longer permitted to carry English sterling out of the country (Symonds 1917, 122). In a June 1602 move to improve the Crown's profit margin, the rate of exchange was increased to twenty-two shillings Irish for twenty shillings of decried sterling coins with the additional caveat that one-fifth of the money presented in Ireland for receipt of sterling in England had to be silver or gold. "Those in the pay of the Queen" were exempted from this last stipulation up to the "extent of their pay or entertainment." But by the following month, with the English treasury still hemorrhaging funds, the exchange of "mere copper moneys" was disallowed, thereby "demonetizing these coins outside the realm of Ireland" (Symonds 1917, 123–124).

The debased coinage scheme for Ireland never gained acceptance by the public and it failed to constrain Tyrone's forces, as they were largely funded by Spanish silver coin (Pawlisch 1985, 147). The program was supposed to help soldiers and government officials in the pay of the English government in Ireland, but they suffered from inflationary rates that merchants who quickly learned to exploit the system imposed. James I enacted new monetary policies for Ireland in 1603 to gradually rid the monarchy of the unpopular and unprofitable scheme. He reduced the value of the billon coinage by one-third but the "moneys of mere copper as pence and half-pence" were to pass at full value, primarily for the "more necessary use of the poorer sort" (Simon [1749] 1810, 110).[2] By the time

Jamestown was settled, the war was over, mint production of the Irish issue had ended, and the Irish economy was again dependent on English currency. A proclamation on May 19, 1607, officially established the need "to revive the use of English money in Ireland; after that, there was monetary union between the two countries" (Ruding 1840, 364–365).

The recalled copper coinage from the failed plan for Ireland would have been stored in the Royal Mint in London to be melted down, either for re-use in another debased coinage or as an alloy for silver coinage emissions. As William Harrison noted in his 1587 *Description of England*, "all coinage is brought into one place, that is to say, the Tower of London, where it is continually holden and perused, but not without great gain to such as deal withal" (Harrison [1587] 1994, 300). Although the way the colony acquired copper coinage is undocumented, recent research has indicated that the Virginia Company obtained some of the Royal Mint stockpiles of scrap copper to conduct metallurgical trials with Virginia ores and to trade with the Virginia Indians, who prized the metal (Hudgins 2005; Straube 2014). A web of kinship, friendship, and business dealings supported this supply, which is particularly illustrated by the fact that the colonist in charge of the metallurgical trials, Captain John Martin, was the son of Sir Richard Martin, master of the Royal Mint. The mint connection is further established by the recovery from James Fort's well (Structure 185), which dates to circa 1608–1610, of a cancelled Royal Mint trial plate for two Elizabethan coins that were never issued (Figure 13.3) (Straube 2014, 272–279). In light of this compelling archaeological evidence, I contend that Rich's "copper coyne" has now been found in the buried 1610 contexts of James Fort.

The Token Money and Its James Fort Archaeological Contexts

The tightly dated contexts of 1607–1624 at James Fort have permitted features and their contents to be closely associated with events documented in the written record. This is especially true for the first three years of settlement, when most of the activity occurred on a one-acre triangle of land enclosed by a wooden palisade. Even burials occurred within the fort walls in the first few months to hide English mortality from the Powhatan Indians. Beginning in 1607, colonists constructed mud-and-stud barracks and storehouse structures, and they dug a well in 1608. In June 1610, a massive cleanup and rebuilding effort followed near-total abandonment

Figure 13.3. Obverses (*top*) and reverses (*bottom*) of farthing and halfpenny coins on the Royal Mint trial plate. Drawing by Caroline Taylor.

of the settlement. Of these, the events of 1610 had the largest impact and can be credited with capturing most of the physical proof of the economic plan (Kelso 2017; Kelso et al. 2012; Kelso and Straube 2008; Straube 2014).

Ninety-nine Irish pennies and halfpennies were found within seven features sealed by the 1610 activities. This constitutes 72 percent of the total 138 Irish coins recovered from the site. Twenty-seven (19 percent) of the token coins were located in disturbed contexts such as plow zones without close dating and were not included in this analysis. The remaining twelve (9 percent) were from three fort contexts that were filled by 1617 and are considered to be residual scatter from the 1610 primary context. Significantly, none of the Irish coins were found in fort contexts dated after 1617 (Straube 2014, 226–233).

Only twelve coins in current circulation were found in the seven 1610 features. This number contrasts starkly with the number of Irish coins and suggests random loss rather than purposeful dumping. Deliberate discard is supported for the Irish coinage by the fact that seventy-two (72 percent) were located in just two contexts—a well associated with a storehouse (Structure 185) and a storehouse cellar (Structure 165)—that were filled during abandonment of the fort and the subsequent cleanup. Another eighteen Irish coins (18 percent) were found in a building cellar (Structure 191) that was adjacent to Structure 185. This structure was related to Structure 185 with ceramic cross-mends and contained evidence of the survival cannibalism (Horn et al. 2013) that occurred shortly before the arrival of De La Warr's rescue party (see below). The token coinage from Structure 191 and the scatter found in four other 1610 contexts appear to be spillover from the two primary deposits in the storehouse locations that took place during efforts to rebuild the fort (Straube 2014, 226–233).

Historical Background and the Need for Token Money

The Virginia Company financed its colony through a joint-stock fund that distributed the risk of the undertaking among investors called adventurers, who bought shares at twelve pounds and ten shillings apiece. This popular method of pooling resources to support expensive ventures while limiting personal liability can be seen in the contemporary use of joint-stock funds to finance the initial voyages of the East India Company and Shakespeare's Globe playhouse (Bowsher 2012, 89–96; Craven 1957, 16–17).

In the first couple of years, the Virginia Company sent commercial and industrial specialists to demonstrate "that Virginia could provide profitable freightage for the ships of England" (Craven 1957, 12). The search for noble metals was emphasized and several goldsmiths and refiners were dispatched to that end, but other commodities such as glass, iron, naval stores, dyestuffs, furs, medicinal substances, and wood products were also sought (Kelso and Straube 2004; Brown 1890, 384–386; Bruce 1935, 2:440–444). The initial results of these endeavors in Virginia were disappointing. There were no valuable resources readily available to offset the company's expenditures and explorations of the Chesapeake Bay watershed had not led to a transcontinental riverine route to the riches of the Far East. Furthermore, the colony had suffered great losses in manpower as many people died from diseases, inadequate provisions, and wars with the Indians. Worst of all were the reports reaching the investors' ears—like those Robert Rich tried to counteract—of the toxic conditions in the settlement created by chronic infighting among the men, lack of incentive, and poor leadership. The high rate of mortality in Virginia was also difficult to hide.

Fearful that King James would abandon the unprofitable scheme, especially in his "desire to placate Spain," a country with which he had negotiated peace just five years earlier and that viewed the colony as a threat to Hispanic New World settlements, the Virginia Company petitioned the Crown for a new charter that would incorporate institutional reforms and, it was hoped, save their investments (Kingsbury 1906–1935, 1:22). The second Virginia charter, granted on May 23, 1609, removed the king's governmental control over the affairs of the colony and placed it with the Virginia Company council. An all-powerful governor was to manage Jamestown, giving the distant settlement more local control of efforts to make the enterprise more productive. The second charter also established a planter membership in the company, which provided shares based on "labor input as well as capital contribution" (Walton and Shepherd 1979, 39). Planters, according to the charter, "goe in their persons" and adventurers "doe adventure their monyes goods or chattels" but all were incorporated in "one bodie or communialitie" (Bemiss 1957, 42). There would be no dividend for the planters and adventurers until 1616, at which time they would receive grants of land in Virginia and a share of the profits (Craven 1957, 17).

Just as it reorganized the structure of management, the company recognized that it needed positive inducements to attract and maintain the colony's labor force (Galenson 1996, 136). Reforms were meant to address the discontent individuals felt who were working for the company in Virginia with no assurances that they would benefit from future profits. With the realization that there were no easy riches to be had, the company was dependent on the colonists' productivity to develop commodities that could provide a healthy return on investment. As a result of the modifications, 600 English were encouraged to sign on as planters, but a few of these individuals "were smart enough to discount the propaganda that had persuaded them" and elected not to participate in future rewards in lieu of receiving wages from the company (Craven 1957, 19). A token currency would have made the most sense for this latter group. With no ability to draw clothing or victuals from the company store based on the value of their shares, these individuals had to wait months until the fruits of their labors could be sold in England and the company sent supplies purchased with the profits to the colony. Payment for work on company projects using coinage would not only instill confidence in the workers that they were being accurately compensated, it would also provide a means of reward and incentive by providing the ability to acquire more goods based on labor expended for the colony.

Sir Thomas Gates, a seasoned military leader, was chosen as the all-powerful governor at Jamestown who would implement these reforms. He was instructed to set up work groups of ten to twenty men to labor on "severall works according to their undertakings in the books by which they were received" (Bemiss 1957, 61). An overseer for each group would "take daily accounte of their laboures." This was to be reported monthly so that the cape merchant could keep track of the "goodes or provisions" that were advanced or gotten above expence" from the company store. From this accounting, the instructions explain, Gates and the cape merchant "shall both knowe how your men are imployed, what they get & where it is, as also the measure of your provision and wealth" (Bemiss 1957, 65).

I maintain that the token currency was intended to be part of these reforms. For seventeenth-century Jamestown, the renewed value of Irish coinage was similar to the use of scrip in the isolated American mining and lumbering communities of the early twentieth century. In those company towns, scrip was offered by management as a "worker perquisite" used to attract labor into remote and inhospitable destinations (Timberlake 1987, 442). Based upon the military mode of imprest money, with which Gates would have been familiar from his recent service as captain for the States General in the Netherlands, the scheme invoked a system of payment for working on company projects. Laborers would receive immediate and tangible compensation in the form of token coinage, which could be redeemed for goods in the storehouse or could be applied as credit to be paid upon the individual's return to England. Gates, however, quickly abandoned any thought of the fiscal plan once he viewed conditions in the colony he had been sent to manage.

Abandoning the Scheme

When Gates and his fellow Bermuda castaways finally reached Jamestown in late May 1610, they were shocked by what they encountered. In the words of colonist William Strachey ([1610] 1973, 63), they found "all things so contrary to our expectations, so full of misery and misgovernment." The previous winter, the Powhatan Indians had besieged James Fort, effectively placing a stranglehold on the colony. With supplies of food from the Indians no longer forthcoming and the threat of death for anyone who ventured from the fort, the colony entered what would become known as the "starving time." Three out of four of the English died that winter and the survivors tell of having to consume all manner of normally taboo foods including dogs, horses, and even each other. These accounts, including survival cannibalism, have been supported by archaeological evidence recovered during fort excavations (Horn et al. 2013).

The appearance from Bermuda of more than 100 additional mouths to feed was too much for the shattered colony to bear and Sir Thomas Gates, as the designated leader, ordered that Jamestown should be abandoned. During evacuation proceedings, artillery was buried, food was prepared for the planned voyage, and unnecessary items were dumped in any open feature. There was barely enough room for all of the colonists on the four available pinnaces, especially with the emphasis on packing "all the arms and all the best things in the store" the Virginia Company could sell in England (Strachey [1610] 1973, 76).

Barely thirty hours after abandoning the settlement, the colonists returned, having been intercepted in the James River by Lord De La Warr, the newly arrived governor. His timely appearance with additional colonists and "provisions . . . sufficient to serve four hundred men for one whole year" not only reestablished the colony but enabled it to evolve from basic survival mode (Strachey [1610] 1973, 85). The energies previously expended on searching for food shifted to rebuilding the ruinous structures of James Fort. When he reached Jamestown, De La Warr ordered laborers in the fort to "cleanse the town," which suggests that the ruined structures were razed and all the debris that had accumulated on the ground was scraped and shoveled into every available pit, thus completing the filling of features that had begun under Gates's orders shortly before (Strachey [1610] 1973, 63). It is in these June 1610 cleanup contexts that the bulk of the Irish copper coinage has been archaeologically recovered. The coins were no longer needed. Because the colony was in chaos and near-collapse, a new military model of settlement was implemented with strict laws that covered all aspects of life and severe punishments for violators. In order to restore order and discipline, the principles of English common law that had been granted to the colonists by the royal charters were no longer recognized. Under this absolute government, the proposed incentive of token coinage was considered irrelevant to maintaining peace and cohesion amongst the colony's laboring forces, so the plan was dropped. The monetary scheme did not die, however; it resurfaced three years later with the plans for settlement of Bermuda.

The Hogge Money of Bermuda

Following the 1609 shipwreck of the Jamestown-bound *Sea Venture* on the uninhabited Bermuda isles, the Virginia Company recognized that the "opulent fertile and pleasant land" could attract new investors to its New World colonizing efforts (Quinn 1966, 144). Interest had been waning in the Jamestown venture for some time as profitable returns from the colony failed to materialize. So in 1612, the Virginia Company revised its charters to include the Bermudas, also known as the Somers Islands, and fifty settlers were sent there under the leadership of Governor Richard Moore. Three years later, the Somers Island Company was formed out of the Virginia Company membership as a distinct corporate entity to administer the new colony. However, the two organizations continued to have membership, interests, and policies in common (Craven 1937a, 176–215; Craven 1937b, 317–362; Craven 1937c, 437–465; Craven 1938, 13–63). By acknowledging the interconnectedness of the two companies, it is possible to reconstruct missing details of the Virginia economic plan by "reading backward" from the more fully documented system applied in Bermuda.

As in Virginia, the governor of Bermuda had jurisdiction over the labor pool of colonists who were initially assigned to company projects. Some worked at fortifying the settlement, building boats for transportation between the islands, erecting structures for housing and storage of company goods, and developing the roadways. Others were engaged in revenue-producing activities, while another group was employed in stocking the common food bank through agricultural activities, hunting, and fishing (Lefroy 1877). All goods, whether shipments from England or locally produced, were deposited in the company storehouse in the town of St. George's, where all the colonists were located, and were allocated to individuals according to their share and to the number of work credits they had amassed by working on company projects (Lefroy 1882). To encourage participation in tasks that did not produce revenue, Governor Moore's 1612 commission specified that the individuals employed "for our business in the saide Plantacon should be reimbursed at a rate not to exceed xxd. for a workman [i.e., skilled worker] and 12d. for a labourer." The company further stated that this system of compensation through wages would be mediated through coinage to be sent with its rates and values on the next supply ship (Lefroy 1877).

The coin, also known as Hogge money because of the image of a wild boar on one side, did not materialize until 1616. By royal charter the previous year, James I granted the Somers Island Company the right to mint coinage "to pass currant in the said Somer Islands betweene the Inhitantes [inhabitants] there for the more ease of commerce and bargaining between them" (Lefroy 1877, 98). The charter stipulated that the form of the coin and its metal would be up to the company's leadership. The iconography of the coin the company chose reflects the "belonging" theme of coin agency identified by Kemmers and Myrberg (2011, 96–99) that is useful in studying biographies of numismatica. In an attempt to appeal to the Bermuda community's sense of group identity, a boar depicted on one side represented "the abundance of hogges" the English found on the island in 1609 and the ship on the other side referenced the *Sea Venture* that had first brought them there (Smith 1986, 362). With the tinned copper Hogge money in denominations of two pence, three pence, sixpence, and shilling came a revised economic policy. The new plan related supplies from England to profits rather than to a set minimal amount (Jordan 2003, 2473). Colonists and company shareholders were to share equally in the proceeds derived from Bermudan commodities such as tobacco, silk, sugar cane, timber, whale oil, and pearls. The colonists' shares were used to procure clothing, food, drink, and other supplies not available in the islands. When they arrived from England, these materials were deposited in the company store, where colonists could "purchase" them with the work credits they had earned (Craven 1937b, 334–335).

The Somers Island Company recognized that the whole populace might not be willing to wait on a promise of future profits while goods were sold in England, so an alternative was offered that allowed them to work for wages. For these individuals the company stated that

> we have appointed a base coyne wch we send rated with our pvisions, whereby you may give to such men there weekly wages when they worke, and as you shall find them to deserve, with wch coyne yt shalbe lawfull and free for them to buy any pvisions out of the Store or any Fishe corne tooles or any other thinge in the Islands where they can get the same. And to that end you shall pclaime the said coyne to be currant to passe freely from man to man throughout the Islands and not otherwise. (Lefroy 1877, 113)

The company tried to make profit-sharing the more attractive alternative by stating that half of the income gained by "contenting soe many with base coyne," and thereby reducing their share, would be divided among those willing "to take theire salrye out of the pffits" (Lefroy 1877, 114). While the control over the company goods was as before, the emission of small change allowed individuals the freedom to purchase goods from each other, encouraging the settlers to be productive during their downtime. This social process of exchange would also reinforce relationships between Bermudans, just as the iconography on the coins reinforced their common identity. Using the colony's legal currency, surplus goods generated in Bermuda could be sold from "man to man," giving more enterprising individuals the ability to live better than their neighbors (Craven 1937b, 336). Since most of the coins were collected at the company store in exchange for goods, they could be recirculated to workers at the next pay period. Thus, there was little need to produce vast numbers of coins (Jordan 2003, 2476–2477). By 1619, Hogge money was replaced by valuations in tobacco, as in Virginia (Sportack 2006, 89). It was a "short term experiment to an economic problem" that provided a tangible way to reimburse workers for laboring on company projects (Jordan 2003, 2487). Especially for individuals who may have been illiterate and thereby totally dependent on the honest bookkeeping of the clerk in the company store, specie was more attractive than a system of credit.

Coins exchanged for goods not only provided workers with direct confirmation of the value of their labors but it provided the Somers Island Company a way to clear its indebtedness to individuals who were not being directly paid in officially issued English coinage for their work. The company benefited in another way since it controlled the prices of goods in the store. In 1617, a new pattern of colonization allowed the colonists to disperse from the town of St. George and made the increasingly unpopular token currency unnecessary. Bermuda was opened up to investors for proprietary planting and was quickly populated by tenant farmers who were freed from laboring on company projects and wasted no time in cultivating tobacco. Supplies from England were no longer offloaded into the company storehouse but were sold directly to the colonists for tobacco. In the end, it proved more advantageous for the company to use tobacco as currency for its colonists rather than a token coinage which cost the company money to produce and was only valid in Bermuda (Craven 1937b, 339; Sportack 2006, 89).

The need for a small-change medium persisted in Virginia throughout the seventeenth century, but there was never an attempt to produce a token coinage there as had been briefly tried in Bermuda. Instead, archaeological evidence suggests that the English government returned to the idea of recycling base metal coins that had been recalled from circulation. Like the scheme using Irish coinage, this later plan is primarily supported by archaeological evidence and provides strength to the argument that token coinage was considered as an economic solution for the colony's first years.

Pattern of Dumping Obsolete Coins in Virginia

Deliberate official dumping of obsolete English coinage in Virginia was first suggested by archaeologist Ivor Noël Hume when he found two 1613 Harrington patent farthings during excavations at Martin's Hundred, a circa 1619–1645 settlement near Jamestown. The copper coins were located in contexts that dated over five years later than their official withdrawal from circulation in England. Noël Hume theorized that the coins had been stored at the Royal Mint and had escaped the melt by being "shipped to Virginia to help satisfy the colony's need for small change" (Noël Hume 1982, 226). At the time Noël Hume lamented that he could not find documentation of or a numismatist who was willing to support his thesis (Noël Hume 1982, 317). But now, with the evidence from James Fort, this seems the most reasonable explanation.

The need in England for denominations smaller than a penny for day-to-day transactions led James I to grant a royal patent in 1613 for the production of copper farthings. The small and underweight coins produced by John Harrington, Lord of Exton, were easily counterfeited and were not popular among the English populace. Harrington recalled the issue within three months and produced a farthing that was larger and heavier but that lasted in circulation for less than a year. The debased English coinage was ridiculed in the popular culture of the day, but since it remained profitable to the patentee and to the Crown, farthing production in various forms continued under a series of monopoly holders until Parliament finally stopped it in 1644 (Fletcher 2003, 44).

The Virginia colony also had a desperate need for a medium of exchange and in 1636, Virginia's new governor, Sir John Harvey, formally requested farthing tokens from the Crown to rectify "the injury to trade in Virginia, caused by little or no money in the colony." The governor was particularly concerned that he had no way to pay laborers until the harvest of the tobacco crop, the primary means of exchange at the time (Sainsbury 1860, 238–239). Harvey's petition may be the reason for the twenty-eight patent farthings that have been recovered from fort-area contexts dating to the second quarter of the seventeenth century or from stratigraphically mixed contexts (Straube 2014, 131–132; 294–295).

Until the excavation of James Fort, only a handful of English patent farthings dating to the early seventeenth century had been recovered from Virginia sites, leading to the impression that few circulated in the colony and that Harvey's 1636 appeal for token coinage had gone unheeded. This notion is seemingly supported by the response of the Virginia House of Burgesses in 1639 to a license granted to Lord Maltravers that year for supplying the colony with farthings "in exchange for such commodities as were readily salable in the English markets" (Bruce 1935, 2:500). The legislators decried the plan, stating that "the mechanics would be unwilling to receive such money in remuneration for their labor, hired servants for their wages, and merchants for their debts" (Bruce 1935, 2:501). Perhaps the burgesses were speaking from personal experiences with the patent farthings that had been sent three years earlier at Harvey's request. If that is so, the large number of recovered pre-1636 farthings at Jamestown suggests that instead of sending the colony only newly minted coins, the Crown also dumped previously issued coins that the Royal Mint had recalled to be melted down when Maltravers' new Rose farthing was emitted (Jordan 2009, 201n24). Some of the farthings still bear the tin coating they were given to appear like silver, indicating that they may represent stores of uncirculated stock (Peck 1970, 26). Just as with the Irish coinage scheme posited here, there is no contemporary documentation to prove the reuse of recalled coinage that archaeology suggests. But there is reference to the practice in the late seventeenth century, when a London newspaper wrote that 400 Quakers leaving Bristol for Pennsylvania in 1682 were carrying "300 pounds worth of Half-pence and Farthings which in that Colony go currant for twice their value." These coins were most likely the English token coinage that Charles II had demonetized in 1672 with the issue of royal copper halfpennies and farthings (Jordan 2009, 259).

Conclusions

Jamestown was an experiment. There was much trial and error in the first few years as the Virginia Company endeavored to help the colony adapt to conditions in the New World. The previous English attempt by Sir Walter Raleigh in present-day North Carolina had been disappointing, leaving no template for a successful long-term colony. Many of the company's adaptive responses to settlement conditions at Jamestown are documented in the historical record. Historians have used these to emphasize the series of failures, providing a negative interpretation in comparison to the later settlements in New England. Failure, however, is part of the experimental process and the knowledge gained from unsuccessful strategies informed new paths forward. Despite numerous setbacks, Jamestown ultimately endured the "messy and incomplete" process of building an English society abroad by finding ways to motivate its settlers to work toward a common goal, thereby becoming the model for all subsequent successful colonies (Kupperman 2007, 327).

The token coinage plan theorized here was the company's adaptive attempt to create an intimate economy that would appeal to the emotional needs of its colonists, particularly to show value for nonshareholding settlers' work on company projects. It was one of the colonial schemes undertaken to better conditions in Virginia and thereby ensure a voluntary labor force that was integral to survival. Traces of the plan's existence have been interpreted from the study of obsolete coinage in context. Without further support from the historical record, this reading of the archaeological evidence can only be regarded as a suggestion, reflective of Haselgrove and Krmnicek's (2012, 238) contention that archaeology can "contribute a solid foundation for discussion by presenting data drawn from the material record and by providing an interpretation."

Jamestown, the tiny English settlement that clung tenaciously to its foothold in the New World, had much in common with the isolated small lumbering and mining communities of the early twentieth century. Both were formed for economic reasons and both discouraged autonomy in favor of schemes of work in common. Both endeavors involved betting on future gain and both necessitated a feeling of trust between the parties involved—those in control and those whose only power was the labor they could provide. The use of internal circulating currencies would not only bind the respective societies together into cohesive inward-looking units, it would also stress the present rather than the future. For the Jamestown settlers, this was especially important. Although most prospective colonists were probably not aware of the true extent of mortality in Virginia—over 40 percent for each of the first three years—enough disturbing information filtered back to England to alert them to the risks (Kupperman 1979).

Laborers working for wages could be assured of their value to the Virginia Company based on what they could purchase from the storehouse. For company officials, an internal token coinage would lessen their indebtedness should any of the workers return to England and seek compensation for their services. This intimate economy would only work in a tightly knit community of individuals with shared expectations as they participated in the exchange of goods for labor. But there was a total breakdown of that community just before the token coinage scheme was to be enacted at Jamestown. Deprivation, sickness, cannibalism, ineffectual leadership, and wars with the Indians during the "starving time" winter of 1609–1610 led to a general malaise and basic survival mode among the colonists. The Jamestown society was immediately reconstituted under martial law and a strict code of behavior. As reflected in the circa 1610 archaeological deposits of the Irish coinage in James Fort, a local economy was no longer viewed as necessary. Cohesion was enforced through clearly stated expectations and severe punishment of transgressors. In a desperate attempt to save its colony, the Virginia Company eliminated plans for a fiscal scheme that would have required reciprocal relationships and instead took complete control. This lasted less than ten years, when the Virginia Company realized that a productive society required incentives and choice. With the

Great Charter of 1618, land was opened up to private ownership, allowing colonists to work for themselves. Land and the tobacco grown upon it became the commodities of value in Virginia. As mentioned earlier, this did not totally obviate the need for small change but it did create an environment where meaningful relationships could be established through economic activities.

Notes

1. Decried coinage was condemned as obsolete or depreciated by proclamation.
2. Billon is an alloy of a precious metal with a high base metal content.

References Cited

Akin, Marjorie H., James C. Bard, and Kevin Akin. 2016. *Numismatic Archaeology of North America: A Field Guide*. New York: Routledge.

Barnard, Francis P. 1916. *The Casting-Counter and the Counting-Board: A Chapter in the History of Numismatics and Early Arithmetic*. Oxford: Clarendon Press.

Bemiss, Samuel M. 1957. *The Three Charters of the Virginia Company of London*. Williamsburg: Virginia 350th Anniversary Celebration Corp.

Berry, Paul. 2002. The Numismatic Record of Ferryland. *Avalon Chronicles* 7:1–71.

Bowsher, Julian. 2012. *Shakespeare's London Theatreland*. London: Museum of London Archaeology.

Brown, Alexander. 1890. *The Genesis of the United States*, 2 vols. Boston: Houghton Mifflin.

Bruce, Philip A. 1935. *Economic History of Virginia in the Seventeenth Century*, 2 vols. New York: Peter Smith.

Craven, Wesley F. 1937a. An Introduction to the History of Bermuda. *William and Mary Quarterly* 17(2):176–215.

———. 1937b. An Introduction to the History of Bermuda. *William and Mary Quarterly* 17(3):317–362.

———. 1937c. An Introduction to the History of Bermuda. *William and Mary Quarterly* 17(4):437–465.

———. 1938. An Introduction to the History of Bermuda. VI, The Revised Plan of Settlement. *William and Mary Quarterly* 18(1):13–63.

———. 1957. *The Virginia Company of London, 1606–1624*. Williamsburg: Virginia 350th Anniversary Celebration Corporation.

Fletcher, Edward. 2003. *Tokens & Tallies through the Ages*. Witham, Essex: Greenlight Publishing.

Galenson, David. 1996. The Settlement and Growth of the Colonies: Population, Labor, and Economic Development. In *The Cambridge Economic History of the United States*, edited by Stanley L. Engerman and Robert E. Gallman, 135–207. Cambridge: Cambridge University Press.

Harrison, William. (1587) 1994. *The Description of England by William Harrison*. Edited by G. Edelen. New York: Dover.

Haselgrove, Colin, and Stephan Krmnicek. 2012. The Archaeology of Money. *Annual Review of Anthropology* 18(2):235–250.

Horn, James, William Kelso, Douglas Owsley, and Beverly Straube. 2013. *Jane: Starvation, Cannibalism, and Endurance at Jamestown*. Williamsburg: Colonial Williamsburg Foundation and Preservation Virginia.

Hudgins, Carter C. 2005. Elizabethan Industries in Jacobean Virginia? An Examination of the Industrial Origins and Metallurgical Functions of Scrap Copper at Early Jamestown (c. 1607–1610). PhD diss., Royal Holloway, University of London.

Jordan, Louis E. 2003. Somer Islands "Hogge Money" of 1616: The Historical Context. *The Colonial Newsletter* 43(2):2465–2493.

———. 2009. Coinage in the English Colonies of North America to 1660. In *Newby's St. Patrick Coinage*, edited by O. D. Hoover, 185–287. Coinage of the Americas Conference, November 2006, Proceedings, vol. 16. New York American Numismatic Society.

Kelso, William M. 2006. *The Buried Truth*. Charlottesville: University Press of Virginia.

———. 2017. *Jamestown and the Truth Revealed*. Charlottesville: University Press of Virginia.

Kelso, William M., and Beverly A. Straube. 2004. *Jamestown Rediscovery 1994–2004*. Richmond: Association for the Preservation of Virginia Antiquities.

———. 2008. 2000–2006 Interim Report on the APVA Excavations at Jamestown, Virginia. Accessed June 1, 2017. Accessible at https://historicjamestowne.org/download/field-reports-3/.

Kelso, William M., Beverly A. Straube, and Daniel Schmidt, eds. 2012. 2007–2010 Interim Report on the Preservation Virginia Excavations at Jamestown, Virginia. Accessed June 1, 2017. Accessible at https://historicjamestowne.org/download/field-reports-3/.

Kemmers, Fleur, and Nanoushka Myrberg. 2011. Rethinking Numismatics: The Archaeology of Coins. *Archaeological Dialogues* 18(1):87–108.

Kingsbury, Susan M., ed. 1906–1935. *The Records of the Virginia Company of London*. 4 vols. Washington, DC: U.S. Government Printing Office.

Kupperman, Karen O. 1979. Apathy and Death in Early Jamestown. *The Journal of American History* 66(1):24–40.

———. 2007. *The Jamestown Project*. Cambridge, MA: Belknap Press of Harvard University Press.

Lefroy, John H. 1877. *Memorials of the Discovery and Early Settlement of the Bermudas or Somers Islands, 1515–1685*. London: Longmans, Green.

Lefroy, John H., ed. 1882. *The Historye of the Bermudaes or Summer Islands*. London: The Hakluyt Society.

Mernick, Philip, and Harold Mernick. 2017. Jettons, or Reckoning Counters. Accessed June 1, 2017. http://www.mernick.org.uk/jettons.htm.

Nelson, Philip. 1905. *The Coinage of Ireland in Copper, Tin, and Pewter, 1460–1826*. Liverpool: W. M. Murphy.

Noël Hume, Ivor. 1972. *A Guide to Artifacts of Colonial America*. New York: Alfred A. Knopf.

———. 1982. *Martin's Hundred: The Discovery of a Lost Colonial Virginia Settlement.* New York: Delta.

———. 2008. Fit for a Queen. In *Ceramics in America 2008*, edited by Robert Hunter, 263–273. Milwaukee: Chipstone Foundation.

Pawlisch, Hans S. 1985. *Sir John Davies and the Conquest of Ireland.* Cambridge: Cambridge University Press.

Peck, C. Wilson. 1970. *English Copper, Tin and Bronze Coins in the British Museum 1558–1958.* London: Trustees of the British Museum.

Potter, Stephen. 1989. Early English Effects on Virginia Algonquian Exchange and Tribute in the Tidewater Potomac. In *Powhatan's Mantle: Indians in the Colonial Southeast*, edited by Peter H. Wood, Gregory A. Waselkov, and M. Thomas Huntley, 151–172. Lincoln: University of Nebraska Press.

Quinn, David B. 1966. Advice for Investors in Virginia, Bermuda, and Newfoundland, 1611. *William and Mary Quarterly* 23(1):136–145.

Rich, Robert. (1610) 1890. Newes from Virginia. In *The Genesis of the United States*, edited by Alexander Brown, 420–426. Boston: Houghton Mifflin.

Ruding, Rogers. 1840. *Annals of the Coinage of Great Britain and its Dependencies.* Vol. 1. 3rd ed. London: John Hearne.

Sainsbury, W. Noel, ed. 1860. *Calendar of State Papers, Colonial Series, 1574–1660.* London: Longman, Green, Longman and Roberts.

Schofield, John, and Alan Vince. 2003. *Medieval Towns: The Archaeology of British Towns in their European Setting.* 2nd ed. London: Continuum.

Simon, James. (1749) 1810. *An Essay Towards an Historical Account of Irish Coins, and of the Currency of Foreign Monies in Ireland (1749).* Dublin: G. A. Procter.

Smith, John. 1986. The Generall Historie of Virginia, New-England, and the Summer Iles. In *The Complete Works of Captain John Smith*, vol. 3, edited by Phillip Barbour, 5–477. Chapel Hill: University of North Carolina Press.

Sportack, Mark A. 2006. The Myth and Mysteries of the Somers' Ilands Hogge Money. In *Money of the Caribbean,* edited by Richard G. Doty & John M. Kleeberg, 21–115. New York: American Numismatic Society.

Strachey, William. (1610) 1973. A True Reportory of the Wreck and Redemption of Sir Thomas Gates, Knight, upon and from the Islands of the Bermudas: His Coming to Virginia and the Estate of That Colony Then and After, under the Government of the Lord La Warr, July 15, 1610. In *A Voyage to Virginia in 1609*, 4th ed., edited by Louis B. Wright, 3–101. Charlottesville: University Press of Virginia.

Straube, Beverly A. 2014. "And he that in Virginia shall copper coin receive": Explicating an Undocumented Fiscal Scheme in the Early English Settlement at Jamestown through the Archaeological Evidence. PhD diss., University of Leicester.

———. 2016. Numismatic Portals to the Past: Archaeological Evidence of an Undocumented Seventeenth-Century Fiscal Scheme for Jamestown, Virginia. In *The Archaeology of Money*, edited by Colin Haselgrove and Stefan Krmnicek, 183–208. Leicester Archaeology Monograph 24. [Leicester]: University of Leicester.

Straube, Beverly A., and Nicholas M. Luccketti. 1996. 1995 Interim Report APVA Jamestown Rediscovery. Manuscript on file, Preservation Virginia, Jamestown, Virginia.

Symonds, Henry. 1917. The Elizabethan Coinages for Ireland. *Numismatic Chronicle* 17:97–125.

Thomas, Keith. 1987. Numeracy in Early Modern England, the Prothero Lecture. In *Transactions of the Royal Historical Society* 37:103–132.

Timberlake, Richard H. 1987. Private Production of Scrip-Money in the Isolated Community. *Journal of Money, Credit and Banking* 19(4):437–447.

Virginia Company. 1890. Broadside Concerning Virginia [1609]. In *The Genesis of the United States*, edited by Alexander Brown, 289–290. Boston: Houghton Mifflin.

Wallis, Helen. 1978. Geographie is Better than Divinitie. Maps, Globes, and Geography in the Days of Samuel Pepys. In *The Compleat Plattmaker: Essays on Chart, Map, and Globe Making in England in the Seventeenth and Eighteenth Centuries*, edited by Norman J. W. Thrower, 1–43. Berkeley: University of California Press.

Walton, Gary M., and James F. Shepherd. 1979. *The Economic Rise of Early America*. Cambridge: Cambridge University Press.

14

Rag, Stone, Water

A Material Study of Holy Wells in Contemporary Ireland

ELEANOR CONLIN CASELLA

> Saint Colman's well and "clootie tree" stand close to the ruins of Cranfield church on the north shore of Lough Neagh [County Antrim]. Protected from the elements by a high circular hedge, the tree is adorned with an assortment of offerings, everything from plastic bags to socks and crisp bags, its branches barely visible under the clutter. The [prayer] Pattern, traditionally held on May Eve, is thought to have died out over two hundred years ago.
>
> (Rackard and O'Callaghan 2001, 98)

The ubiquitous presence of holy wells is a distinctive characteristic of the rural Irish landscape. Constructed of both natural and manmade materials, these vernacular religious grottoes typically mark a ritually significant spring of fresh water. Known as *an tobar* ("the well or spring") or *na toibreacha* (plural) in Irish Gaelic, these sites are typically associated with miraculous cures and dedicated to Christian saints—most frequently the Virgin Mary, St. Patrick, or St. Brigid, although locally significant patron saints are also identified with well sites. General surveys of holy wells have identified over 3,000 across the island, although many are now disused and largely forgotten (Aalen 1997, 176).

From a purely descriptive perspective, Irish holy wells could be described using Colin Renfrew's model for an "archaeology of cult" (Renfrew and Bahn 1991, 359–60), as a number of the necessary material indicators are commonly present, including the repeated use of ritual iconographic symbols, representation of the deity in abstract form, special votive

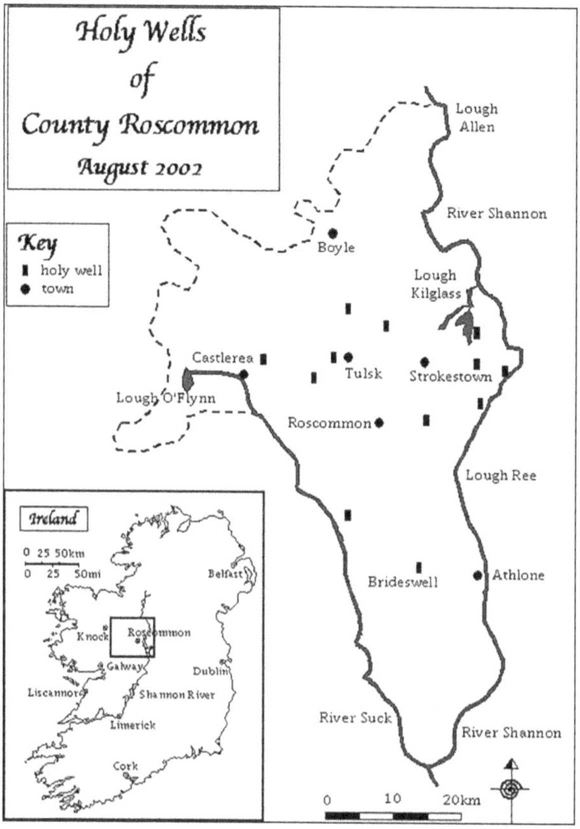

Figure 14.1. Project study area and recorded sites, County Roscommon. Map by Eleanor Conlin Casella, 2002.

deposits, and the presence of built spaces to focus attention (Lane 2001, 160). In 2002, I supervised a brief training field survey of holy well sites in the western Connaught region of Ireland, during which students and local community participants recorded the material culture, folklore, and oral histories of *na toibreacha* in County Roscommon (Figure 14.1). Drawing from results of the 2002 field season, this chapter offers an expanded interpretation of the intimate economies that surround these emotive places.

Of Myths and Meanings: A Diachronic Perspective

Both the pilgrimage practices and associated landscapes of most holy wells suggest pre-Christian origins (Walsham 2011). Diverse archaeological examples of ritual deposits and megalithic monuments can be found in association with springs, rivers, and lakes throughout Western Europe

(Richards 1996). Additionally, scholars have long observed enduring symbolic correlations of water with concepts of purity and cleansing that ultimately became ritually assimilated into the Christian practice of baptism (Lane 2001, 166).

Spring sanctuaries and "cult wells" were common throughout Iron Age Europe. Archaeological evidence has been recorded from continental La Tène (or late Celtic type) Iron Age sites from the first century BC. Bronze figurines, snake imagery, wooden votives, and human skulls are frequently recovered from sites associated with fresh water springs (Green 1986, 150–161). Following Roman colonization, prehistoric European holy wells were quickly integrated within new geographies of ritual practice (Rattue 1995, 23–32). Over the first century AD, Celtic spring sanctuaries throughout England became appropriated as sites of Romano-British bathing and healing. Bath (Aquae Sulis) in Somerset is the obvious and most iconic example, although other Romanized pre-Christian sacred springs were located at Buxton (Aquae Arnemetiae) in Derbyshire and at Coventina's Well in Carrawburgh, Northumberland (Green 1986). Because the Romans did not expand into Ireland, *na toibreacha* underwent a very different process of diachronic transformation.

Current Irish folklore and oral histories trace the origins of holy wells to the syncretic fusion of Celtic and Christian faiths that emerged throughout the island from around the fifth century AD. Indeed, most scholars of the early Christian era have observed a marked continuity of religious practices throughout this transitional period. These studies cite the ubiquitous presence of *na toibreacha*—in addition to their association with local deity "saints," and prehistoric cairns, mounds, and standing stones—as primary evidence for the accommodation of preexisting Celtic religions during the rapid Christianization of Ireland (Swan 2001, 96; Walsham 2011).

At Tulsk (County Roscommon), Tobar Ogulla commemorates the spring of fresh water in which St. Patrick baptized Fidelma and Eithne, princess daughters of the High King of Ireland (Figure 14.2). These mythic characters have been formally incorporated into Irish Catholic traditions and are locally commemorated through the Tulsk parish's Church of Saints Eithne and Fidelma. This holy well is situated within the prehistoric Neolithic to Iron Age settlement of Ráth Cruachan, or Rathcroghan, the fortified seat of the O'Connor royal dynasty of the Connacht region of western Ireland (Waddell 1998). The immediate archaeological neighborhood of

Figure 14.2. Tober Ogulla, Tulsk, County Roscommon. Photo by Eleanor Conlin Casella, 2002.

Tobar Ogulla is as significant and monumental as the nationally iconic sites of Tara and Newgrange; it consists of more than thirty prehistoric ringforts, palace compounds, and earthen barrows situated within two miles of Tobar Ogulla.

Located in southern County Roscommon, Brideswell has a similarly unique significance for the early church because of its association with St. Brigid, who appears in folklore as the first Irish-born evangelist. The traditional prayer cycle of Brideswell incorporates a prehistoric mound with curbstones, a standing stone monument, and the bedrock side of the spring, in addition to a roof gable of the local school and a concrete and marble statue of St. Brigid erected by the community in 1957 (Gacquin 2001; Logan 1980, 31–32).

Many Irish holy wells commemorate the arrival of Christianity with a sacred topographic feature inscribed by the bodily presence of the first evangelist of that local region. At the now-disused St. Barry's Well, which is associated with the evicted village of Ballykilcline on Lough Kilglass, the waters sprang up where St. Barry's knee touched the ground as he smote the evil serpent (*oll-phiart*) from Slieve Bawn, the nearest mountain. Similarly, at St. Patrick's Well in Kilmore (near Athleague) the central shrine contains the hoof print of St. Patrick's horse, as indicated by a cupule (or circular depression) in the limestone bedrock. Another of his sacred hoof prints is immortalized by a second vertical cupule that is also preserved in limestone, but located within a quarry site approximately 300 meters to the northwest. It is perhaps important to note that the medieval parish boundary lay between these two evocative "hoofprints," with each polity retaining half of this mythic imprint. Holy wells associated with St. Patrick very commonly contain some remnant of his bodily presence. In Patrick Logan's descriptive compendium of holy well folklore, he records the frequent presence of stone imprints made by St. Patrick's knees, hands, fingertips, feet, head, and, in the case of Cross Patrick church in Killaha parish (of County Mayo), imprints of the saint's buttocks (Logan 1980, 38).

The physical inscription of the saintly journey across these rural spaces forged an intimate bond between local inhabitants and the land itself.

> The wandering Irish saints prophesy, cure, win battles, even raise the dead. They also curse. They are indissolubly associated with the landscape, and share its ambivalence and bouts of temper. In that they are more like the ancient Hebrew heroes and prophets than the saint-martyrs of Mediterranean Roman civilization. Like the Hebrews they were tribespeople, not townspeople, the shamans of a pastoral folk who themselves moved in the landscape. (Taylor 1995, 43)

Such inscriptions create a sense of belonging through familiar memories (Tilley 1994, 27–29). A saint's legendary movements transform the Irish landscape into interconnected sets of sacred monuments that link inhabitants both to the topography itself (as residual physical evidence of the saint's presence) and to the sedimented layers of history and meanings embedded within these sacred features. Or, as Chris Tilley has observed, drawing from Parmentier's (1987) ethnographic work in Polynesia, "paths form an essential medium for the routing of social relations, connecting up spatial impressions with temporally inscribed meanings" (Tilley 1994, 31).

Arguing from a comparative perspective, Carole Crumley has noted the particularly effective use of water springs for intergenerational communication of cultural meanings.

> Even when the connection between memory and meaning is severed (as when a ritual is retained but its meaning lost), information can still be delivered to future generations. The most effective carriers of social memory are landscape elements that have both practical utility and cosmic meaning, such as caves, springs or gardens. Such elements offer a personalized mnemonic that is "good to think." (Crumley 1999, 271)

The absent presence of the saint at an Irish holy well—as represented through the sacred stone imprints of head, hands, or buttocks—can be thus interpreted as an augmented mnemonic. The marks provide materialized evidence that etch a continuous social memory of the saint's intimate sacred activities over generations, even as specific social meanings and practices diachronically transform.

These mnemonic continuities occurred in the context of Ireland's difficult history of dispossession and social upheaval. Over the latter part of the sixteenth century, the militaristic, religious, and mercantile aspirations of Elizabethan England resulted in the imposition of new sectarian political economies throughout the rapidly expanding Atlantic world (Horning 2013; Parno and Fortenberry 2013). In Ireland, enduring antipathies emerged as rural Gaelic and Old English chiefdoms were forcibly replaced. In exchange for Her Majesty's land grants, loyal Scottish and English Protestant landlords promised to settle the Catholic Irish into ordered townlands and to expand annual agricultural exports (Foster 1989). By the end of the seventeenth century, these colonial ventures combined with anxiety over Ireland's support for the deposed Catholic king James II and ultimately culminated with the imposition of the Penal Laws (1695–1793). This series of religious restrictions was designed to enforce Protestantism as the official state religion of Ireland. All Catholic religious orders were disbanded and the English Crown seized their substantial land holdings. Catholics were excluded from holding property or engaging in professional trades and Catholic religious services were forbidden inside all townland buildings.

Indeed, from the seventeenth century on, the colonial experience of "being Irish" became so associated with religious confrontation that Irish scholars now often use the term "politico-religious" to describe the experience of modern Irish ethnicities (Cecil 1993, 146). Particularly outside the Anglo-Irish towns, poverty excluded most Catholics from what haphazard medical provisions existed. As a result, folk remedies, herbalists, and faith healers predominated (Foster 1989, 220), as did the diverse folklore surrounding the curative power of holy wells reflecting this traditional dependency.

As the Irish historian R. F. Foster has noted, however, the Penal Laws were intended to humiliate, not eradicate, the Irish Catholic Church (Foster 1989, 205–208). Catholic services continued to be held in open-air fields at Mass Rocks. These places of community worship were never hidden. Today they form a common type of listed historic monument; their locations can be found in local tourism heritage publications and current Irish Ordnance Survey maps (Bishop 2016). While Catholic parish churches were formally abandoned, archaeological evidence demonstrates local reuse of these ruins as burial grounds throughout the eighteenth and nineteenth centuries, in addition to quiet examples of building repair and maintenance (Costello 2017). Similarly, over the difficult era of the Penal Laws, devotional activities at holy wells, while officially discouraged, were reluctantly acknowledged as "backward" but harmless folk traditions. For Irish Catholics, *na toibreacha* emerged as important physical mnemonics of Gaelic continuity (Walsham 2011). Aidan O'Sullivan's archaeological work on *crannogs*, or fortified island settlements, has suggested similar metaphorical significance during this British colonial period. He interprets the enduring continuity of settlement on these manmade fortified lake dwellings as a stubborn Gaelic resistance to the imposition of a new English geopolitical landscape order throughout the sixteenth and seventeenth centuries (O'Sullivan 2002).

With the advent of the famine years (1845–1849), Ireland suffered a cataclysmic moment of transformation. Over a five-year period, approximately one-quarter of its population was lost through hunger, disease, and emigration (O'Tuathaigh 1990, 204). Entire towns were abandoned through a combination of charitable relocation schemes and forced evictions by landlords. For this survey project, the effect of this rapid period of social upheaval was manifest in the consolidation of devotional practices around certain wells and the abandonment of others. Wells attached to surviving towns gained in popularity, while more local or rural devotional sites dropped from active usage. For example, Ballykilcline, a populated hamlet near Strokestown, was cleared of its tenants and demolished by the local landlord in 1846 (Orser 2005). Although the exact location of this abandoned holy well was very recently rediscovered by the current farmer while clearing brush, traditional folklore recorded by Patrick Logan in 1980 remembered the general existence of the Ballykilcline well, its association with St. Barry, and its associated cure for headaches (Logan 1980, 73).

The spread of automobile transportation in Ireland during the 1930s hastened the consolidation of religious activities around certain prominent holy wells. During our field interviews, a number of residents and site visitors suggested that the smaller local wells fell out of use because of duplicated cures associated with other wells, and because of the growing commercialization of nationally and internationally profiled holy wells. Perhaps the significance of the pilgrimage itself featured in this issue of continuity. The intercession or cure requested at a holy well is traditionally accompanied by a display of personal sacrifice—an intimate quid pro quo of sorts. The journey to the holy well often forms part of this sacred offering. As road and air travel grew more common, greater distances to increasingly foreign holy wells became required to demonstrate the magnitude of the sacrifice and the potency of the cure. The display of nonlocal offerings at many of the Irish holy well sites we surveyed—including keychains advertising business addresses from distant regions and holy water or medallions collected from continental sites such as Lourdes (France), Fatima (Portugal), and Medjugorje (Bosnia-Herzegovina)—offered powerful material evidence of the extended journeys undertaken by supplicants to forge this intimate exchange.

The few scholarly books on holy wells published over the last twenty years tend to differentially focus upon Irish holy wells from the southern and western counties (Healy 2001). This regional attention may reflect a higher survival of traditional Gaelic sites and practices in locations distant from the primary center of English colonial control. This distribution may also reflect a romantic focus of study on those rural counties most celebrated as "wilder and purer" regions by nationalist writers, artists and heritage bureaucrats (O'Sullivan 2002; Duffy 1997).

Notebook observations from the 2002 field season suggested four possible forms of contemporary significance for Irish holy wells. First, for the vast majority of foreign summertime visitors that drive and cycle their way across Ireland, a brief stop at a holy well added an exotic experience of Celtic folklife to their tourist itinerary. These visitors were frequently accompanied by their Irish hosts. This second group described the sites as important to their own sense of a distinctive national folklore—part of what creates a general sense of Irishness.

These two forms of significance were distinguished from a significance linked to a third group we encountered: local Irish residents for whom the primary significance of *an tobar* lay within its role as a focus of community for both current and previous neighbors. Finally, there were visitors for whom the holy wells are a significant religious experience and who actively and openly engaged in their religious devotions while we were conducting our fieldwork surveys and interviews.

A Spring of Waters, a Body of Prayers

Working from this historical and ethnographic context, holy well sites can be interpreted as a central locus for intimate exchanges materialized among and between individuals, the corporate body of the Irish Catholic community, and saintly deities of another realm. As noted earlier, the origins of many *na toibreacha* are the bodily presence of the first evangelist: the mythic saint's body literally generates the holy water. Images of sacred bodies are frequently left as votive offerings, taking the form of statues, two-dimensional icons, and candles. A highly popular candle icon depicts the reclusive Italian monk Padre Pio, who became the focus of a postwar era devotional cult following his revelation of stigmata, or wounds perpetually embedded in his hands and feet representing the nails of the crucifixion.

The Well of St. Barry at Whitehall Parish (County Roscommon) is closely associated with the ruined stone church and graveyard of Kilbarry. At this site, the upper cranium of a human skull is encased within a niche built in the exterior side of the remaining nave. Local traditions claim this relic to be the earthly remains of a local monk who held curative powers over tooth and jaw ailments (Logan 1980, 85). The faithful supplicant reaches into the niche to touch the skull, then touches those fingers to their own teeth and makes the sign of the cross. The gesture must be made three times to activate the potency of this cure.

Irish holy wells offer miraculous cures for bodily ailments—typically eye problems, wounds and sores, throat problems, and headaches—although the ancient St. Brigid's Well at Brideswell (recorded as one of the most important festival sites for the early eighth-century Church) offers a

Figure 14.3. St. Cholin devotional window, Castlerea, County Roscommon. Photo by Eleanor Conlin Casella, 2002.

cure for fertility problems. Inappropriate bodily encounters with the holy well can desecrate the holy site. All such sacrilegious encounters involved either the violation of a sacred body, or the washing of non-persons in the holy well. For example, St. Cholin's Well, near Castlerea (County Roscommon) was reportedly dry because of the rape and mutilation of a nun from a nearby convent. Her eyes were blinded during this violent attack. The clootie tree and dry well associated with this brutal folktale remain a powerful sacred site. A window in St. Patrick's Church of Castlerea was sponsored by James Keenan of Kansas City (United States) to commemorate the infamous legend. Donated during the 1890s, it also offered his devotional gratitude after his eyesight was cured through a visit to this local holy well. Within the Church window, St. Cholin offers her own violated eyes up as symbolic evidence of her own original embodied and deeply intimate sacrifice (Figure 14.3).

Such despoiling of *an tobar* frequently results in a cycle of punishment and redemption. At St. Brigid's well in Kilteevan, near Roscommon town, the local people we interviewed linked their split well to a shameful misuse committed by the nineteenth century Protestant landlord, Robert Ormsby of Kilmore (Ryan 1997, 222). The original well offered a cure for skin wounds and sores. Ormsby discovered a woman bathing her child,

Figure 14.4. Pattern Day, St. Brigid's Well, Liscannor, County Clare. Photo by Eleanor Conlin Casella, 2005.

who was inflicted with scurvy, at the well. Upon learning of this miraculous cure, Ormsby plunged his mange-inflicted greyhound into the well, thereby mocking the Catholic faith of the Irish woman, and desecrating *an tobar*. As a punishment, the well dried, only to eventually reemerge across the roadway as a symbol of sacred redemption. While an obvious historical context can be read through the Protestant desecration of a Catholic holy site, both the motif of a dog as the nonhuman agent of desecration, and the relocation of an "insulted" holy well frequently appear in Irish folklore (Logan 1980, 67–68).

While the majority of devotions to holy wells occur throughout the year as private and individual encounters, each well retains a feast day when the community of believers congregate to celebrate, respect, and commemorate the patron saint of *an tobar* with intimate offerings. Patterns, or prescribed cycles of prayers, are recited as the faithful walk through networked stations of the site. At St. Brigid's Well in Liscannor (County Clare), supplicants literally walk the rosary during this pattern, ascending steps to a carved sandstone cross which must be circled, touched, and kissed five times before descending the pathway back to the well shrine, where sacred waters are collected and anointed in the sign of the cross upon one's head and torso (Figure 14.4).

During our field survey, the antiquity of this cross was visible in the extensive surface polish and wear patterns along its body and base. While my students were recording this site in August 2002, a local resident explained that the pathway itself formed a sacred geography; its shape represented the oval created when a rosary was set to rest. For the pilgrim, the annual St. Brigid's pattern thus creates an embodied rosary through its very enactment. Patterns thereby become a very personal offering, a particular "art of walking" that is simultaneously an "art of consciousness, habit and practice, that is both constrained by place and landscape and constitutive of them" (Tilley 1994, 29).

At more formalized wells, the holy pattern will take the form of the Stations of the Cross—a standardized cycle of prayers endorsed by the Vatican to commemorate the crucifixion of Jesus. Each round of the pattern is marked through depositing a stone next to *an tobar*, scratching a cross onto the central shrine, or swallowing three sips of the sacred water. We recorded the ubiquitous presence of cups and fragmentary ceramics in all active holy well sites we surveyed. Interviews with local female residents confirmed that old cast-off teacups and mugs had been quietly placed for visitors to use at these wells, suggesting an intimate offering of household goods.

A Very Arduous Pilgrimage

An intercession by the relevant saint typically requires some form of sacrifice to maximize the potency of an intimate prayer. For example, at St. Kieran's Well in County Meath, a large ash tree associated with *an tobar* assumed the duty by seeping blood from its trunk. According to local folklore first recorded in 1849 by Sir William Wilde (the father of Oscar Wilde), thousands flocked to the well to witness the miracle and collect the "blood" for cures (Rackard and O'Callaghan 2001, 72).

Feast days require special fasting in preparation for the pattern. A state of spiritual purity may only be achieved through abstinence from food throughout the novena day. The most traditional form of pilgrimage is undertaken barefoot, particularly for the annual pattern walks—or in the case of "The Reek," a rugged mountain pilgrimage hike up the iconic sacred mountain Croagh Patrick in County Mayo. This embodied practice is believed to communicate the humbled attitude of a supplicant before the patron saint. The barefoot pilgrimage also serves as a mortification of flesh—a penance for past misdeeds or addictions, and a sacrificial offering toward a future holy intervention by the associated deity. Intimate physical suffering thus offers a bodily sacrifice in exchange for a sacred cure or benediction, a blessing toward hopes for an improved future, or a passionate remembrance of those loved and lost.

Votive offerings at holy wells typically include material representations of the bodily imperfections cured by the holy well—crutches, eyeglasses, and even asthma inhalers. Bodily indulgences and physical addictions are also frequently sacrificed. The offerings of sweet wrappers, alcohol bottles, and cigarette packages demonstrate a material yearning for deliverance, moral improvement, and health. These polyvalent votives can be also read as both authentic evidence for and material advertisements of the miraculous curative powers believed to infuse *an tobar*. Until recently, holy wells specialized in specific cures (Logan 1980, 69). However, certain more active wells recently seem to have had their curative value "expanded" by transforming into more generalized cure-alls—a sort of "general practitioner" approach to folk medicine possibly intended to attract more pilgrimages to the area.

Most holy wells are associated with an adjacent rag tree, upon which the supplicant ties a scrap of cloth, a hair tie, a handkerchief, or a segment of tissue paper (Figure 14.5). These clootie ("strip of cloth or rag") form polysemic votive offerings. Traditionally they represented the humility of sacrifice—a strip of cloth torn from the supplicant's clothing in exchange for the intercession of the saint. Another version forwarded by a local resident claimed the clootie represented a sacrifice of the most personal item held by the individual while engaged with *an tobar*. This explanation was offered when we asked about the modern practice of fastening various types of hair ties (ribbons, scrunchies, elasticated bands, etc.) to the rag trees.

Other informants argued that the clootie commemorated a supplicant's request—the prayer remembered by the saint until the "rag" had decayed. Another explanation reflected the curative powers of the holy well: the inflicted person would wash their wound with the rag and thereby cast their disease into this humble offering. Once this surrogate clootie had decayed from the tree, the wound would be cured. Our project survey located

Figure 14.5. Tober Ogulla, Clootie Tree, Tulsk, County Roscommon. Photo by Eleanor Conlin Casella, 2005.

only one rag tree at a site unrelated to a well. Its presence at the cave of Ownegat (near Tulsk, County Roscommon)—known in Irish folklore as both the mouth of the otherworld, and the gate of hell—suggested an additional protective meaning whereby sacred offerings were made away from any holy well. Regardless, these otherworldly clootie symbolically acknowledged the powerful material presence of an early pre-Christian landscape—with the underside of the capstone of Ownegat incised with Ogham script, an Iron Age form of writing that appeared from circa 300 AD on stone monuments across Ireland and the Celtic fringes of Britain (Waddell 1998).

The emotive theme of decay was significant at all the holy wells we recorded. Traditionally, *an tobar* offerings are left to intentionally decay. They enact a specific moment of sacrifice, commemoration, or request: they both retain and create the lifecycle of that personal prayer. Votives (as private offerings) are not generally objects that require maintenance or conservation. They are respectfully left alone to decay as the intention behind them achieves fulfilment. Results of our survey suggested that only within the last fifty years have permanent memorials become erected.

Such "improvements," as termed by the local residents, occurred only at the most active and regionally known holy wells.

Our Missing and Much Loved One

Ultimately, *na toibreacha* provide a public forum for the performance of individual religious experience. As such, the material culture associated with these sites represents an accumulation of intimate prayers, intentions, and exchanges. For example, it is customary to leave a stone at the close of one's pattern. The stone fabric itself then becomes materially infused with mythic power (Brenneman and Brenneman 1995, 54). Seven smooth cobblestones lie behind the spring of Angel's Well at Bindoo (County Donegal). To activate the curative powers, a supplicant will pass a stone "around their heads, arms, legs and torsos, blessing themselves with the stone and kissing it to finish" (Rackard and O'Callaghan 2001, 66). The piles of stones curated at the sides of Irish holy sites thus represent a gradual collection of individual actions and intimate exchanges.

Similarly, at both St. Barry's Well of Kilbarry and Cluain Patrick of Kilmore (County Roscommon), rounds of the pattern are counted by drawing a cross on the central shrine. Resulting etched markings therefore represent a slow sedimentation of individual patterns into a materialized corporate expression. Personal votive offerings join a material community of Irish Catholic spiritual activity. In a sense, they form "citations" of Catholic beliefs, laws, and norms that guide an appropriate exchange with the impalpable deity linked to *an tobar*. If materialization defines a process of sedimentation, over time these intimate offerings accumulate seemingly fixed or bounded meaning (Butler 1993, 15)—they produce a "surface we call matter" (Butler 1993, 9).

As places for miraculous cures, Irish holy wells have also evolved as places of material commemoration of the deceased. The absent presence of the patron saint is emotively invoked through the death notices, graffiti, and scapulars (personal baptismal accessories) left as votive offerings—all artifacts that intimately re/member those lost from family and community. Relationships between individuals and those no longer present are thereby sedimented at *an tobar*. They provide a place for materially expressing both longing for and belonging to.

Thus, it is the accumulated piles of stones, the amassed votives, and gradually etched medieval cross at Cluain Patrick that represent, produce, and commemorate both individual and corporate bodies of Irish Catholics. As Butler observes,

> When can we say with confidence that an identification has happened? . . . Identification is the phantasmatic staging of the event. In this sense, identifications belong to the imaginary; they are phantasmatic efforts of alignment, loyalty, ambiguous and cross-corporeal cohabitation; they unsettle the "I"; they are the sedimentation of the "we" in the constitution of any "I." (Butler 1993, 105)

Although the recitation of a rosary during the enactment of a pattern is in itself an intimate solitary act, it simultaneously imagines the "we" (Irish Catholics) and the "I" as a member of that collective body. In that sense, *na toibreacha* have a special role in the production and maintenance of Irish Catholicism. Unlike churches—where the community of believers performs a public mass service codified by the Vatican that is uniform throughout the international Church—these vernacular Irish holy wells are sites of deeply individual and deeply intimate worship.

It is through regular reiterations of these material actions by individual supplicants that a corporate identity, a sense of belonging to a communal body of belief, becomes literally sedimented through the rag, the stone, and the water. Once a year, on Pattern Day, the community gathers to publicly reiterate themselves as a Catholic body that belong to the spring of fresh water. For the remaining 364 days, *an tobar* is a site of intimate longing: the material culture sediments, commemorates, and yearns for the absent presence of the sacred body, the healthy body, the deceased body, and the community body.

The People Still Occasionally Visit: Transgressive Continuity

Judith Butler's work was critiqued (Lloyd 1999) for its emphasis on the individual process of identity construction, for primarily reading forms of personal reiteration as "discontinuities"—or as "gender trouble" (Butler 1990). In her analysis of Butler, Moya Lloyd argued for an appreciation of historical context in order to understand the fine (yet vital) distinction between a repetitive performance and a transgressive parody (Lloyd 1999).

Expanding Lloyd's critique into this specific Irish historic context, the continuous intimate economy of holy wells may have been as transgressive as any material performances of discontinuity or parody. Dramatic

Figure 14.6. Detail of altar stone, Cluain Patrick, Athleague, County Roscommon. Photo by Eleanor Conlin Casella, 2002.

periods of colonization and social upheaval marked the history of Ireland from medieval through modern periods. These historic contexts etched new layers of sociopolitical meaning onto *na toibreacha* across the island. Conversions required by the rapid establishment of Christianity were echoed in later attempts to replace Catholicism with a new Protestant state religion. Through both transitional periods, individual and corporate citations of preexisting religious practices reinscribed the holy wells as stubborn places of Irish Catholic social memory (Figure 14.6), transforming these intimate sacred places into transgressive sites of cultural *continuity*.

This reiteration of previous ritual practices became transgressive in its tenacious refusal to accept the radical disjunctures colonization brought. While tremendous geopolitical transformations wrenched the previous social order, *an tobar* allowed intimate exchanges among individuals, their corporate community, and their beloved (and feared) deity to all be recited, reinvoked and re-created. As traditional offerings of intimate votives, personal prayer cycles and shared feast days to the local saints continued, these embodied continuities of practice became assimilated into a new syncretic and distinctly Irish form of Catholicism. It is ultimately through these fundamental, embodied, and polysemic *continuities* of rags, stones and waters that *na toibreacha* have retained their intimate power within Ireland's rural landscapes.

References Cited

Aalen, F. H. A. 1997. Buildings. In *Atlas of the Irish Rural Landscape*, edited by F. H. A. Aalen, Kevin Whelan, and Matthew Stout, 145–179. Cork: Cork University Press.

Bishop, H. 2016. Classifications of Sacred Space: A New Understanding of Mass Rock Sites in Ireland. *International Journal of Historical Archaeology* 20:828–872.

Brenneman, W. L., and M. G. Brenneman. 1995. *Crossing the Circle at the Holy Wells of Ireland*. Charlottesville: University Press of Virginia.

Butler, Judith. 1990. *Gender Trouble*. London: Routledge.

———. 1993. *Bodies that Matter*. London: Routledge.

Cecil, R. 1993. "The Marching Season in Northern Ireland: An Expression of Politico-Religious Identity." In *Inside European Identities*, edited by S. MacDonald, 146–166. Oxford: Berg Press.

Costello, Eugene. 2017. Medieval Memories and the Reformation of Religious Identity: Catholic and Anglican Interactions with Parish Church sites in County Limerick, Ireland. *Post-Medieval Archaeology* 51(2):332–353.

Crumley, Carole L. 1999. Sacred Landscapes: Constructed and Conceptualized. In *Archaeologies of Landscape*, edited by Wendy Ashmore and A. Bernard Knapp, 269–276. Oxford: Blackwell.

Duffy, J. 1997. Writing Ireland: Literature and Art in the Representation of Irish Place. In *In Search of Ireland: A Cultural Geography*, edited by B. J. Graham, 64–83. London: Routledge.

Foster, Roy F. 1989. *The Oxford Illustrated History of Ireland*. Oxford: Oxford University Press.

Gacquin, W. 2001. The Pattern of Brideswell. In *A Century of Education: Brideswell National School*. Unpublished local council pamphlet, Brideswell (County Roscommon).

Green, Miranda. 1986. *The Gods of the Celts*. Surrey, UK: Bramley Books.

Healy, Elizabeth. 2001. *In Search of Ireland's Holy Wells*. Dublin: Wolfhound Press.

Horning, Audrey. 2013. *Ireland in the Virginian Sea: Colonialism in the British Atlantic*. Chapel Hill: University of North Carolina Press.

Lane, Paul. 2001. The Archaeology of Christianity in Global Perspective. In *Archaeology and World Religion*, edited by Timothy Insoll, 148–181. London: Routledge.

Lloyd, Moya. 1999. Performativity, Parody, Politics. *Theory, Culture & Society* 16(2):195–213.

Logan, Patrick. 1980. *The Holy Wells of Ireland*. Buckinghamshire, UK: Colin Smythe, Gerrards Cross.

Orser, Charles E., Jr. 2005. Symbolic Violence, Resistance and the Vectors of Improvement in Early Nineteenth-Century Ireland. *World Archaeology* 37(3):392–407.

O'Sullivan, A. 2002. Crannogs: Places of Resistance in the Contested Landscapes of Early Modern Ireland. In *Contested Landscapes: Movement, Exile and Place*, edited by Barbara Bender and Margo Winer, 87–101. Oxford: Berg Press.

O'Tuathaig, G. 1990. *Ireland Before the Famine, 1798–1848*. Dublin: Gill and Macmillan.

Parmentier, R. 1987. *The Sacred Remains*. Chicago: University of Chicago Press.

Parno, Travis G., and Brent R. Fortenberry. 2013. Catholic Artefacts in a Protestant Landscape. In *Historical Archaeologies of Cognition*, edited by James Symonds, Anna Badcock, and Jeff Oliver, 15–27. Sheffield: Equinox.

Rackard, A., and L. O'Callaghan. 2001. *Fishstonewater: Holy Wells of Ireland*. Cork: Attic Press Ltd.

Rattue, J. 1995. *The Living Stream: Holy Wells in Historical Context*. Woodbridge, UK: Boydell Press.

Renfrew, A. Colin, and Paul Bahn. 1991. *Archaeology: Theories, Methods and Practice*. London: Thames & Hudson.

Richards, C. 1996. Henges and Water. *Journal of Material Culture* 1:313–336.

Ryan, H. A., ed. 1997. *Kilteevan: A Look at a School and Its Parish*. Dublin: School Board of Management.

Swan, D. L. 2001. *The Book of the Burren*. 2nd ed. Kinvara, County Galway: Tir Eolas.

Taylor, L. 1995. *Occasions of Faith: An Anthropology of Irish Catholics*. Dublin: Lilliput Press.

Tilley, Christopher. 1994. *A Phenomenology of Landscape*. Oxford: Berg Press.

Waddell, J. 1998. *The Prehistoric Archaeology of Ireland*. Galway: Galway University Press.

Walsham, A. 2011. *The Reformation of the Landscape*. Oxford: Oxford University Press.

15

Concluding Thoughts

Reframing the Archaeology of Intimate Economies

MARY C. BEAUDRY

Early approaches to intimate economies focused on households. The interests of economic anthropologists tended toward small-scale economies of groups such as hunter-gatherers and they used the term "sharing," as distinct from "reciprocity," to characterize the sorts of exchanges that took place in intimate economies. In such studies, sharing was seen as "an integrative or coordinating process that makes the parts of the intimate economic system congruous and effective without calculating returns, within an intimate social group, and patterned by the general role structure of that group" (Price 1975, 4). It has become clear, however, that intimate economies are pervasive in larger-scale complex societies and in simpler ones and that such economic systems can be far-flung and may operate wholly in the shadows of capitalism or beyond them (Henry 1987; see also Wright 2010). They may be known but tacitly overlooked and may or may not involve illegal or illicit activities as defined by Dawdy and Hartnett (2013). The contributions to this volume demonstrate clearly that acknowledgment of these facts has afforded historical archaeologists an important entrée into this topic and opportunities to make substantive contributions to research on intimate economies (see, e.g., Casella 2010).

Focus on intimate economies is a relatively recent development in the social sciences. Zelizer (2002, 276) points out that

> since the nineteenth century social analysts have repeatedly assumed that the social world organizes around competing, incompatible principles: Gemeinschaft and Gesellschaft, ascription and

> achievement, sentiment and rationality, solidarity and self-interest. Their mixing, goes the theory, contaminates both; invasion of the sentimental world by instrumental rationality desiccates that world, while introduction of sentiment into rational transactions produces inefficiency, favoritism, cronyism, and other forms of corruption.

In intimate economies we see sentiment, solidarity, and self-interest operating simultaneously and beneficially for the parties involved, in most cases without any of the ill effects that entrepreneur and competition models of economic exchange predict.

Contemporary approaches to intimate economies (see, e.g., Bloch 2017, 76–111; Cabezas 2011; Loza 2016, 63–94) often focus on the sorts of interactions studied by Ara Wilson in *The Intimate Economies of Bangkok: Tomboys, Tycoons, and Avon Ladies in the Global City* (2004). Wilson's research is heavily focused on sexual and ethnic identities as they are produced and transformed through the modernity of the non-Western world and on the key intersections of social identity and relationships (see also Wilson 2012). She looks at architecture, material objects, primary texts, secondary texts, and the business press; commercial sites such as shophouses, retail stores, and tourist sex trade go-go bars; and a popular downtown shopping mall, a telecommunications marketing office, and direct sales companies such as Amway and Avon. Wilson's notion has taken hold throughout much of the social sciences and in gender and sexuality studies, legal studies, and economics. In a similar vein, Lyttleton (2014) has explored the material economies in Asia that intertwine culture, sexuality, and health in response to the global pressures of modernization.

Intimate economies based on the commodification of bodies, emotions, and sexualities are seen as high value–producing forms of exchange in contemporary global capitalism. New technologies of communication, transport, and medicine make new types of commodification possible, producing new subjects and social relations among various actors in the global economy. One of the key features of this conception of intimate economies is self-commodification. For instance, in her chapter in this volume analyzing the assemblage from a nineteenth-century brothel context, Jade Luiz has found considerable evidence not just of embodiment but also of self-commodification through the economic choices that both the madam and working women made in creating and manipulating sensual experiences for brothel clients.

Another contemporary notion of what constitutes an intimate economy involves the recent emergence of peer-to-peer marketplaces for items such as clothing and home goods, a system that is viewed as an "intimate economy" characterized by a new willingness of people to participate in one another's lives: "We're using one another's resources, and the stigmas associated with used items have fallen by the wayside. Now, there's this intimacy of sharing [personal items] with one another" (Fallon 2014). As archaeologists, however, we are well aware that sharing and the reclamation and resale of used goods, at times goods quite personal if not intimate in nature, is hardly a new feature of alternative economic networks. One can think of rag pickers, gleaners, and so on throughout time, including the nineteenth-century Parisian purveyors of leftover food from the tables of the French court (Beizer 2015; see also Stobart and Van Damme 2010).

Bridge and Smith (2003) consider that the commodity is at the heart of intimate economies, noting that recent research along these lines has been heavily affected by the material turn in anthropology and other disciplines. They cite especially the influence of Daniel Miller's work (e.g., Miller 1987, 1998) on their field of geography and on scholars in many other disciplines who have developed their own approaches to materiality and the notion of economies as "intimate encounters with things" (Bridge and Smith 2003, 258–260). Their approach to intimate economies attends more closely to culture writ large than to the subcultural nature of intimate economies and the forms they take. Overemphasis on commodities obscures the human individuals and their participation as embodied actors in intimate economic interactions.

What the most recent contemporary studies of intimate or sharing economies have in common with the archaeological approach brought forward in this book is a focus on materiality, embodiment, and contingency. What historical archaeologists do *not* do is use their studies of intimate economies as the basis for a critique of the negative impacts of capitalism. Their aim is to bring intimate economic networks out of the shadow of capitalism and to examine how such networks operate and how the connections formed in such interactions foster human connections and linkages that benefit all of the parties involved.

Contemporary notions of intimate economies are not wholly congruent with the intimate economy approach historical archaeologists take in this volume—the contributors refer to the economies they study as "diverse, intimate, and autonomous" (Reilly), "internal and illicit" (Fogle), or as characterized by "otherness and liminality" (Hyttinen et al.). Even so, the exchange networks discussed in all of the chapters shared key elements with the intimate economies of today. They all, regardless of how independent, liminal, or subordinate they may have been, linked their participants with the global political economy and the capitalist market. This is especially apparent in the case studies involving commodity production and resource exploitation, be it sugar manufacture, seal hunting, whaling, or liquor production and exchange carried out in locales in Finland, the U.S. East Coast and Southeast, the Caribbean, and Antarctica. Another characteristic these exchanges share with contemporary intimate economies is that they involve face-to-face or even more intimate interactions, inventive and mixed strategies for survival and/or profit, and unbridled opportunism, including, at times, the sale of goods obtained by theft.

Nyman's chapter offers a contemporary, autobiographical account of how "new" persons can be incorporated into intimate economies based on barter and exchange of services. This is based on his own experience of how he and his wife, "incomers" to a New Hampshire town, became enmeshed in thick webs of exchange as they were gradually introduced to how the local "market" operates alongside and often out of the gaze of larger market forces. He uses his personal experience as a lens through which to examine how descendants of the indigenous peoples of northern New England employ their own survivance strategies as they have done since first European contact—by adapting and responding to Euroamerican desires and needs for "Indian-made" goods. In McGovern's chapter, we see a different example of Native American survivance strategies, this time among Montauket whalers, who through ties of kin and association constructed dense and powerful social networks that promoted their own survival though exchange within an intimate economy that was subordinate to the larger capitalist sphere.

Lakomäki, Ylimaunu, and Kylli's examination of how the exchange and consumption of beverage alcohol among the early modern Sámi of Fennoscandia and northwest Russia reveals that exchange of liquor was not solely a mechanism whereby colonizing Europeans were able to incorporate Sámi into global capitalist networks. Close examination of archaeological evidence indicates that liquor played a critical role in Sámi culture. It was incorporative and integrative in that culture and featured not just in internal economic exchanges but through lived experiences and social relations, independent of European colonialism. The networks the Sámi wove through alcohol distribution and consumption functioned in ways similar to the networks by McGovern's Montauket whalemen formed in the sense that they were linkages forged by both economic and social interactions. McGovern examines relationships among consumers, laborers, and merchants that were linked by labor, production, and consumption as well as by kinship and community. Webs of social and economic activity among whites, indigenous Americans, and African Americans fostered and supported a form of intimate economy that operated both within and outside the broader global economy.

French's case study of the moonshine industry in southern Appalachia pairs very nicely with Lakomäki, Ylimaunu, and Kylli's of the Sámi. French's work is contributing to our understanding of how widespread illegal whiskey production and consumption was in communities in the western North Carolina and how folk knowledge of the practice was as vital as the commodity was to the local informal economy in the region.

Hyttinen, Ylimaunu, Kallio-Seppā, Mullins, and Kuorilehto write about the pitch tar industry of Oulu, Finland, which was sited away from the mainland town because of the fire hazard it presented. The location also attracted iron workers. Ostensibly these were both highly industrial processes and very much linked to the eighteenth- and nineteenth-century global capitalist system, but, as the authors point out, both iron working and making pitch tar had taken place for many generations before either of these processes took the form of heavy industry and hence retained the spiritual and ritualistic associations that had long been attached to them. They describe the evidence of animistic ritual in association with the eighteenth- and nineteenth-century operations on Pikisaari Island, reminding us that every highly industrialized process linked to global economies arises from longer-term craft and artisanal traditions. They tend to be carried out by generationally linked skilled operatives whose work combines folk or traditional beliefs and practices of intimate economies with the routinized practices required of the capitalist economy of industrial labor.

In their chapters, Reilly, Fogle, and Gibson and Kelly consider forms of subordinate, internal, and illicit economies embedded within or peripheral to the overarching economy of plantation systems. Reilly offers a rare glimpse of an underexamined element of plantation economies, that of so-called poor whites, who have largely escaped the attention of archaeologists, especially in the Caribbean. He discusses poor whites in Barbados whose lives and livelihoods, while formed by the capitalist economy, were not fully enmeshed in it, providing through evidence recovered from two nonplantation locales a fascinating image of a lively, intimate, interactive, interracial "subordinate" economy. In their research on French sugar plantations in Martinique and Guadeloupe, Gibson and Kelly examine the implications of the creole concept of *se débrouiller* or "getting by," which enslaved communities developed to survive difficult circumstances, provide for their material needs, and develop important intimate social and economic networks that extended far beyond the boundaries of their individual plantations.

Fogle's archaeological study of the enslaved community at Witherspoon plantation in South Carolina is enriched by an abundant documentary record that sheds light on the "internal economies" that the enslaved conducted through both their own productive activities and through sale of items pilfered from their masters. Of particular interest is the much-documented attitude the enslaved expressed that they felt it was their right to appropriate the goods of the master, which seems have been justified on the basis that sale of the master's goods permitted them to acquire items such as liquor that the master declined to provide, not even through the credit voucher system, and actively worked to prevent them from acquiring.

Salerno, Cruz, and Zarankin's close examination of ways nineteenth-century seal hunters created their own microeconomies aimed at personal survival within the capitalist enterprise of providing seal skins for the world market focuses on the manifold strategies of formal and informal exchange sealers devised to feed and clothe themselves in order to overcome the meager provisions supplied to them by the sponsors of sealing voyages. In this instance, the capitalist system that demanded profits over all else fostered and even encouraged the development of intimate economic relationships among sealers: greater profits were to be had if workers in the enterprise had to fend for themselves. The outcome was a sense of solidarity among sealers and ships' crews that largely evaporated when the industry turned to a much more highly organized and closely managed factory system.

Loren's consideration of glass beads as bodily objects makes a valuable contribution to ways of rethinking approaches to glass beads as objects entangled with human bodies in various ways, not merely as trade goods. That label highlights the acquisition of beads through global markets, closing down interpretations of these artifacts at the point when they leave the hands of European traders, ignoring the fact that they had subsequent social lives and were critical in how Native Americans constructed, presented, and performed identity. Loren examines how glass beads were critical to the French colonial project in Louisiana and how native Tunica valued and deployed beads in intimate ways that triggered a range of sensory experiences and communicated bodily identities through various entanglements, among themselves and in encounters with French traders and diplomats.

Straube's research into the inordinate number of casting counters and jettons that had been dumped into a well at Jamestown, Virginia, as part of its beleaguered residents' deliberate yet short-lived abandonment of the Jamestown Colony provides incontrovertible evidence, if any were needed, that archaeologists can bring to light unacknowledged if not previously unknown forms of intimate economies. Seeking to explain the material finds, Straube discovered overlooked corroboration that prior to the abandonment attempt, Jamestown's leaders had sought to make use of a token currency scheme in order to establish an alternative sort of economy at the settlement whereby workers would be paid in scrip that could be exchanged for real money at an unspecified future date. Whether the scheme would have worked is impossible to judge, but it was elaborate and, in the end, useless. While it may not seem apt to think of the proposed scheme as an intimate economy, it is important to remember that the inability of Jamestown's leaders to engage its colonists in a basic, straightforward exchange of labor for pay compelled them to consider imposing something out of the ordinary (although far from completely novel) in order to bind the community's laborers together in the ways that exchange relations regularly do.

Another form of exchange, at first glance one-sided, comes to light in Eleanor Casella's evocative examination of the Irish Catholic tradition of pilgrimage to and reverence toward holy wells and places deemed holy through association with specific saints. Deposits of offerings and votives at such places by believers is inspired by the most intimate of impulses to seek intervention from a revered saint on behalf of themselves or loved ones. There is an embodied aspect to this, Casella notes, both in the performativity of the rituals and prayers (the "patterns") and in the fact that many requests are not aimed at spiritual matters but rather are pleas for bodily healing. What is interesting is that believers often assert that their bargain is a two-way one and that the object of their prayers and supplications has responded and healed them. This is of course a prime example of the power of faith and of the power of belief in an intimate and somewhat unbalanced form of reciprocity through a "personal" relationship between saint and supplicant.

Contributors to this book have worked to reframe the archaeology of intimate economies as a legitimate topic of study for historical archaeologists and have demonstrated that such economies are key features of early modern and modern industrial and rural cultures. Essays in this volume explore a diverse range of case studies of different types of alternative yet embedded economic systems, some of them genuinely intimate in nature. Yet no matter how removed from the mainstream, participants in each of these intimate economies were nevertheless subject to if not victims of the larger processes of capitalism and globalization. As Comaroff and Comaroff (1999, 294) have noted with regard to occult economies, "it is important not to forget that 'the local' and 'the global' do not describe received empirical realities. They are analytic constructs whose heuristic utility depends entirely on the way in which they are deployed to illuminate historically specific phenomena." Intimate economies, like occult economies, are a means through which "human beings *create* community and locality and identity, . . . they *fabricate* social realities and power relations" (Comaroff and Comaroff 1999, 295; italics in original). In exploring examples of intimate economies, we are reminded of the linkages between the local and the universal, of how likely we are to find intimate economies wherever we look—so long as we look beyond capitalism's overarching globalized market. In intimate economies we see resourcefulness, illegal activity, and especially strategies based on the practice of multiple modes of producing, consuming, and surviving—and of resisting the dominant order.

References Cited

Beizer, Janet. 2015. The Emperor's Plate: Marketing Leftovers in Nineteenth-Century Paris. In *Food & Markets: Proceedings of the Oxford Symposium on Food and Cookery*, edited by Michael McWilliams, 15–34. London: Prospect Books.

Bloch, Alexia. 2017. *Sex, Love, and Migration: Postsocialism, Modernity, and Intimacy from Istanbul to the Arctic*. Ithaca, NY: Cornell University Press.

Bridge, Gavin, and Adrian Smith. 2003. Guest Editorial: Intimate Encounters: Culture—Economy—Commodity. *Environment and Planning D: Society and Space* 21:257–268.

Cabezas, Amalia L. 2011. Intimate Encounters: Affective Economies in Cuba and the Dominican Republic. *European Review of Latin American and Caribbean Studies* 91:3–14.

Casella, Eleanor Conlin. 2010. Broads, Studs, and Broken Down Daddies: The Materiality of "Playing" in the Modern Penitentiary. In *The Social Archaeologies of Trade and Exchange: Exploring Relationships among People, Places, and Things*, edited by Alexander A. Bauer and Anna S. Agbe-Davies, 165–182. New York: Routledge.

Comaroff, Jean, and John Comaroff. 1999. Occult Economies and the Violence of Abstraction: Notes from the Postcolony. *American Ethnologist* 26(2):279–303.

Dawdy, Shannon L., and Alexandra Hartnett. 2013. The Archaeology of Illegal and Illicit Economies. *Annual Review of Anthropology* 42:37–51.

Fallon, Nicole. 2014. In the New "Intimate Economy" We're All Potential Entrepreneurs. *Business News Daily*, February 2. Accessed January 3, 2015. https://www.businessnewsdaily.com/5860-sharing-economy-marketplace-businesses.html.

Henry, Stuart. 1987. The Political Economy of Informal Economies. *Annals of the American Academy of Political and Social Science* 493:137–153.

Loza, Mireya. 2016. *Defiant Braceros: How Migrant Workers Fought for Racial, Sexual, and Political Freedom*. Chapel Hill: University of North Carolina Press.

Lyttleton, Chris. 2014. *Intimate Economies of Development: Mobility, Sexuality and Health in Asia*. London: Routledge.

Miller, Daniel. 1987. *Material Culture and Mass Consumption*. Oxford: Blackwell.

———, ed. 1998. *Material Cultures: Why Some Things Matter*. Chicago: University of Chicago Press.

Price, John A. 1975. Sharing: The Integration of Intimate Economies. *Anthropologica* 17(1):3–27.

Stobart, Jon, and Ilja Van Damme. 2010. *Modernity and the Second-Hand Trade: European Consumption Cultures and Practices, 1700–1900*. London: Palgrave MacMillan.

Wilson, Ara. 2004. *The Intimate Economies of Bangkok: Tomboys, Tycoons, and Avon Ladies in the Global City*. Berkeley: University of California Press.

———. 2012. Intimacy: A Useful Category of Transnational Analysis. In *The Global and the Intimate: Feminism in Our Time*, edited by Geraldine Pratt and Victoria Rosner, 31–56. New York: Columbia University Press.

Wright, Sarah. 2010. Cultivating Beyond-Capitalist Economies. *Economic Geography* 86(3):297–318.

Zelizer, Viviana A. 2002. Intimate Transactions. In *The New Economic Sociology: Developments in an Emerging Field*, edited by Mauro F. Guillén, Randall Collins, Paul England, and Marshall Meyer, 274–300. New York: Russell Sage Foundation.

Contributors

Mary C. Beaudry is professor of archaeology, anthropology, and gastronomy at Boston University. Her research interests include the archaeology of colonialisms; the archaeology of households and domestic life; archaeologies of gender relations, personal identity and self-fashioning; and the archaeology of cookery and dining.

Eleanor Conlin Casella has specialized in the archaeology of historical and contemporary societies for over twenty years. She has directed field projects in Ireland, Britain, North America, and Australia. She is currently adjunct professor of humanities at the University of Tasmania.

M. Jimena Cruz is a doctoral student at the University of Minas Gerais in Brazil. She is part of the Landscapes in White research project on Antarctic archaeology.

Historical archaeologist Kevin R. Fogle has a PhD in anthropology and is a research affiliate and instructor at the University of South Carolina, Columbia. His research focuses on many aspects of the African Diaspora in the southeastern United States, from cultural landscapes to foodways.

Kirk D. French is associate teaching professor at Pennsylvania State University, where his research focuses on the small-scale production and cultural meanings of alcoholic beverages. His work examines the social and economic impact of alcohol through a comparative lens.

Heather Gibson is cultural resources director for the California and Pacific Islands region at SWCA Environmental Consultants. She received her PhD in anthropology from Syracuse University and focuses on the historical archaeology of the American West and the Caribbean.

Marika Hyttinen is a doctoral student in archaeology at the University of Oulu, Finland. Her PhD dissertation focuses on the early modern pitch mills along Finland's Gulf of Bothnia.

Titta Kallio-Seppä received her PhD in archaeology at the University of Oulu, Finland. Her research interests are in the fields of historical archaeology and dendrochronology.

Kenneth G. Kelly is professor of anthropology at the University of South Carolina. He is an anthropological archaeologist who studies the impacts of the slave trade on coastal African societies and the ways enslaved people in the Caribbean endured the conditions of slavery.

Markku Kuorilehto is a licentiate in philosophy, a master in theology, and a doctoral student in archaeology. He works in the Oulu University Teacher Training School. He specializes in medieval and early modern history and place-name studies.

Ritva Kylli is university lecturer of Arctic and northern history and adjunct professor of Finnish and North European history at the University of Oulu.

Sami Lakomäki is senior university lecturer in cultural anthropology at the University of Oulu, Finland. He specializes in Indigenous histories and the histories of colonialism in North America and Fennoscandia.

Diana DiPaolo Loren is curator and director of academic partnerships at the Peabody Museum at Harvard University. She specializes in North American archaeology, focusing on issues of colonialism, identity, embodiment, and materiality.

Jade Luiz is a collections assistant at the Peabody Museum of Archaeology and Anthropology at Harvard University. She received her PhD in archaeology from Boston University. Her research interests include archaeology of the senses, of prostitution, and of costume and dress in nineteenth-century America.

Allison Manfra McGovern is a senior archaeologist at VHB in Hauppauge, New York. She received her PhD in anthropology from the Graduate Center at The City University of New York. Her research focuses on the archaeology and history of Long Island.

Paul R. Mullins is professor of anthropology at Indiana University-Purdue University, Indianapolis. His research in historical archaeology examines the relationship between racism and material consumption.

James A. Nyman received his MA in historical archeology from the University of South Carolina. His independent research concerns interactions between Europeans and Native Americans, cultural accommodation, identity formation and rearticulation, and cultural persistence during European expansion into the New World.

Matthew C. Reilly is assistant professor of anthropology, gender studies, and international studies at the City College of New York. He is a historical archaeologist studying the modern Atlantic World in the Caribbean and West Africa.

Melisa A. Salerno is a researcher at the Multidisciplinary Institute of History and Human Sciences, National Council for Scientific and Technical Research (IMHICIHU-CONICET) in Argentina. She is part of the Landscapes in White research project on Antarctic archaeology.

Beverly A. Straube is an independent archaeological curator and material culture specialist and a research associate with the James River Institute for Archaeology. She is currently serving as curator for the First Colony Foundation and for the Jamestown-Yorktown Foundation.

Timo Ylimaunu is a docent in post-medieval urban archaeology and senior lecturer in historical archaeology at the University of Oulu, Finland. He is an international associate at Indiana University-Purdue University Indianapolis.

Andrés Zarankin is associate professor and runs the Laboratory of Antarctic Studies in Human Sciences at the University of Minas Gerais, Brazil. He is the director of the Landscapes in White research project on Antarctic archaeology.

Index

CPSIA information can be obtained
at www.ICGtesting.com
Printed in the USA
LVHW030805140519
617333LV00002B/3/P

9 780813 056326